Four Seasons

Four Seasons

A Ming Emperor and His Grand Secretaries in Sixteenth-Century China

John W. Dardess

ROWMAN & LITTLEFIELD
Lanham • Boulder • New York • London

Published by Rowman & Littlefield
A wholly owned subsidiary of
The Rowman & Littlefield Publishing Group, Inc.
4501 Forbes Boulevard, Suite 200, Lanham, Maryland 20706
www.rowman.com

Unit A, Whitacre Mews, 26-34 Stannary Street, London SE11 4AB,
United Kingdom

British Library Cataloguing in Publication Information Available

Library of Congress Cataloging-in-Publication Data
Names: Dardess, John W., 1937–
Title: Four seasons : a Ming emperor and his grand secretaries in sixteenth-century China
    / John W. Dardess.
Description: Lanham : Rowman & Littlefield, 2016. | Includes bibliographical references
    and index.
Identifiers: LCCN 2016004888 (print) | LCCN 2016011802 (ebook) | ISBN
    9781442265585 (hardcover : alkaline paper) | ISBN 9781442265592 (paperback :
    alkaline paper) | ISBN 9781442265608 (electronic)
Subjects: LCSH: Ming Shizong, Emperor of China, 1507–1567. | Ming Shizong, Emperor
    of China, 1507–1567—Friends and associates. | Ming Shizong, Emperor of China,
    1507–1567—Political and social views. | China—History—Ming dynasty,
    1368–1644. | China—Politics and government—1368–1644. | Political leadership—
    China—History—16th century. | Emperors—China—Biography. | China—Kings and
    rulers—Biography. | Public officers—China—Biography. | China—Officials and em-
    ployees—Biography.
Classification: LCC DS753.6.M49 D37 2016 (print) | LCC DS753.6.M49 (ebook) | DDC
    951/.0260922—dc23
LC record available at http://lccn.loc.gov/2016004888

Printed in the United States of America

Contents

Introduction

World population in 1550 numbered some four hundred million, about a quarter of whom were subjects of Ming China's Jiajing emperor (r. 1521–1567). Ming China was the largest organized political entity on the sixteenth-century globe—the biggest in population, territory, and wealth. No one in China knew of any true rivals. Rulers elsewhere in the world knew nothing of Jiajing, though of course they'd heard of China.

"Four Seasons" is a way of saying that, once he seized firm control of the reins of state, there were four phases in the long rule of the Jiajing emperor. Each phase featured a different powerful chief grand secretary, with whom the ruler cooperated in order to cope with what was by far the world's most demanding political responsibility.

The ruler's name was Zhu Houcong, although no one ever called him that. He was always addressed, or referred to, by some epithet: *shang* (the one above), *sheng* (sage), *tianzi* (Son of Heaven), *bixia* (the throne), and such like. For the sake of convenience, we will just call him by his reign title, Jiajing.

The reign title was reportedly chosen by the young ruler himself, from his favorite chapter, "Wu yi" (No Frivolity), in the Confucian classic *Shujing* (*Book of Documents*). *Jia* means "to improve, make splendid," and *jing* means "to pacify." His main palace in West Park was called the Wuyi Dian. This was really a terse policy statement about what the ruler was going to focus on and the seriousness with which he was going to act. He meant it. [1]

Western Europe in Jiajing's time was torn by religious conflict and dynastic wars. This was the age of Luther and Calvin, Henry VIII and Charles

1

V. Politically, Europe was an unhappy patchwork of a few big states and some five hundred tiny sovereignties. But the opening by Spain of the silver mines in present-day Bolivia, in addition to the silver produced in Japan, flooded China with so much of the metal that the silver tael became a standard monetary unit of account. India came closest to China's size, but there was no contact at all between the Ming court and the Mughals, Babur and his successors, who were busy conquering the subcontinent during Jiajing's time. Under Suleiman the Magnificent, almost an exact contemporary of Jiajing's, the Ottoman Turks pressed into southeastern Europe, and, although they achieved their high point of power in the mid-sixteenth century, never did they make any direct contact with China. Ivan the Terrible was setting in motion the exponential expansion of Russia, but again, no contact was made or attempted with China—not yet. Ming China's own expansion phase had ended a century earlier. China was off by itself and, compared to the other big political systems, was a mature power, its institutions developed and settled, its political thinking anchored in the civilization's Golden Age, and its geostrategic posture fixed. The great bureaucratic machine that governed Ming China was mature, too, indeed even overripe, and while it was certainly functional, it harbored a range of rust spots, some merely unsightly, others potentially crippling.

It was the young emperor's job to command this machine. It was not in his plans to consolidate or expand its territory any more, but to ensure that it did what the Ming founders had designed it to do. That meant fixing its faults and breakdowns. There were detailed provisions to watch over—for revenue and defense; for infrastructure and its management (Yellow River flood control, the Grand Canal lifeline, the communications system, etc.); and for internal policing and judicial administration (two metropolitan regions and thirteen provinces, divided into 159 prefectures, which oversaw 240 subprefectures, 1,114 counties, and some 150 million people). The Ming government also managed civil religion and its panoply of public rituals—a national repository of cosmic symbolism with implications for collective human needs and relationships that Jiajing considered to be of vital importance nationwide. The machine comprised upward of twenty thousand ranked and salaried bureaucrats who became bureaucrats by way of state-managed schools and a state-run system of written examinations designed to capture the most promising of China's young talents for careers in state service.

The machine as a machine was to a high degree self-regulating, with detailed procedural codes. The Ministry of Personnel had charge of appointments and periodic evaluations, while censors and supervising secretaries (in short form, *kedao*) impeached the ineffectual and corrupt, and as "speaking officials" (*yan'guan*) offered ideas, plans, and advice, some of which was unwanted, disruptive, and punishable by higher-ups. Jiajing was the supreme and sole executive and judge of last resort. To provide indispensable help, he had a small board of advisors, the Grand Secretariat.

Jiajing did not come to the throne in the usual way. When he was thirteen years old, his cousin, the Zhengde emperor, died childless. Chief Grand Secretary Yang Tinghe and the Empress Dowager Zhang issued him an edict, summoning him and a modest entourage up to Beijing from his princedom in Anlu, six hundred miles south. That was in 1521.

During the opening years of his long tenure on the throne, the young emperor showed his mettle. In 1524, he faced down a protest demonstration mounted by some two hundred Beijing officials. Young as he was, Jiajing was determined to defy their demand that he break ritually from his own dead father and agree to make himself heir to the defunct line of his father's elder brother, the Hongzhi emperor, by way of an act of posthumous adoption. Jiajing prevailed. The issue raised as much emotional heat as, say, our recent (early twenty-first-century) debates over gay rights or abortion, as it affected filial and family order all over China. But by warring successfully for his own side in the confrontation, the ruler defined himself as a determined autocrat. Without the help of Chief Grand Secretary Zhang Fujing, however, he probably could not have pulled it off.[2]

In the "spring" phase, Jiajing went on to reform all of Ming China's public religious observances; to build or rebuild Beijing's altars, temples, and shrines; and to improve and make splendid China's sense of itself as the world beacon light of advanced civilization. Ritual was not simply decorative. It was a totally serious matter, absolutely essential both to internal social order and to the national sense of superiority over all things foreign or barbarian. Zhang Fujing was chief grand secretary, and he provided a powerful guiding hand in that endeavor.

In the "summer" phase of Jiajing's reign, things turned rather sour. Jiajing retreated from the Forbidden City to West Park, leaving many public duties behind but remaining attentive to his executive duties. Under Chief Grand Secretary Xia Yan, ritual reform wound down, and China turned to military muscle flexing, successfully in the case of Annam, disastrously in the case of the plan to reconquer the Ordos. The collapse of that plan cost Xia Yan his life.

The third, "autumn" phase of Jiajing's long reign featured lassitude and complacency under the increasingly corrupt guidance of Chief Grand Secretary Yan Song. Zhang Fujing had been a hard warrior in a righteous cause—sincere, austere, and enormously erudite—and Jiajing felt close to him. Xia Yan was brilliant and energetic but a bon vivant, easily bored, and insouciant. Jiajing was impressed by him but never felt close to him. Yan Song wormed his way into the ruler's favor by his attentive diligence and his warm embrace of Jiajing's turn to religious Daoism and all its special prayers and rituals, which his rival Xia Yan, for all his brilliance, failed to see the need for. Serious surges of violence along the coast and northern frontier in the 1550s elicited from Yan Song a flaccid policy of negotiation and compromise. Yet he enjoyed the longest tenure of any Ming chief grand secretary—1548 to 1562, fourteen years.

The final phase, the "winter" of the Jiajing era, featured a refreshing turnabout from Yan Song's rancid legacy to a renewal of the ruler's early springtime interest in good governance. This was Chief Grand Secretary Xu Jie's achievement, the result of his skill and energy in convincing the ruler to veer away from the old ruts. Xu was on the job at the time of Jiajing's death (January 23, 1567), and it was he who wrote Jiajing's last will, which cleaned up much of the foul detritus that had accumulated over the course of so many years of one-man rule. I've already written a book about Xu Jie,[3] and I won't repeat here all that I said about him there. Considering him in the light of his three predecessors, however, allows me to introduce some new material and bring to light some dimensions of his story that I could not develop earlier.

What sort of man was Jiajing? He is very hard to know except in the context of the many written messages he exchanged with his chief grand secretaries. All four left behind large collections of documents, which their descendants or other interested parties printed up for general circulation. Even so, some of their writing does not put them in a very good light. From Jiajing's remarks and the secretaries' responses, a researcher today can learn many intimate details of how China was managed from the perspective of the men at the very top of the system. Not every question can be answered, but many can.

Primary documents are any historian's treasure trove. This book uses them to interweave Jiajing's story with those of the four chairmen, so to speak, of his board of intimate advisors. Except for the first of them, Zhang Fujing, a scholar-ideologue with no prior bureaucratic experience, the others—Xia Yan, Yan Song, and Xu Jie—entered the Grand Secretariat after years of service in the Ministry of Rites, in Jiajing's time a privileged holding pen and training ground for future grand secretaries. Reading not only their correspondence with Jiajing, but also their letters, memorials, and policy proposals from earlier in their careers provides a fine-grained look into their life stories and records their reactions to many of the things, important and not so important, that were going on all during their active lifetimes. By the time each enters the Grand Secretariat, we have a good idea of the kind of men they were—their flaws, their skills, and their individual experiences.

This book offers one approach into a vastly complex era of China's history, fuller coverage of which awaits future historians. I hope that this probe, which is a little like so many test borings into layers of rubble, clay, and rock, proves effective as an aid to understanding some of the issues and crises at stake during the Jiajing era. Not a single topic, but a large assemblage of them, should convey something of the real world that China's top managers had to deal with.

I would end with this thought: After finishing the draft of this book, I was struck by an unlikely comparison that might be made between Jiajing's four seasons and the span of Soviet history. People of my generation (I was born in 1937) will have retained vivid memories of the Soviet leaders from Stalin's time on. Soviet ruling modes arced from Stalin's harsh drive to achieve an ideologically perfect communist society, to Khrushchev's ebullient muscle flexing, to Brezhnev's complacent corruption, to Gorbachev's new path of benign reform. The four chief grand secretaries of Jiajing's time showed roughly similar profiles—Zhang Fujing's ideological ferocity, Xia Yan's exuberant expansionism, Yan Song's complacent corruption, and finally Xu Jie's new path of benign reform, his "opening the avenue of speech" rather akin to Gorbachev's glasnost. One cannot overdo this; the Soviet Union lacked a tsar, after all. But perhaps giant autocracies may at times trace similar paths as they evolve.

Finally, let me thank Sarah Schneewind for her help and support, Vickie Fu Doll for her librarian's expertise, Pam Le Row for her skills with Word, and the superb editorial staff at Rowman and Littlefield: Susan McEachern, Janice Braunstein, and Audra Figgins.

NOTES

1. See, too, the extended discussion in James Geiss, "On the Significance of the Reign Title Chia-ching," *Ming Studies*, no. 30 (1990): 37–51.

2. Chinese lineages often arranged posthumous adoptions for men who died without sons. But in Jiajing's case, he was an only son. So his posthumous adoption by the Hongzhi emperor necessarily deprived his father of a direct filial successor.

3. *A Political Life in Ming China: A Grand Secretary and His Times* (Lanham, MD: Rowman & Littlefield, 2013).

Chapter One

A Young Emperor Shows His Teeth

Never before had the Ming imperial house, founded in 1368, suffered a fertility failure, but in 1521 the Zhengde emperor, an only son, died childless at age twenty-nine. Chief Grand Secretary Yang Tinghe and the senior empress, nee Zhang, quickly agreed to call in a cousin of Zhengde's, thirteen-year-old Zhu Houcong, whose father was the younger brother of the Hongzhi emperor. (The Hongzhi emperor was Zhengde's father; Empress Zhang was his principal consort.) Good things had been heard about the young fellow. For over a month, the throne of Ming China lay vacant, awaiting the arrival of the new appointee.[1]

Zhu Houcong was the only surviving son of his father, the Prince of Xing, who died in 1519. The Xing princedom was seated in Anlu (nowadays Zhongxiang in Hubei Province) some six hundred miles south of Beijing on the Han River. A delegation bringing the invitation and a gold tally departed Beijing on April 15, the day after Zhengde's death. It consisted of a mix of dignitaries emblematic of the different key components of the Ming power structure, military, civilian, and eunuch. They were Dingguo duke Xu Guangzuo (a descendant of the Ming founder's top general); Shouning marquis Zhang Heling (one of the senior empress's younger brothers); the commandant-escort Cui Yuan (husband of a daughter of Zhu Houcong's grandfather, the Chenghua emperor); Grand Secretary Liang Chu; Minister of Rites Mao Cheng; and three senior eunuchs. They reached Anlu on May 2. The call to the throne, ghostwritten for the dead Zhengde, was in Mao Cheng's safekeeping. Cui Yuan bore the gold tally.[2]

The young ruler-to-be met the delegation at the Anlu city gate, where Mao Cheng presented him with the edict. He took the document into the palace and there read it out in front of the delegation and his own entourage. Everyone was impressed with how well the boy rose to the solemnity of the occasion. Members of the delegation were given gifts of silver and cloth.

If Zhu Houcong felt joy at the news that he was specially chosen to rule China, he kept it well hidden. What he showed publicly were tears and sadness—not at the death of his cousin, whom he'd never met, but at leaving behind his mother, still very much alive, and the tomb of his father for a new life and an unknown fate. Thus on May 6, he visited his father's tomb, fell prostrate in a fit of weeping, and had to be helped to his feet. Everyone who watched this performance was reduced to tears as well. The next day, May 7, he wept again as he bade his mother farewell. She counseled him to be a good ruler, a Yao or a Shun. She would come to Beijing later.

The party left that same day for Beijing. Zhu Houcong's own entourage numbered some forty people, including two eunuchs; the Xing princedom's chief administrator, Yuan Zonggao; and the ceremonial guards commander, Lu An. The rest were guardsmen and functionaries of various sorts. They proceeded north up the Han River. The boy ordered one of the senior eunuchs to ensure that no one harassed the local officials or harmed commoners along the way. A senior eunuch of the Beijing delegation placed the surveillance vice commissioner of Huguang Province under arrest for failing to show proper respect as the party passed through his territory.

On May 26, the cortege reached Liangxiang, about twenty miles south of Beijing. There an emissary from the Ministry of Rites presented the protocols for entering Beijing. Because Zhu Houcong was Prince of Xing, he was directed to enter through the Dongan Gate, the designated portal for all visiting princes—a side gate, that is, not the front gate. Reportedly the young prince read the program and said to Yuan Zonggao, his mentor, "The edict makes me, an orphan, succeed to the imperial position. But it doesn't consider me an imperial son." Yuan agreed.

The next day, the prince and his traveling palace reached Beijing's outskirts, where Chief Grand Secretary Yang Tinghe twice invited him to enter through the Dongan Gate. Yuan Zonggao demurred. "He's directly succeeding to the imperial position," he argued. "How can he still be treated with the ritual due a prince?" He shouted for the central entry through the Daming Gate to be opened.[3] The Empress Zhang, informed of this dispute, yielded to young Zhu. In he came, through the central Daming Gate. This was a first small victory in the young ruler's long struggle to define Ming ritual and establish his supreme authority over it.

The enthronement took place without incident the same day. An elaborate edict of succession, put together by kingmaker Yang Tinghe, granted nation-wide tax relief and promised a substantial list of expense-cutting and abuse-eliminating reforms. The new emperor would indeed carry these out over the first few years.

From this point, we can start calling the new emperor Jiajing, after his reign title. For the next eight months, however, the reign title Zhengde would remain in force. The first year of the Jiajing reign would begin on a day corresponding to January 28, 1522. (The Ming rule was never to change reign titles in midyear.)

Already, however, the seeds of conflict between Jiajing, who would turn fourteen in September 1521, and Chief Grand Secretary Yang Tinghe, age sixty-one, had been sown. Yang had been a grand secretary since 1507, and chief since 1518. These had not been happy years for either the Grand Secretariat or the civil bureaucracy as a whole. The Zhengde emperor, from the moment he came to power in 1505, also as a thirteen-year-old, hated over-bearing civil officials and for the next sixteen years ruled China through his palace eunuchs and military aides and treated civil officialdom with neglect, contempt, and occasional brutality. Yang Tinghe and most of the bureaucracy were determined to ensure a revival of the dignity and authority of the civil officials, reining in young Jiajing as they had never been able to contain his headstrong cousin. And indeed, Jiajing proved, over the long haul, to be amenable to working in tandem with his grand secretaries in his rule of China. On this, Jiajing and Yang were in agreement. What, then, led them to clash? Much of the blame has to be laid upon Yang Tinghe, for misjudging the character of the boy emperor and for mishandling the technical ritual details of the imperial ancestral cult.

There is no question about the depth of Jiajing's sense of loss in the death of his father, the Prince of Xing. The prince had lavished personal attention on his son, giving him his first lessons in the classics, showing him how to wield the writing brush, and serving as a model of a kindly and compassion-ate lord of the manor, before he died of "summer illness" at the age of forty-two. Jiajing's love and respect for him knew no bounds. This fact failed to register with Yang Tinghe.[4]

The issue that nearly ripped China apart stemmed from Yang Tinghe's hasty assumption, without deep thought or careful research, that because a

father-to-son line of succession had come to an end with the childless Zhengde, the line had to be restored to wholeness by way of a posthumous adoption. Jiajing had to agree to become the adopted son of his uncle, the Hongzhi
emperor, who was Zhengde's father and his own father's half-brother. The
ritual devotion Jiajing would normally offer his father would terminate, and a
clansman would perform the filial observances in his place. Because Jiajing
was a prince's son, and the prince had no claim to the throne himself, posthumous adoption would make the boy a rightful ruler, a son now in an unbrok-
en line of emperors. The rites due a dead prince were just a private family
matter. The rites due an emperor overbore the rites due a father. Rites of filial
respect offered to the Hongzhi emperor were national in scope, completely
transcending in gravity and importance Jiajing's merely personal devotion to
his family.

Yang's argument made some sense. But was it correct? Were the rules for
it embedded somewhere in the classics? And could clear precedents be found
somewhere in China's long history? Most important, would Jiajing agree to
it?

That was not all: there was the boy's mother. On May 30, Jiajing sent off
two senior eunuchs to Anlu to escort his mother up to Beijing. On October
24, she and her cortege finally arrived at Tongzhou, twenty miles east of the
capital. There the commandant-escort Cui Yuan and Grand Secretary Jiang
Mian officially greeted her. The Ministry of Rites proposed to Jiajing that his
mother should enter the left-hand entry at the Zhengyang Gate, then proceed
through a series of side gates to her palace quarters in the Forbidden City.
Another ritual power game, no less. Jiajing rejected the proposal. The ministry was treating her as a prince's consort, which was indeed correct. She
hadn't yet been elevated to the rank of empress.

Jiajing ordered that his mother must take the central entry at the Daming
Gate, then pay her respects at the Taimiao, the imperial ancestral temple. The
court officials raised a storm of protest. So Jiajing asked her to wait at
Tongzhou. Meanwhile he ordered the Embroidered-Uniform Guard to provide her with the carriage and robes due an empress who was the ruler's
mother.

Jiajing's mother, nee Jiang, had married the Prince of Xing in 1491. She
was a daughter of a Beijing family that included minor officials. She had
some education. When she arrived at Tongzhou, she heard about the clamor
being raised by the Beijing officials that Jiajing be made the posthumous son
of the Hongzhi emperor. In anger, she reportedly said, "How can you make

our son someone else's son? You officials, with your favor and glory, why haven't you given the prince proper respect?" She adamantly refused to enter Beijing under such humiliating conditions.

This was a crisis moment indeed. Jiajing wept in frustration. He told Hongzhi's widow, the senior empress nee Zhang, that he was going to abdicate and take his mother back to Anlu.

Just at this juncture a learned tract bearing the title "Questions and Answers on the Great Rites" burst through a crack in the phalanx of official opinion and called into serious question the correctness of the demand that Jiajing be made Hongzhi's son by posthumous adoption. The author was Zhang Cong (later renamed Zhang Fujing). He'd just now won his *jinshi* degree. His early attempts to gain Jiajing's ear went nowhere, as Yang Tinghe's partisans at first blocked his memorials and then demanded that Jiajing not respond to them, though the ruler did silently agree with those he was able to read.

On November 1, Yang Tinghe capitulated and agreed to a compromise. He really had no choice. There was Jiajing's mother, refusing to enter Beijing; Jiajing, threatening abdication; and, very worrisome, the availability of a well-argued tract taking Jiajing's side. So Yang arranged to raise both Jiajing's grandmother, nee Shao, and his mother, nee Jiang, to empress rank. He also directed the Ministry of Rites to grant the above and also posthumously promote Jiajing's father to the rank of emperor.

So finally on November 2, after nearly two weeks' delay, Jiajing's mother proceeded into the city of Beijing. She took the central entryway at the Daming Gate and rode on into the Forbidden City where Jiajing was waiting for her. She agreed not to visit the Taimiao, a quasi-public ancestral shrine. Instead she visited the more private ancestral temples, the Fengxian and Fengci, dedicated to the dead Ming rulers and their empresses.

* * *

Thus, within barely a month of his enthronement, a by now fourteen-year-old Jiajing was headed toward full domination of Ming government. Young as he was, he instinctively understood power: how to use his personal resources to get his way over men (and women) much older and vastly more experienced than he.

Tops on Yang Tinghe's agenda was cleaning up all the accumulated corruptions and excrescences of the Zhengde era—the bloated rosters of eunuchs, soldiers, and artisans, and all the rest. Jiajing backed it for a few years, but his commitment to it was shallow. The one set of reform issues that riveted Jiajing's attention was centered on imperial ritual. It was perhaps indicative of an overall climate of peace and security in Ming China that ritual could override such existential matters as, say, military defense or internal security. It was indeed an unbridgeable dispute over rites that would soon lead to the bloody crackdown on the Great Rites demonstrators of 1524 and the triumphant emergence of Jiajing as Ming China's undisputed decision maker.

The ruler could not hope to remake ritual unaided. He understood that he needed help. He would soon need someone akin to a personal attorney, who could argue his case with learning and vigor. He would need someone who could also act as a manager and coordinate an ambitious program of ritual reform and revival.

For years afterward, Jiajing resented the memory of Yang Tinghe for having taken advantage of his youth and bullying him. After having given in to Jiajing on the issue of the respect due his mother (as the mother of an emperor, not the wife of a prince), Yang and the other grand secretaries, and many official cosigners of supporting statements, dug in their heels and refused to budge on the posthumous adoption matter. Early in 1522, Jiajing unwillingly caved in. It appeared the dispute might be over.[5]

But it was hardly over. Yang Tinghe retired in March 1524 (yet the resentful emperor stripped him of all honors in 1528, and he died the next year). Slowly, Zhang Fujing[6] and a handful of like-minded scholar-officials pressed their well-argued case favoring Jiajing's wish not to be the Hongzhi emperor's posthumous adoptee. Zhang was not, under normal conditions, a likely candidate at all for the highest post on offer in Ming China. It was the so-called Great Rites controversy that propelled him there.

* * *

Zhang Fujing's origins were plebeian. His family, registered as salt workers, lived in Yongjia County, Zhejiang Province, near the coast. Zhang's father, Zhang Sheng (1427–1509), owned a small farm, thirty *mou* (about five acres), of what his son referred to as low-grade fields. Zhang Sheng referred to himself as a peasant. But he was not a poor peasant, because he served as an unpaid tax collector and forwarder, sported a literary name (*hao*), and paid from his own granary the laborers hauling stone to build a memorial honoring Zhang Fujing for achieving his provincial degree in 1498. Zhang Sheng had three successive wives and one concubine, who gave him four sons and two daughters. The sons all survived to maturity. Zhang Fujing was the youngest. Both daughters were married off. No poor peasant could have managed all that, even an abstemious vegetarian like Zhang Sheng.

Still, Zhang Sheng's resources were limited. His son had to accept charity, boarding for a while with the rich Shao family, who ran a local school. Wang Yangzhi (1433–1515), the husband of one of Zhang's cousins, also took him in as a boy and tutored him in his bamboo-shaded library alongside his own young sons. Wang was a well-off peasant and tax collector. Zhang Fujing's uncle, Zhang Ji (1431–1504), was richer than Zhang's father, and his son Zhang Shan, Zhang Fujing's first cousin, used his wealth to fund local public works and to help cover the expenses of Zhang Fujing's family. Zhang Sheng was pleased when his son was accepted as a prefectural stipend student in Wenzhou. As a stipend student, Zhang Fujing finally had the bare resources necessary for marriage, and so he married a peasant girl of the Cai surname (1480–1530). According to Zhang's epitaph for her, they lived wretchedly. Yet she never complained. All this suggests that Zhang Fujing came from an immediate family of limited means, but his family was embedded in a wider kin network that was generous with its resources. All the members were striving to rise from peasant or salt worker to elite (*shi*) status. Only Zhang Fujing succeeded, and only after many years trying. [7]

Zhang passed his provincial *juren* degree in 1498, at the age of twenty-three, a rather low seventy-eighth on the ranked list. Then from 1499 to 1517, he failed seven consecutive times at the metropolitan exams held triennially in Beijing. It is not clear what he did during all that time besides accept Imperial University status and study on his own. In 1518, he formally announced to the local mountain and river gods that he was building an academy (*shuyuan*) at a rural spot where he was going to gather students. His cousin Zhang Shan helped him with that. Who the students were, and how and what they were taught, is not known. Some locals laughed and doubted that the label "academy" was appropriate. Possibly it was just a primary school, and Zhang needed the income from tuition fees.

At the exams held in Beijing in 1521, Zhang finally passed. He was forty-six, more than a decade older than average. He was not one of the top three winners, who received Hanlin Academy posts. Nor was he one of the elite group of twenty-four made Hanlin bachelors. He finished seventy-sixth overall on the ranked list of 330. His future did not look promising.

There was a delay between the metropolitan exams (he finished ninety-sixth) and the final round, the palace exam, over which the emperor was supposed to preside personally and sign off on the final rankings. The metropolitan exam was held while Zhengde was still alive, but his illness and death forced several postponements of the palace exam until June 9, 1521, under Jiajing, when it was announced that the graduates would first assemble at the Xijiao Gate to pay their respects (five bows and three kowtows) and then enter the Vermilion Steps in front of the Fengxian Dian inside the Forbidden City to take the question for the exam. Then on June 22 they would reassemble at the Xijiao Gate, where Jiajing would preside. The Court of State Ceremonial would provide a table; the Hanlin Academy would hand the ranked list of results to the Ministry of Rites, who would place the list on the table. Because of Zhengde's funeral, there would be no banquet or reading aloud of names. All the civil and military officials would gather in plain robes, and the musicians would attend; but no music would be played. Then the new degree winners would pay their respects again. The Ministry of Rites would carry the list outside the Chang'an left gate and post it there. The number one winner would be given a special escort. Four days later, he'd get a special cap and robe. On June 24, all the *jinshi* would go to the Court of State Ceremonial to rehearse the next steps, and on June 25, the top man would lead everyone to the Xijiao Gate to offer thanks; then on June 26 he would lead them all to the Confucian temple to conduct a sacrifice. The Ministry of Rites would tell the Ministry of Works to cut a stela bearing everyone's name for placement at the Imperial University. [8]

Zhang's presence in Beijing during all this, and at this particular time, surely gave him an opportunity to ferret out the state of the emerging rites crisis, to learn about whom he should contact, and to figure out how to get his message through to Jiajing personally. It was no hard task to spot the flaws in the prevailing argument that Jiajing must ritually desert his father and mother. That violated human feeling (*renqing*), without question. Nor could any classical rules clearly justify it.

Zhang's first official assignment was as an observer trainee in the Grand Court of Revision. While still a trainee, not yet a holder of an official position, he sent up his first long statement, the "Questions and Answers on the Great Rites," or *Dali huowen*. It was dated August 2, 1521. It took some bold courage to defy prevailing opinion. This was followed by a second installment, dated October 30. The censors and supervising secretaries (*kedao*) impeached him for his first statement on grounds that it "deflected and disordered the ruler's mind." Jiajing refused demands from the Ministry of Rites that he chastise Zhang. He met with Yang Tinghe in an effort to get him to change his mind. Yang refused to give an inch. Then in October 1522, while the emperor's mother had halted her journey at Tongzhou and was refusing to enter Beijing by side entrances, Zhang sent up the second installment. He had trouble getting anyone to take it in. Finally he went personally to the Zuoshun Gate and submitted it. Yang Tinghe tried but failed to get Hanlin compiler Yang Weicong, the top-ranking *jinshi*, to stop him. So Jiajing got to see Zhang's tracts. He simply marked them "noted." The Ministry of Rites and Yang Tinghe decided to remove Zhang from Beijing for his troublemaking, and so they exiled him, in effect, down to Nanjing as a bureau secretary in the southern Ministry of Justice.[9]

* * *

Vanishingly few officials backed Jiajing's desire to remain true to his father and be an adoptee of a former emperor. Zhang was one, and he was not popular. There were a bare handful of others. Who were they? Why would they challenge the prevailing consensus on the rites? Early in 1524, Jiajing learned of five such men and summoned them to Beijing.

He found out who they were because of his periodic practice of calling for the officials to gather and consolidate their opinions on controversial issues. Jiajing was already aware of Zhang Fujing, of course. Then he learned about Gui E. From his post as a bureau secretary in the Ministry of Justice down in Nanjing, Gui E sent up a long statement in support of Jiajing's position on the Great Rites. On February 24, 1524, Jiajing forwarded his statement to Minister of Rites Wang Jun and instructed him to gather all the high civil and military officials and the *kedao* (supervising secretaries and censors, the "speaking officials") and poll them for their views.

On March 2, Wang reported the results. Eighty-two memorials came in, featuring the views of some 250 writers and cosigners. The Beijing officials were absolutely unanimous in opposing Gui E. Only four writers took the side of Gui E and Jiajing. He gave their names: Zhang Fujing, Huo Tao, Xiong Jie, and Gui E himself. They were not present in Beijing and weren't included in the poll, so their statements must have been on file, made earlier. Two more were discovered later: Xi Shu and Fang Xianfu.

For two weeks, Jiajing said nothing. Then on March 17, he told Wang Jun that he wanted the matter discussed again, that some sort of compromise needed to be made, such that the integrity of the imperial line was preserved, while the ruler's emotional need to revere his dead father was met. Meanwhile, on his own authority, Jiajing ordered his supporters to come up to Beijing.[10] This was a sixteen-year-old boy playing a complex power game. It is not clear who might have been advising him.

Who were these men? They were an interesting group. At the outset, the most prominent among them was Xi Shu (1461–1527), a native of Sichuan, a midlevel official with a long and distinguished provincial career behind him, a friend of both the renowned Wang Yangming and his philosophical adversary, Luo Qinshun. Aware of the developing rites controversy in Beijing, Xi Shu had prepared a statement supporting Jiajing, but he feared submitting it. In 1522, while a vice minister of war in Nanjing, he was put in charge of a massive famine relief effort for flood victims north of the Yangzi, and drought victims south of it. Meanwhile, his colleague, Gui E, a bureau director alongside Zhang Fujing in the Nanjing Ministry of Justice, enthusiastically sent Xi Shu's statement up to Beijing. (Xi Shu, capable and sympathetic, was no firebrand himself.)

Gui E (1478–1531) was very different. He was regularly yoked with Zhang Fujing as one of the two prime movers in the pro-Jiajing faction. At the outset, memorialists and chroniclers often listed him ahead of Zhang (later the order was reversed: Zhang and Gui). Gui was hotheaded to the point of occasional mental breakdown. After passing his *jinshi* degree in 1511, he was made a county magistrate, a typical first assignment for a degree winner who placed somewhere low on the list. His superiors found him obstreperous and twice dismissed him. Under Jiajing, he returned to office, and in 1521 he was made a bureau secretary in Nanjing. A year later, Zhang Fujing joined him in the same capacity.

Xiong Jie (1478–1554), a Jiangxi native, won his *jinshi* in 1514 and as a supervising secretary played a major role in the Zhengde era, uncovering cases of crime and malfeasance. In 1522, he composed a statement supporting Jiajing. It was rejected. He was sent away as assistant administrative commissioner in Henan Province. He resubmitted his statement, but family mourning obligations forced him to postpone coming to Beijing until 1527. Xiong was an active and sincere devotee of the Cheng-Zhu Neo-Confucian orthodoxy, always seeking to "realize [the Way] through personal experience."[11]

Huo Tao (1487–1540), a *jinshi* year-mate of Xiong Jie's, was like him a man of vehement disposition. Like Xiong, he expressed his support of Jiajing early on, in 1521, so the ruler knew about him. The year 1524 found him at home in Nanhai, Guangdong Province, on sick leave. There would not have been time for him to send up a new statement from Guangdong 1,200 miles away to the south. There must have been an earlier statement of his on file. He finally arrived in Beijing in 1527.[12]

Fang Xianfu (c. 1485–1544), a high-ranking young *jinshi* of 1505, a Hanlin bachelor, and later a bureau vice director in the Ministry of Personnel, was, like Huo Tao, a native of Nanhai County in Guangdong. He had been at home ten years on sick leave when Jiajing came to the throne in 1521. The new government recalled him to his old position in the Ministry of Personnel. On the way to Beijing that summer, Fang had gotten wind of the developing Great Rites controversy, and so he composed a statement supporting Jiajing. When he arrived in Beijing, he found the political atmosphere too intimidating, and so he decided not to submit it. But a copy of it had somehow come into Gui E's possession, and so Gui sent it up, together with Xi Shu's statement. Gui was corralling reluctant warriors to the pro-Jiajing cause.

This all made for a small core group of pro-Jiajing officials: Gui, Zhang, Xi, Huo, and Fang. As of March, Fang was the only one personally in Beijing. Xiong Jie, at home in Jiangxi, was never a member of the leading circle. The Ming dynastic history (*Ming shi*) says he lacked the partisan spirit. Huo Tao was still down in Guangdong. Xi, Zhang, and Gui were in Nanjing. They at once answered the summons that Jiajing issued, purely on his own authority, leaving Beijing officialdom completely out of the loop. That was certain to raise a din of protest. How would the spurned officials react?

* * *

The kingmaker and chief grand secretary Yang Tinghe retired from office on March 15, 1524. He was getting old at sixty-four and felt frustrated as Jiajing asserted himself and Yang's personal authority, great but always contingent upon imperial favor, eroded. He was a holdover from the Zhengde era, too, and not Jiajing's personal appointee. None of his immediate successors as chief grand secretary could exert command and control over Ming government to the same degree. Jiang Mian had had enough, and he resigned on June 2. Mao Ji stepped down on August 26. That left Fei Hong, who served as chief until 1527, maneuvering unsteadily between Jiajing and the many officials who were opposed to him. So the Grand Secretariat was not in a position to stop erosion in the anti-Jiajing ranks as Jiajing began leavening those ranks with appointees of his own choosing.

Around April 24, the anti-Jiajing minister of rites, Wang Jun, fell sick and begged to resign. Until he died soon after, Jiajing thought he might be feigning his illness. He scolded him for "perversely flouting the canons, and treating me with arrant contempt," and dismissed him. The Ministry of Personnel sent up two nominees to replace him. Jiajing rejected both and, on his own authority, appointed Xi Shu to the post. That was a big first blow to the opposition.[13]

Meanwhile, arguments raged over the proper titles of respect to be given Jiajing's birth parents, and over the question of whether, as an adopted son, Jiajing still had the right to build a shrine to his own father inside the Forbidden City. On March 17, after having called in his supporters Zhang and Gui from Nanjing, he issued an edict stating that he dared not disturb the imperial ancestral temple or the direct line of imperial succession, but hoped nevertheless to express his deepest feelings for his own natal father, so he directed the officials to come up with an appropriate solution to his dilemma.[14] He sent a notice down to Gui and Zhang, who were on the road heading north, telling them not to come after all. Xi Shu, traveling separately, was also ordered to stop.[15]

Zhang and Gui received the message on April 15, upon their arrival at Fengyang, still some five hundred miles from Beijing. From the prefecture's copy of the *Capital Gazette* (*Dibao*, the informal official newspaper), they read Jiajing's compromise edict. Gui was incapacitated by a serious attack of something like rheumatoid arthritis, but finally, on April 27, he and Zhang sent up by way of a personal houseman a memorial scolding Jiajing for forgetting that the word *bensheng* (natal; one's own parent), which appeared in the compromise edict, was a trick; that is to say, "natal" implied the existence of another parent by adoption, who was not natal. Jiajing got their memorial, realized his mistake, and decided he'd better let the two proceed up to Beijing after all. Jiang Mian, who would retire a month later, warned him that the two might be physically assaulted on arrival, but Jiajing paid no heed. He also ordered Xi Shu to resume his journey.[16]

Meanwhile, in Beijing the struggle intensified. As Jiajing for the moment had compromised on his father's titles, the question of whether he could build an inner palace shrine to his father rose to the top of the list of disputes. Minister of Personnel Qiao Yu protested that an inner palace shrine negated any need for a shrine at the prince's home in Anlu and mixed Jiajing's family line with the greater imperial line. Other luminaries chimed in.

The Ministry of Rites would soon become the launching site for Jiajing's whole effort at remolding the Great Rites, and indeed beyond that, for his further plans for the ritual remaking of China. Jiajing appointed Wu Yipeng, vice minister of rites and an oppositionist, as Wang Jun's temporary replacement. At the same time, he took the extraordinary step of directly issuing from the palace an order appointing Xi Shu to that post, whenever he should arrive.

This provocative display of imperial authority ignited a small firestorm of protest. It was pointed out that established Ming precedent had it that ministers of rites were always Hanlin men recommended by the Ministry of Personnel. Xi Shu was neither. Protesters demanded that Jiajing rescind the appointment. He refused. [17]

Xi Shu was no narrow polemicist but a man of ability and wide experience in the provinces. As an educational official in Guizhou, he built an academy for the celebrated official, thinker, and teacher Wang Yangming. He helped suppress a tribal revolt in Yunnan. In Huguang he handled flood control, bandit suppression, and corruption. Then he was transferred to Nanjing, where he met Zhang and Gui. Xi Shu wanted the promotion, but he followed custom in twice declining it. Then on July 8, opponents charged him with gross corruption and mismanagement in the handling of the great famine north and south of the Yangzi. On August 13, Jiajing received Xi Shu's answer to that accusation: "I was sent to offer relief in the Fengyang region," replied Xi, "and I worked day and night in an area wracked by epidemic disease. I saved a million people, I did my job, but the officials hate me because of [my statement about the] Great Rites; they attack my motives, and I have no way to clear myself, so I ask to be investigated, and if killed, I'll have no regrets." Xi's statement, made public on June 10, accused the anti-Jiajing bloc of purveying unclear ideas, which many officials knew to be wrongheaded but they feared to challenge the majority. Only Zhang and Gui, he said, have dared to speak out, and they are hated like enemies for having done so.

Jiajing ordered the eunuch Directorate of Ceremonial, the Ministry of Revenue, the judicial organs, and the Embroidered-Uniform Guard to send one top official each to join the provincial authorities and conduct an investigation into the facts about the accusation against Xi. [18]

As already noted above, Chief Grand Secretary Jiang Mian asked to resign on June 2. He said he was frustrated by Jiajing's insistence on building a
palace shrine to his father, by his peremptory appointment of Xi Shu, and by
his ordering Zhang and Gui to resume their trip to the capital. He said
suspicions about the ruler's intentions were on the rise everywhere, and those
orders must be rescinded. Jiajing agreed to Jiang's plea to resign and, for
good measure, scolded him for wanting to desert his job at a very busy time
and for putting blame on the ruler for the growing crisis.[19] Grand Secretary
Mao Ji replaced him as chief.

The controversial shrine to Jiajing's father was declared finished on June
10. Room for it in the inner palace ancestral temple, the Fengxian Dian, had
been set aside and renamed, and a delegation of officials (including a reluctant Wu Yipeng) was chosen to go to Anlu and fetch Jiajing's father's spirit
tablet for installation in the new shrine.[20] Clearly the anti-Jiajing position
was eroding.

Zhang Fujing and Gui E finally arrived in Beijing in late June. Gui E was
still too weak to walk. On June 21, his boat reached Jiangjiawan (Jiang
family cove) east of Beijing, a major freight and passenger hub at Tongzhou,
about twenty miles away. There he hired a sedan chair and the next day
found a place to stay outside the Zhengyang Gate. He let Jiajing know that he
would make a personal court appearance when he felt stronger.[21] Zhang
appeared for the daily dawn court lineup on June 25, bearing his and Gui's
joint statement.[22]

Beijing officialdom reacted in fury. The *kedao* led the charge. Some thirty
supervising secretaries cosigned a vehement protest. The chief supervising
secretary of the Office of Scrutiny for Rites, Zhang Chong, charged the two
new arrivals with making false and deceptive statements, with fomenting evil
plans to wreck the imperial ancestral temple, with sowing enmity between
Jiajing's mother and the Hongzhi emperor's widow, with criticizing and
challenging the ruler's edicts, and with destroying the "good species" of
office-holding officials. Forty-three censors laid into Zhang, Gui, Xi Shu,
and several other sympathizers as so many shameless flatterers with no more
than self-advancement in mind.[23]

Jiajing merely "noted" receipt of these memorials; then he released them
for general discussion. He did not release any of Zhang and Gui's statements.
This was a new battle tactic.

On July 9, Zhang and Gui sent in a sharp reply to all the attacks sent
against them. They reminded Jiajing that the rites officials were stubbornly

defending a position that was wrong from the start. The *kedao* were merely "eagles and dogs" using slanders and threats on behalf of high officials who aimed above all to stay in power. They urged Jiajing to convene the grand secretaries and the rites officials in some convenient place inside the Forbidden City where the two could openly plead their case. Jiajing pigeonholed this idea.

Then, on July 13, he launched a torpedo into the mix. He announced the appointments of Zhang, Gui, and Fang Xianfu to Hanlin Academy positions—Zhang and Gui as chancellors, Fang as academician reader-in-waiting.

Among the Hanlin men already on duty, the reaction was swift and unforgiving. Chancellor Feng Xi and three others refused to attend court, in effect going on strike. The *kedao* weighed in with warnings. Censor Liu Qianheng said rewarding ambitious strivers with skewed views threatened to demoralize the elite classes (*shi*) nationwide.

Feng Xi and the others offered to resign. Jiajing said no. Minister of Personnel Qiao Yu demanded that Jiajing dismiss all the deviant, place-seeking new appointees. Jiajing refused, ordering everyone to stay on the job. He informed the realm that Zhang and Gui and the others were loyal and capable men of deep learning whose ideas were based in the classics. They were not obsequious careerists.

Twenty-nine supervising secretaries and forty-six censors answered back with fire, demanding executions for the craven rogues who dared mislead the ruler, just on the basis of one idea. Minister of Justice Zhao Jian said he was eager to begin prosecuting Gui and Zhang. Jiajing ordered him to back off. Vice Director Xue Hui of the Ministry of Personnel sent up a long statement in two parts refuting the views of Zhang and Gui on the rites of succession. Jiajing was not pleased to receive this. He said Xue Hui exceeded the limits of his job and spoke wantonly. He ordered him imprisoned and interrogated under torture.[24] Zhang and Gui submitted a reply that Jiajing again retained but did not make public.

Clearly the Great Rites dispute was growing uglier by the day, and it was young Jiajing himself who was ratcheting up the process. Worse was to come. Threats of physical violence against Zhang and Gui filled the air. The two absented themselves from court for a few days, claiming they were ill. Then they used side entrances to come and go, avoiding the crowd. Marquis Guo Xun let them stay in his mansion for safety's sake. He is also said to have arranged a nighttime interview for them with Jiajing. "I'll share every danger and blessing with you," the ruler reportedly said. "Never mind the roar of the crowd." Zhang replied, "They're just administrators, while you're most revered, as bright as the sun, as powerful as a thunderbolt. Who dares defy you? A few Embroidered-Uniform Guards will suffice to take care of them!" And the emperor nodded his agreement. [25]

On July 22, thirty-six junior Hanlin appointees and bachelors asked to be allowed to resign because they could not accept Gui E and the others as colleagues. Their leader was none other than Yang Tinghe's son, Yang Shen. An unbridgeable gulf divided them: on the one side, the standard Neo-Confucianism of Cheng Yi and Zhu Xi, and on the other, perverted learning. Jiajing scolded the young men, most of them trainees. He docked their salaries. [26]

There were more protests. On July 25, a junior official from the Court of State Ceremonial spoke out. On August 1, two physicians from the Imperial Academy of Medicine thought "Guande Dian" (Hall for Observing Virtue) a poor name for Jiajing's father's shrine, and they asked Jiajing to change it. That stung the ruler. "I fixed that name myself," he replied. "It expresses filial piety, and the sign has already been put up. Those two forget their main jobs; they exceed their station and speak recklessly, and they treat me contemptuously." The protesters were all sent to prison for questioning under torture. [27]

On August 3, Fang Xianfu, still in the Ministry of Personnel, asked for permission to resign and go home. It will be recalled that he was a staunch supporter of Jiajing and was on the verge of taking up a new post in the Hanlin Academy. He said that the Great Rites should not be used as a path for advancement in office. He also said that he simply had no way to respond to all the attacks, and that the longer he stayed, the worse things would get, to the detriment of the whole rites issue. Jiajing ordered him to stay. [28] Fang was a devoted follower of Wang Yangming, and like Wang, he was not confrontational. He had little of Zhang Fujing's zest for bureaucratic warfare.

Jiajing was retaining all of Zhang and Gui's statements, releasing only those sent up by the opposition. So Zhang and Gui knew everything the attackers were saying, whereas the opposition was reduced to firing their bullets in the dark. It was not a fair fight.

On August 5, Minister of Personnel Qiao Yu, completely frustrated by Jiajing's stand on the rites, was finally allowed to resign. [29]

Six days later, the political heat in Beijing flared even higher. By fiat, Jiajing ordered the Ministry of Rites to prepare and submit a program for conducting a formal announcement to Heaven, Earth, the imperial ancestors,

and the gods of soil and grain that the word *bensheng* (natal) was to be erased
henceforth from his mother's title. That of course meant he was disavowing
the Hongzhi emperor's consort as his adopted mother. The ceremony was to
be staged on August 15.[30] At the moment, the minister's post was vacant, as
Xi Shu hadn't yet arrived. So Vice Minister Zhu Xizhou protested on the
ministry's behalf that for three years Jiajing had recognized the Hongzhi
emperor as his father and his consort as his mother; that this new order had
come by way of palace fiat, making all earlier public edicts void and mean-
ingless; and that the gods and spirits would surely spurn a corrupted rite.
"The word *bensheng* is not a disparagement," the ministry said. "It does not
block the correct line of descent, and it expresses the emotion one feels for so
close a relative. Why erase it and stir controversy in the realm?"[31]

That certainly sounded reasonable, but Jiajing would have none of it.
Zhang and Gui had succeeded in changing his mind on why the word *natal*
had to go. Jiajing sent a eunuch to ask the grand secretaries to endorse the
ceremony. Mao Ji and Shi Yao both declined. Jiajing then arranged to meet
them personally. "You ignore me," he scolded. "And you want to deprive me
of my father?" The grand secretaries had no response to that. The young
emperor then gathered the officials at the Zuoshun Gate and proclaimed that
the ceremony for changing his mother's title would take place four days
hence.[32]

Much of the rest of Beijing officialdom rushed at once to the support of
the Ministry of Rites. Hanlin chancellor Feng Xi led off. "Your edict [on the
rites] has been in force for three years, yet now on the basis of reckless
statements made by one or two men, you erase the word *bensheng* as a way
to exalt your own mother exclusively. This order of yours alarms us. We
don't know how to deal with it, but we venture to say that you rule the
ancestral temple and the spirits in it, and you must hold the rituals there in
high respect, so you must not misunderstand the idea of succession that it
stands for. If you pervert the sacred rites, and leave a legacy of controversy
for future generations, won't you be ruining your virtue?" All the speaking
officials (*kedao*); bureau directors from the Ministries of Personnel, Revenue, War, and Justice; and the assistant minister of the Court of Judicial
Review joined in the protest. Jiajing ordered eight of them arrested and
imprisoned.[33]

At some point during these days, Zhang Fujing sent in a detailed thirteen-
point rebuttal of all the matters of controversy raised thus far by Jiajing's
opponents. As usual, Jiajing did not make it public. Zhang treated each

opposition argument as a "deceptive fraud" (*qiwang*). No one recognized an honest difference of opinion. Obviously the politicization of the debate was becoming toxic. The thirteenth and last point of Zhang's left no doubt on that score:

> The reason a faction has formed about rites is because we consider you to be a ruler who came in to resume the great succession and should not be made a son of Emperor Xiaozong [the Hongzhi emperor]. The partisans of fraud maintain that you are Emperor Xiaozong's son, and did not come in to resume the great succession. This disagreement has gone on for three years without being resolved. The idea that you're Xiaozong's son began with just one powerful and evil grand secretary [i.e., Yang Tinghe]. The Ministry of Rites officials sided with him. The Nine Ministers and the *kedao* sided with him. From the outset, they didn't grasp the importance of the affair, or how mistaken their ideas were. We respect your sagely brilliance, and how pure your mind is for filial piety. How can we ignore that? That's why we struggle, not caring for our own safety, to make this dispute clear. Sixty or seventy percent of the officials of the two capitals, high and low, know that the prevailing court opinion is wrong. Only twenty or thirty percent cleave to it out of ignorance. But those who know it to be wrong look on dissenters as evil and deviant. They use rumors to get them demoted and sent away, and the periodic evaluations to get them dismissed. Those ignorant of rites take advantage of that to launch attacks, not letting anyone speak out. Then the Nine Ministers and *kedao* officials sign joint memorials. Do they really all share the same opinion? The heads of the Nine Ministries draft memorials which they don't let anyone see. They just write the names of the offices on a blank sheet of paper. Then they send clerks out to collect signatures. Anyone who refuses to sign is impeached by their supporters among the *kedao*. Even high officials resign, none daring to voice his anger. The joint memorials of the *kedao* fall into this same pattern. One of them does the writing, while the rest feel forced to follow along. Many at court right now agree with me, but they just glance to the front and rear and then nod, saying nothing. Anciently, the Three Dukes would speak of the Way, the Nine Ministers would take office and govern, and the Censors would look and listen with great care. Doesn't that cause us shame now? This is the thirteenth evil fraud. [34]

It certainly appears that Zhang Fujing's reading of the political atmosphere at the Ming court was spot on. He was, after all, a practical man of action and an astute analyst of politics, as well as a scholar of the rites.

With the title change for Jiajing's mother scheduled for August 15, an explosion could no longer be contained. Jiajing was withholding Zhang Fujing's long memorial. Vice Minister of Personnel He Mengchun heard something about it, however, and somehow managed to obtain a copy of it at the Office of Transmission. That of course was in violation of procedure. It defied Jiajing's prerogative to "declassify" memorials. The vice minister then stayed up all night composing a point-by-point rebuttal. Mainly he denied that Jiajing's opposition constituted any sort of "faction." He insisted that everyone's opinion was freely arrived at, with no coercion involved. (Jiajing retained this memorial, too.)

Indeed, even if Chief Grand Secretary Yang Tinghe had wrong-footed the rites at the outset of Jiajing's succession in 1521, by 1524 those who had followed his lead had developed powerful arguments around the idea that imperial succession was one thing, while family succession was quite another. The one was public and impartial, the other private and self-serving. It was passionately asserted that nothing short of the utter collapse of civilization would soon follow if Jiajing should choose the path of selfishness. Zhang Fujing had that one wrong. It was not pure good facing down deliberate evil. It was two totally sincere, indeed death-defying rallies of officials— Jiajing and Zhang Fujing and a handful of others on one side, facing a seething bloc of aroused and indignant opponents on the other.

Why was direct succession such a touchstone issue? Unclear signals from the classics and histories, including early Ming history, had created a seed-bed for a scholarly controversy, but why did things explode from there into a partisan battle? A partisan battle was probably going to happen anyway. Any controversial issue might have ignited it.

The explosion occurred on August 14. A good portion, perhaps 10 percent, of the officials on duty in Beijing stopped work and staged a demonstration. After dawn court was dismissed and the officials began drifting back to their offices, He Mengchun acted, apparently on the spur of the moment, to rally them for a demonstration. Everyone was assuming that Jiajing's refusal to release He's memorial meant that he was going to forge ahead with his larger plan to disavow the Hongzhi emperor and break the direct line of dynastic succession. Partly in despair and partly with a slim hope that a demonstration might move Jiajing to change his mind, some 232 officials of high rank and low, outside the Zuoshun Gate, fell to a kneeling position with arms extended and began wailing the names of Taizu and Xiaozong, the first and last emperors in the direct line. Jiajing, nearby in the Wenhua Pavilion, could hear it. For hours the din went on. Eunuchs were sent out to tell everyone to leave, but to no avail. Eight arrests were made. That stopped the din momentarily, but then it started again. Finally, in midafternoon, Embroidered-Uniform Guardsmen moved in and arrested all of them.

The demonstration failed. Jiajing took it as a gesture of contempt directed at him personally, but his retaliation was measured. Twenty-one high-ranking participants, and sixty-five very low-ranking ones, were placed on probation. The rest, 134 middle-ranking officials, were taken on August 19 from prison to the Meridian Gate, and there each was flogged thirty times. Most were then dragged to the edge of the Imperial City and released. Seven were taken back to prison and flogged again on August 27. Seventeen men in all died of their wounds. The rest were variously demoted and transferred to the provinces, removed from civil service, or exiled for life to the frontiers.[35]

That broke the back of the resistance. On August 15, the formal ceremony for the erasure of the *bensheng* designation went ahead as scheduled.[36] On the same day, the ruler personally scolded He Mengchun for his leading role in the demonstration, but for the moment he let him off with a fine of a month's salary. Chief Grand Secretary Mao Ji and his colleague Shi Yao had come out and for a while knelt alongside the demonstrators. Mao Ji was sympathetic with their cause. Frustrated with Jiajing's autocratic behavior, he wrote a long and heartfelt protest and was finally allowed to retire honorably on August 23.[37] Shi Yao stayed on; Fei Hong became the new chief grand secretary.

* * *

So an unbeatable combination of effective scholarly research and brute force settled the Great Rites issue. But the utter sincerity that good and upright men had invested in a losing cause did not dissipate. It smoldered on among the defeated and disaffected officials for some years thereafter.

Already on August 16, the ruler had to deal with nine high officials, among them He Mengchun, for staying away from the retitling ceremony for Jiajing's mother. They all acknowledged their guilt. Jiajing just scolded them, then let them go.[38]

The delegation bringing Jiajing's father's spirit tablet from Anlu reached Beijing on August 20 and was installed with great ceremony in the Guande Hall he had built inside the Forbidden City. Jiajing ignored memorials begging him to forgive all the imprisoned demonstrators in honor of this solemn occasion.[39] Honors to Jiajing's father mounted over the years following, ending eventually in a new and better shrine, and further posthumous imperial honors.

The failed demonstration of August 14 left two different developments in its wake. The first was an all-out effort by Jiajing to explain and justify his view of the ritual of succession by way of compiling and publishing a comprehensive casebook documenting the dispute and making it clear to everyone in China how and why Jiajing's was the correct line. The other was a continuing fight by the losers against Zhang and Gui and their allies, but avoiding rites and targeting instead their alleged self-serving opportunism and corruption.

The casebook was edited by Zhang Fujing. Jiajing provided the title of it: *Great Canon for Clarifying Human Relations (Minglun dadian)*. Because it was narrowly focused on a technicality in the chain of imperial succession, a matter not likely to rise again, it was never challenged. Perhaps it validated once again for all Chinese the central importance of filial piety in their lives.

Collecting all the documents and compiling the work was demanding and exhausting. It was no slapdash job. Zhang was the de facto general editor of it, but Jiajing was a constant and perceptive critic of the work as it progressed. Its aim at the outset was to educate all the realm's elites.

Fang Xianfu, Hanlin reader-in-waiting, produced an early prototype. He argued that the whole rites issue had not been well articulated and was not widely understood. Jiajing approved Fang's request to gather the memorials of Zhang Fujing and the others and have the Ministry of Rites print them up for distribution.[40]

That was scarcely enough. A definitive casebook was needed, as Zhang argued in a long memorial. Fang's compilation was incomplete; plus it included statements by Xi Shu and others that were sufficiently off target as to leave loopholes that oppositionists might easily exploit. Many of the editors who were expected to work on the new casebook were among the crowd that had knelt and wailed on August 14. Zhang claimed they still harbored evil in their minds and would likely sabotage the project. There was, however, no need to recall from circulation Fang's version. The new casebook should be compiled quickly, minus the participation of underground opponents in the Hanlin.[41]

The editing, undertaken personally by Zhang and a few trusted others, turned out to be complicated and demanding of time and thought.[42] Zhang and the emperor exchanged confidential messages about it. Jiajing wanted it to be a monument, a testamentary guide for all future generations. On July

26, 1527, Jiajing wrote the Grand Secretariat about a draft Zhang had submitted called "The Complete Book of Correct Rites." Wrote Jiajing, "This rite is not just for today, but forever. It clarifies human relations, rectifies correct order, and is very important. But the title isn't quite right. I'd call it the *Ming lun dadian*. I don't know if that's all right or not. You all need to meet with Zhang and Gui and discuss that and reply."[43] The new title was adopted. On August 1, the ruler directed editor Zhang to repair the flaws in Xi Shu's statement and to add statements of Han and Song vintage and praise them if they were acceptable or criticize them if not. Then future generations won't be misled, he said.[44]

On September 9, Jiajing responded to another draft. "I've read the draft," he wrote, "but you need to clearly indicate which memorials are solo and which are coauthored, which ones stem from official discussion meetings or were written in response to imperial directives, and which ones are blatantly wrong. You have to discriminate right from wrong, orthodox from deviant. This is how a well-grounded book must be. You have to accept the difficulties and reedit this."[45]

The work was completed and published on June 17, 1528, with the grand secretaries of the time (not Zhang Fujing) listed as principal supervising editors.[46] Jiajing provided a preface, and Zhang Fujing a colophon. Promotions in rank went to Zhang, Gui E, Fang Xianfu, and the grand secretaries. Yang Tinghe and the other high figures in the opposition were punished by reduction to commoner status. The Great Rites dispute thus came at last to its grand finale. With his casebook, the young autocrat laid his moral and intellectual claim to sagehood.

* * *

The other consequence of the failed demonstration of August 14, 1524, was the creation of a seething opposition underground. Jiajing was reluctant to authorize an all-out witch hunt to root them out. On September 19, 1524, a firebrand supervising secretary by the name of Chen Guang sent Jiajing a list of ten prominent officials, Chief Grand Secretary Fei Hong among them, who, he claimed, were involved in dissent, were members of a deviant clique, and should be punished forthwith. Fourteen men he singled out as still suffering the deviant clique's hatred and as therefore deserving of promotion. So here was a clear invitation to launch a purge. But Jiajing declined to act on it. He reassured Fei Hong of his continued backing and retained the others as well.[47]

A few months later, Chen Guang himself came under assault as an attack dog for Minister of Rites Xi Shu, and as notoriously corrupt in private life. Jiajing ordered an investigation of the charges. Xi Shu and Fei Hong begged to be allowed to retire because of the controversy, but Jiajing retained them. Pleas from various officials for mercy and amnesty for those flogged and exiled for what they did on August 14 were ignored. The outbreak of troubles along the northern frontier and the need for the cooperative attention of the officials may have helped dampen enthusiasm for a witch hunt.

In a long memorial of November 29, Xi Shu, now at last in Beijing as minister of personnel, urged a war on corruption. Jiajing didn't want that sort of purge, either. He said the cleansing of the abuses of the Zhengde era was over and done with. It would not benefit governance (the *zhengti*) to overdo it. We're looking, he said, for the rise of a "Jiajing order" of peace and harmony in the realm. Your fixation, said Jiajing to Xi Shu, is on "disorderly change" (*fengeng*), and an upheaval of that sort is not wanted.[48]

* * *

Jiajing, for all his quick temper and occasional cruelty, never set in motion a big purge in the paranoid style of Stalin, or of Ming Taizu, the dynasty's founder. He wanted to put an end to controversy and move on to other projects. But a major flare-up burst unexpectedly upon the scene in 1527, three years after the 1524 demonstration. This was the so-called Great Case (*da yu*). The facts of the case are rather murky, but the passionate bureaucratic hatreds it rekindled, and the outcome of it, are clear.

The Great Case involved a fugitive White Lotus cult leader and outlaw by the name of Li Fuda. He was a native of the northernmost reaches of Shanxi Province, on China's steppe frontier. He and an uncle had allegedly gathered a large following of worshippers of the Maitreya Buddha, whose rebirth was believed to presage the end of the world as we know it. They went on a rampage of killing and destruction in central Shaanxi Province. Ming forces suppressed them. The uncle was caught and executed. Li Fuda escaped into hiding not far from his home. There he allegedly paid someone of the Zhang surname to admit him into the Zhang lineage book under a new name, Zhang Yin.

Li was entrepreneurial and wealthy. At some point, he made his way to Beijing and bribed his way into both Shanxi military rank and the Beijing registry as an artisan. Artisan registry allowed his three sons to engage in alchemy and drug manufacture there. They were said to have concocted drugs for Marquis Guo Xun, a powerful inside protector of Zhang Fujing and Gui E and a key ally of Jiajing in the Great Rites dispute. It is this connection that turned a regional criminal case into a national cause célèbre.

Someone back in Shanxi fingered Zhang Yin as in fact the wanted fugitive Li Fuda. Two sons were arrested in Beijing. Back in Shanxi, the local and provincial authorities were divided over whether Li's (or Zhang's) accuser was telling the truth or not. Eventually, Regional Inspector Ma Lu made a strong case that Zhang was Li after interrogating him and consulting locals who knew Li Fuda. Guo Xun, acting on behalf of the drug-making sons, wrote Ma Lu, asking him to drop the case. If a bribe were on offer, Ma Lu refused it. Worse, he charged Guo Xun with treason for protecting a rebel wanted for mass murder! He produced Guo's letter as evidence.

Jiajing was at first inclined to endorse Ma Lu's statement that Zhang Yin was Li Fuda and that Li should be executed and his family enslaved. Back in prison in Shanxi, Li awaited his fate. Guo Xun's involvement, however, gave the ruler pause. Minister of Personnel Xi Shu came to Guo's defense. A case reviewer in the Court of Judicial Review impeached both Guo and Xi and asked the ruler to convene the whole court to consider the case. The Censorate made a similar recommendation. Jiajing ignored them. He called in Guo Xun and demanded an explanation. The marquis made excuses, argued that Zhang Yin was not Li Fuda, and begged for mercy. Jiajing took no immediate action.

Then one of Li's (or Zhang's) sons, acting on Guo's advice, submitted a plea on his father's behalf. The plea was made public. That prompted a blizzard of memorials from the speaking officials (*kedao*) in both Beijing and Nanjing, demanding Li's execution and heavy punishment for Guo as well. In response, Guo now argued that all these angry accusations were the crowd's retaliation for having lost out earlier in the Great Rites showdown. Jiajing was inclined to agree with that explanation. So the Li Fuda/Zhang Yin case metastasized into something of a referendum on the Great Rites.

The Li Fuda case was removed from Shanxi and brought to Beijing for court discussion and trial. Ma Lu submitted a fierce argument for the prosecution. The speaking officials agreed and impeached Guo Xun.

Behind the scenes, Zhang Fujing and his close ally Gui E told Jiajing that the court officials were acting in conjunction so as to ruin Guo Xun, in the expectation that they could further implicate all the advocates of the Great Rites and so slake their desire for revenge. Jiajing agreed with them.

Meanwhile, Li Fuda/Zhang Yin was brought in custody to Beijing where ten high officials plus the Embroidered-Uniform Guard interrogated him. Li confessed to all charges. They recommended immediate execution. Jiajing stalled. He demanded a trial before a full gathering of court officials. The original accuser and the locals who disputed him were interrogated again. One local man recanted his testimony. He denied that he ever challenged the accuser. Jiajing was told of this new testimony, but he doubted its veracity. He announced that he was going to conduct the investigation himself. Grand Secretary Yang Yiqing talked him out of it, arguing that it was too petty a matter for the emperor to take a direct role in it.

Tang Shu, a bureau secretary in the Ministry of Justice, sent in a well-researched and reasonably argued memorial to the effect that Li Fuda's guilt was clear and that he must be executed.[49] In anger, Jiajing removed Tang Shu from the civil service. That reaction frightened Minister of Justice Yan Yishou and various others. An amended statement was sent up, together with all the conflicting evidence, with a new conclusion that the case was unclear. Even that concession did not mollify Jiajing.

In May 1527, the emperor sent the Embroidered-Uniform Guard out to Shanxi to bring to Beijing, imprison, and interrogate under torture Provincial Inspector Ma Lu plus all the other officials involved in the original indictment fingering Zhang Yin as actually the fugitive Li Fuda. Minister of Justice Yan Yishou restated his original opinion, that to let Li off the hook would encourage another sectarian rising out west. Jiajing rejected Yan's argument, accusing him of cliquism. Yan asked for another court discussion. Jiajing agreed. Ma Lu and Li Fuda were placed side by side. Ma Lu repeated his charges, and Li made no effort to refute them. So again Yan made his plea.

Jiajing reacted with force and fury. He accused Yan of deceiving his ruler in the interest of clique politics. He remanded Yan and seven other officials of the Ministry of Justice, Censorate, and Grand Court of Revision to the Decree Prison. The situation was turning ugly.

The young emperor's next move was blatant in the extreme. He stuffed the judicial organs with his close supporters in the rites in the expectation that they would firmly declare Zhang Yin and Li Fuda to be two different men, rescue Guo Xun from imminent ruin, and salvage the ascendancy of the pro-Jiajing side in the Great Rites dispute.

Thus on August 31, 1527, Jiajing made Gui E acting minister of justice, Zhang Fujing acting censor in chief, and Fang Xianfu acting chief minister of the Court of Judicial Review, for the explicit purpose of delivering a verdict of guilty upon Ma Lu for falsely identifying Zhang Yin as Li Fuda. And indeed, Zhang Fujing conducted a wider purge, removing some twenty speaking officials from their positions as, among other things, onetime partisans of Jiajing's old nemesis, Yang Tinghe. Then he had Ma Lu put to torture, forcing him to confess to making a false indictment. In a memorial to Jiajing, Zhang Fujing explained that by law Ma Lu could not receive the death penalty (his victim was still alive), but the ruler could sentence him and his family to perpetual exile in a malarial frontier garrison. Jiajing agreed and did just that.[50]

Further arrests, imprisonments, and torture in the Great Case led to the removal and blacklisting of some forty more officials for having supported Ma Lu—and, by the same token, for opposing the Great Rites. Zhang Yin/Li Fuda was released from prison. To show that Jiajing commanded the moral high ground in this ugly affair, Zhang Fujing proposed editing a casebook justifying the crackdown; the ruler agreed, and a small volume was put together collecting all the relevant documents and printed in 1,700 copies for distribution in Beijing, with orders for the provinces to print further copies for their own reference. The casebook was titled *Record of the Great Case as Clarified by the Emperor (Qinming dayu lu)*.[51]

* * *

Such was the grand opening of the Jiajing reign, as the ruler grew from boyhood to young manhood. With the last chapter of the rites turmoil finished, he was twenty years old and had crushed a stubborn opposition. He achieved a grip on power that he would hold for the next four decades.

It was within his authority as an emperor to define for mankind now and for all time what filial piety was and to insist that it was so fundamental a right that it could not be overridden by any higher consideration whatsoever. Generally the Ming realm accepted, or at least acquiesced in, that ruling through the rest of its time on earth.

The victory did not come without a cost, however. It was achieved at the expense of the dead bodies and ruined lives of good men who had sincerely disagreed with Jiajing and were willing to suffer grievously for their beliefs in 1524 and again in 1527. Zhang Fujing, Gui E, and Jiajing's other backers could not escape the imputation of crass careerism, of using the Great Rites to propel themselves from obscurity into high office, not on the normal basis of recommendations, but at Jiajing's personal beck and call. Marquis Guo Xun was no paragon of virtue but an extremely wealthy bon vivant and schemer. That Jiajing had to work with such men to achieve his victory put a sour coating on the ethical and philosophical rationale for his interpretation of filial piety. But Jiajing was sincere, despite his methods. In the end, it was power that trumped all.

NOTES

1. On this, see F. W. Mote, *Imperial China, 900–1800* (Cambridge, MA: Harvard University Press, 1999), 658ff.

2. For much of what follows here, see under the relevant dates, *Ming shilu* (hereafter cited as *MSL*) (Taiwan Academia Sinica reprint, 1962), vol. 70; Tan Qian, *Guo que* (hereafter cited as *GQ*) (Beijing: Guji chubanshe, 1958), vol. 4; Xia Xie, *Xinxiao Ming tongjian* (hereafter cited as Xia Xie) (Taipei: Shijie shuju, 1962), vol. 4; *Ming shi* (hereafter cited as *MS*) (any edition), ch. 17; Gu Yingtai, *Mingshi jishi benmo* (hereafter cited as *MSJSBM*) (any edition), ch. 50; *Dictionary of Ming Biography*, ed. L. Carrington Goodrich and Chaoying Fang (hereafter cited as *DMB*), 2 vols. (New York: Columbia University Press, 1976); *The Cambridge History of China*, vol. 7, *The Ming Dynasty, 1368–1644, Part I* (Cambridge: Cambridge University Press, 1988); Carney T. Fisher, *The Chosen One: Succession and Adoption in the Court of Ming Shizong* (Sydney: Allen & Unwin, 1990).

3. Jiao Hong, ed., *Guochao xianzheng lu* (hereafter cited as *GCXZL*) (Taipei: Taiwan xuesheng shuju, 1965), 1.632 (epitaph for Yuan Zonggao).

4. Yang Tinghe made one error that somehow never figured in the emerging controversy. According to a strict reading of Ming house law, Jiajing was not a legitimate candidate for enthronement. His father's mother was a concubine who was never elevated to the rank of empress, and it was forbidden for an agnatic successor to be the grandson of a concubine. But Jiajing had no rival, and his right to succeed was never once called into question.

5. See Mote, *Imperial China*, 662–663.

6. For convenience's sake, I will call Zhang Cong, Zhang Fujing from here on. Jiajing gave him the name Fujing in 1531 at Zhang Cong's request because the second part of his name was homophonous with the second part of Jiajing's given name, Houcong, and Zhang felt that the similarity was unsettling and presumptuous.

7. Zhang Fujing, *Taishi Zhang Wenzhong gong wenji* (Siku quanshu cunmu congshu, 4th ser.), 77.294–305 (epitaphs).

8. *MSL*, 70.74; *Mingdai dengkelu huibian* (reprint Taipei, 1969), 6.2999–3002, 3041. This latter is a collection of examination class yearbooks, with descriptive accounts and a listing of all the graduates.

9. Wang Shizhen, biography of Zhan Fujing, in *GCXZL*, 1.549.

10. *MSL*, 72.884–886, 900–902; Xia Xie, 4.1896–1897.

11. *MS*, ch. 197 (biography); *GCXZL*, 2.1033–1034 (epitaph).

12. *DMB*, 1.679–683 (biography).

13. *MSL*, 72.933.

14. *MSL*, 72.900–902.

15. *MSJSBM*, ch. 50.

16. For dates, I follow Gui E's memorial, as the *MSL* dates are unclear.

17. *MS*, ch. 197 (biography of Xi Shu).

18. *MSL*, 72.996–998, 1042; *MSJSBM*, ch. 50.

19. *MSL*, 72.985–986.

20. *MSL*, 72.989, 994–995.

21. Gui E, *Wenxiang gong zouyi* (Siku quanshu cunmu congshu, 4th ser.), 60.44.

22. *MSL*, 72.999–1003.

23. *MSL*, 72.1006–1007.

24. *MSL*, 72.1013–1022.

25. *GQ*, 4.3302.

26. *MSL*, 72.1022.

27. *MSL*, 72.1024–1032, 1035.

28. *MSL*, 72.1036.

29. *MSL*, 72.1036.

30. *MSL*, 72.1041.

31. Xia Xie, 4.1913.

32. Ibid., 4.1914.

33. Ibid., 4.1913–1914.

34. Chen Zilong, ed., *Huang Ming jingshi wenbian* (reprint Taipei, 1964), 12.48–50.

35. John Dardess, "Protesting to the Death: The *fuque* in Ming Political History," *Ming Studies*, no. 47 (Spring 2003): 109–118.

36. *MSL*, 72.1051–1052.

37. *MSL*, 72.1079–1083; *MS*, ch. 190 (biography of Mao Ji).

38. *MSL*, 72.1074.

39. *MSL*, 72.1080–1081, 1084; Xia Xie, 4.1917.

40. *MSL*, 73.1178–1179 (December 31, 1524).

41. Zhang Fujing, *wenji*, 51–52.

42. Ibid., 56–57.

43. Zhang Fujing, *Yudui lu* (Siku quanshu cunmu congshu, 2nd ser.), 57.57–58.

44. Ibid., 58.

45. Ibid., 61.

46. The grand secretaries were Yang Yiqing (1454–1530), Jia Yong (1464–1547), and Fei Hong (1468–1535).

47. *MSL*, 72.1104–1105.

48. *MSL*, 73.1158–1159.

49. The details are in Xia Xie, 4.1987–1989.

50. Zhang Fujing, *Taishi Zhang Wenzhong gong ji* (Siku quanshu cunmu congshu, 4th ser.), 77.66; *MSJSBM*, ch. 56 (the Li Fuda case); Xia Xie, 4.1996–2001.

51. Zhang Fujing, *Taishi Zhang Wenzhong*, 77.67, 73.

Chapter Two

Spring

Grand Secretary Zhang Fujing

So, young Jiajing, by force of personality, by making full use of the traditional prerogatives of the Ming throne, and with the help of a bare half dozen key supporters, forced his will on a recalcitrant bureaucracy of many thousands, and, through them, on all the millions of people of China. Ritual correctness was a serious matter.

A small group of supporters, not an army—they were all that was necessary. There was, however, a reserve force of unknown size consisting of low-ranking opportunists, intellectual crackpots, and sundry others eager for a chance to exploit the Great Rites cause and ride it to power and riches. None of the leadership wanted anything to do with such men. But that meant that Jiajing and his partisans, even after the big crackdowns of 1524 and 1527, had continually to deal with a subdued but by no means dead bureaucratic opposition, who seized on any chance to vent their anger against the young emperor's inner circle.

The springtime, so to speak, of Jiajing's long reign coincided with Zhang Fujing's elevation to the Grand Secretariat in 1527 and his occupation of Ming China's highest post, chief grand secretary, from 1529 to 1535. Under severe attack, he was forced to step down temporarily several times. Gui E joined him as a grand secretary in 1529, but he died in 1531. Fang Xianfu came aboard in 1532 and retired in 1534. The other grand secretaries were mostly low-key workhorses like Li Shi and Chai Luan. The crucial Ministries of Personnel and Rites were usually occupied by Jiajing's personal appointees, at times Gui E and Fang Xianfu.

What was Ming China's agenda during those years? Things in China and along its frontiers were fairly quiet. Wang Yangming brought his campaign against various southwestern tribes to a successful conclusion in 1528. He died the next year, a target of continuing controversy despite his successes. Wang's legacy would ignite future partisan turmoil. However, the one big event of those years was the second mutiny among Ming troops at the northern frontier garrison city of Datong in 1533 (the first took place in 1524). An internal uprising in southern Shanxi, the Blue Sheep Mountain (Qingyang Shan) affair of 1528–1529, caused turmoil and controversy, too. However, the matter that grabbed everyone's attention and focused their efforts was none of the above but Jiajing's ambitious determination to bring off nothing less than the ritual reconstruction, architectural and programmatic, of Ming China's entire heritage of civil religion.

To carry this program out, Jiajing rode the momentum he had just gained in the Great Rites victory. The reconstruction of the rites was labeled a *fugu*, a "restoration of antiquity," or a *zhongxing*, a "midcourse revival." The idea behind the latter was to restore China to what it had been like before the disastrous fifteen-year reign of Jiajing's older cousin, the Zhengde emperor, who had let everything go to rot in a swamp of militarism, wantonness, and corruption. But ritual reconstruction meant more than that. The label *fugu* meant that no existing ritual, even those sanctioned by the Ming founder himself, was safe from revision in the light of what earnest research could unearth of the rites established in the Golden Age dawn of China's civilization. It was heady stuff. It was also of course controversial, a maker or breaker of men's careers.

* * *

The first of Jiajing's great ritual reforms showed this clearly. Early in his reign, the Ming founder ordered that Heaven and Earth should be sacrificed to conjointly, in a single ceremony at a single site. This ruling held for the next century and a half. But was it correct in the light of ancient precedent?[1]

The leader of the effort to restructure this most solemn of the imperial observances was, no doubt about it, the young emperor himself. He needed help with it, however. One midlevel bureaucrat sensed Jiajing's intentions and rose to the occasion. This was Xia Yan, who was, as of 1530, chief supervising secretary of the Office of Scrutiny for Personnel. (He would eventually ride ritual reform, with Jiajing's backing, to the post of chief grand secretary nine years later and preside during the "summer" phase of the Jiajing era.)

As early as 1522, when Xia Yan was a supervising secretary in the Office of Scrutiny for War and was busy confiscating farmland from the eunuchs and palace favorites who had seized it during the Zhengde era, he proposed to Jiajing that some of that land be set aside for the planting of mulberry trees to feed the silkworms that might be used in a revived silkworm rite for the empress to conduct. This was an ancient practice, long in abeyance. Jiajing liked the idea, but the Ministry of Revenue objected to it because of its cost, so the emperor dropped it.

On February 3, 1530, Xia raised the suggestion again. He took part that day in the joint suburban sacrifice to Heaven and Earth, held at an altar in Nanhai, a suburb south of Beijing. That provided him an opportunity to gain the emperor's attention. How better to do that than to lavish sincere-sounding praise on the young ruler? The rejection of the mulberry proposal of 1522, he reassured Jiajing, had come about because the young man had just come to the throne, and things were very busy and there was no time for it. Now, eight years later, he reminded the ruler that he, Xia, had the privilege of being included in the imperial entourage, so he was able to view clearly how earnest and strict the emperor's attitude was; how, that evening, clouds of incense mounted to the sky, inviting Shangdi and all the lesser gods to come down and accept the offerings; and how the ruler had exercised due care in changing the date of the rite to make it precede the new year's court assembly. Xia said that it was the utter sincerity Jiajing showed in carrying out this highest of the civic sacrifices that prompted his renewed request to institute the silk rite. He asked the emperor to have the Ministries of Rites, Revenue, and Works gather and discuss the idea. He also asked that officials familiar with the ancient ritual texts add their opinions. A week later, Jiajing replied to all this favorably.[2]

Official opinions about this rite diverged. Zhang Fujing, by now chief grand secretary, thought an altar for the silk rite could be built outside the Anding Gate. From his post in the Hanlin Academy, Huo Tao objected. The proposed site was too far away, he insisted. The Ministry of Revenue agreed. There was no water there, either. Tang and Song precedent suggested a site inside West Park. Jiajing replied that the Tang precedent was convenient but nonclassical and therefore should not be followed. Li Shi, the low-key minister of rites, sent up an elaborate plan and program, suggesting that the altar be placed outside the Xuanwu Gate. Jiajing agreed to that, and so, two months later, protected by five thousand guards along the route and another five thousand encircling the altar, the empress conducted the silk ritual.[3] So, thanks to Xia Yan, and at great expense, one minor bit of the program to re-create the ritual face of ancient China came back to life. There was much more to come.

* * *

From silk, Xia Yan pressed ahead immediately with big plans to revise and rebuild the sacrifices to Heaven and Earth. It was perfectly safe to do so. Jiajing and Chief Grand Secretary Zhang Fujing were engaged in intense discussions of the matter, as they had been earlier about the silk ritual, in which Jiajing was no passive onlooker but intimately involved in every de-tail.

Xia's memorial was sent up on February 26, 1530. He said we must establish a correct system valid for all future time. The rite needed to con-form to the hearts and minds of the people below and accord with Heaven's intent above. Antiquity had to be the guide, not the errors introduced in Han, Tang, and Song times. However, the program involved many intricate details that had to be gotten right, so Xia urged the ruler to solicit opinions from all quarters—civil and military officials high and low, and imperial in-laws too—as often the ancient ritual texts leave too many questions unanswered.[4] Meanwhile, with Zhang Fujing's unenthusiastic concurrence, Jiajing put the question to the shade of the Ming founder, Taizu, by way of divination in the Fengxian Dian. Twice he got the reply "not propitious." Zhang had said divination wasn't necessary, but apparently Jiajing got better results on the third try, on March 9.[5] No matter. Jiajing liked Xia's memorial and followed its suggestion for open discussion.

On April 8, the Ministry of Rites reported its count of all the replies received. In favor of dividing the ritual to Heaven and Earth were 192 offi-cials. Preferring the retention of the combined sacrifice, but not strongly opposed to dividing it, were 206 officials, among them Minister of Personnel Fang Xianfu. Those wholly neutral numbered 198.

Interestingly, no respondent voted a clear no. Officials seem to have been frightened away from that choice by what was happening to that hot-tem-pered contrarian Huo Tao. Huo had sent up a long, well-researched, and impassioned plea not to divide the rites to Heaven and Earth. He blamed Zhang Fujing and Xia Yan for misguiding the ruler. Jiajing replied with a long statement of his own, denying that Zhang and Xia were to blame for anything and stating that the idea to separate the two rites was his own personal decision.[6] Huo apologized for not having made sufficiently clear the rationale for his position, and so he restated it by appending a copy of a long personal letter he'd written Xia Yan, disputing Xia at great length.[7]

Challenging the emperor this way was not a wise move politically. Xia Yan was indignant. Jiajing was offended. He had tried to warn Huo away from his objections; why didn't he listen?[8] On April 7, the emperor had Huo arrested and sent to the Decree Prison for interrogation under some form of duress. There he remained for a month until he recanted. In the light of Huo's earlier support in the Great Rites, Jiajing then ordered his release.[9]

* * *

So rites reform proceeded in an atmosphere sown with fear. Confidential messages exchanged between Zhang Fujing and the ruler also mention this fear. On April 6, Jiajing sent Zhang a three-part query, the first part asking whether Zhang knew what Minister of Rites Li Shi's position was. On the same day, Zhang replied. He said Li's original opinion was that separating the sacrifices to Heaven and Earth was in line with ancient practice, but then he became frightened and backed away:

> I told him your opinion. Li then said that on March 3, he was at the Imperial University for the sacrifice to Confucius, when opposite him, Gu Dingchen [at the time supervisor of the Household of the Heir Apparent] said in the hearing of everyone present, "I understand the court wants to separate Heaven and Earth [on the grounds that] this is the fixed ancestral system. You, Li Shi, must know about this and its seriousness. Earlier when [the Prince of Ning] asked [on the same grounds] for a protective guard, only Minister of Personnel Lu Wan agreed, and later his whole family was confiscated." I saw that his obvious intent was to indict me [Zhang Fujing] publicly. Afterward when I saw him, he said, "If a meeting is held to discuss this, I'm certainly not going to sign on. There are only one or two men in the Hanlin Academy who favor the division. The rest don't dare." Also he said that he went to Vice Minister of Rites Yan Song's house and told him, "You'd better not manage this affair, because sooner or later the court will change its mind, and you and your colleagues will be in for it." After that, Yan Song and [Yan's colleague, Junior Vice Minister of Rites] Zhan Ruoshui both took fright, and so they prepared

statements about the mistake of dividing the sacrifices, for possible future use. Also, he said that the Supervising Secretary Tian Qiu had said, "The original opinion of us *kedao* officials was that the court wanted to divide the sacrifices, that [the divided rite] was the ancient rite, and we all agreed, but later, because one Hanlin official [Huo Tao] issued a warning threat, we all changed our minds." Also he said, "On top of that, Huo Tao's memorial shocked and frightened people inside and outside."

So I [Zhang Fujing], said to Li Shi, "You're a rites official; you're surely going to grasp the principle of things clearly, and you'll send up settled opinions and put all this talk to rest. The court is reviving the canons of the Three Dynasties [of antiquity] and restoring the original system of the Ming founders. The discussion is settled. Everyone will sign on, though they haven't done so yet. Over several days of talks I was able to convince [Minister of War] Li Chengxun that this was a big and glorious affair of the court. Also, [Censor in Chief] Wang Hong made a powerful public statement supporting the court and refuting the crowd's wrong opinions. At today's general discussion meeting, those two acted on Li Shi's behalf, so most of the gathering signed on to the proposal to divide the rites.[10]

From Zhang's detailed report to Jiajing, one can see that not everyone agreed that state ritual needed reforming. Enacting reform was hampered by an undertow of opposition to it. The bureaucracy needed to be frightened into at least a grudging acquiescence. But as Zhang often reminded Jiajing, it was fully within the scope of the legitimate power of the emperor to single-handedly determine and shape ritual. And Jiajing was determined to leave no stone unturned in his attempt to get it absolutely right and leave a solid religious legacy for ages to come.

* * *

Work proceeded at once on the separate altars to Heaven and Earth, first the one called the "round mound" in the southern suburb, then the other, the "square mound," in the north. It was decided to follow ancient clues and also build altars in the eastern and western suburbs for sacrifices to the sun and moon, respectively.

These were huge projects. Over them, Jiajing presided as though he were the director of some Hollywood epic. No detail of the grand production was too small for him to consider over and over. He so interested himself in it that he became knowledgeable enough to discuss exact measurements, the relative merits of stone and glass bricks, and the precise formats of the sacrificial programs to be used—the acoustics, the choral music, singing, the harmony, the libretti, and on and on. Xia Yan outside, and Zhang Fujing inside, acted as Jiajing's chief architects and planners.

Xia sent up a report of a discussion meeting held on April 7, the day after Jiajing's exchange with Zhang Fujing. The Ministry of Rites conducted the discussion in the Dongge, inside the Forbidden City. That the sacrifices to Heaven and Earth would be split was firmly decided and closed to further debate. The question now was how to arrange the tablets of Taizu and Yongle as accessory recipients (*pei*) of the sacrifices. Minister of Rites Li Shi led the discussion. He argued that, in effect, the Ming had two meritorious and virtuous founders, not just one, and that both had been and should continue to be joint and equal recipients at both the southern and northern suburban altars. But Xia Yan and others disagreed. Fathers, they said, must always precede sons, merits and virtues notwithstanding. They decided to lay the matter before Jiajing and get his final ruling.

For nine days, the emperor did not respond. A report or rumor had it that the Grand Secretaries Zhang Fujing and Chai Luan were not in favor of making a father-and-son hierarchy of Taizu and Yongle. The rumor was correct. Zhang Fujing and Jiajing were indeed involved in a furious argument over the question. Their confidential messages leave no doubt of that.

On April 20, Jiajing's message to Zhang stated that while Taizu had founded the Ming, his son Taizong (the Yongle emperor) had saved it from collapse and reestablished it, so that their merits were surely equal; nonetheless, even Yongle would insist on keeping the father-son hierarchy.[11] Jiajing said he'd given the matter deep thought. He said he'd seen, apparently in a dream, four men carrying yellow banners inscribed with song lyrics, of which he could recall only the first line of one, which read, "Joy at our sacrifice to Heaven and to Earth as well." He said this must have been a personal message from the ancestors. He said Zhang wasn't following the correct line because he was afraid of the danger of the inevitable controversy. He suggested that Zhang inform Li Shi of these thoughts.

To this, Zhang replied the next day. He artfully held his ground. He said he was uneasy with the idea of making Taizu and Taizong recipients of separate suburban sacrifices. He had stated this earlier, and, getting no reply, he was living day and night in fear. On April 14, after the daily tutorial, when tea was served, he had asked the eunuch Bao Zhong to convey his thoughts to Jiajing again, and so now he was deeply grateful for the ruler's merciful reply. He agreed with Jiajing, but with great finesse he suggested that suddenly removing Taizong as a recipient of the sacrifices was too abrupt. As to the line from the lyric that the ruler reported, what did it really mean? Zhang said it was indeed a message from the ancestors, just like a response to a divination. He discussed it with Li Shi, and he lay awake all night thinking about it. Couldn't it mean that Taizu and Taizong were really asking Jiajing to make them joint recipients? The next morning, Zhang said, he discussed this interpretation of the line with Li Shi, who agreed with it. They also agreed that the matter should be kept totally secret, because if it ever leaked, evil rumors would surely arise. Plus note that we've had eclipses and reports of dearth everywhere. Dissidents love these omens and disasters. "If I fear the danger of controversy, and can't follow what is right, and so change my original opinion, I deserve death."

Three days later, on April 24, Jiajing answered. He appreciated Zhang's diligence and loyalty. He thought the line in the spirit message was sent from the world beyond in approval of dividing the Heaven and Earth sacrifices. He had also had another dream. This one was of a strange written character. What did it mean? Jiajing used some convoluted reasoning together with an impressively erudite reference to the Tang writer Han Yu to confirm the view he held all along. No surprise there. The ruler also noted that Xia Yan disagreed with Zhang on this issue, and that he, Jiajing, agreed with Xia, because he believed Xia's stance was the correct one. If not, then the gods and spirits will surely exact revenge!

The next day, April 25, Zhang respectfully acknowledged Jiajing's opinions without actually endorsing them. He did agree not to dispute Xia Yan. He looked up the weird character that appeared in Jiajing's dream and found its pronunciation, but not its definition. He asked Jiajing not to overtax himself over trifles like this given the press of other business. The emperor needed to guard his health, he said.

Five days later, Zhang sent up a very worried communiqué. A wrong arrangement of the suburban sacrifices would affect all future time and ruin the Ming dynasty, and Zhang forthrightly unloaded a scolding on Jiajing. "Your mind of loving ritual and restoring antiquity is too eager for quick results," he warned. "You, the ruler, need to handle slowdowns and frustrations better." He said the ruler shouldn't be so quick to let on what his intentions are. Xia Yan and other supporters are just trying to win recognition and favor. "If the ruler finds me, Zhang, to be insincere about this, he must punish me."

On May 3, the emperor came down hard on Zhang. The chief grand secretary's draft responses to Xia Yan's memorials were not acceptable. Why was Zhang so supportive on the question of dividing the sacrifices to Heaven and Earth, and now so contrary in insisting on retaining the Hongxi emperor's ruling of a century before, making Taizu and Taizong joint recipients of the sacrifices? This was not how to give good service to one's ruler.

Zhang answered back later the same day. He said he was weeping with frustration, but he forcefully stood his ground. The emperor was making a grievous error. How does he explain having Taizu as the sole accessory in the two suburban rites but having both him and Taizong as joint recipients in a lesser rite? A learned and impassioned plea followed.

The next day Jiajing fired off a long retort. He rejected all loose talk of bad omens and reports of the construction workers' resentments as lies inspired by "small men" who were gathering the minister of rites and the grand secretaries into their clique. He said the only Confucians whose views were sound were Confucius, Mencius, Cheng Yi, and Zhu Xi. Zhang Fujing must carefully rethink the issue and change his mind. He ought not to cling to deviant ideas and show such overweening stubbornness.

Zhang thought about this. On May 4, he thanked Jiajing for his instructive teaching and for sparing him the death penalty. But he thought Jiajing was becoming overwrought and counseled him to take care not to endanger his health.[12]

The issue was then dropped. Jiajing had his way. The confidential correspondence between the emperor and his chief grand secretary resumed on a friendlier note. Through it, Jiajing had forcefully defended his views and, with the powers of life and death at his fingertips, had pressed an older and much more learned man to the wall. But there was a strong bond between the two, and their argument did not ruin it.

* * *

From Xia Yan's long and detailed reports to the throne, it is obvious that the construction of the four suburban altars, starting with the most important one, the altar to Heaven in the southern suburb, was a huge undertaking. Work on it began on June 8, 1530. Some ten thousand soldiers from the capital training battalions were mobilized to haul construction materials to the building site. A thousand others worked at the site itself. A thousand more Embroidered-Uniform Guardsmen were added. It wasn't enough. Fortunately, Beijing swarmed with destitute drifters and beggars who could be and were recruited for the job. It was like disaster relief for them. Luckily, too, it seems the dynasty was momentarily awash in silver reserves, making it unnecessary to raise taxes. The Court of the Imperial Stud had two million taels silver on hand. Construction costs for all four suburban altars were estimated to amount to five hundred thousand to seven hundred thousand taels. At the moment, on June 21, the work had barely begun, and it must be sped up under more efficient management. Jiajing responded positively with encouraging comments. [13]

On July 14, Xia Yan reported that he had just visited the construction site and had discussed various questions of materials and building methods with the artisans and their supervisors. The main objective was to make the altar durable. He submitted architectural drawings for Jiajing's inspection. Again, Jiajing thought this looked all right, but he asked that the construction overseers meet and discuss and report. [14]

On July 18, Xia Yan, Marquis Guo Xun, Zhang Fujing, and Minister of Rites Li Shi all visited the building site and then went to inspect the glass factory. There they got into an argument. Xia Yan opposed the use of glass bricks. Only "white jade stone" was durable enough, he insisted. The others wouldn't listen. They demanded the use of blue-colored glass. The eunuchs in charge of the kilns were terrified of imperfections in the firing of the glass bricks, the workmen were giving trouble, rainy weather was slowing the drying, and though they were afraid to say so, it was clear they preferred stone, because it was more durable, cost less, and could be laid faster. To this plea, Jiajing partially agreed; he thought facing the stone with glass should be feasible. [15]

Finally, on July 27, Xia Yan raised some financial issues. Jiajing had agreed to the Ministry of Works' request to lay a silver assessment on the provinces and send officials out to expedite delivery. Xia protested. The silver assessment on the provinces was for next year's rebuilding of the Renshou Palace, he explained. The southern suburban altar was about half done and could be completed in three more months, and all the other altars could be finished inside a year. The building supervisors' consensus was that three hundred thousand more taels from the canal transport funds of the Ministry of Revenue should suffice to do it all. Jiajing changed his mind and fully agreed with Xia Yan. [16]

Jiajing's communications with Xia Yan were sporadic. With Zhang Fujing, he exchanged notes nearly every day over the most intimate details of the construction. Jiajing wanted a resplendent altar, not just a sturdy one. He did not like Xia Yan's argument in favor of "white jade stone." On July 18, Zhang visited the kilns and reported that the workers had successfully produced one hundred beautiful blue glass bricks that were nearly unbreakable and "shone like Heaven." It could take the place of the white stone. But Jiajing was doubtful and thought that blue stone shipped from south China was a better option. Zhang disagreed; the blue stone had never been tested and could split in Beijing's harsh winter, whereas the glass wouldn't.[17] (The choice of glass may have prevailed. Space will not allow further consideration of the thick file of messages on this topic—the construction of the altar in an alfalfa field just south of the Chaoyang Gate, its exact dimensions, the road leading to it from the Forbidden City, the choice of ritual and musical instruments, the long and elaborate program to be followed, and on and on.)

On November 12, as the time for the inaugural sacrifice to Heaven at the new altar drew near, Xia Yan submitted a list of matters that needed to be attended to: arrangements for the emperor's participation, orders for all officials to bathe and fast, the invitation list, and clean robes for the singers and dancers.[18] All imperial visits to the four suburban altars took place in the predawn darkness and were brightly illuminated by long lines of lantern and torch bearers, turning night into day. The cost of the illumination was borne by local residents, who should be given a break on their other service obligations. Uniformed guardsmen should replace the servants, lowlifes, and unsightly homeless drifters, with their tangled hair, bare feet, and clothes made of rags, who had been holding the lanterns and torches. The road taken by the ruler's sedan chair should be cleared and the alleyways temporarily blocked to keep away gawkers.[19]

Jiajing conducted the inaugural sacrifice to Heaven in the southern suburb, with Ming founder Taizu as sole accessory, on December 12, 1530. The next day, he distributed rewards and promotions to the officials and artisans, issued amnesties for certain categories of prisoner, and granted tax remissions for the commoners. A large banquet in the Fengxian Dian regaled civil and military officials and foreign envoys. Everything seemed to proceed without a hitch.[20]

* * *

The solemn sacrifice to Heaven was the big keystone in China's catalog of rites. But there was much more to the face-lifting, many more problems to discuss, much more research to do, many more sites to construct. The time, effort, and expense invested in all this, from the emperor down to the lowliest laborer, staggers the imagination. The cost in silver taels seldom came up for discussion. These further ritual arrangements could be related at great length, but a brief look at a few of them will have to suffice.

Early in 1531, Jiajing ordered that the ancient imperial plowing rite be conducted in West Park, and that the empress's silk rite be carried out there was well. It fell to Xia Yan to take the main hand in arranging all this. In December, Xia, since promoted to Hanlin reader-in-waiting, submitted a report on the work done thus far. On March 17, Xia accompanied palace eunuchs and government artisans and measured out 7.945 *qing* of land (roughly 20 acres). The Ministry of Revenue and the Directorate of Imperial Parks planted 780 small mulberry trees along the road to the silk altar. Then dry fields and paddy were prepared for planting grain. The two metropolitan counties (Daxing and Wanping) provided the peasants, tools, oxen, and seeds. When the planting was done, the oxen were sent back, and sixteen plow mules were brought in. By early October, all the harvested grain was threshed, and 858.827 *shi* of grain (approximately 57 tons) were put in storage for use in the suburban and ancestral temple sacrifices. It remained to regularize all this in fixed directives. These Xia Yan supplied, and Jiajing endorsed them on December 27.[21]

The empress's earlier trip to a suburb for the silk rite was declared to have been "inconvenient," which is why Jiajing ordered the altar relocated in West Park, a site he had previously rejected. East of the altar was built a "mulberry-picking terrace"; east of that a robe-changing hall; to the north a silkworm room, with alcoves to the right and left; and in the rear another room for the silkworm women. Three matrons staffed a silkworm office under eunuch direction. Female musicians attended. At the end, there were kowtows, but no congratulatory celebrations.[22]

Meanwhile, thinking and planning about how to rearrange and rebuild the Imperial Ancestral Shrine (Taimiao) and the appropriate observances there went forward with great passion and intensity. It will have to suffice here to say that this work began in 1530 and continued on for many years thereafter. Xia Yan was a major force behind it, but much of the work took place after 1535, when Zhang Fujing retired and Xia was made a grand secretary.

* * *

It will be convenient at this point to shift topical gears. Just what sort of person was Jiajing in his early years? His drive to control the government in the Great Rites affair and, following that, his determination to remake the ritual face of China in themselves tell us a great deal—that this was a young man of iron will and fierce ambition, with an instinctive understanding of power. But there were further edges to his personality. These come through in his correspondence with Zhang Fujing, which Zhang's heirs printed up many years later as the *Yudui lu* (*Record of Replies to the Emperor*).

The *Yudui lu* features a line-drawn portrait of Zhang, plus pictures of the big seals issued to him in 1527 and 1531 to stamp on the covers of his messages. Jiajing explained that his own handwriting was poor, but he was concerned to prevent leaks and was afraid copyists might breach security, hence the need for secrecy. Other business, of which there was a great deal, Zhang wrote up as memorials, which the emperor typically read first, then shared with the rest of the bureaucracy.[23]

A message datable to 1527, when the ruler was twenty years old, affords an unfiltered window into his state of mind. He said he was getting all kinds of suggestions about new advances to make in governance (*zhengzhi*), but the problem was finding the right men to staff the Grand Secretariat and the ministries so that new measures could be put into effect. He wondered aloud to Zhang (probably right after raising him to the Grand Secretariat on October 28) why, in his six years on the throne, he'd not been able to bring in supportive Grand Secretaries. He'd recently had trouble with Jia Yong and Yang Yiqing. He said some grand secretaries took advantage of his youth to deceive him. Others misappropriated his authority to issue their own orders to those below. They were apparently urging him to lie back and enjoy life. "By nature I don't like entertainment, and I especially avoid dissipation, and like anyone else I love what's good and hate evil, and I'm personally the leader of men, I bear the Mandate of Heaven, so how can I just relax and not aim for good rule and so glorify the ancestors?" He pleaded for Zhang's help in selecting the right men for key positions. Zhang in confidence recommended eleven such men, all supporters of Jiajing in the Great Rites dispute. He agreed with the ruler that opposition figures should be avoided.[24]

To this, Jiajing replied that he found Zhang very useful and helpful, a man he could lean on. He and Zhang then conducted candid evaluations of top officials. Jiajing wanted men who were conscientious, hardworking, and loyal. The ruler abhorred the opposition underground, which survived despite the two big repressions of 1524 and 1527. "Recently because of the Great

Rites dispute," wrote Jiajing, "and the rise of deviant talk, the flock of vil-lains cling together, and if they get posts and salaries, they'll surely link up with others of like mind, ignoring me totally. Good men denounce them, upright opinion ridicules them, yet they gather and yammer as they lay their accusations, just as though Heaven above and the ancestors aren't behind the scenes backing me, which is how I was able to get you and a few others to fight for what's correct, and you've led that, and without you, I don't know where I'd be." Zhang replied with much practical advice as to how to pro-ceed, and for some days, he and Jiajing continued the discussion. [25]

Zhang wanted to press ahead to eliminate corruption. He told Jiajing just what he'd said to twelve circuit censors about to depart Beijing for the provinces. "Today corrupt officials fill the realm," he said to the censors. "They gouge the common people terribly, and they don't let the ruler hear of it, so the people grow poorer, and banditry breaks out. The key to this lies with the Grand Secretariat. If the grand secretaries, with the generous salaries the court provides them, act impartially and let no one carry on intrigue and traffic bribes, then the heads of the ministries won't dare demand payments, and if they don't, then you censors can impeach the local officials who demand payments, the money can be recouped, and the ministries and grand secretaries won't be willing to intervene to save them, and they won't dare gouge the people anymore. Today the court wants peace for the people. You censors must heed that. If you just turn a blind eye as before, I'll have you arrested." Jiajing replied the next day, November 1. He said he appreciated Zhang's having "absorbed my mind to act in behalf of the people."[26] Actual-ly, Jiajing was never eager to press down hard on official corruption. (Like-wise, his repressions of dissenters always fell short of a thorough purge.)

On November 13, Jiajing shared two new confidential matters with Zhang. Early in his reign, Jiajing made it a habit, except when he was sick, to meet the daily dawn court assembly. Each dawn, before the day's work began, the officials would line up before the emperor in strict order of rank. Jiajing said he could gauge the officials' attitudes from visual clues that only he could see. Some of what he noticed he shared with Zhang Fujing. "Of your four colleagues [in the Grand Secretariat], wrote Jiajing, "Yang Yiqing I know to be loyal and sincere, but one or two aren't exerting themselves as you do. Also, earlier, I said Dong Qi [vice minister of personnel] wasn't satisfactory. Standing in court ranks, he talks to those next to him, and when he looks up, he laughs. That's disrespectful. He walks out of line, he does bows and kowtows out of turn, which, if not disrespectful, is arrogant. Unfortunately, he's a high official. Song Cang [vice censor in chief] is like this too. I'm afraid you don't know all this, so I tell you. And I notice your colleague [Grand Secretary] Chai Luan." Chai was stepping back into the wrong file after coming forward to perform his kowtows. Perhaps his attention had wandered.

Zhang answered the next day, November 14. He had some appropriate words about the officials' deportment. Then he launched into something different—an analysis of the question how a phalanx of Great Rites and Great Case oppositionists could ever have gotten started and organized. His research into the records of the Grand Secretariat showed that it all began in 1511 in the preceding Zhengde era when the Grand Secretariat (in which Jiajing's nemesis Yang Tinghe played the leading hand) seized control of the appointment of Hanlin bachelors (i.e., trainees, the cream of the crop of new metropolitan degree winners). They assigned thirty of them (out of a total of thirty-seven) to positions: nineteen to regular posts in the Hanlin Academy, and seven to posts as *kedao* (supervising secretaries and censors). In 1517, the numbers were thirty-four selected, fifteen posted to the Hanlin and thirteen as *kedao*. In 1521, the numbers were eight Hanlin and ten *kedao*.[27] "These three classes provided ninety-one bachelor appointees," wrote Zhang. "All this I found in the Grand Secretariat records. This is how through the years the inside clique of Great Rites disputants were mostly Hanlin, while the outside clique were mostly *kedao*. That's how their arguments grew so unchallengeable and why they could so freely ignore the emperor. Only you had the upright determination to stop this. The twenty bachelors on hand now are mostly clients of the Grand Secretariat. Eventually, they'll get high positions and cause trouble. I'm afraid [Grand Secretary] Yang Yiqing doesn't see this. If we get rid of all these partisans and fill positions with men of talent and good behavior wherever they may be found, then favor will again be the court's prerogative, and the appointees will strive to requite you."

This was interesting political analysis. There was indeed some truth to it. In response, on November 26, Jiajing ordered all the bachelors sent to posts elsewhere in China. Chief Grand Secretary Yang Yiqing protested that it was customary to post a few of them to Hanlin and *kedao* positions. Zhang Fujing, the newest grand secretary, but clearly Jiajing's favorite, challenged that in his memo: "These types are brazen and ambitious, their mouths still reek of their mothers' milk, and they shouldn't be placed in the Hanlin and *kedao* as speaking officials. Is it wrong to change the rules? They should be put in the ministries and local government, so in future they won't be such opportunists." Jiajing wasn't yet ready to dismiss Yang Yiqing. He accepted Yang's objection. "I mustn't summarily change the ancestors' regulations," he directed. And so the issue was dropped.[28]

This shows Jiajing's radicalism had its limits. His desire for change was heavily focused on ritual reform, where he was inclined to dictate, even when it meant changing ancestral regulations. In other respects, as here, he was cautious and not eager to pursue major reforms, partly for fear of the likely reaction. "Yang Yiqing clings stubbornly to precedent, and I'll have to be patient and try to get him to change his mind," he wrote. "I can't just defy a chief grand secretary, especially when he says I must not change the ancestors' rules. If I order the abolition of the bachelors, then it will be said, wrongly alas, that I make arbitrary decisions." Discussions continued in detail but in a lower key about how to appoint good grand coordinators for the provinces.[29]

* * *

Jiajing was twenty years old in 1527, when he appointed Zhang Fujing to the Grand Secretariat. He was twenty-eight when, in 1535, and some 360 secret messages later, Zhang retired as chief grand secretary for the final time. During those years, as the emperor grew from youth to young manhood, he shared with Zhang a surprising amount of very personal information, relating both to himself and his immediate family. Zhang's role was to serve not just as a policy advisor, but also as Jiajing's writing instructor, life coach, and even his doctor and psychotherapist. Jiajing felt free to expose his ignorance, fears, and vulnerabilities to Zhang's gaze.

Jiajing often spoke of his relationship with his mother, the empress nee Jiang (it will be recalled how in 1521 she refused to enter the Forbidden City through a side gate). The mother of the emperor was not a "private" person in a separate family sphere shielded from public concern. The requirements of ritual and people's expectations dictated otherwise. So Jiajing saw no problem in describing to Zhang how he treated his mother and asking whether he was behaving correctly toward her or not. Some of this seems trivial and time wasting, but it was not. Every son in China knew that filial devotion was very nearly the highest ethical obligation of them all. How the emperor fulfilled that obligation had to conform to the highest standards possible; otherwise ugly rumors would soon give the green light to bad behavior and endanger family order nationwide.

On December 20, 1527, Jiajing told Zhang of a talk he had with his mother about whether to move his father's remains from Anlu and rebury them in the Ming tombs near Beijing. Jiajing had long favored such a move, and the rites officials had discussed and endorsed it, but his mother wept in protest against it. She didn't want his father's soul (*ling*) disturbed, and she wanted to be buried in Anlu beside him when she died. "I told my mother to rest easy," Jiajing reported, "to take care of herself and live long. That she shouldn't worry about this; any fault is on me." According to Jiajing, his mother replied, "How can you, the emperor, say that? I know your mind. Moving his remains is a serious matter. It would disturb the common people. You must let me join him in the south [when I die]. Then I will be free of worry." So Jiajing asked Zhang whether he had done right in caving in to his mother's wish. The same day, Zhang assured him that he had.[30]

Two months later, on February 25, 1528, Jiajing presented Zhang with a sticky family problem. Xie Zhao, all of fifteen years old, had just been married to Jiajing's younger sister, the Yongchun princess, but he was neglecting his studies and disrespecting his tutors. The princess, meanwhile, was being encouraged by the empress to practice Buddhism. "Whenever I admonish [my mother] about that, she remains adamant, and my sister shows no mind to break with it either. Unless my mother scolds her, I fear the collapse of family order. This incriminates my parents and imposes blame on me. I'd like to write a formal notice to my mother, asking her to teach my sister, but I don't know if that's all right or not. I tell you this in secret. Please give a full reply."

Jiajing prefaced all this by underlining its larger meaning. He echoed a key passage from the *Great Learning*: "I think rulers [must] first regulate the family, then the lineages of the in-laws are improved by that, and then the whole realm further blossoms because of it." (Jiajing's hostility toward Buddhism would deepen in future years.)

Zhang wrought a careful reply. He reminded Jiajing that Buddhism taught compassion, nonviolence, reincarnation, and consequences for good and bad deeds. It was suitable for the simpleminded, and thus it had traditionally been tolerated, although Jiajing himself was too intelligent to fall for it. It was a good idea to write such a note to his mother, asking her to instruct the princess. Zhang wrote: "Your mother believes this doctrine because she's looking for blessings and long life, that's all." He advised Jiajing to have his mother read Han Yu's Tang-era essay on the Buddha's bone. He attached a copy of it. That should change her mind, and she'll instruct your sister

likewise. As for Xie Zhao, his tutors needed to impose a strict regimen on him.[31]

Three days later, Jiajing confided that he'd had no luck with his mother. He was reluctant to press her. She was afraid Buddha might seek revenge. Zhang couldn't help much. He cited Mencius and Zhu Xi about how to admonish one's parents. Other palace people might be held accountable for failure to instruct the princess. Reading Han Yu should cure mother of her delusions. At all events, Jiajing was taking the right steps in regulating his family, and so pacifying the realm should proceed smoothly.

On March 1, Jiajing confessed he'd made no headway. He had sent a secret letter to his mother via a palace matron, and apparently his mother told the princess of its contents when the young girl came to court; but her mother continued her own worship of the Buddha, and so accordingly did her daughter. So Jiajing, faced with a minor family rebellion, did not know what to do. He didn't want to increase the pressure on his mother and offend her. Zhang's reply was sensible. The delusional allure of Buddhism, he said, runs deep. It's hard even for great sages to demolish it. Your mother's will can't be changed so easily. As a filial son, you can only persist, but gently.[32] That put an end to the matter for the time being.

On August 7 of that year, his mother asked Jiajing if it were all right if she set up a small shrine to her dead husband so that morning and night she could visit it and make offerings. "Let me think a day or two," he replied, "then I'll respond to your order." He put the question to Zhang, who answered the same day. This was a convoluted matter ritually. Zhang noted that Jiajing's father's spirit tablet was kept in the Shimiao shrine, his spirit seat in the Chongxian Dian, and that in the seasonal sacrifices to him, his wife, Jiajing's mother, was not a qualified participant. So setting up this small shrine is an excellent idea. Jiajing should grant her request. Zhang advised setting up a spirit seat in a quiet room somewhere in the palace. Daily sacrifices might be too tiring for her, so seasonal sacrifices should be the rule.[33]

There was more. On September 12, Jiajing told Zhang that he'd ordered workmen to make a spirit signboard and build the shrine, and on a lucky day, he'd formalize the installation. He needed a detailed program and an inscription for the signboard. Would he need a prayer reciter, or could the ruler manage the inaugural rite unassisted? The same day, Zhang green-lighted Jiajing's presiding solo, after which his mother could take over. The program should be the same as that regularly used in similar connections, with the offering consisting of minced meat. The next day, Zhang sent along a suggestion for the inscription, using a relevant citation from the classic *Record of Rites* (*Li ji*), which he attached.

So what began as a simple request from Jiajing's mother for a personal dispensation was turning into a formalized affair embedded in classical precedent and transformed into a quasi-public ceremony. Zhang and Jiajing continued to discuss the details. Jiajing didn't like Zhang's wording for the signboard. Plus he asked Zhang to critique a pronouncement as well as a litany for the inaugural that he'd composed by himself. Zhang thought the litany and other pieces excellent, with only a few minor changes needed. They still differed over the signboard inscription. Jiajing wanted to have his father styled *zunzhu* (revered lord). Zhang explained that was what a secondary wife would use. The discussion ended there.

On September 21, Jiajing took his mother for a stroll somewhere out on the palace grounds. She asked whether it would be all right for his father's Pure Consort (Shufei, a second-ranking concubine) to come along with them. Jiajing had no idea, and so he asked Zhang, who replied the same day that it was permissible for her to follow along after the sage-mother, but because she'd given birth not to a son but to an eldest daughter, she should not be accorded any undue respect.[34] Palace life was not sequestered but a bit like life on an open stage.

On December 7, Jiajing's mother thrust a sharp prod into her son. His empress, nee Chen, had died childless. The funeral and burial were over, yet he'd done nothing to replace her. "The ancestral line is very important; the empress's palace can't be kept empty, and you should keep that in mind," she said. "I've been remiss, unfortunately," Jiajing replied, "causing you worry. I ask for your order." "What do you propose to do about it?" she asked. "This can't be delayed." So Jiajing asked Zhang what he should do.[35] (We will turn later to the question of Jiajing's relationships with the palace women, which would nearly occasion his murder.)

For some reason, Jiajing felt it appropriate to confess to Zhang his lapse in filial care. On February 24, 1530, he said that despite his awareness that nothing was so loving and close as the mother-son relationship, he'd recently failed to visit her twice daily, and he'd only just learned she'd been sick. He blamed himself. He ordered the palace pharmacy (Neiyao Fang) to send her medicine. She recovered, and at noon on that day she went to the palace shrine she'd had set up for her husband and did the rites. Jiajing led his new empress to do the same and congratulated his mother. "I'm dull and I definitely lean on your strength to guide me," Jiajing confessed to Zhang. "I fear

you don't know all this, so I tell you, to reassure you in your loyal support."
Zhang expressed his gratitude. [36]

On March 19, the sage-mother showed she shared her son's punctilious
concern for ritual correctness. She wanted to hold a birthday banquet for her
sister-in-law, the Empress Zhang, widow of the Hongzhi emperor. She had
questions about the ritual. Jiajing didn't know and didn't want to suggest
something that might turn out to be mistaken, so he consulted Zhang. Zhang
replied that the two women held the same title, so Jiajing should bow to both
of them together, and at the banquet they should sit side by side. [37]

The next day, Jiajing had another question. What should he say at the
banquet for his aunt? Also, his mother had said, "I should sit facing west and
present the cup to her as I would to my mother-in-law." Jiajing replied, "I'll
yield to whatever you say." But he had second thoughts. "Maybe I humbled
myself too much," he confessed. "Maybe I harmed the rite. Maybe when I
appear and do the rite, I wait for my aunt to take her seat, and mother should
sit facing a bit to the southeast. An attendant should present the cup. But
mother isn't sure about this. So I ask you to consider it again for me." Zhang
lavished praise on mother and son and counseled the ruler that ritual should
aim at a middle ground between excess and deficiency. Jiajing should modify
the attendant's role; otherwise he had it pretty much right. [38]

But on March 24, Jiajing still had questions. Other people, apparently,
had voiced their opinions on the banquet ritual. Jiajing reported that some
thought that he himself should fetch and pour the wine and hand the cup to
his mother, who would pass it on to the honoree. Jiajing thought that perhaps
his mother should pour while he held the cup. Zhang replied, no; it would
symbolize the acme of filial piety if Jiajing poured while his mother held the
cup. [39]

All these exchanges, it should be emphasized, did not supplant other
important business. The banquet messages were usually sandwiched somewhere inside multipart queries and replies. Still, the overall context for policy
at this time was the ritual makeover of China. Thus it was a detail in a larger
picture, not a distraction from it.

On October 2, Jiajing reported feeling better after a bout of illness, and he
said he would entertain his mother at a banquet three days hence, after the
rites to distant ancestors. Zhang replied that he'd heard the ruler was spend-
ing all day with his mother, and while his filial piety was exemplary, he
shouldn't overdo it. Four days later, Jiajing acknowledged Zhang's advice.
He admitted going too far to make his mother happy. He reported that his

mother said, "I'm all right, but I fear you overdo your ritual duty. You go to all lengths to fulfill that duty, but how can I rest easy knowing that?" So Jiajing agreed to ease up. Zhang answered on October 5, reporting that he'd gone to the eastern suburb to inspect the ongoing construction of the altar to the sun when he happened to look up and spotted Jiajing and his mother atop the Xiangfeng Lou (soaring phoenix mansion), taking in the view. What a joyous sight! He thought Jiajing was indeed totally attentive to his mother's needs.[40]

On April 5, 1531, the emperor showed his mother a file of prose poems that he, Zhang, and a few others had composed during a visit to inspect the silk and plowing rites arrangements in West Park. According to Jiajing, she read it and said, "I'm so happy to see this. Your giving effort to this will please all the high officials; it's a model for posterity." Replied Jiajing, "I'm no sage or worthy; the high officials helped me." Also, at Zhang's request, Jiajing had renamed Zhang Cong, Zhang Fujing. The emperor's mother asked him about that. "[He] thought his name too similar to mine, so he had it changed." She asked why her son chose "Fujing" ("confidence" plus "respect"). "Because of his reverent service to me, I gave him that name," Jiajing replied. His mother was very pleased.[41]

Jiajing's mother died in 1538. There is more of her story in chapter 4. To this point, it can be said about her that she was literate, that she shared and surely reinforced her son's deep concern for ritual and etiquette, and that she and Jiajing were, at the same time, deeply devoted to one another, as a matter of sentiment. Jiajing's filial piety was not feigned.

* * *

If the mother-son relationship at the Ming court was a semipublic affair, such that it had to be conducted absolutely flawlessly, the ruler's relationship to his empress and other palace women, and the obligation that he produce progeny, sons preferably, of course, were semipublic matters as well.

Jiajing early on confessed to Zhang that he hadn't much of a sex drive. He said he treated his empress and two secondary consorts (*fei*) with courtesy, but, he said, "I don't care for sex, and perhaps I overdo the warning that too much of it is unhealthy. Besides, my endowment of *qi* (vital energy) is weak and thin, so I'm really afraid of sexual indulgence. I've now been married seven years, and I'm still young, but the succession is important, and I fear the crime of filial impiety (i.e., having no progeny). I confess this to you, so you know I have it in mind." That was on January 15, 1528.

Zhang replied the next day, with the simple suggestion that the ruler was driving himself to exhaustion with his scrupulous observance of all rituals. His mother was uneasy sitting while Jiajing knelt before her. His aunt thought one bow before her was enough; four was too many. Plus, daily obsequies at the Fengxian Dian, Fengci Dian, and Chongxian Dian, all of them full of tablets to dead ancestors, was causing the emperor knee collapse and panting, such that his voice was failing at the dawn court lineups. Zhang said children would be forthcoming if Jiajing just took rest and allowed eunuchs and others to substitute for him at some of these rites.[42]

The progeny issue came up again on March 29, 1508. Low-ranking officials were expressing concern and sending up helpful memorials, presumably angling for favor and promotion. Jiajing shared with Zhang some thoughts on the physiology and ethics of procreation. Medical experts stated that the male attained reproductive capacity at age fifteen, the female at thirteen, at the time of first menstruation. But if the male is a teenager, any child he fathers is likely to die early. The father should be in his twenties or thirties, in the prime of life; then the child would be robust. (Jiajing was just then twenty-one.) He noted that the emperor stood above all mankind; everyone in the realm is affected by him, so his family order must be upright, and everyone in it correctly placed, with the husband principled and firm, the wife submissive and wise. That would make the gods and ancestors extend their blessings. "This [childlessness] is caused by my lack of virtue," concluded Jiajing. "But I'm still young, not in good health, but you can relax; we'll proceed slowly." Zhang cheered him on.[43]

On October 21, 1528, Jiajing's empress, nee Chen, died childless, as was mentioned above.[44] Officially it was due to some sort of illness. Rumor had it she'd lost her fetus and died of shock after a severe scolding by Jiajing. He took the blame but showed no grief. A long discussion among the officials and the ruler took place over how long the mourning should last, what colors and types of robe should be worn, and how and where in the imperial necropolis west of the capital she should be buried.[45]

His mother pressed Jiajing about selecting another empress. On December 7, Jiajing again turned to Zhang for advice. Zhang urged that the empress's palace shouldn't stay empty; that all of China, officials and common people, were expecting an heir; and that of the two consorts, whoever was the wiser and purer should be installed very soon.

The next day, Jiajing confessed to self-doubt. "My virtue is mostly faulty, no matter what choice I make. I inherited the ancestors' throne. Then I caused the empress [Chen] to die suddenly without heir. Maybe I could put this difficult affair [of choosing a new empress] off for a month or a year. That won't be too late, will it? I must obey what my mother tells me, but I'm afraid it will turn out badly. Whether people do good or evil comes from their nature. Few people turn from evil to good anymore. If a gentleman's wife must be a pure woman, that's even truer in the case of a ruler. Earlier when I first got married, palace women long steeped in evil had exclusive charge of it [as go-betweens], and day and night they spoke to my mother, who never checked into it. If this repeats, it's best not to press forward with the succession. I love the virtuous and wise. I have no personal thoughts of favorites or sex. . . . If I pick a virtuous one, [those passed over] will be angry, and ridicule and slander will follow." Jiajing asked Zhang to discuss this, plus what his mother had said, with his colleagues and give a reply.

Zhang replied at once, though he said he was too ill to come to court. He thought Jiajing needn't worry about ridicule or slander, that his mother was right to urge him not to delay, and that soon the minister of rites would submit a formal request to install a new empress. [46]

* * *

Fire broke out on November 21, 1529, in seven small housing units on the west side of the Qianqing Palace. [47] The units housed young palace girls. The fire woke and frightened Jiajing's aunt. It angered Jiajing. The next day he told Zhang that he thought this might be an omen, that maybe his faults had caused the fire. The girl or girls responsible were now in custody, and he asked whether he should punish them. Zhang doubted it was an omen, as Jiajing didn't hoard treasure, consort with eunuchs, or give himself up to sex and entertainment. He should hold his anger in check, because anger adversely affected his health.

The next day, at the imperial tutorial, Zhang noticed a look of worry and fear on Jiajing's face. He insisted the emperor wasn't to blame. The girls' carelessness was the sole cause of the fire. A regular trial process should limit any punishment to the actual culprit or culprits.

On the day after that, November 23, the emperor gave Zhang further details. He said managers, eunuchs probably, arrested eight girls for carelessness with fire. The matron in charge had been sick at the time. Under questioning, the girls said they had lit lanterns and gone outside, but before they could go back in, their places were on fire. Jiajing thought they'd said this out of fear of being punished. The next morning, they were all in custody. "I thought about this for several days," Jiajing confessed. "It wasn't Heaven. It wasn't other people. It wasn't fate. It was I who really caused it. That's why I asked you about it, and you've replied. But the palace girls are very frivolous and careless and should be given some measured punishment. And you saw the worry on my face and my cough. The fire did scare me. My virtue is bad. But the cough came on because of the wind that hit me that night. I didn't get to sleep until the fourth drum sounded, so I got the cough. Anger didn't cause it. In the palace, I've tried never to be too delighted or too angry. In delight I might grow lax; anger I have to let dissipate. I tell you all this to reassure you."[48]

Five days later, Zhang resumed his role as life coach. He said he'd given the palace fire much thought. The blame really had to be placed on us bureaucrats, he said. It was just one of many recent bad portents—floods, drought, locusts, comets, eclipses—and it's not clear how to interpret them. So Zhang offered a four-point regimen for the ruler to follow. First came his health: stay calm, don't get too hot or cold, eat and sleep regularly, and take some relaxation. Second, he must ensure offspring by emotional control, choosing suitable consorts, finding pleasure, but avoiding falling in love. Third, keep up his sincere study of the sages' texts; and fourth, improve governance by controlling his emotions, taking care with decisions, and checking into lies and concealments.

Jiajing read and accepted Zhang's four-point program. He had some further thoughts, however. He'd noticed there was a gate called the "Hundred Sons Gate" next to the seven fire-damaged housing units the girls had vacated, so it looked to him as though Heaven were protecting him because as yet he had no heir. Jiajing added that his new empress (nee Zhang, earlier the "Complaisant Consort," one of the two who had served the tea and angered Empress Chen) was not in good health, so he was reluctant to impregnate her. To this matter, Zhang Fujing (no relation to the empress) suggested to Jiajing that he ask his mother to select some healthy girls to serve as consorts and produce backup sons. If Empress Zhang should at any time produce a son herself, that son would of course become the heir to the throne.[49]

No pregnancy was immediately forthcoming. In April 1530, Zhang endorsed a suggestion sent up by the Ministry of Rites, originally written by a well-meaning local Confucian student who shared the concern of Jiajing and his mother for the absence of an heir, that a very ancient sacrifice to the god Gaomei, a son giver, could be revived and carried out. Jiajing was doubtful. He didn't think the gods should be appealed to for an heir. He thought pregnancy was a matter of physiology. A good fetus will have received placental instruction. He'll have the benefit of harmony between his father and mother. Heaven will give him his mandated life span (*ming*), and his parents will give him his body. No prayer is needed. Zhang changed his mind and agreed.[50]

Jiajing asked the Hanlin Academy to prepare a program for teaching and improving the behavior of the young palace girls. A program was done up and presented on October 23, 1530. It included easy poems on goodness for the girls to memorize and recite. The empress would lead the girls to Jiajing's mother and to the palace matrons, who would lecture them. There was more, and it was all very formal.[51] Jiajing thought it a good idea to give each chosen girl a title and position. Zhang heartily agreed.[52]

Having pondered the matter, Jiajing came up with some practical questions about the teaching program for the girls. He urged that the lessons be postponed until early the next year. Also he thought that now was the time to recruit a new group of girls. Zhang agreed and offered to write a memorial urging the emperor to order the Ministry of Rites to conduct a roundup of young virgins from high-ranking families of the Beijing area and give them titles of rank.[53] Three days later, Zhang told Jiajing that the whole realm was rejoicing at the news of the girls' recruitment. After discussing the matter with Minister of Rites Li Shi, Zhang thought it best to extend the area of recruitment beyond Beijing to include the provinces of Henan, Shandong, and Nan Zhili.[54] On October 31, Jiajing told Zhang of his mother's joy at hearing of what was afoot.[55]

Then, during the night of December 30, Zhang had a portentous dream. He dreamed of the character *xu* in a glow in the southeast sky, which morphed into two characters, *taizi*, "heir apparent." In his dream he kowtowed to it in joy many times. Then he awoke and at once wrote it down. Was this prior notice of the birth of a successor? The character *xu* contains four bits, of which three mean "person." Does that mean a crowd of progeny? Maybe a newly selected virgin has the surname "Xu"? Or perhaps she comes from Xuzhou in Shandong? Zhang wasn't sure. To this promising omen, Jiajing replied that while pleasantly surprised, he was also afraid that he lacked virtue and so couldn't get the descent line started. But his mother, when told of Zhang's dream, was certain it was good news, and she prayed about it at her husband's palace shrine. Jiajing thought "Xu" might be the name of a Daoist god. No recently recruited girl had "Xu" for a surname. He asked Zhang to explain further.

Zhang thought Jiajing's reverent affection for his mother, and his mother's heartfelt desire for a grandchild and heir to the throne, were going to have a good outcome eventually. What *xu* meant would come clear as well. Ancestors should be prayed to, not the gods.

Zhang went on to sketch out a remarkable scene. He said that the day before he happened to be in the Translators Institute when Peng Ze, chief minister of the Court of Imperial Sacrifices, showed him a painting recently done by his brother-in-law, an assistant postal official at Henanfu, of a spectacularly brilliant cloud. The accompanying letter said the cloud appeared one noon, and no one had ever seen anything like it before. "This [cloud] appeared," Zhang explained, "because you've perfected the rites and music, and have revived the old [norms of] civil and military governance." The cloud joins reports of lucky wheat and clear Yellow River water and Zhang's dream as preparatory signs of great blessings. These omens hadn't been memorialized through the regular channels, explained Zhang, because the officials feared impeachment for obsequiousness if they did so. Zhang sent Jiajing the cloud painting.

Jiajing received the news and the painting with due modesty and circumspection. Emperor and minister then discussed the best way to pray to the ancestors for progeny. Zhang urged that it was now time to recruit the virgins and announce that move at the ancestral shrines, the Taimiao shrine to the dead Ming emperors, and the Shimiao shrine to Jiajing's father. This would not be a minimal private ceremony. It would be a full-blown public event involving all Beijing officialdom. For three days preceding, the officials were to wear special dark red robes and then gather at the Meridian Gate on the appointed day. And so it was done, on January 12, 1531. Zhang Fujing was too sick to attend.[56]

Then tragedy struck. Forty-eight virgins were selected and admitted into the Forbidden City. They were not housed in any of the palaces there, but instead were made to stay in wooden cells of sorts lined up cheek by jowl along one of the interior streets. Zhang heard of a fire somewhere on the west side of the emperor's palace during the night of February 11–12, 1531. He wanted to know if Jiajing was all right. A much shaken Jiajing replied that the fire was to the east of his palace, caused by his own faults and misrule. It alarmed the ancestors and panicked the women. Come noon, Jiajing would report this to Heaven, Earth, and the ancestors. "I was asleep when fire was reported," confessed the emperor. "I broke out in a sweat of fear; then I felt weakness. My cough returned. . . . When the ladies came looking for me, I was lying in bed and couldn't get up to meet them. My mind is disturbed. Send me a text to use for the rituals at once."

Zhang reassured him. Jiajing was too respectful of Heaven and Earth to have caused the fire. The girls' carelessness had caused it. Jiajing must guard his health. February 13 was a lucky day for canceling court and making the ritual announcements. If the emperor was unwell, he could have substitutes perform for him. (It turned out that Jiajing was well enough to do the rites himself.)

Still upset, Jiajing wrote Zhang a detailed report of the fire. He said he felt all right except for a lingering cough due to congestion in the lungs. The fire, he said, broke out in the room of a girl surnamed Guo, who was totally drunk and died in the fire. The other girls jumped out the windows and escaped. The street along which the housing was built was very narrow and the units were interconnected, so it was hard to control a fire. Some units were close enough to water to be saved, but fourteen units burned down. The girls who were housed there have spent the last two nights sleeping rough in the street. He thought a detailed rebuilding program with fire safety in mind needed to be worked on.

Zhang agreed to all this. The ruler, he said, needed to rest to clear his lungs. The culprit was the dead girl. All the other girls needed to be forgiven. Temporary shelter for those made homeless needed to be arranged at once. Reconstruction should use stone and brick rather than wood, he advised.

Jiajing visited his mother on February 14, and she asked him to cancel her birthday celebration that year on account of the fire. This put Jiajing in doubt: should he obey his mother or not?

To that, Zhang Fujing had a firm answer. It was not Heaven but carelessness that caused the fire. If you ascribe the fire to Heaven's doing, you just excite the mouths of the "small men." The opposition partisans have already denounced the lucky grain and other omens. They'll just use the fire to mislead people. Jiajing should explain this to his mother. "If you overdo worry and fear," he counseled, "you'll be misled and render yourself helpless."

Jiajing agreed. He went so far as to write a short tract, which he titled *Yuzhi huojing huowen* ("Questions and Answers about the Fire Scare, Composed by the Emperor"). He sent Zhang a copy. Zhang liked it. Why wouldn't he? It closely echoed his argument, blaming the girl Guo. Jiajing added the details that the girls' housing was tight and crowded, some units housing not one but three or four girls; that they didn't all get along; that one girl was too drunk to wake up and was burned to death (referring, presumably, to the Guo girl); and that at three drums a watchman discovered the fire, reported it to security, and yelled "fire." Thirty-five contiguous units were burned to the ground. Jiajing might have blamed himself if he'd banned wine and then failed to enforce the ban, but that was not the situation. Only scoundrels, for partisan reasons, would interpret the fire as a sign from Heaven. So Jiajing informed the realm and recovered his mental balance. [57]

* * *

Eventually, over his lifetime, Jiajing produced eight sons and five daughters, of whom two sons and two daughters survived to become adults. [58]

Jiajing took advantage of a temporary absence of Zhang from court to break with his earlier decision not to appeal to the gods for progeny. He arranged an elaborate Daoist service in the Qin'an Pavilion. Minister of Rites Xia Yan was master of ceremonies. Vice Ministers Zhan Ruoshui and Gu Dingchen presented early examples of the later infamous *qingci*, Daoist prayers written in gold ink on dark paper. Incense was presented on successive days by Marquis Guo Xun, Grand Secretary Li Shi, Minister of War Wang Xian, and two others. That was in late December 1531. [59] No explanation was offered as to why, if sacrifice to the classical god Gaomei was inappropriate, it was all right to entreat the Daoist gods. But Jiajing had another spiritual guide hovering in the wings, and neither his name nor his presence was ever mentioned in Jiajing's correspondence with Zhang Fujing. He was Shao Yuanjie (1459–1539), a Daoist priest whom Jiajing invited to Beijing and the Forbidden City in 1524, and upon whom he lavished deep reverence and rich rewards. [60] Almost certainly it was Shao who arranged this rite.

On March 19, 1531, nine of the recently recruited virgins were chosen, following classical precedent, as the Nine Concubines. Each was given a title and placed in rank order. Their leader was Virtuous Concubine Fang, later Empress Fang.

A few days earlier, Jiajing stated to Zhang that he didn't think the fathers of the Nine Concubines should be given military positions, which they didn't earn or deserve, but something else.

Zhang replied that he got this message that night while he was lodging in the eastern suburb waiting for the emperor's dawn arrival to conduct the solar sacrifice. He answered at once that in light of the need to inform the ancestors about the offices conferred on the girls' fathers, it was best to conform to traditional hierarchical norms, such that the fathers of empresses, consorts (*fei*), and concubines (*bin*) should all get military offices of descending rank. So the concubines' fathers should be made battalion commanders. Anything lower, or any nonmilitary post, would diminish the preeminence of the imperial court.[61]

Jiajing asked Zhang to confer with Li Shi about all this. Zhang did so and the same day, August 3, 1531, suggested that some concubines be promoted to consorts and that the fathers of all the virgins be given start-up positions as acting judges in the Embroidered-Uniform Guard, then battalion commanders when their daughters were raised to concubine, and then commanders in the guards when their daughters were made consorts.[62]

On January 23, 1534, Jiajing drafted his own proclamation to the realm concerning the installation of a new empress, Virtuous Consort Fang. His draft underlined the importance of the empress's role as a necessary participant in the imperial sacrifices, as manager and instructor of the palace women, and as prospective mother of an heir to the throne. The position of empress was currently vacant due to the death of Empress Chen from "illness" and the dismissal of Empress Zhang due to "misbehavior" (*zuo nie*). Zhang Fujing and Li Shi, since promoted to grand secretary, both reviewed the draft and gave it their full approval.[63]

The removal of Empress Zhang had to be explained. An official statement of Jiajing's to the Ministry of Rites stated that "she was seldom compliant, she was disrespectful and unyielding, and though warned in a kindly way, she refused to reform, and regarded me as nothing. A woman like this cannot be empress. She has stepped down. Her seal of appointment has been rescinded, and her use of special stationery stopped."[64] Nine days later, Empress Fang succeeded her.

The last note from Jiajing to Chief Grand Secretary Zhang Fujing, who had since retired to his native home, is dated June 23, 1536. It is just a friendly report on the imperial family's latest doings, the latest four concubines taken on, the ruler and his mother's trip out to the Ming tombs, and his beginning construction on his own sepulcher there. He said nothing of policy or politics. A special messenger reached Zhang on July 24 with the message. Zhang died early in 1539.[65] That their last piece of secret correspondence should have sounded so warm, the ruler treating Jiajing as though he were a senior family member, is a good indication of the success of both in sustaining their relationship despite the many challenges to it.

* * *

Jiajing and Zhang had fierce arguments over how to respond to rebellion and mutiny out in the provinces. Zhang was stern and repressive, Jiajing much less so. Two controversial war-related issues arose during Zhang's tenure as chief grand secretary. One was the Blue Sheep Mountain (Qingyang Shan) affair of 1528–1529. Blue Sheep Mountain was located in a spectacular landscape of sheer crags, ravines, and forest in southern Shanxi Province, some 350 miles southwest of Beijing. A report received March 2, 1528, stated that government troops going after bandits there had been beaten off, and that several leading civil and military officials had been killed.[66] Beijing's response was to order Regional Vice Commander Zhao Lian to lead a retaliatory strike, with Censor in Chief Chang Dao in charge of provincial forces to assist him. On November 15, eight months later, victory was declared.[67] This was but one of many violent local disturbances that erupted during Jiajing's long reign. Often they took place in mountain areas that were underserved by local government and were filling up with new settlers as a result of continuing growth in Ming China's population.

There were actually two contentious issues connected with Blue Sheep Mountain. The first had to do with how severe a repression to conduct. Having ordered troops to the area, Jiajing wanted them held back in hopes that the disorder might be settled through negotiations. Zhang reacted in horror to this approach. His disagreement was not secret but part of an open debate. Zhang was at this time a grand secretary under Yang Yiqing, who would soon resign.[68] Zhang argued in alarm (and here I paraphrase) that negotiation with bandit leaders was wrong. The ruler needed to get angry and activate the *zhongxing* (dynastic revival) program. This was a critical moment, as examples from Tang history showed. Blue Sheep Mountain was too close to Beijing to leave in the hands of a bandit. Bandits everywhere were watching events unfold, seeking opportunity. Even if Li Keji's plan worked, it was not how a dynasty in all its majesty should respond to an uprising against it. (Li Keji was a lowly Imperial University student and a native of the area, whose plan to settle the affair peacefully made its way up through channels and won Jiajing's endorsement.) Zhang demanded a decisive and bloody crackdown. He noted that in the Datong Mutiny of 1524, the court dallied and did not fully punish the rioters, with the result that to that day, violent men had been encouraged by the leniency. And now we are repeating this misguided policy. These bandits sit at the juncture of three provinces, they've killed thirty to forty government troops and many innocents, and they must be exterminated.

The other contentious issue regarding Blue Sheep Mountain was how to sort out all the claimants for merit and restore civil authority. That was mainly Xia Yan's work (see chapter 4). But the episode highlights Zhang Fujing's aggressiveness. His alarmism was excessive, and Jiajing ignored his advice. But in 1533 a second Datong mutiny, involving some of the same soldiers who had rioted back in 1524, broke out in the Great Wall garrison city of that name in northern Shanxi Province. Again, a fierce argument erupted in Beijing over how best to suppress the uprising. At this time, Zhang was chief grand secretary. He had lost none of his penchant for purposeful violence. He never discussed the issue in his secret messages, but he was vocal about this second Datong mutiny in an open discussion channel, while addressing his remarks to Jiajing. In fact, he devoted five statements to it.

What happened was this. On October 23, the army at Datong mutinied. Led by soldiers Ji Fuzi, Wang Fusheng, and Wang Bao, upward of fifty troops refused to dig a thirteen-mile ditch along one side of the city and do it inside of a three-day deadline. That night, they killed their commanding officer, Regional Commander Liu Jin. They set fire to the office of Grand Coordinator Pan Fang, who fled into hiding, and then they went on a looting rampage. Word of this got out when the Prince of Dai managed to escape to Xuanfu, about 150 miles east. New at his job, Pan Fang didn't know what to do other than to send up a report.

The purpose of the ditch was to protect the walled city of Datong from a recent upsurge in Lu (Mongol) raids. The minister of war, Wang Xian, had sent out Vice Minister of War Liu Yuanqing as supreme commander, and Military Commissioner Que Yong as regional commander. It was Liu who agreed to Liu Jin's idea to dig the ditch. [69]

Pan Fang sympathized with the mutineers. He thought Liu Jin's harsh treatment the cause of the uprising. His memorial asked for leniency. Outraged and disturbed by Liu's murder, Liu Yuanqing demanded suppression. Jiajing sent the dispute to the Ministry of War for discussion. Minister Wang Xian argued that only some of the troops had mutinied, that they must be rooted out and destroyed, and that all the rest should be let go. He sent orders to that effect to Liu Yuanqing and Pan Fang, but the principals on the scene mishandled a very delicate situation. Liu Yuanqing's publicly displayed placards were unnecessarily provocative: "When the 1524 mutiny occurred, the court was lenient in managing it," read the signs. "That has nurtured the present leaders in evil. Heaven's suppression must fall on them." The words steeled those involved in the earlier mutiny to resist to the end.

A dozen or so captured mutineers were forced to name the leaders of the riot. Pan Fang noted that not all of those they named were in fact guilty. No matter. All the mutineers now felt vulnerable to false accusations. So when Liu Yuanqing sent an officer into Datong to demand that everyone surrender to the imperial forces, rumors flew that those forces were going to come in and conduct a general massacre, and so the mutineers refused to give in. Liu then had his men force a gate and commence slaughter and pillage. The mutineers forced them back out. There was no stopping the bloodshed now. Everywhere lay victims of wanton killing inflicted by imperial soldiers greedy for merit.

It was at this malignant moment that Zhang Fujing weighed in with his open-source advice for Jiajing. His first message, undated, acknowledged that many years of maladministration and mistreatment lay behind the mutiny, but the mutineers were holding members of the imperial clan, local officials, and many innocent commoners hostage. Yet if we withdraw our forces to allow everyone to exit, the mutineers will just spread their evil everywhere, causing an even worse disaster. More planning was needed; the aim, he said, was to exterminate leaders and protect the innocent.

His next message, also undated, protested Jiajing's decision to recall and replace Liu Yuanqing and Que Yong. Changing leaders while a battle rages is always bad practice, he advised. Both Liu and Que have good career records. Dismissing them will demoralize our forces. The Ming army has so far penetrated two of the three outer walls. The mutineers' situation is deteriorating. The good are managing to flee or hide. Zhang also noted that the mutineers had established contact with the Lu raiders and had sent forty interpreters with gifts of cloth to entice them into making a foray. Que Yong caught a spy, who gave him this information. Defense against the Lu was part of Liu and Que's responsibilities, so they shouldn't be dismissed.[70]

Critiquing a military operation from a distant command post in Beijing was a hazardous procedure. Datong was some 150 miles west. Neither Zhang nor anyone else could monitor developments there very closely. Pan Fang and two other officials managed to capture some mutineers, of whom they flogged to death ten or so and delivered seventy or so others, including the leader named Wang Bao, to Liu Yuanqing's camp at Yanghe, a military base about twenty-five miles east of Datong. They argued that this capture should suffice to make further military operations unnecessary. Liu firmly disagreed. He cited the disastrous results of the leniency policy of 1524. He sent the captives to Censor Su You for interrogation. Much of the information they gave was false. But on the basis of it, Liu sent Assistant Regional Commander Zhao Gang to Datong to find and arrest those named. This provoked rumors inside Datong that a massacre was coming, and so the resistance stiffened.

Meanwhile, Que Yong threw a siege around Datong, and fighting began in earnest. Ming troops were wantonly killing people, but Liu rejected pleas to call the assault off. He posted police around Datong so as to intercept and block any memorials sent out by imperial clansmen or officials caught inside Datong that begged for mercy and a lifting of the siege. He asked Beijing to send him fifty thousand more troops. Jiajing at first agreed, then changed his mind.

While this was going on, the court debated whether Pan Fang and others were right, that it was wanton killing by Ming troops that ignited the mutiny and that if the troops were withdrawn the mutiny would fizzle out. Zhang Fujing and most of the other officials at court disagreed and supported Liu Yuanqing's hard line. Jiajing deferred a final decision, but he seemed to show his hand when he dismissed Pan Fang on October 28.[71] Zhang thought Pan Fang no better than a message bearer for the mutineers.[72]

Inside Datong, turncoat Ming officers rejected Pan Fang's offer to negotiate. They managed somehow to send a delegation to the Lu leader, styled "the Little Prince," and offered him gold, cloth, and singing girls in return for an alliance. They reportedly said that China was richer than the steppe and that the Little Prince could become an emperor with a base at Datong, using the vacated residence of the Prince of Dai as his palace.

During December–January 1532–1533, the situation lay unresolved. Three thousand troops under the command of Regional Military Commissioner Shi Jun came from their base in Liaodong to help beat off the Little Prince. They captured and beheaded 137 mutineers who had come out to join him.[73]

The Datong Mutiny raised issues that forced a split in the ranks of those officials who had backed Jiajing in the Great Rites controversy. Gu Dingchen, the wily vice minister of personnel, favored a conciliatory line.[74] So did Huang Wan, vice minister of rites, an original pro-Jiajing discussant. But he and Zhang Fujing, once partisan allies, came to have a falling-out, never more so than over Datong.[75] After personally visiting Datong, Huang argued that while the reaction to the 1524 mutiny had indeed been too lenient, Liu and Qiu and the others were going too far in the opposite direction. The mutineers are not raiders or bandits. Most of Datong's people are good people of ours. The leaders of the mutiny number no more than a few dozen, and their involuntary followers are but three hundred or so. It would have been easy early on for Liu and Que just to enter Datong and make arrests. But they botched it completely. Their talk of cleansing the city, plus the looting by their troops, provoked the city into resistance. So the Grand Secretariat (he meant Zhang Fujing) called for a punitive campaign, and the ruler agreed to that, and they assaulted Datong as though it were a bandit's nest, slaughtering innocents and thus intensifying the resistance. They got Pan Fang and others like him cashiered. The ruler had to dismiss Liu Yuanqing, but Que Yong's siege still held, and the Little Prince would be warmly received if he ever managed to enter Datong. Remove Que Yong and end his siege, and the mutiny would soon be over.[76]

In a follow-up memorial, Huang urged imposing harsh measures on the leaders of the mutiny only, avoiding the extremes of leniency and cruelty. Go after the top leaders. Put up wanted posters for the others. Warn local officials not to overdo it. Let the escapees go, and don't let them return. Fears of their joining the northern Lu are unfounded. That fear shows ignorance of both Lu and Chinese. Chinese captured by the Lu either become slaves or are traded to distant nomads in exchange for horses, so they'll never come back. Defecting to the Lu is not a pleasant option. And the Lu, for their part, doubt their loyalty. (I omit Huang's further interesting remarks about the poor quality of the current masters of the steppe and the uselessness to them of the Chinese defectors.)[77]

During February 1534, fuel ran out inside Datong. People began tearing apart the Prince of Dai's residence, government offices, and private buildings for firewood. Some three hundred people were allowed out to scrounge for firewood, and Que Yong's men in an act of bad faith seized them. Others inside the city refused to surrender. Fighting ensued. The Lu took part, but, surfeited with loot, they soon left. Liu Yuanqing's request to add a commander to battle the Lu was rejected. He tried mining the city, but to no avail. He tried flooding it. Nothing worked.[78]

By February 18, Jiajing had had enough of it. He now echoed Huang Wan's minority opinion. He told the grand secretaries that while the murderers who started all this could not be forgiven, the rest of the city was not to blame for the trouble. Liu Yuanqing and Que Yong, bloodthirsty and greedy for success, have turned the affair into a serious revolt, bringing the Lu into it. What kind of idea is it to flood the city? Does Liu want to destroy what the ancestors have built and kill everybody? Even if he succeeds, how will we ever rebuild the place? We must dismiss both of them. Appoint new frontier defenders. Make covert arrests of the main culprits.

So Jiajing finally made his position clear. Zhang Fujing and his hard line lost out. Liu Yuanqing resigned in disgrace. Que Yong was for the moment kept on. New officials were sent out. Huang Wan and others readied relief for all those trapped inside Datong. The resistance ended. The Prince of Dai returned from Xuanfu.[79] And that pretty much ended the affair. It was not so much that Zhang and the emperor differed on strategic philosophy. It was, rather, that Zhang misread the facts on the ground and jumped to his preferred posture of severity.

* * *

While Zhang and Jiajing had conflicting views about the Datong Mutiny, with Jiajing rightly rejecting Zhang's unthinking hard line, they were also at odds over how to respond to the egregious misbehavior of Zhang Yanling, younger brother of the Zhaosheng empress, the Hongzhi emperor's widow. On this, ironically, Jiajing took the hard line. Zhang Fujing (no relation) tried to persuade him to ease up. Again, even though this was an imperial family matter, it was handled as a public issue.

The Zhang brothers, Heling and Yanling, were beneficiaries of every title, honor, emolument, and privilege the Ming dynasty could conceivably lavish on undeserving in-laws. But the Hongzhi emperor had loved his empress, and in his eyes, her family could do no wrong. They became well known as devotees of wealth accumulation and corruption of every sort. Jiajing hated them.

On October 23, 1533, the younger one, Zhang Yanling, Marquis of Jianchang, was arrested and put in prison. The case against him had a history that dated back to 1515, when a soothsayer named Cao Zu, for unclear reasons, allegedly took poison and committed suicide. Cao's son, Cao Ding, was a slave of Zhang's who introduced his father into the household. Then he and the other slaves all had a falling-out with Cao Zu, and they got Zhang Yan-ling to expel him. In revenge, Cao Zu denounced them all for secretly plot-ting treason. Arrests were made. Cao Zu was put in the Ministry of Justice's prison, while other slaves were put in the Embroidered-Uniform Guards prison, and yet others, including Cao Ding, in the eunuch-run Eastern Depot. None of them was put to torture. Only when it was ordered that they were all to be interrogated in open court did Cao Zu take poison. Or was it murder? Three prison officials were indicted, and the case was dropped. Zhang Yan-ling reportedly paid big bribes to two senior eunuchs who had been helpful.

Later, Zhang Yanling flogged to death both a Buddhist monk and the slave woman who had stolen money to give him. He had their corpses cre-mated.

Early in Jiajing's reign, when the homes and estates of top Zhengde-era eunuchs were being confiscated, Zhang was able, in the style of a post-Soviet oligarch, to acquire their properties at a very low price. Reportedly his gar-dens and pavilions exceeded all bounds.

Then, allegedly, a low-level military commander who was also a slave of Zhang's, Si Cong, lent money on Zhang's behalf. He fell five hundred taels behind on his repayments, and Zhang pressed him for it. So Si Cong got one Huang Zhi, son of a onetime astrology student, to threaten to resubmit the case involving Cao Zu so as to force Zhang Yanling to bribe him. Zhang refused. He had someone go capture Si Cong and search his house for the documents. Then he had Si flogged a hundred lashes and put in a dark room where he died. He ordered Si's son Si Sheng to burn the corpse. As a reward, Zhang canceled the debt and treated the son generously. Si Sheng was too afraid to say anything against Zhang, but he voiced such deep hatred for Huang Zhi that Huang fetched the memorial his father had written for Si Cong and submitted it. That was in October 1533.

So the Ministry of Justice arrested Zhang Yanling and all his slaves. Interrogation brought to light his illegal property acquisitions and his mur-ders of the slave woman, the Buddhist priest, and Si Cong. Allegations of a secret plot of regicide couldn't be substantiated, however. Minister of Justice Nie Xian sent the case up to Jiajing.

Jiajing's reaction bordered on the apoplectic. "Either there was a plot or there wasn't," he thundered. "It doesn't matter whether it was carried out or not. Nie Xian is partisan and dishonest." He demanded a reinvestigation. He said that the plea that Si Cong wasn't beaten to death, and that Cao Zu died of self-poisoning, seemed a distortion of the facts done at someone's behest at the time.

A chastened Nie Xian interrogated two more of Zhang Yanling's slaves. Now the testimony was that Si Cong killed Cao Zu by strangling him, and that Si Ding and others had concocted the treason plot. So there was no proof that Zhang Yanling had been involved in such a thing. Still, there was no doubt of his indulgence in luxury or his cruelty. These called for the death penalty. His older brother Zhang Heling had a mansion just next door yet did nothing to restrain Yanling. Seven senior officials who did nothing about any of this should be investigated. The slaves deserved a range of punishments. So Nie reported.

An angered Jiajing thought it was as clear as daylight that Zhang Yanling's crimes fell within the scope of the Ten Abominations, for which death was the penalty. But "those who accused him [of treason] have no proof of it. So for now, his murdering of innocents and his sumptuary excess will earn him the death penalty under ancestral law. His brother Heling will have his dukedom rescinded. His slave Ma Jing, who spread prophecies, is to be executed. The other ten slaves are to be exiled to the frontiers as soldiers" (and various other penalties were imposed). Zhang Yanling was forbidden to file exculpatory appeals. [80]

Chief Grand Secretary Zhang Fujing thought Jiajing was doing his own imperial family grievous harm by this verdict. Four times he openly interceded on Zhang Yanling's behalf, mainly because he thought his execution would have a serious effect on the Great Rites settlement. He argued that while Jiajing had refused to cut ties with his natal family and to become the Zhaosheng empress's son by adoption, he nonetheless accepted her role in his enthronement, and he always accorded her a due measure of filial respect. Even his own mother befriended her. The whole realm knew this and acclaimed it. But she was the Zhang brothers' own older sister. What terrible end must befall her if indeed Zhang Yanling were convicted of the crime of treason! (As a traitor's sister, enslavement at the least.) He was guilty of murder, and that called for the death penalty, but he'd done the murders back in the Zhengde era, so a kind of statute of limitations applied here. The chief grand secretary therefore recommended depriving him of his marquisate, confiscating his properties, reducing him to commoner status, and sending him into military exile. [81]

Jiajing was not convinced. So Zhang reminded Jiajing how in 1521, having just achieved his degree, he had braved death to champion Jiajing's own mother's rights at the expense of the Zhaosheng empress. She has never forgotten that, nor have all the vengeance-seeking court officials. Their plot is to maneuver Jiajing into exterminating the whole distaff Zhang family, and thereby place the whole Great Rites settlement in a very bad light. They accuse me and Grand Secretary Fang Xianfu of being Zhang Yanling's secret friends and partisans. The ruler hasn't seen into this. Does he think I'm a member of a treason gang? The treason charge is based on Cao Zu's supernatural claim that he was raising ghost troops, and thus it has no credibility. At least get Zhang Yanling out of Beijing. Think about what kin extermination means for the Zhaosheng empress. Could you rest easy with that?

Clearly Jiajing was in a foul mood with thoughts of treason clouding his judgment. Two more such cases were pending. One involved Feng En, the other Qin Tang. Feng En was a Nanjing censor whose memorial of November 1532 in response to the appearance of a comet singled out Zhang Fujing and Fang Xianfu for the death penalty, for which Jiajing ordered Feng arrested and subjected to torture. Feng won wide acclaim for withstanding the torture. Qin Tang was a lowly office manager in the Nanjing Censorate. Jiajing thought Feng En's real target was himself and the Great Rites and Great Case settlements. Zhang Fujing urged clemency here. How could he, Zhang Fujing, be protecting traitors as charged if the alleged traitor called for his own head? He simply asked that Jiajing do the right thing. But Jiajing was still sure Zhang Yanling's ultimate aim was to seize the throne.[82]

Zhang Fujing's final word on the matter reemphasized points he'd already made. He reminded Jiajing that the Great Rites and Great Case settlements had not entailed a single death penalty (never mind the deaths due to flogging; the sentence was flogging, not death). Feng En's execution would needlessly terrorize the speaking officials. Qin Tang was just a pedant out of his depth. Zhang Yanling's death will make his sister weep, and the realm will sympathize with her. Leniency was the best option for all these cases.[83] Zhang Fujing lost out on the Datong Mutiny, but in this instance his views prevailed.

* * *

From 1521 to 1524, a very young fledgling emperor came into his own as an autocrat, as he fought hard to force his own interpretation of imperial family ritual upon a Ming realm full of doubters and resisters. It was Zhang Fujing, a middle-aged nobody, his newly won *jinshi* degree in hand, who, along with a mere handful of like-minded officials, created around Jiajing an iron guard of explainers, advisors, and policy enforcers that, as Jiajing freely admitted, made it possible for him to prevail. That laid the grounds for the springtime, so to speak, of his reign, with Zhang Fujing at his side and ritual reform and reorganization at the forefront of national policy.

A final question to consider is this: Zhang Fujing paid a heavy price for the unfailing support he gave Jiajing. Zhang was not a popular official. Many detested him and tried as best they could to ruin him. Zhang really had no friends. He had hangers-on, but no party or faction. As he often said, his only supporter and rescuer from certain death was Jiajing. Jiajing's need for Zhang was almost as desperate, but not quite. Jiajing was not naive about power. His suspicion of all high officials, Zhang included, while not Stalin-like, ran deep. He always cultivated counterbalancing alternatives. Zhang was not the only official with rights of secret correspondence. Evidence for the ways in which Jiajing handled Zhang Fujing can be seen in the three times he was made to step down from office.

The first time came in 1529. Grand Secretaries Yang Yiqing, Gui E, and Zhang all came under savage attacks from various supervising secretaries. On September 15 came a venomous bombshell from one Lu Can, supervising secretary in the Office of Scrutiny for the Ministry of Works. He asserted that

> Grand Secretaries Zhang Cong (Zhang Fujing) and Gui E are evildoers of skewed learning. As minor officials, they won the ruler's favor in the Great Rites dispute. In a mere three or four years, they rose to the highest positions, enjoying unprecedented favor, which even the fullest measure of service would not suffice to repay. Yet they deceive the ruler, act in their own interest, monopolize power, take bribes, reward friends, and harm enemies. Zhang Cong is fiercely self-willed, obstinate, and self-centered. His technique is to make it look as though he's not causing much harm. Gui E appears mild on the surface, but he's violent on the inside. Whenever the poison of anger erupts in his mind, like a snake or tiger he kills all who offend him. Let me cite a few instances.
>
> The minister Wang Qiong was corrupt and vicious in the Zhengde era, joining powerful villains to befoul the realm; he should have been executed, but Gui E accepted a huge bribe from him and repeatedly recommended him. Zhang Cong helped with that and got him hired. His excuse was that Wang Qiong's talent outweighed his guilt.
>
> The Earl of Changhua, Shao Jie, is a foster son who, as everyone knows, vied to inherit the earldom. Gui E got a big bribe from him, and so a lowly house slave by origin got to usurp the title, and all of the other hereditary

nobles are ashamed to associate with him. (Lu Can here cites Gui E's connections with various lowlifes, co-locals, relatives, and promotion seekers.)

The Nanjing vice minister of rites, Huang Wan, adheres to the popular perverted learning [of Wang Yangming]. He dazzles with his vain lectures. Peng Ze became advisor to the heir apparent.

All this has come about through covert sympathizing with Zhang and open allying with Gui. Cliques have become customary and corrupting. Gui E wields great power, so he has many adherents. The realm fears him. Everyone freezes. No one dares speak up about the wrong. He has to be done away with, or else the realm will be in danger. Destroy him. Punish all his adherents. Make the way of impartiality bright and so gladden men's minds. [84]

Lu Can seemed to take Gui E as the main villain. Surprisingly perhaps, Jiajing openly and fully endorsed Lu Can's assault on his two great paladins, Gui and Zhang. He acknowledged the positive role both had played in the Great Rites struggle and the favor he'd shown them for that. "But," he said, "they've since abandoned their early resolve; they've begun acting recklessly, betraying me, forgetting righteousness, and committing transgressions." He penalized everyone Lu's memorial accused. He asked Zhang Cong (Zhang Fujing) to "go home and introspect and mend his ways, in hope of someday returning to office." Gui E he forced to retire altogether. [85]

Jiajing, all of twenty-two years old at this juncture, was showing the realm who was boss. Zhang and Gui were certainly eager to pack officialdom with Great Rites supporters and squeeze out dissenters. Zhang was like a master of hounds, Gui his alpha attack dog. As a later commentator pointed out, they thirsted for ever more power and forced Chief Grand Secretary Fei Hong into retirement in 1527. They were pressuring his successor, Yang Yiqing, to retire as well. [86] Clearly Jiajing, with his intuitive understanding of power, was not about to become a prisoner of his own support group and thought this a good moment to flash a sign of independence from it.

However, Zhang was also Jiajing's life coach and psychotherapist. After Zhang's departure, Jiajing felt lost. Zhang had only traveled as far as Tianjin, a hundred miles southeast of Beijing, when Jiajing sent a messenger to order him back to the Grand Secretariat. Before he left Beijing, Zhang did his introspection and confessed that he'd been "too hard and impatient"; that hardness means fragility, and impatience leads to failure; and that he needed to ease up and slow down. Zhang was accompanying his wife's coffin back home to Yongjia County in Zhejiang, and his son was too sick to continue the trip, so he abandoned both coffin and sick son at Hexiwu and rushed by land conveyance back to the Grand Secretariat. Jiajing gave him back his seals for stamping on secret messages. [87]

Meanwhile, with Zhang and Gui out of power for the moment, Huo Tao (supervisor of the Household of the Heir Apparent) sent up an advisory statement to Jiajing. He defended Zhang and Gui. He castigated Lu Can as a partisan of Chief Grand Secretary Yang Yiqing. He denounced Yang for having accepted large gifts of money from several place seekers. He went on to note Yang's hostility toward Zhang and Gui, his efforts to encourage the speaking officials to impeach them, and his forming links with various palace eunuchs. Huo said his own days as a pro–Great Rites advocate were numbered, seeing that Zhang and Gui were gone. He asked to resign. Jiajing kept him on. [88]

Yang Yiqing also offered to resign, He denied Huo Tao's charges:

> Huo Tao thinks I'm responsible for the ouster of Zhang and Gui. He accuses me of many crimes. If what he says is true, I deserve death. Early on, I was on friendly terms with Zhang and Gui. Over time, we developed differences, but we always composed them and restored harmony as before. For two years, we have had nothing but cordial relations. Huo says they attacked me, but I never saw that. He says I brushed them aside, but you, the ruler, know that's not so. As for my linking up with eunuchs and speaking officials, you are quite immune to eunuch pleadings. The speaking officials are the eyes and ears of the court; if they take direction from grand secretaries, they betray their responsibility and their own selves as men. . . . When you issued the order dismissing Zhang and Gui, [Chai] Luan and I exchanged glances, wondering what was going on. We thought Gui was perhaps guilty of some things, but Zhang was too loyal just to be rejected like that. You personally wrote the stern rescript that day, so we didn't dare request that they be kept in office. Plus you asked Zhang to go home, introspect, reform, and return someday. We didn't dare quibble with that. When Zhang left, we both choked up. Our relations stayed as friendly as ever. Why does Huo Tao say such things? He charges me with corruption. I don't dare protest that, but if it turns out to be true, I'll gladly undergo execution. I note Huo Tao is famous for his high and upright rhetoric, but he's been criticized for overdoing it. He needs to think of harmony and the distant future. How can he harbor such anger? He charges others with motivations they don't have and acts they never did. His accusations are groundless. I'm old and sick and beg to retire.

Jiajing reaffirmed his trust in Yang and disallowed his request to retire. [89] Yang's reply was artful. He did not quite deny Huo Tao's allegations altogether. Jiajing was perplexed.

On October 15, Jiajing secretly consulted Zhang Fujing about how to respond to Huo Tao's charges against Yang Yiqing and Gui E. The problem was sensitive, and Jiajing wanted to get it right. He was indebted to Gui E, he said, but Gui had indeed done some self-centered things. It appeared to Jiajing that Yang's receiving huge gifts of gold and silver was based in fact, and that put an emphatic end to his ability to lead and inspire government. Jiajing understood that it would be a hard thing for Zhang to draft a reply, given his closeness to the accuser, Huo Tao, so he proposed to send Huo's memorial down to the ministries for discussion.

Zhang replied at length the next day. He thought the dismissal of high officials should be done politely, so as to preserve the *guoti* (the image of good governance). Zhang confessed that he too had recommended the rehiring of the capable Zhengde-era eunuch Zhang Yong, but unlike Yang, he described in detail how he had time and again refused all the gifts of gold and silver the eunuch and his brother had tried to foist upon him. He urged Jiajing not to put Yang, who was old and sick, through an exhausting prosecution and trial.[90] That was an artful way to get rid of Yang.

Jiajing pretty much followed Zhang Fujing's advice. Zhang wrote back in deep gratitude, noting that Yang Yiqing had been an important early supporter in the Great Rites dispute. By going easy on him, said Zhang, the ruler shows his compassion and his continued backing of the Great Rites champions and staves off a likely partisan counterrevolution.[91]

Yang retired, honors intact, on October 22. Gui E was recalled to the Grand Secretariat on December 8. Zhang Fujing replaced Yang as Ming China's top official, chief grand secretary. Gui E, a much changed man, turned silent and depressed. He became ill, resigned, and died at home on October 3, 1531.

* * *

Zhang's next forced departure from the Grand Secretariat came on August 18, 1531. Missing from both his secret correspondence and his collective writings is any mention of the matter, perhaps because it put him in a very bad light. What lay behind his dismissal was a developing challenge from Xia Yan, the assiduous rites scholar and future chief grand secretary, at the time chief supervising secretary of the Office of Scrutiny for Personnel. Jiajing's esteem for Xia was on the rise. Xia was alert for opportunities to get Zhang Fujing in trouble.

What set the dismissal in motion was an advisory memorial sent up by one Xue Kan, an avid disciple of Wang Yangming and director of the Messenger Office. In view of Jiajing's failure to produce an heir thus far, he suggested that an imperial clansman be designated to come live in Beijing as a standby until such time as an heir was produced. It made sense, and there were Ming precedents for such a precautionary policy.

Xue showed a draft copy of this memorial to Peng Ze, chief minister of the Court of Imperial Sacrifices and a fellow Cantonese. Peng, Xue, and Xia Yan were all *jinshi* year-mates. Peng was a supporter of the Great Rites and an adherent of Zhang Fujing's, and he was aware that Zhang disliked Xia Yan, that Jiajing was busily praying for an heir, and that this memorial would surely offend the emperor and provoke him into starting a big housecleaning, in which Xia Yan would surely get caught up because of his tie to Xue Kan. So he got Xue Kan to agree to his showing the draft to Zhang Fujing. Peng told Zhang that the actual author was Xia Yan. Zhang believed the lie and said that it was an important matter and that he would use his influence as chief grand secretary to support it. He told Jiajing of the memorial's existence. But several days passed, and the memorial wasn't sent in. Zhang asked Peng about it. Xue Kan had meanwhile been fasting and taking divination to determine the right day to submit such a risky document. Peng, in a state of panic, visited Xue Kan and told him that Zhang Fujing liked the memorial and that he had to write the final version and submit it immediately.[92] On or about August 12, Xue submitted it and asked that the whole court discuss it.

Jiajing exploded in anger. He said Xue Kan's memorial was wanton, disruptive, and villainous in intent. Xue was put under arrest, and the entire court gathered at the Meridian Gate, where the well-meaning but politically naive Xue was placed under interrogation. Jiajing was sure some prince's bribery was behind this. Xue had to be forced to reveal the prince's identity. Meanwhile, Jiajing conferred along with Zhang in the Wenhua Palace about whether the memorial was genuine and how to answer it. Zhang supposedly told the emperor that he, Jiajing, was in the prime of life and that he should not follow Xue Kan's advice. Zhang then proceeded to the Meridian Gate where the interrogation of Xue Kan was going on. He demanded to know who directed Xue to write the memorial. "I wrote it myself," Xue replied. "I've found out Xia Yan planned this with you. Why don't you admit that?" asked Zhang. "Xia Yan is a year-mate," replied Xue, "but I haven't seen him lately. Peng Ze asked you whether [my memorial] was acceptable, and you thought it was, so I sent it up."

Zhang hastily departed through the Zuoyi Gate to find Jiajing. Xia pushed the gate open and followed him in. They came to the front of the Wenhua Palace. A eunuch said Jiajing was taking a nap and couldn't be disturbed. Zhang then went to his office to write a report. Xia went to his office in the History Office to do likewise. Then he went home, where police greeted him and placed him under arrest. He was taken to prison. Jiajing gave orders that he not be tortured.[93]

Under torture, Xue Kan maintained that Xia Yan had nothing to do with his memorial.

On Jiajing's order, Marquis Guo Xun, Grand Secretary Chai Luan, and a palace eunuch representative conducted another mass meeting of the court. This time all the facts were said to come clear. So Xia Yan was released. Peng Ze was exiled to serve as a soldier in the Datong garrison. Xue Kan was removed from officialdom and sent home (Jiajing refused all pleas to amnesty him, or any of the others sentenced in the various crackdowns). Zhang's two secret memorials were made public and shown to be mendacious and perverse. Jiajing ordered him to retire.[94]

What Jiajing said about Zhang was extremely damaging. He said he'd relied on Zhang in the Great Rites dispute and had raised him to the highest position. "He was not just a supporter but a teacher. He'd been ordered earlier [in 1529] to rethink, yet [on his return to office] he didn't watch his thoughts or rectify his nature; instead, he turned away from uprightness and presumed upon affection, which is not what the ruler needs to rely on. He devoted himself to his hatred [of Xia Yan] and forgot his supporting role. That cannot be condoned."[95]

So Zhang was dismissed and sent home again, under the dark cloud of a scolding. While he was gone, his comrade-in-arms in the Great Rites, Fang Xianfu, took over as chief grand secretary, alongside Grand Secretaries Li Shi and Chai Luan. His nemesis, Xia Yan, was promoted to minister of rites.

Jiajing recalled Zhang back to office on February 6, 1533. On April 26, he arrived in Beijing and resumed his old position as chief. His secret correspondence privilege was restored. His exile had lasted about half a year. Jiajing was not a man to hold a grudge.

The third and final dismissal of Chief Grand Secretary Zhang Fujing took place on May 5, 1535. Though Zhang was sick and begged hard to be allowed to resign, and though Jiajing's affection for him had not waned, still he left under a cloud. Jiajing consulted with Li Shi about whether to allow Zhang to retire, and Li Shi, long on Zhang's side but in his shadow, now agreed that he was dictatorial and widely hated, that he suppressed certain talented men, and that he should be allowed to go. Li Shi further recommended that the empty slot in the Grand Secretariat be filled by none other than a talented old enemy of Zhang's, Fei Hong. Li Shi himself took over for the next three years as chief.[96]

Zhang's hostility toward Fei Hong casts a revealing light on just where Zhang had long stood on policy and other matters. Fei Hong, a grand secretary in 1521, and chief from 1525 to 1527, though much liked by Jiajing, had been forced out of office by Zhang and Gui after some intense intrigue and maneuvering.[97] In 1527 or so, Zhang attacked Fei Hong for his soft line on the 1524 Datong Mutiny and for usurping the emperor's authority. He told Jiajing that his own group of Great Rites supporters (Zhang, Gui, Fang Xian-fu, Huo Tao, Huang Wan, and Xiong Jie) had met together and agreed that though they all came from different parts of China and held different offices, they were at one on the Great Rites because "right principles are rooted in human minds." He said the ancestral Ming institutions were sacrosanct and could not be changed, but they must be rescued from collapse. Too grand a reform plan would be dangerous. "Gentlemen are in harmony but not in tight unison, because that makes for faction." Reform and a total makeover (*fengeng*) are very different, the one restoring order, the other leading to breakdown. Lofty but impossible ideas must be laid aside.[98] This assault on Fei Hong was successful, and Zhang's statement stood as a credo of sorts for Jiajing's Great Rites partisans from that point on.

The year 1535 marked the end of the "spring" phase of the Jiajing reign period. With Zhang's final departure, all of the Great Rites champions were finally gone from the scene. By 1535, Zhang had had serious differences with his onetime close comrades in arms and with Xia Yan over the handling of the Datong Mutinies and the Blue Sheep Mountain affair. Zhang blamed the rioters and the outlaws; everyone else blamed the security organs for their misrule and then their provocative severity. All "harmony" had vanished. There were other differences as well. Indeed, it was time for Zhang to go.[99]

* * *

What was the verdict on Zhang Fujing from the perspective of commentators later in the Ming? On the whole, it was favorable. The editors of the "veritable records" (*Ming shilu*) placed a short biography and summing up in the annals at the time of Zhang's death in 1539. They said he was deeply learned in the study of rites, was physically imposing, and that his views on the Great Rites were sincerely held. He skyrocketed to high favor, whereas the opposition was severely punished. He made himself extremely unpopular when he acted as a judge in the Great Case affair. But he was brilliant, hard, and incorruptible; he acted wholly impartially and carried out his duties valiantly despite the hatreds he kindled. . . . In the Grand Secretariat he was candid with the ruler, but much of his dealings with the ruler were secret, such that even his colleagues didn't know of them. . . . Heavy criticism failed to deter him. Jiajing appreciated his sincerity and trusted him. He'd call him *Shaoshi* Luoshan, familiarly, and not by his given name. [100]

Other commentary was a bit less effusive, but still positive. Wang Shizhen (1526–1590) thought Zhang had halted a drift toward mediocrity. The effect of his presence is appreciated at court, even now, fifty years later, and thanks to him, the people enjoy peace and security. Li Weizhen (1547–1626) compared him to Zhang Juzheng, the controversial and powerful chief grand secretary of the early Wanli era. Both were strong men. Jiajing trusted Zhang Fujing, but officialdom didn't like him. However, seventy years later, his reputation was stellar, while Zhang Juzheng's was not. He Qiaoyuan (1558–1632) wrote that Jiajing found Zhang to be persuasive and so he favored him highly, and Zhang made use of Jiajing's anger and power to achieve his aims. Zhang was overbearing, harsh, and incorruptible. He deferred to the ruler and was sincere and impartial. He said what he thought, and he was a great and awesome official. Sun Chengzong (1563–1638) was impressed as well. [101]

On balance, the opinion of posterity weighed heavily in Zhang's favor. And the Great Rites settlement, as well as most of the ritual reforms devised mainly by Xia Yan while Zhang was in power, were still in force years after their sponsors and creators had passed away.

NOTES

1. The complexity of this matter is well developed by Romeyn Taylor, "Official Religion in the Ming," in *The Cambridge History of China*, vol. 8, *The Ming Dynasty, 1368–1644, Part 2*, ed. Denis Twitchett and John K. Fairbank (Cambridge: Cambridge University Press, 1998), 840–892; also Ho Yun-yi, "Ideological Implications of Major Sacrifice in Early Ming," *Ming Studies*, no. 6 (1978): 55–73.

2. Xia Yan, *Guizhou wenji* (Siku quanshu cunmu congshu, 4th ser.), 74.547–549; also in Xia Yan, *Guizhou xiansheng zouyi* (Siku quanshu cunmu congshu, 2nd ser.), 60.420–421.

3. Xia Xie, 4.2049–2050. The full story of Jiajing's silk rite revival has been recounted in Joseph S. C. Lam, *State Sacrifices and Music in Ming China: Orthodoxy, Creativity, and Expressiveness* (Albany: SUNY Press, 1998), 55–74.

4. Xia Yan, *Guizhou wenji*, 74.492–494.

5. Xia Xie, 4.2052; Zhang Fujing, *Yudui lu*, 57.210–211, 213–214.

6. Huo Tao, *Weiyai wenji* (Siku quanshu cunmu congshu, 4th ser.), 68.556–564.

7. Ibid., 68.565–569.

8. Xia Yan, *nianpu*, in *Guizhou wenji*, 74.176–178.

9. Xia Xie, 4.2054.

10. Zhang Fujing, *Yudui lu*, 57.220–222.

11. Peter Ditmanson, "Imperial History and Broadening Historical Consciousness in Late Ming China," *Ming Studies*, no. 71 (2015): 23–40, shows that imperial succession matters such as this one were not confined to court circles but were drawing national attention.

12. All this correspondence is in Zhang's *Yudui lu*, 57.220–228.

13. Xia Yan, *Guizhou xiansheng zouyi*, 60.276–277.

14. Ibid., 277–278.

15. Ibid., 278.

16. Ibid., 278–279. Also in Xia Yan, *Guizhou wenji*, 74.565–567.

17. Zhang Fujing, *Yudui lu*, 57.265–266. There was corruption at the kilns; cf. 57.306–307.

18. Xia Yan, *Guizhou wenji*, 74.538–540.

19. Traffic control remained a problem, vexing Jiajing's visits to the four altars. On February 13, 1532, Xia Yan reported that the specially built lanes for the emperor's exclusive use had not been kept clear. Civil and military officials in sedan chairs and on horseback heedlessly used them. Starting ten days before the emperor came through, the lanes needed to be scraped, swept, and sprinkled to allay the dust. The road leading out of the Zhengyang Gate was so uneven and so narrow in places that puddles formed, carts tipped over, and traffic jams resulted. Detours needed to be arranged. Jiajing agreed to order all the roads cleared ten days before the suburban sacrifices. Carts were forbidden (Xia Yan, *Nangong zougao* [Siku quanshu zhenben, 5th ser., 1973], 1.50b–52b). This account gives a good eyewitness picture of the scale, difficulty, and disruptiveness of the new Ming rituals.

20. *MSJSBM*, ch. 51; *MSL*, 77.2843ff.

21. Xia Yan, *Nangong zougao*, 2.1a–4b, 2.5a–8a.

22. Xia Xie, 4.2071–2072; *GQ*, 4.3438, 3440. Further details of the rite may be found in *MS*, ch. 49. The rite was canceled in 1559.

23. Zhang Fujing, *Yudui lu*, 57.16–20.

24. Ibid., 57.61–62.

25. Ibid., 57.67–68.

26. Ibid., 57.62–64.

27. See Du Lianzhe, *Mingchao guanxuan lu* (1966), 64–67.

28. Xia Xie, 4.2006–2007.

29. Du Lianzhe, *Mingchao guanxuan lu*, 36–37, quoting Jiajing's statement of November 24.

30. Zhang Fujing, *Yudui lu*, 57.81–83.

31. Ibid., 57.98–99. Xia Yan, *Guizhou xiansheng zouyi*, 60.374–375, has a long memorial of 1534 about appointing a new tutor for Xie. Xie Zhao (1512–1563) grew up to be a member in good standing in the military aristocracy. Jiajing's sister died in 1540. See Li Chunfang, *Li Wending gong Yian tang ji* (Siku quanshu cunmu congshu, 4th ser.), 113.206–208, for Xie's epitaph.

32. Zhang Fujing, *Yudui lu*, 57.100–101. For later anti-Buddhist measures, see Xia Yan, *Guizhou wenji*, 74.634–637; and *Guizhou xiansheng zouyi*, 60.383–384.

33. Zhang Fujing, *Yudui lu*, 57.135–136.

34. Ibid., 57.139–140.

35. Ibid., 57.147.

36. Ibid., 57.209.

37. Ibid., 57.217.

38. Ibid., 57.219.

39. Ibid., 57.219.

40. Ibid., 57.278–279.

41. Ibid., 57.370–371.

42. Ibid., 57.87–89.

43. Ibid., 57.107–108.

44. Xia Xie, 4.2026.

45. *GQ*, 4.3385–3386. The *Ming shi*, biography of Empress Chen, ch. 114, says he was seated beside her one day, as the two consorts, Zhang and Fang, offered tea. Jiajing stared at each of their hands. The empress, out of jealousy no doubt, grew angry, tossed her cup, and got up, so provoking Jiajing's rage. On December 5, with the weather having turned extremely cold, Jiajing took pity on the laborers building her tomb, and Zhang Fujing agreed the work should be suspended until spring (*Yudui lu*, 57.146–147).

46. Zhang Fujing, *Yudui lu*, 57.147–150.

47. *MSL*, 67.2517.

48. Zhang Fujing, *Yudui lu*, 57.179.

49. Ibid., 57.179–182.

50. Ibid., 57.236–237.

51. *MSL*, 77.2790–2791.

52. Zhang Fujing, *Yudui lu*, 57.283–285.

53. Ibid., 57.285–286.

54. Ibid., 57.286–287.

55. Ibid., 57. 288.

56. Ibid., 57.321–324; 327–329.

57. Ibid., 57.347–351; *Yuzhi huojing huowen* (Siku quanshu cunmu congshu, 2nd ser.), 57.1–4; *MSL*, 77.2904.

58. *DMB*, 1.320; the children are listed in *GQ*, 1.15–16.

59. *GQ*, 4.3455; *MSL*, 77.3134–3135.

60. *DMB*, 2.1169–1170 (biography of Shao Yuan-chieh).

61. Zhang Fujing, *Yudui lu*, 57.363–364.

62. Ibid., 57.392–393.

63. Ibid., 57.397–398.

64. *MSL*, 78.3535–3536.

65. Zhang Fujing, *Yudui lu*, 57.415–416.

66. *GQ*, 4.3374.

67. Xia Xie, 4.2014, 2026.

68. Xia Yan, *Guizhou xiansheng zouyi*, 60.441–468; Zhang Fujing, *Taishi Zhang Wenzhong gong ji*, 77.85–87.

69. Details in, inter alia, *GQ*, 4.3489–3490.

70. Zhang Fujing, *Taishi Zhang Wenzhong*, 77.167–169.

71. *GQ*, 4.3491.

72. Zhang Fujing, *Taishi Zhang Wenzhong*, 77.169.

73. *GQ*, 4.3942–3945.

74. *MS*, ch. 193 (biography).

75. Ibid., ch. 197 (biography). Huang was a follower of Wang Yangming; see Huang Zongxi, *Mingru xue'an* (any ed.), ch. 13.

76. Chen Zilong, ed., *Huang Ming jingshi wenbian* (reprint Taipei, 1964), 10.736–743; *MSL*, 78.3615ff.; *MSJSBM*, ch. 54 ("The Datong Mutiny").

77. *Huang Ming jingshi wenbian*, 10.743–750.

78. *MSL*, 78.3559.

79. *MSL*, 78.3560–3562; *GQ*, 4.3497–3498; *GCXZL*, 8.4799–4800 (epitaph for Que Yong).

80. *MSL*, 78.3502–3505. Zhang Heling died in prison in 1537, and Zhang Yanling was finally executed in 1546. See their biographies in *DMB*, 1.74–77.

81. Zhang Fujing, *Taishi Zhang Wenzhong*, 77.162–163. He recommended the same for elder brother Heling, and he thought the eunuchs serving the Zhaosheng empress in the Renshou Palace should be replaced.

82. Ibid., 77.165–166.

83. Ibid., 77.166–167. There were later ramifications of the Zhang Yanling case; see *GQ*, 4.3534–3535, under date of October 30, 1536.

84. *MSL*, 76.2443–2445.

85. *MSL*, 76.2445.

86. *GQ*, 4.3407. Indeed, Yang retired on October 22.

87. Zhang Fujing, *Taishi Zhang Wenzhong*, 77.96–100.

88. *MSL*, 76.2460–2463. Supervising Secretary Liu Shiyang sensed that a big purge of Great Rites supporters might be under way, and he weighed in with congratulations to the emperor for ousting Zhang and Gui and their evil following of opportunists. He urged that Yan Song and a long list of others be removed as well. Jiajing sent this memorial out for discussion. See *MSL*, 76.2464–2467.

89. *MSL*, 76.2466–2467.

90. Zhang Fujing, *Yudui lu*, 57.177–179; *DMB*, 1.111–113 (biography of Chang Yung).

91. Zhang Fujing, *Taishi Zhang Wenzhong*, 77.102–103.

92. Peng earlier registered Xue's memorial under Xia Yan's name as author. Also he told Zhang that Hanlin junior compiler Ouyang De, a Wang Yangming disciple, had read the draft and thought it submissable and he got Companion to the Heir Apparent Liao Daonan to testify that there was evidence Xia Yan had links to the Jiangxi princely estate, and that the ruler should do nothing until the actual memorial came in (*MSL*, 77.3048–3049). The plot was concocted to look like a rerun of the Prince of Ning's conspiracy of 1519, with Xia Yan as the key operative.

93. Xia Yan, *nianpu*, in *Guizhou wenji*, 74.181–182. The pages here are in part blurred and unreadable.

94. *MS*, ch. 207 (biography of Xue Kan).

95. *MSL*, 77.3047–3051.

96. Xia Xie, 4.2118. Fei Hong died later that same year.

97. *MS*, ch. 193 (biography of Fei Hong).

98. Zhang Fujing, *Taishi Zhang Wenzhong*, 77.49–50, 54.

99. Ibid., 77.172–173; *Yudui lu*, 57.403–405.

100. *MSL*, 81.4576–4577.

101. *GQ*, 4.3568–3569.

Chapter Three

Summer

Grand Secretary Xia Yan

Xia Yan entered the Grand Secretariat early in 1537, rose to chief the next year, and was dismissed for the fourth and last time in 1548. Jiajing, age twenty-nine in 1537, turned forty-one in 1548. Having left youth behind, he felt he need not lean any longer on a mentor and life coach like Zhang Fujing. He was never emotionally attached to Xia Yan, though he was deeply impressed early on by Xia's erudition, energy, and skill.

It will be recalled that Zhang Fujing brought but a shallow portfolio of administrative accomplishments with him when he entered the Grand Secretariat. By contrast, Xia's experience of government in several demanding capacities was twenty years long, and both wide and deep. Much of his thick file of official papers relates to the things he did and said during those twenty years, which included the years in which Zhang Fujing was in power. Their relationship was cooperative early on, but as noted in the previous chapter, it eventually turned very sour.

Through Xia Yan, the researcher these days can drill many test borings down into the rubble, the clay, and the bedrock of life in sixteenth-century China, starting with the year of Zhengde's untimely death in 1521, when Xia was a supervising secretary in the Office of Scrutiny for War, a post he held for the next ten years. During Jiajing's earliest years, Yang Tinghe was chief grand secretary and setter of national policy, which involved mainly cleaning up the mess left by Zhengde, and Xia was heavily involved in assisting with that. Indeed, he was a superachiever. He played a forceful hand in purging the military of some of the corruption and resource-draining excrescences that had grown like lichen during Zhengde's time on the throne (1505–1521). He showed a meticulous, detailed, vehement, and rather long-winded approach that he would exercise to good advantage ever after.

An early impeachment of his targeted with great partisan heat Zhengde's minister of personnel, Wang Qiong. Yang Tinghe and Wang Qiong were not mutually friendly. Xia's attack on Wang Qiong was lavish in its fury. It said he was a "small man," a power-hungry liar who as minister of war brokered bribes on the rebel Prince of Ning's behalf, who made huge payments to Zhengde's palace favorites, and who incriminated good officials, misled Zhengde, shut down the "avenue of speech," and retaliated against all his critics, so that "people seethed and gnashed their teeth." To escape from disaster to blessing, Wang paid, Xia alleged, a huge bribe to one of Zhengde's favorites to get a new appointment as minister of personnel. The talk of the streets and markets was that Wang Qiong grew fat on the Prince of Ning's bribes, and he had military power and villains relied on him. Such a man, concluded Xia, could not lead the Ministry of Personnel. Wang Qiong's replacement as minister of war was Wang Xian. Xia charged Wang Qiong with corruption and treason. He was poised, Xia asserted, to join the dead emperor's favorite, Jiang Bin, and carry out a coup d'état!

Acting on young Jiajing's behalf, Chief Grand Secretary Yang Tinghe arranged both men's dismissal. Wang Qiong was imprisoned and then sent into military exile. Wang Xian was made to retire. These actions were taken in June 1521.

These were overwrought partisan attacks, however. Wang Qiong was actually responsible for arranging and supporting Wang Yangming's successful defeat and capture of the rebel Prince of Ning. Wang Xian, if truly a traitor, should have been arrested, tried, and executed. Both were men of talent. Both had impressive accomplishments. Perhaps the best that can be said of Xia Yan's reckless venom is that it was in tune with the post-Zhengde cleanup policy, one that also engaged his energies and was aimed at real sources of infection.[1]

Eager to clean out all the deadwood and corruption that had accumulated since 1505, Yang Tinghe had the boy emperor order the Ministries of Personnel, Rites, War, and Works to check all their rosters thoroughly and eliminate all civil and military personnel, Buddhist and Daoist priests, and artisans and musicians, plus all relatives of empresses and children and grandchildren of princesses, who had no legitimate authorization to occupy their positions.

Xia Yan's responsibility was to audit the military registers, and that he did, with meticulous attention to precedents, past actions, and a one-by-one examination of each officer's credentials, his purpose being to remove all the relatives and hangers-on of Zhengde's eunuchs and palace favorites. At the end of his long report, Xia said he'd identified some 3,199 "city foxes and country rats." Some of them were accomplished whiners whose likely protests should be denied. All these types must be removed forthwith from the military rolls.[2]

But some months later, as Xia put it, "the flies, driven away, have come back." They complained and used corrupt connections and other resources to resist the purge. In a very long and detailed accounting, Xia described the situation, going so far as to accuse young Jiajing himself of issuing toothless edicts. A crackdown, if imperially ordered, must be seriously carried out, he insisted.[3]

Three years later, Xia sent up another long report, arguing that the military purge was not effective, in that a gang of protesters, far from being punished, was forcing an interminable delay. Jiajing, or whoever was drafting his directives, was reluctant to insist on a thorough purge of all those holding dubious military credentials. Xia again named names and circumstances. He seethed with indignation at the situation and demanded a complete refocusing of court attention to the matter.[4]

In reply, the palace temporized and demanded a further investigation. Again, Xia Yan exploded. "We are shocked at this directive," he said, "and we don't know what to do. . . . The security of the state is involved here. The Zhengde court gave out posts under false pretenses, merits weren't based on combat, registries were obtained from powerful favorites, rewards were given to the undeserving, and salaries were wasted on supernumeraries." Xia said probe after probe into all this had so far yielded nothing. And on and on he raged.[5] Indeed, Jiajing himself had allowed eleven nephews and housemen of the recently deceased eunuch grand commandant at Nanjing, Dai Yi, to become military officers. This was resuming the very Zhengde-era abuse Jiajing had promised to abolish! This new dispensation threatened to grow and become uncontrollable![6]

Xia also objected, "in shock" as he said, to the news that Jiajing was appointing two younger brothers of his old nursemaids hereditary battalion commanders in the Embroidered-Uniform Guard. This was unconscionable! Neither appointee "had ever served in the ranks, had ever seen battle, so how do they deserve five-rank posts? Their sisters urged this. . . . Although the two ladies have given many years of service, this reward is excessive." He begged Jiajing to rescind the order.[7]

* * *

Any bureaucrat with career aspirations in these years had to keep a steady eye on the partisan situation. While he and most others were in Yang Tinghe's camp, they were all very much aware of the rise of Zhang Fujing and Gui E in Jiajing's favor. It would definitely not do to jump ship, desert Yang Tinghe, and join Zhang and Gui in the metastasizing Great Rites business. The partisan game had to be played with finesse and perspicacity, but luck counted for more. We will soon see how Xia Yan managed it.

Meanwhile, in addition to his work purging the military rosters, Xia took on the difficult task of confiscating and redistributing the many illegally occupied farming estates in and around Beijing and the Northern Metropolitan Province (Bei Zhili). Again, his effort is notable for the extensive detail he provided in his reports to the throne. The throne had ordered a thorough check of all privileged estates (*huangzhuang*) in the control of favorites and schemers of the Zhengde era, the impeachment and punishment of their proprietors, and the return of the properties to the soldiers and civilians from whom these lands had been seized.[8]

It was in the style of Xia Yan to embrace this order with diligence, determination, and a deep commitment to its purposes. His long report included a description of the north China ecology together with an analysis of how the *huangzhuang* abuse originated. North China is flat and broad, he explained. Much of it is saline and poor, with marshy and reedy places. Just a few days of rain will create flooding and ruin the crops, which is why early in Ming times no field measurements were made or taxes levied, so peasants could easily relocate and escape floods. But in recent years, powerful court favorites inveigled evil commoners into yielding these untaxed properties. They also seized pastures for horses, taxable land, and saltworks. Commoners were dispossessed, starving and homeless, some turning to banditry or dying in the ditches if they didn't become scheming accomplices and housemen of the new proprietors, or joining military units as supernumeraries. Meticulous investigation has turned up some 209,019.28 *qing* (about three and a half million acres) tied up in *huangzhuang*. A tenth of that was confiscated and given to the commoners, to great rejoicing. This was a big part of Yang Tinghe's renewal (*weixin*) program. More needed to be done, he said.

And playing to Jiajing's devotion to ritual, as mentioned in the previous chapter, he suggested earmarking confiscated land near the Beijing city wall for planting to mulberry for the empress's silk rite.[9]

Xia provided follow-ups: an impeachment of a palace eunuch and his control of pasture entailed a long history of the estate in question, and an impeachment of the Jianchang marquis Zhang Yanling (his notoriety is discussed in the chapter preceding) and another grandee in connection with their *huangzhuang*, again describing the history in exhaustive detail.[10] But as in the case of discharging unneeded military officers, here too Jiajing backed away from a thorough crackdown. Eighteen influential eunuchs had made an effective protest. Xia chided the ruler. He insisted that Jiajing withdraw his protection.[11] And some estates, once confiscated, were retaken: Xia impeached the assistant surveillance commissioner Li Ji for this (Li was a onetime protégé of the notorious eunuch dictator Liu Jin). His behavior was unbelievably cruel. Such a man, said Xia, cannot remain another day in his position.[12]

For this and other services, Xia was deservedly promoted early in 1523 to supervising secretary of the right in the Office of Scrutiny for War.

* * *

In June 1524, Xia's mother died, and he went home for the obligatory year's mourning. He left in the wake of his departure a crowd of angry and revenge-seeking supernumerary officers of the Embroidered-Uniform Guard and other units, whom he had investigated and discharged. And while he was on leave, the Great Rites work stoppage and demonstration of August 14, 1524, took place, in the aftermath of which Yang Tinghe's backers were crushed and the pro–Great Rites group of Zhang Fujing and Gui E came into power. Xia had been a Yang Tinghe sympathizer, but since he was no ideological zealot, he might not have taken part in the demonstration had he been in Beijing at the time. From his home in Jiangxi Province, he judged the factional situation in Beijing as too uncertain for him to think about rejoining government right away. So for the next several years he built a hall and a pavilion at home and devoted himself to study and to writing social and landscape poetry. Finally boredom—and a sense that success or failure was in the unpredictable hands of fate—propelled him back into action. He ignored the warnings of well-meaning friends about the dangers and arrived in Beijing in the late spring of 1528. He resumed his old position in the Office of Scrutiny for War. He decided that he could put his great energy and skills to work in behalf of the ritual reprogramming of Ming China, as well as in other matters.[13]

First, however, there was important work for him to do as a supervising secretary. The Blue Sheep Mountain fracas of 1528–1529, including its suppression and aftermath, as mentioned in the previous chapter, elicited from Xia Yan the most exhaustive, detailed, and lengthy reporting and archival research—featuring on-the-scene investigation, proposals for a fair allocation of rewards and penalties, and plans for the reconstruction of the whole stricken region—that he had ever undertaken and accomplished. It was truly a command performance, monumentally impressive. No wonder Jiajing would eventually invite him to assume the Ming state's highest position.

Buried inside Xia's book-length report dated April 4, 1529, is a whole history of the trouble that brewed for years in and around Blue Sheep Mountain. It is a veritable anatomy of a criminal enterprise, the story of the rise and spread of an outlaw movement that bears some resemblance to a present-day Mexican gang, in that it focused on plundering operations, terror, and the development of fighting capacities and lacked any larger political aims. His report is based on interrogations of twelve gang members and much else.

The leaders of the Blue Sheep Mountain gang were members of a local lineage of the Chen surname. They began as moneylenders to local villagers. Then they discovered from outside bandits seeking refuge in the mountains that robbery was much more lucrative. So their first known raid took place in the fall of 1515, when a Chen uncle joined an outside bandit and looted silver and clothing from well-off commoners in Lingchuan County nearby, in the far south of Shanxi Province. The bandit, named Wang Tinglu, was caught by Shanxi provincial troops some months later and executed, but not before he named two local Chen accomplices, including Chen Qi, father of the soon-to-be gang kingpin Chen Qing. The Chen remained at large.

Criminals though they may have been, the Chen had connections to county government. Through his father's influence, Chen Qing was put on a waiting list for a clerical vacancy in Lingchuan. At length he was made a clerk (*dianli*) in the county rites section (*lifang*). His service at that function completed, he was next taken on in 1520 as a clerk in the punishments section (*xingfang*) in the Administrator's Office of the Shen princedom, based nearby in Luzhou. Then he got into some unspecified trouble and fled prison for sanctuary in the mountains. Another Chen was an attendant (*zhihou*) of some sort for the Lucheng county magistrate and remained at large.

Another was in prison awaiting trial for killing a woman. But through their clerical work, some of the Chen surely gained important information and useful know-how.

By 1522, Chen Qi and his outside bandit allies began looting and killing well beyond Blue Sheep Mountain, targeting villages and rich villagers in Henan Province, too. Arrest teams killed four marauders and wounded sixteen others.

In the early summer of 1523, Assistant Surveillance Commissioner Wang Lin got the Licheng county magistrate to put up placards offering amnesty to "good people" whom the outlaws had corralled into their camp up in the mountains. Chen Qi had six hundred people, males and females, under his control. Wang Lin led troops and captured his son Chen Qing, plus another bandit leader, and imprisoned them, pending trial and execution. At the formal request of his mother, Chen Qing was transferred from Luzhou to the headquarters of the Surveillance Commission for prosecution under the death penalty. Two policemen escorted him. Chen bribed one of them with four taels silver to look the other way, and on October 26, 1523, he escaped and hid in Blue Sheep Mountain. There he joined his father and brothers and some sixty-three other outlaws (Xia lists all their names) and put together a plunder machine, raiding villages far and wide; robbing families; torching their homes; seizing, raping, and occasionally killing their wives and daughters; and forcing their menfolk to march in captivity back to the mountains with them.

The local, regional, and provincial authorities put together a poorly coordinated coalition of troops and had some success bottling Chen Qing up in the mountains, but they didn't dare enter. This allowed Chen to strengthen his fighters, as they all set to work making weapons and practicing martial arts. By the late spring of 1527, they resumed raiding—mounted this time, looting villages, killing defenders, setting fires to homes in Henan Province, and then raiding Lingchuan back in Shanxi. The Lingchuan loot came to 170 taels silver, 36,000 copper coins, 400 silk garments, 200 *shi* of mixed grains, and 16 horses, mules, and donkeys. This the bandits carried back to the mountains.

This latest burst of brazen predation prompted the regional authorities (all listed by name and position) to organize an army. One unit managed to penetrate Blue Sheep Mountain. Chen Qing and his father led three hundred men and routed them. They stabbed and killed some, wounded others, and made off with their clothing and weapons. The Ming forces then beat a retreat. A bigger and better-organized campaign was clearly going to be needed.

Plus another attempt at negotiation. The mountain's dense vegetation was a barrier to any large army. Censor in Chief Chang Dao, on or about August 6, 1527, sent a country magistrate with an offer of amnesty up into the mountains. Chen Qing provided him with a list of 1,079 names of local villagers, and 248 names of outsiders, but he refused to lay down arms or cease raiding. Chang Dao and his colleagues decided a campaign would be necessary. First, they offered Chen Qing a two-month deadline to release all his captive villagers.

Xia Yan's job was to reevaluate merit claims after Chen Qing surrendered and the Blue Sheep Mountain sanctuary was eliminated. One of the claimants was Chang Dao, and for fairly clear reasons Xia gave him a very poor rating. While the two-month deadline pended, Chang Dao helped to organize a sizable coalition of forces drawn from various parts: one thousand *weisuo* garrison troops from Taiyuan further north, two thousand local Luzhou men, and one thousand peasants from nearby Huguan County. Two officials were to follow the men as reporters to record merits and failures. Notices were posted in the mountains offering amnesties. A few men were coaxed to come out, but Chen Qing, learning from an informer what was up, rallied his men and put up an effective defense. Chang Dao, "sitting placidly at the wall of the provincial capital [Taiyuan]," a hundred miles north, directed what turned out to be an utter and disastrous rout. That was in early January 1528. Chen Qing, his father, and two of his brothers led three hundred men armed with spears and swords and in the mountainous terrain killed twenty-three government troops and put the rest to flight. They captured 154 suits of armor, 82 spears, 52 swords, 49 bows, 3,452 arrows, and 3 pack animals. Then they began raiding villages again.

The Ming forces regrouped for another assault. Xia Yan lists all thirty-nine commanders, plus two officials to record merits. Again, the bandits were tipped off. Chen Qing launched a surprise attack. The government forces were uncoordinated and were unable to rally. Xia lists all the casualties, common soldiers as well as commanders. Chen Qing this time captured 14 horses, 20 long spears, 29 large swords, 28 small ones, 83 bows, and 3,225 arrows. This took place on or about February 8, 1528.

Discouraged by Chen Qing's rout of the Shanxi troops, the commander of the Henan soldiers, who were supposed to assist, instead turned tail and went back home.

Informed of the rout, the Ministry of War back in Beijing ordered that the salaries of Chang Dao and all the other commanders be stopped until such time as they began showing better results.

Chen Qing's gang began raiding again. Three hundred of them looted twenty-one families, killed eight men and women, and, for their efforts, fetched 300 taels silver, 250,000 copper coins, 300 silk garments, 400 bolts of cotton cloth, 170 *shi* of grain, and 32 horses, mules, and oxen. This raid is dated February 21, 1528.

Further attempts to negotiate terms with Chen Qing came to nothing. Raids continued. This time he targeted villages in Linxian in Henan Province. Desiring some entertainment, he abducted a woman and a musician from nearby Shanxi.

Meanwhile, the Ming authorities began assembling forces for a bigger campaign. Merchants were asked to buy up stores of hay and grain. Five hundred "fire carts" were manufactured. Training began. Notices were posted, warning civilians to stay away from any place where fighting was going on. Posters were again placed in the mountains offering amnesty for deserters from the bandit side. All this got under way in June 1528.

Chen Qing's response to this mobilization was to force upward of 2,300 local people, male and female, to join his side. (The Veritable Records note that Chen Qing, obviously drawing on what he'd learned as a clerk, registered these captives, organized them into standard groups, and selected seven hundred to eight hundred of them as able-bodied men to help defend against the coming assault.[14]) Raids continued. A clash with the Ming forces went well for the bandits.

However, during the autumn of 1528, at long last, the various Ming commanders met and carefully planned a four-pronged attack on Blue Sheep Mountain. This turned out to be the long-awaited success. Chen Qing and his father and brothers were all captured. Thousands of coerced villagers were released. The hard-core bandits were imprisoned, and most of them died in custody. Large holdings in farmland, houses, weapons, livestock, silk, silver, and other goods were seized and much of it returned to their original owners or resold. This took place during the winter of 1528–1529. Xia Yan's report went on to detail all the names, battle sites, and merits as well as the derelictions and atrocities committed by apathetic or unruly Ming forces.[15]

* * *

Xia Yan's work had just begun. His assigned mission was huge. It was to review the merits and faults of all the civil and military officials involved, as they had sent up to the Ministry of War a stream of conflicting claims for rewards. It was also to assess the needs of the local people, many of whom were homeless and destitute due to all the raiding and fighting. And third, his job was to inspect Blue Sheep Mountain personally and determine what should be done to ensure its resettlement and peaceful integration into the Ming realm.

Xia did all this with great determination, clear thinking, and extraordinary attention to detail. Space will not allow a full recital. Suffice it to say that before he left Beijing he had a firm idea of who the top mistake makers were. Censor in Chief Chang Dao forced people to rebel because he didn't clearly separate Chen Qing and his small gang of hard-core criminals from all the hapless local civilians whom they pressed into service, but targeted all of them as rebels, thus turning a police matter into a military one, which may actually have been his intent. Commissioner in Chief Lu Gang, "a stupid military man, flamboyant and violent," purposefully delayed and refused to engage his troops because he wanted to wait until he could conduct a big massacre and so enhance his stature and rewards. And there were many more claims to sort out and evaluate.

He asked Jiajing to make all necessary preparations and issue orders beforehand, as meetings had to be held involving many officials from different places, and merit assessments and relief orders had to be made and carried out immediately and on the spot. Referring everything back to Beijing for approval would take too long.[16]

Xia wrote up an itinerary. He left Beijing on December 14, 1528. Eight days later he reached Zhending Prefecture, about 150 miles southwest. He was delayed there two days by a snowstorm. Originally he was to proceed further southwest to Luzhou in Shanxi, but the terrain, river, and cold weather forced him to travel instead to Zhangde Prefecture in Henan, another 150 miles directly south, which he reached on December 25. There he met with a large gathering of officials and commanders, sent bandits to prison, released their captives, and had them escorted and resettled in their home places. A lot of them were dying of cold and starvation. Clothing and grain were given to the survivors. On January 15, 1529, he reached Linxian in Henan, forty miles west on the Shanxi border. Three days later he reached a village in the Shanxi mountains, where he joined up with several regional commanders. On January 19, Xia and the commanders reached Guduidi, the home village of bandit leader Chen Qing. On January 21, they reached Blue Sheep village, scene of the bandits' defeat. Then they descended from the Taihang mountain range to Luzhou, twenty-five miles further west, which they reached on January 23. There the main work began. Fully empowered by the emperor, Xia could act however he saw fit.

Relief was the first priority. He sent local officials into every village in the mountains to register everyone, issue them individual tickets, and direct them to Luzhou where relief supplies were available. There were thousands of good people needing rescue whose homes and tools had been destroyed by fire, their grain stores gone, their cows and sheep stolen, and who no longer had any way to make a living. All of them feared an uncertain future.

Xia posted notices of what the official policy was going to be. He reassured all the villagers of Blue Sheep Mountain that the turmoil was in large part the fault of official malfeasance, that only Chen Qing and a hundred or so men of violence faced execution, and that everyone else, victims or former bandit followers who had been coerced, were going to be given a blanket pardon. Poor civilians who had been ravished by the raiders were advised to swallow their hatreds and not make accusations. A new county government and Confucian school were going to be set up, along with a three-year tax holiday. This was all thanks to Jiajing's "regarding all the world with equal benevolence," turning "tigers and wolves into good species, and crows into songbirds."[17]

Xia Yan had an eye for topography. On the way to Luzhou, he and his party had spent four nights and five days in the mountains, and so they had a good look at the rivers and streams, the villages, the roads, and the choke points. The area was thinly settled, with the sole exception of Blue Sheep Mountain village, which was fertile and well watered, with a good climate. That was where the new county seat should be placed. Other local officials came to the same conclusion. Xia consulted geomancy texts to get an idea of how to lay out the main buildings, the school, and the Confucian temple, plus walls, streets, alleys, ditches, and so on (this interest in architectural planning Xia would put to use later in designing Jiajing's temple building in Beijing). Also in the plans were three walled forts in Henan Province, three police offices in the mountains, and a new and improved road network.[18]

On March 9, 1529, Xia submitted an annotated map and plan for the area's reconstruction to Jiajing. The ruler liked these and forwarded copies to the appropriate ministries.[19]

Xia also provided an interesting analysis, based on interrogations of ex-outlaws, of what kinds of men these fellows were. His aim was to show that they were not all evil and should not all be tarred with the same brush. Toward the end of the war, they were all registered and organized by Chen Qing into mutual security units (*baojia*), which had the effect of turning captives into gang members. Some outlaws, the hard core, were by nature and habit evil men. Some were simply ignorant and fell under the evil men's influence. Some were just "outlaw youths" who clung together. Others were simpleminded and easily coerced. Isolated in the mountains as they had all been, beyond the reach of government, they had all become like so many wild animals. When we attacked them, their discipline broke down; many surrendered or were easily captured, while the hard core scattered and disappeared into the wild like so many birds or fish. Xia urged that Chen Qing's registers be publicly burned so that the people's lingering fear of being unjustly accused of banditry might be assuaged. Jiajing forwarded Xia's memorial to the Ministry of War for their reaction. [20]

Xia submitted a list of the names of everyone—civil and military, of high rank and low—who deserved rewards or should be penalized on April 4. Jiajing clearly was in no position to assess such a mass of data, and so he handed it off to the appropriate ministries for their comment. [21]

Xia Yan also readied plans for the implantation of an apparatus of local government in Blue Sheep Mountain, and these he sent to Jiajing on March 8, 1529. In turn, Jiajing sent the document and attachments to the ministries. Xia said the plans were based on wide consultation with regional and local officials. The area measured 100 *li* (33 miles) east to west and 140 *li* (47 miles) north to south, with a dense population at Blue Sheep village, thirty or so miles away from any existing county center of government, and thus beyond reach. It was a haven for local outlaws and wandering bandits from everywhere who made a nest there and launched raids. He noted four primitive trails through the mountains, along which were spotted some hundred tiny villages (which he listed). The new county would be carved from three existing counties: Huguan, Licheng, and Lucheng.

Xia decided against creating military bases, because farmland was too scarce and the soldiers might cause trouble. Instead he proposed placing three police offices at choke points that he described in detail, each with one hundred archers on patrol to keep out fake priests, undocumented drifters, and such like.

He further proposed building two stone gateways at strategic entry points for troops from Henan Province. Eight interior roads needed to be built or improved so as to reduce the inaccessibility upon which the raiders had relied.

At Linxian in Henan Province, three forts (*junpu*) should be built to guard the three roads leading west through the precipitous Taihang range into Blue Sheep Mountain. At each fort, 130 troops should be organized into two sections for rotation. Construction costs could be met from the unspent portion of the twenty thousand silver taels authorized for relief.

The new county should be set up as quickly as possible to accommodate upward of four thousand people who were earlier under Chen Qing's control. The county magistrate, once appointed, can work out the details of compiling tax registers and maps. These common people love their mountain home, and it would be disastrous to make them live elsewhere, as some have proposed.

Xia noted that space for farming was very limited. Most of the fields were not on level ground. There are marshes sporting oak and chestnut trees, which can provide food in a famine but cannot be put to the plow. The commoners are very poor and rely heavily on cattle and sheep. Idle space is hard to find. Even the fields once occupied by Chen Qing and his kinsmen don't amount to much.

As to construction costs for timber, stone, tile, and wages, the Luzhou subprefectural resources have been depleted, and the ten thousand taels needed can't be met there. Recently Beijing released fifteen thousand taels for relief for the truly destitute, and of that amount, Xia already issued four thousand taels, so that's done. And he issued 120 taels to build the two stone gateways, so that left 10,879.5 taels that, if authorized, could be used for construction. If not, the grand coordinator might be asked to fund everything from fines money and other resources at his disposal. Luzhou also had on hand several thousand taels in commerce tax, which could be used. That would avoid further burdening the peasant population.

Finally, he recommended that someone knowledgeable from the general area should be chosen to serve as the new county's first magistrate. He also asked that the Ministry of Personnel pick some young, talented, and sharp men to serve as the first Confucian instructors and police chiefs. [22]

And by a memorial of the same date, March 8, 1529, Xia Yan proposed raising Luzhou from a subprefecture to a full prefecture (*fu*), because Luzhou's span of control over six counties could not be stretched to include a seventh. Besides, no one respected a subprefectural magistrate who lacked the metropolitan *jinshi* degree. Xia said he talked to many local authorities about this matter, and they agreed that only a full prefecture could adequately rein in a greatly increased population and a large and growing Shen princedom, plus garrison soldiers, and prevent a recurrence of the banditry that had just been suppressed at such cost. Xia argued that Luzhou's city wall needed repair, its garrison was far short of the needed men and horses, and security was in effect nonexistent. So a special military defense circuit vice commissioner (*bingbei fushi*) needed to be placed there for at least three years to get this big task done. Putting up additional buildings on vacant space in the city would cost only five thousand taels, and that amount was already at hand in the form of already collected commerce taxes. Last, Xia made a cogent argument for abolishing the *minzhuang* military draft as cruelly burdensome as well as ineffective. The draftees should be replaced by smaller rotational postings of permanent garrison troops.[23] He also had specific recommendations about who the new vice commissioner and the new county magistrate should be.[24]

Almost all of this was done just as Xia had proposed. The new county was named Pingshun (pacified and obedient). Construction began in October 1529 and was declared done on February 24, 1533. Included was a special shrine (*shengci*) put up in Xia Yan's honor.[25] The county was a great success. No big trouble ever broke out in that region again.

* * *

About a month later, Xia returned from Blue Sheep Mountain to his post in Beijing. Late that year (1529), Jiajing shifted him from the Office of Scrutiny for War to the post of chief supervising secretary in the Office of Scrutiny for Personnel. That was an unusual sort of transfer. Everyone was "astounded and amazed" by it.[26]

A bureaucrat of vaulting ambition, would Xia Yan be content fulfilling the formal requirements of his new position? He would not. Immediately he involved himself in Jiajing's plans to reform Ming China's public rituals, starting with his request to revive the silk rite, as mentioned in the previous chapter. Right after that, on February 26, 1530, he submitted a general outline for national ritual reform. Here he placed religious rites (*qi*) at the top of the list of dynastic priorities, and the suburban sacrifices to Heaven and Earth at the top of the list of rites. Jiajing's concern for these rites was truly inspirational; surely the souls (*ling*) of the ancestors would be put at ease, and

the virtue of the gods (*shenming*) would be placed on full display. Much of
the program currently being followed, however, was incorrect in the light of
ancient texts and orthodox commentary. The suburban rites to Heaven and
Earth must be divided. They must be conducted in the open air, not under a
roof. Sacrifices to the imperial ancestors should be conducted early in spring,
not at the solstices. Xia urged Jiajing to ease men's minds below and obey
Heaven's intent above, to solicit everyone's opinions, and to follow Golden
Age precedents, not the errors of the Han, Tang, and Song. The main responsibility lay with the Ministry of Rites, but Xia wanted to participate too, even
though his formal responsibilities lay elsewhere.

Jiajing liked this memorial, and he ordered the Ministry of Rites to include it in its printing of all the other submitted discussions.[27]

There followed a heated dispute with Huo Tao and others in which Jiajing
took Xia Yan's side (see the "Spring" chapter). Indeed, Xia Yan's impressively learned contributions to Jiajing's ritual reforms inspired the editors of
the Qing Imperial Library (the Siku Quanshu) to single out most of his
memorials on the topic and preserve them under the title *Nangong zougao*.
That volume consists of some sixty-four memorials he wrote while he was
minister of rites, from 1531 to 1536.[28] Most of these deal with rites, ritual
reform, and temple construction, but the Rites Ministry was also tasked with
managing foreign relations and monitoring the civil service recruitment system. In order to get a better idea of how China was ruled and achieve a fuller
appreciation of Xia Yan's energy and competence, as well as the experiences
he brought to the Grand Secretariat, we need to check into these matters.

* * *

First, foreign relations, but leading into that, let's start with some background. Ming governance considered foreign relations to be quite separate
from internal security or frontier defense, which lay in the domain of the
armed forces and the Ministry of War, but of course there are interconnec-
tions among them. Before joining the Rites Ministry, Xia served in the Office
of Scrutiny for War for ten years, so he had much experience in that sector.
Besides his important work at Blue Sheep Mountain, he also weighed in on a
riot of some thousand garrison troops in Yunnan, who knelt and pleaded for
their regular food allotment, which had been delayed for two months. They
stoned the gate of Ouyang Zhong, the grand coordinator, when he failed to
respond. Xia's memorial is dated November 11, 1529, and it argues against

Jiajing's harsh order to punish the riot leaders and dismiss Ouyang Zhong and several other officials. But a close study of the Yunnan riot, said Xia, gives a better understanding of how and why it happened, and shows that Jiajing must modify his angry response to it. There has recently been a breakdown in the military food supply nationwide. Protest riots have broken out in Gansu, Datong, two prefectures in Fujian, Baoding (in Bei Zhili), and Zhejiang. Something has to be done to fix this problem, he insisted, or else we'll soon be faced with the late Tang situation of defiant and autonomous provincial military governors. To this, Jiajing vehemently disagreed that he'd been too harsh.[29]

Xia raised the food crisis issue again in connection with a call-up of twenty thousand combat veterans to respond to a massive Lu (Mongol) raid on Datong. Datong was in horrible shape thanks to gross mismanagement during the Zhengde era. The officers are corrupt. There have been successive years of drought. Grain prices are sky high. Cannibalism has been reported among the civilian population. There have been raids on grain markets. Troops lie starving at the camp gates, too weak to take part in combat. We've issued some hundred thousand taels for relief, a stopgap measure only, and more has to be done to stabilize the situation and prevent mutiny. A secure system of grain transport has to be set up to forward Grand Canal grain from Beijing up to the frontier. The recent dismissals of some hundred thousand excess soldiers, Buddhist and Daoist priests, artisans, and various other parasites should free up enough grain to save the situation. Jiajing forwarded this memorial to the Ministries of Revenue and War for their reaction.[30]

On May 14, 1530, Xia reported another military food breakdown, this one in the Yulin area, on the Great Wall in Shaanxi Province. It was awful. Empty granaries, deserted fields, merchants unable to get there, smoke from cooking fires extinguished, reports of cannibalism, grass roots and tree bark completely stripped and eaten, people grinding stones to powder to alleviate hunger pangs, soon to collapse and die. Told of this horror, Jiajing issued one hundred thousand taels silver from the Taicang treasury to help ease it, but the present grand coordinator was a poor administrator, and a better man needed to replace him so that what until recently had been the strongest of the frontier garrisons could be nursed back to health. The problem, said Xia, was that throwing silver at stricken regions doesn't necessarily fill stomachs at all. Corrupt officials skim the funds, and we don't know how the silver is spent. Grain stores aren't maintained. A special appointee needs to monitor all this very carefully. Xia recommended two excellent men for those jobs. Jiajing sent his statement to the Ministry of Personnel for their reply. [31]

Probably Xia Yan's vivid and compelling memorials, alongside the efforts of others, helped alleviate the worst famine conditions along the frontiers. But the question came up again in 1534, when Xia was minister of rites. The food supply did not normally fall within his purview anymore, but managing the Ming princedoms did. So in response to a statement sent up by the Prince of Dai in the wake of the latest mutiny at Datong asking for relief for his suffering clansmen, Xia noted that the four months of siege had cost over a million taels, with fire damage and casualties beyond counting, forcing many civilians to flee to the Lu, so the Prince of Dai's request for aid should be granted. But Xia took issue with a request of the Ministry of War to recruit tens of thousands of braves so as to bring the troop presence at Datong back to normal. The problem was that Ming government would be unable to feed such a gathering. Better planning was needed. This statement is dated April 4, 1534. Jiajing agreed and rescinded the recruitment order he had just authorized. [32]

Thus Xia Yan found it impossible to suppress a sense of responsibility for the whole realm in order not to exceed his formal powers as minister of rites. His prior experiences led him to identify military food security as an issue he was equipped to rivet his attention upon.

* * *

Foreign relations proper he was prepared to handle, too. A long, perceptive, but undated memorial of Xia Yan's took up the thorny issue of Ming trade relations with Japan and its interconnection with problems of northern frontier defense. Internal evidence suggests 1523, when he was supervising secretary in the Office of Scrutiny for War. This was a rites responsibility, but it was also a military issue, and Xia leaped to the challenge. What happened was this: the employees of two rival Japanese families, the Ouchi and the Hosokawa, on a periodic tribute mission to China came to blows in the port city of Ningbo, then turned to pillaging it. [33] The leader of the Hosokawa group, a Chinese named Song Suqing, was caught and imprisoned. The leader of the Ouchi, Shusetsu Gendo, and a gang of a hundred men plundered unopposed the great city of Hangzhou, fifty or so miles west.

Xia Yan thought this violence symptomatic of a major collapse in China's maritime defense, and he was nearly beside himself with apoplexy at the listlessness, complacency, mendacity, and corruption of all the responsible civil and military officials. His long memorial, presaging his later involvement in Blue Sheep Mountain, rehearsed the whole history of China-Japan relations and expressed deep shame that the king of Korea had put up an effective defense against Japanese violence, whereas China hadn't. He said the northern frontier raiders will get wind of this failure and despise us all the more. Xu urged that a special official with plenipotentiary powers be sent down to Ningbo to punish all the guilty officials, and especially to crack down on all the Chinese, like Song Suqing, who were mixed up with the Japanese traders. Their severed heads should be mounted on poles and publicly displayed as a warning to all. Beijing officialdom should collectively discuss the question whether official links to Japan should be terminated altogether.

What is notable here is Xia's emotional outburst of shame and anger— shame that a mighty giant like China should be a hapless victim of mere handfuls of violent foreigners, and anger that the responsible authorities did nothing about it, while villainous Chinese traitors made common cause with the Japanese enemy. It was an image and prestige issue, not so much an existential threat to Ming security, although if left unattended, that danger couldn't be ruled out.[34]

* * *

Years after, as minister of rites, Xia Yan found himself a bit constrained, as he no longer had a direct voice in military affairs. As minister, on April 21, 1532, however, he joined a discussion of whether to recognize a breakaway Mongol group that for the past twenty years or so had been occupying Xihai, the area around the great Qinghai Lake (also called Kokonor), southwest of the present-day province of Gansu. Reports from the field said the Mongols' occupancy was by theft (even though Xihai lay beyond Ming China), that farming had ceased there, and that the occupiers had been using the area as a staging base for raids on China's frontier. Now, however, their behavior seemed to have improved, and they were seeking tributary privileges and recognition as a *wei* (Ming garrison), with office and seal, and were offering their chief's son as a hostage. Xia thought the Ministry of War should speak up about the implications of this for China's security and that the whole question should be turned over to a general court discussion, because the

Xihai Mongols were not a traditional Ming tributary. Four days later, Jiajing replied that he had already ruled on the matter. What he meant is not clear.[35]

Tributary relations with the turbulent, politically splintered, and now increasingly Muslim statelets of central inner Asia (present-day Xinjiang, Uzbekistan, Tajikistan, etc.) were a major headache for the Ministry of Rites and its Bureau of Receptions. Xia Yan's long statement of November 1, 1532, argued that these particular tribute missions had to be very carefully monitored, because China's prestige was at stake, and China could not be seen to be victimized by scams and deceits inflicted upon it by villainous foreigners. Missions bloated with idlers, with mission leaders claiming to represent kings of states no one had ever heard of, carrying meager and inferior goods into China in return for overly generous rewards were at the heart of the problem. Two days later, Jiajing agreed that China's *guoti* (national prestige) was vexed by these dubious missions, which must be stopped at the frontier.

Further memorials by Xia delved deeper into the difficulties. The Central Asians were acting outrageously in Beijing. Yet if we handle them roughly, they may well go back home bearing grudges and start trouble against us. Again, we must carefully check into how the frontier officials are managing the embassies at the entryways into China. Jiajing mostly agreed, replying two days later to Xia's statement of March 13, 1533.[36]

On May 6, 1533, Xia explained that the *Da Ming huidian* (the principal administrative thesaurus) recognized only three Central Asian "kings" (*wang*): those ruling Turfan, Samarkand, and Tianfang (the Ka'aba, i.e., Mecca and the Red Sea coast of Arabia). Lower local authorities were called "chiefs" (*toumu*). But now Turfan claimed seventy-five kings, and Tianfang twenty-seven. Things were clearly getting out of hand. The three legitimate kings needed to be officially informed that they must downgrade all these other so-called kings to chiefs again.[37] On May 22, Xia reported fifty-three more "kings" from Samarkand. China cannot afford this, he maintained. He said he went in person to the Zuoshun Gate to witness the gifts being distributed to the Turfan and Tianfang envoys. Expensive embroidered silk dating from the Yongle era, featuring fresh colors and fine gold thread, unmatchable by weavers of the day, was being handed out. The storehouse men said their stock was exhausted, while the foreigners were offering iron pans, not an equal exchange at all. Xia suggested that the ruler politely tell the three states (*guo*) that they must call their local authorities chiefs, not kings, and that the size of the embassies and the timing of their arrival must follow the old rules.

On May 27, Jiajing agreed.[38] A pileup of envoys waiting at the Gansu frontier for entry permits had to be ironed out; Xia discussed the problem with the grand secretaries, and a simplified procedure was devised, which Jiajing endorsed, on June 10.

Xia was fond of historical backgrounders (cf. his historical sketches of the Blue Sheep Mountain gang and China-Japan relations). Late in 1536, the minister of rites provided a denunciatory overview of China-Turfan relations since Yuan times. He accused the current sultan, Mansur, of violence and deceit, but he argued that the best way to deal with him was to continue to allow tribute missions, only on a tightly restricted basis and under heavy guard.[39]

On July 29, 1535, Xia replied to a request from a different population: Tibetans settled at the Minzhou Guards (*wei*), in present-day Gansu Province, wedged between the Tatars (Daren) and Muslims (Huiren). A Tibetan Buddhist monk complained on his people's behalf that the current payment rate for their horses was unfair. For each horse, the Tibetans were only getting one bolt of silk and one tub of butter. The Mongols and Muslims got much more than that. Also he asked to be allowed to buy more tea. Each member of the embassy was allowed to buy thirty catties. They wanted ten times that amount. Xia thought this excessive and asked Jiajing instead to authorize a tight inspection of all the baggage the envoys were carrying. Jiajing agreed.[40]

Some thousand straight-line miles southeast of Minzhou lay "outer" Tibet, dBus-Gtsang, in and around the city of Lhasa. As did Turfan, Tianfang, and Samarkand, with their oversized embassies, so too the "four kings" of outer Tibet had been sending missions, not with the stipulated ten monks each, but as many as a thousand. Ming border officials, possibly paid off, just let them and other oversized Tibetan missions come through unchallenged. Jiajing agreed that this could not go on.[41]

In Guizhou Province, some thousand miles southwest of Beijing, lay the Kaili Pacification Office. This was territory settled by the Miao people, who had just concluded a civil war, and the Pacification Office was a new Ming creation. As with other such offices in southwest China, Kaili was drawn into the Ming tributary system as a sort of second-class foreign country, and as such it was obliged to send up congratulatory messages on the emperor's birthday and on seasonal occasions and to offer war matériel, horses in the case of Kaili. The new chief of the office, a Miao aristocrat bearing the Chinese name Yang Zhang, sent up through channels a complaint that if he imposed on his war-torn people the cost of securing the expensive paper and preparing the messages, paying for a courier, and providing the horses, the people would rebel. After a thorough review of this whole question, Jiajing agreed on November 19, 1531, to follow Xia Yan's advice and cancel the horse tribute for seven years.[42]

One grasps from all this a strong sense of how the huge size of China, like an overpowering magnet, drew into its orbit tribes and kingdoms, and smaller countries of all sorts, from every point of the compass. So off to the northeast, a mere three hundred or so miles from Beijing, was the steppe homeland of the so-called Three Guards of the Uriyangkhad, wedged between the Lu ("raiders") of Mongolia (with whom there were few to no tribute relations until 1571) and the turbulent Jurchen tribes of Manchuria. As Xia Yan explained, the Three Guards were set up early in Ming as a defensive "hedge for China," and in return they were granted exceptionally generous tribute privileges, including twice-yearly missions to Beijing. But as Xia reported on January 20, 1533, some of the Uriyangkhad (here called Dazei, "Tatar bandits") had raided the Miyun area (inside China, forty miles northeast of Beijing), killed troops, stolen their weapons, and abducted people and cattle. Why on earth had they done that? For one thing, the overseers of the Ming defenses had relaxed their vigilance. Another reason, alluded to by Xia, was that much as China might wish to punish the Uriyangkhad, it could not really afford to do so; if it did exact revenge, China could lose its "hedge" and thus jeopardize its security. That was the Ming dilemma.

An Uriyangkhad chief named Donga, arrested in Beijing and interrogated through an interpreter, was asked which leaders and which tribes (*buluo*) were responsible for the raiding. "I don't know what men did the evil," he said. "It wasn't us. Otherwise we wouldn't have dared come offer tribute. Now that we've been told of it, we'll tell commander Gelantai. If we find out who did this, we'll [arrest them] and send them to the frontier." Xia thought a thorough investigation of the trouble was absolutely necessary. Two days later, Jiajing agreed to send a new grand coordinator and *kedao* (supervising secretaries and censors) to the frontier to ferret out the facts and report.[43]

As for the Jurchen in Manchuria, there was a problem with their annual tribute mission, as Xia reported on March 12, 1536. The Jurchen at issue were those based in the Jianzhou region, five hundred miles northeast of Beijing. (A century later, under the new name of Manchu, these Jurchen would commence their conquest of all of China.) Eighty of them came to Shanhaiguan, the eastern gateway into China, and complained that they were unable to buy their quota of tribute horses because of heavy snow. They said there were four hundred more people following behind, who wouldn't be able to buy horses either. The first group was allowed to enter Beijing. The others appeared to exceed the quota for legal entry (surely another bloated mission, like those from Turfan, Tianfang, Samarkand, and Tibet). Jiajing agreed that their credentials needed to be carefully checked before any of them were allowed in.[44]

Five hundred miles over the East China Sea lay the Ryukyu archipelago. On August 20, 1535, Xia forwarded, on behalf of the Bureau of Sacrifices, a vivid description by Supervising Secretary Chen Kan of his harrowing voyage to the islands to enfeoff the king as legitimate ruler of that *guo*. (The king was Sho Sei, r. 1527–1555.) The mission was a success, despite huge storms coming and going, thanks to the protection of the sea god, who appeared before the terrified hundred or so passengers on board as first a butterfly, then a bird. Ultimately, of course, the god was under Jiajing's command, and a description of the whole experience must be sent to the ruler and a stela put up to reward the god. Xia Yan urged that the Hanlin Academy be directed to compose the inscription and that the Fujian Provincial Administration Commission conduct the sacrifice to the sea god. Jiajing agreed.[45]

Three days later, Xia replied to Jiajing's solicitation of comment upon Chen Kan's report about the Ryukyu kingdom. The report for the first time gave an accurate picture of the islands and their king, destroying the prevalent but false legends that the place and its ruler were barbaric. Added was a vocabulary. Xia thought this was valuable information to have, and Jiajing agreed that Chen's account should be deposited in the History Office for future reference.[46]

The Ryukyu kingdom and Korea should have been subjected to the same procedural rules for their China missions, but they weren't, and so Xia initiated a reform. Korea had been submitting horses to the Ministry of Rites for its inspection, but they had long been handing their memorials of congratulations on the emperor's birthday and on the winter solstice to the Court of State Ceremonial, which passed them up to the palace eunuchs. That was incorrect. These papers must instead be presented to the Ministry of Rites, which would forward them to the Grand Secretariat. On March 21, 1534, Jiajing agreed to the change. This was mainly an internal matter involving bureaucratic turf, but Xia insisted that the intent was to deprive Korea of too cozy and privileged a pipeline to the Ming throne.[47]

Xia palliated the Koreans by lifting a prohibition that confined their envoys to the Interpreters Institute (Huitong Guan), not allowing them out into the streets of Beijing to buy and sell. Violent behavior by Jurchen envoys had led to the blanket imposition of this rule years earlier. Xia argued that the Koreans were a civilized people, and an exception should be made for them. He suggested that every five days the educated Korean envoys be let out to sightsee in the streets and markets, accompanied by one interpreter. Their servants, however, should be kept confined. This would mollify the Koreans' offended feelings and also sustain China's laws. On March 25, 1534, Jiajing endorsed this proposal.[48]

Finally, there was Annam (Vietnam). On October 20, 1536, Jiajing's second son was born. Heaven, Earth, the gods, and the realm were informed of the birth a month later, when it appeared the baby might live. On December 9, Jiajing called in Xia and told him that foreign countries should be informed of the birth now, not just later on when the baby received his official title. He told Xia to prepare a proposal. On December 18, Xia proposed sending a Hanlin official as head of mission, and a supervising secretary as deputy, bearing the imperial proclamation, one mission to Korea, and another to Annam, and again later, when the child received his title. Jiajing agreed to this.

Then Xia followed with a statement that while it was feasible to send such a mission to Korea, sending one to Annam was not. Annam was in violent revolutionary turmoil. Roads were blocked. Legitimate authority there, if any, couldn't be identified or located. In a long review of China-Annam relations past and present (another historical backgrounder, a Xia Yan specialty), Xia argued that it would injure China's *guoti* (national dignity) to send a mission into the teeth of certain disaster. The China-Annam frontier was riddled with corruption and lax vigilance, and the Rites and War Ministries needed to gather and discuss long-range plans about how to restore the traditional tribute relations.[49] Jiajing suspended the mission and ordered the discussion.

The discussion was held a few days later. Xia was in his final days as minister of rites. He contributed a long statement, dated November 1, 1536, with another long review of the history, plus an inventory of known facts and uncertain intelligence about the current situation, and a strong endorsement of a plan to preposition arms and supplies on the border and organize a very large army, ready to invade the country if the situation should call for that.

Twenty years of Annam's failure to send tribute missions was compelling proof of its hostile disloyalty. Jiajing agreed.[50]

Xia was promoted to the Grand Secretariat on January 23, 1537. Annam would figure as a major military problem during his tenure there (I defer further attention to this question to the following chapter on Yan Song).

But to review all that Xia Yan did with respect to foreign relations during the six years he was minister of rites, 1531 to 1536, it is well to recall that satisfying Jiajing's ritual reform demands soaked up by far the greater part of his time and energy. Still, he managed somehow to fit in detailed attention to vexing problems in managing China's tribute system, from Japan to Samarkand, from Tibet to Guizhou, from the Uriyangkhad to the Jurchen, to the Ryukyus and Korea and Annam. These experiences must certainly have given him a practical grasp of China's proper place in the larger world, excellent background for the duties he would assume in the Grand Secretariat. (Zhang Fujing never had that arrow in his arsenal.)

* * *

If foreign affairs were troublesome, the minister of rites' responsibility to help manage the huge bureaucratic recruitment system may have been even more exhausting and difficult. As with foreign relations, however, much of this was guided by fixed written regulations. It was the minister's job to suggest to Jiajing remedies for systemic kinks as they arose, for which the existing rules offered no clear guidance, or else were clear but were being ignored.

It may be safe to say that the system for recruiting new bureaucrats, constantly rejuvenating Ming China's governing apparatus of some twenty thousand higher-level mandarins, was the preeminent shaping feature not just of government, but of society at large. So the mechanisms of recruitment were forever in need of some readjustment or other.[51]

Every three years, the metropolitan and palace exams yielded a crop of roughly three hundred *jinshi* degree winners (about 10 percent of all test takers). The top three finishers were given salaried positions in the Hanlin Academy. The next twenty or so were appointed unpaid Hanlin trainees (bachelors; *shujishi*), given special advanced instruction, tested after three years, and then typically offered good positions in Beijing. The trouble here was that the trainees came to be viewed as a privileged and snobbish clique, a breeding ground for Yang Tinghe's side in the Great Rites controversy. So in

1527, at Zhang Fujing's urging, the class was canceled, and all the trainees were instead appointed to salaried starting positions all over China.[52] Now in 1532, with Zhang Fujing temporarily forced out of office, Xia Yan and others begged the emperor to restock the depleted Hanlin with young and talented trainees as had traditionally been done. Jiajing agreed to do that.[53]

Regarding that year's exam, soon to be held, Xia sent up on February 26, 1532, a detailed three-item reform proposal aimed at changing the criteria by which the examiners graded the candidates. First, they should look for un-adorned, straightforward, mild, and generous modes of written expression. They should reject the current trend toward obscurity, cleverness, and convoluted thorniness. Second, Xia noted the traditional tripartite format of the exams: questions on the Four Books and Five Classics; on discourses, memorials, and adjudications; and last, five questions on policy, which Xia said were the hardest, because passable answers required responsiveness, relevance, and wide knowledge. Only one of a hundred examinees could write good answers in the brief time allotted to them. It was customary that successful exams got printed up and distributed as models for future students, but these were often so riddled with sloppy responses to poorly designed questions as to contaminate the whole process. So besides better-written questions, the answers need to be edited before they're printed, and that would be feasible if the public announcement of the exam results is delayed until the editing can be done. Third, some changes are needed in how we choose examiners. As things stand, the Ministry of Rites proposes two main examiners from among the Hanlin academicians, and the Grand Secretariat proposes seventeen associate examiners, eleven from the Hanlin, three from the offices of scrutiny, and three from the six ministries. Often a designated examiner can't take part for some reason, so we need to appoint three or four backups. The provincial degree winners will soon be arriving, Xia noted, and we need to put up placards at the ministry and at the gate to the examinations cells so that both examiners and examinees are informed. Two days later, the ruler agreed to all of what Xia proposed.[54]

Then in 1533, two problems involving the conduct of the provincial exams prompted Xia to urge removing the authority to nominate examiners from provincial-level officials and instead centralizing it in Beijing. He also thought it necessary to tighten the provincial standards for acceptable written expression. Jiajing refused the first proposal, but he agreed to tighten standards.[55]

However, it was not the examination system per se but its ancillary systems that ate up much of Xia Yan's time and attention—the imperial universities in Beijing and Nanjing; the so-called tribute system for bringing local students into the universities; and the great mass of *shengyuan*, the Confucian students attached to prefectural and county schools all over Ming China who aspired to make it through the tight examination quotas or enter one of the imperial universities if they couldn't. Here, social pressures threatened to swamp administration as a large mass of students accreted about the central mechanism of examination-based bureaucratic recruitment pure and simple. Competitive written tests alone could never meet all of Ming China's staffing needs, and something also needed to be done to reduce the competitive pressures.

On January 18, 1532, Xia responded to Jiajing's order to reply to complaints coming up from the field that the system of "annual tribute" (*suigong*), whereby prefectural and county students were in order of seniority brought up to the universities, had gotten clogged with elderly, feeble, and learning-deficient students, who were in no way suitable for even the lowest posts in Ming bureaucracy.

There were three hierarchical categories of local students: stipend students, their stipends awarded on the basis of seniority; "added" students without stipend, doubling the original local quotas, twenty in the case of counties; and "supplementary" students, an open category with no quota. The younger and better students were seldom the stipend students, and that was the problem. All *shengyuan*, irrespective of category, if they tested out well, were eligible to take the provincial exams, so the exam system siphoned off the best and the brightest. The relative youth and vigor of those who passed at the provincial and metropolitan levels equipped them for the higher and more demanding positions. Stipend students tended to be repeated failures at the provincial level. Counties, by quota, sent up to the universities one aging stipend student every two years, prefectures one every year. This became a social problem. Many *suigong*, tested on arrival, were found deficient in learning and demeanor and were summarily denied entry. So they were turned loose, with no resources, some so poor they died in the ditches.

What to do about this? Xia did not favor a major overhaul. He thought the right approach was to keep the existing system intact and just order the education intendants (*tixue*) and provincial officials to make more rigorous their standards at the students' places of origin. And what of the *suigong* who, even so, got rejected when they came to Nanjing or Beijing? Xia's streak of compassion for the hapless and hopeless shone here: let the failures retire with robe and headband as tokens of honor; let the aged and decrepit retire with the higher honor of cap and belt if they so choose. Three days later, Jiajing agreed and directed that he wanted to read no more time-wasting reform proposals on this issue.[56]

What kinds of places were the imperial universities? They were something like holding pens for tribute students and provincial degree holders (*juren*) who failed their metropolitan exams. Student status carried certain fiscal privileges and social prestige back home, so many of the students stayed home, leaving the universities with a depleted student body and the students with dim prospects for ever getting a good job.

A formal imperial visit to the Beijing university would surely help to revitalize it. The commander of Jiajing's security detail suggested that he make such a visit. The ruler forwarded the suggestion to Xia Yan. In reply, on December 21, 1531, Xia praised the ruler's recent gestures of support for Confucianism—a shrine to the doctrine's founders in an east room in the Wenhua Palace, which he was visiting monthly and also twice a year to hear special lectures, and also the recent building of the Wuyi Palace in West Park, specifically to hear the grand secretaries discuss the *Book of Odes* and the *Book of Documents* and thereby "improve customs." So a visit to the Imperial University (Taixue) was wholly appropriate. It was just a question of when to schedule it. The first month of the coming year was not good because officials would then be arriving from everywhere to undergo their periodic performance reviews. Nor would the second month do because the metropolitan examinations would be taking place. So Xia asked Jiajing to order the Directorate of Astronomy to pick a lucky day during the second ten-day period of the third month for the ruler's visit by sedan chair. Meanwhile, the ministry would prepare the program.

Jiajing decided to make the visit early in the year after that, 1533.[57] When the next year rolled around, the date was fixed for April 7. The visit was duly made. Xia Yan proposed to have it written up as a tract commemorating an important moment in Jiajing's dedication to ritual renewal. Copies should be printed, distributed to each province for reprinting and further distribution to all the local schools in China so that people everywhere will be informed of the ruler's state of mind. Jiajing gave his approval on May 21.[58]

Jiajing sent the Ministry of Rites a memorial from a censor who objected to proposals to "cleanse" (*shatai*) the *shengyuan* ranks nationwide of all poor performers and overaged students. Xia Yan agreed and again exercised a spark of compassion for those stuck in the Confucian school pipeline. A general purge was too cruel, he maintained. The fathers and older brothers of these students worked hard early on to teach them, and will their efforts come to nothing? Shall we deprive all these students of robe and cap and make them all peasants laboring in the fields? History shows examples of purging the ranks of monks and nuns, never the ranks of *shengyuan*.[59] To be sure, there are cases of laziness and irreverence among the students, but these need to be dealt with on a case-by-case basis, and we must make the education intendants and other officials responsible for putting an end to literary cleverness and philosophical deviance. That was Xia Yan's reply on January 28, 1532. Jiajing agreed two days later.[60]

But some zealous officials had already carried out some cleansing. On November 14, 1532, Xia memorialized that overeager education intendants were still ruthlessly and indiscriminately rejecting young and untested students in order to shrink swollen *shengyuan* rolls, and that was a sad and regrettable waste of possible talent. He asked that new intendants be appointed and the expellees put on a waiting list for reinstatement, after which a simple test could be applied to weed out the aged and unqualified. It took Jiajing the usual two days to agree.[61]

A long memorial of Xia's, dated July 18, 1532, focused on problems connected to the flow of *shengyuan* coming up as prospective tribute students to the Imperial University in Beijing. In batches over the years 1529–1532, tests were given them after they reached Beijing to ensure their fitness. Grand Secretaries Zhang Fujing, Li Shi, and Chai Luan reported to Jiajing the overall numbers: 50 grade A, 45 grade B, and 641 grade C, with 59 failures to be sent back home. The question was what to do about the failures. Jiajing solicited the Rites Ministry's opinion. In reply, Xia Yan listed all fifty-nine by province, together with the names of the education intendants who had certified them. Xia suggested a sliding scale of penalties, as an excess of harshness would make them afraid to certify anyone at all. And Xia took care to encourage people from poor and remote places, home to many of the failures, who had brought along their wives and children. The trip back home would be long and costly, so why not let the failures from border provinces (Yunnan, Guizhou, Sichuan, Liangguang, and the northwest frontier) stay in Beijing and await another test? Jiajing agreed to the sliding scale of penalties, said nothing of the failures from remote parts, and denied Xia's request to palliate the disappointed with robes or any other tokens of honor.[62]

Indeed, Xia had a consistent soft spot for schools and students from faraway places. On November 24, 1531, he sent Jiajing a plaint submitted by a distressed student from a guards school in Liaodong (Manchuria), speaking on behalf of a party of examinees, who by rule had to travel to Shandong Province for the provincial examinations: "We started our journey in the sixth month [June–July 1531] and entered the pass [Shanhaiguan] in the next [intercalary] month [July–August]. There was steady rain and flooding everywhere, and we trudged through the mud and heat and finally arrived [in Shandong] at the end of the seventh month [late August]. But due to the heat and damp, half of us were sick and couldn't finish the exams. Those who did finish were weak and barely made it, so only one *shengyuan* from our school passed. The rest of us failed because we wrote poor exams, which we admit, but we'd traveled six thousand *li* (two thousand miles) from Liaodong to Shandong, which took four months, and all our suffering was beyond telling."

Xia took pity. He said that when Liaodong first sent candidates to Shandong in 1447, sea travel was possible. For the last forty years, however, the sea route has been shut down. For poor students to pack food and books for such a long trip overland is too much, so he asked the ruler to let them come to Shuntian Prefecture in Beijing and take the exams there. Jiajing agreed to this.[63]

Students whose home was a Guards community in Dezhou, located at a land and water junction between Nanjing and Beijing, were too economically distressed to afford a Confucian school, so Xia proposed that those students attend the civilians' school in Dezhou proper. Jiajing, in the usual two-day turnaround time, agreed to this dispensation.[64] This would seem to be too trivial a matter to engage the attention of the ministry, the Grand Secretariat, and the emperor himself in such a question, but quite obviously, it was not. None of the problems involving schools and students that Xi Yan handled bubbled up from any of the richer and more central regions of China.

Thus Guizhou Province, deep in the southwest, heavily populated by non-Chinese, came to Xia's attention on September 2, 1535. Created in 1415, Guizhou saw its Chinese population grow to the point that it was no longer necessary to send its provincial exam candidates on long treks through the mountains, bamboo forests, the malarial heat, and the danger of robbers to neighboring Yunnan Province to take their exams. There were now at least three thousand students, of whom seven hundred were qualified to take the exams. They study the Five Classics, they have already produced a few metropolitan degree winners who have entered the Hanlin and Censorate, and they are every bit as good as any from Jiangnan or the Central Plains. It will cost 2,800 taels to build examination cells in a vacant space in the south part of the provincial capital (Guiyang), and enough funds for that are on hand there. In addition, the quotas for both Yunnan and Guizhou should be raised from thirty-four and twenty-one to forty and twenty-five, respectively. Jiajing agreed.[65]

A growth curve like Guizhou's was evident in Liaodong, too. The Shandong regional inspector, Chang Shiping, had made a personal tour of Liaodong. He noted that every city or walled town had a Confucian school, with the exception of the Right Encampment Guard at Guangning, some three hundred miles northeast of Beijing. He reported that the population there had grown, customs were pure and simple, the students were all devoted to their studies, and the commoners were well behaved, unlike before. The forty *shengyuan* in that community had to make a costly and difficult trip of 130 *li* (forty or so miles) to Guangningzhen or Yizhouwei to attend school. Last year, he said, nine candidates from the various guards communities of Liaodong passed their provincial exams in Shuntianfu (Beijing), and one of them came from the Right Encampment Guard, proof of its readiness to have its own school. Jiajing agreed to Xia Yan's request of September 9, 1535, to spend government money to build and staff such a school. The ministry promised to cut a dedicatory inscription for it.[66]

Again, it was troubles with marginal and second-rate educational institutions that caught the attention of the minister of rites when in spring 1536 he tried to fix a continuing breakdown in the tribute system's funneling of *suigong* from the nation's local schools to the imperial universities in Beijing and Nanjing. Xia had all the statistics in hand, sorted by province. There was a shortfall of 1,193 students over the last four years. The reason for the shortfall was the education intendants' fear of blame and demotion if their nominees failed the testing. So it was safer for them not to send anyone at all. This policy affected remote and small places especially hard. Students there lose all hope, the schools dissolve, and customs erode. Any blame for failures should shift from the education intendants and fall on government teachers and provincial inspectors. It's not clear how Jiajing responded to that.[67]

The Imperial University chancellors were at times leading Confucian intellectuals. Lü Nan (1479–1542), an outstanding Zhu Xi apologist, was Beijing chancellor in 1535–1536, and Jiajing ordered Xia Yan to critique his five-point proposal for university reform. On April 3, 1536, Xia did so. He agreed with Lü to tighten requirements for all *juren* (provincial degree holders) who failed their metro and were waiting for another try at them. He agreed that currently the university students who entered via the *suigong* route tended to be young men with literary aptitude but lacking in refined behavior. They were prone to ambition, arguments, and shallow go-getting. This seriously disadvantaged students of good character from small places and frontier military communities. So, once again, character needed to be considered as important as literary ability. Xia agreed that residency needed to be tightened for students who paid silver to enter the university. As it was, too many of them were going home and using their status for corrupt purposes. Fourth, the sons of the military nobility were skipping out as well, and Xia agreed that they too needed to attend and study the rites. Last, and most interesting, Lü urged resurrecting the ancient and neglected *Yi li*, a text on etiquette and rites. It had been fleshed out with pictures and explanations by Yang Fu in Song times, so it was possible now to use it to re-create the ancient gestures and dances. Xia was a bold champion of Jiajing's passion for ancient ritual and music, so he heartily recommended printing up a few hundred deluxe copies of the *Yi li* and manufacturing the ritual utensils needed for it.[68]

It is uncertain how much of this was actually done. But we've been seeing much of Xia Yan in action, a virtual dynamo, always exhibiting his tireless energy, his skills, and his penchants—a soft spot for the disadvantaged and an appetite for deep and probing inquiry.

As minister of rites, there was much more Xia did, which for reasons of space cannot be covered in detail here. The Ming princedoms, for instance, came under his purview and involved time-consuming quasi-legal proposals for adjudicating succession disputes, criminal misbehavior, and such like.[69] He also weighed in with proposals on a number of one-off issues, such as the occasional disruptive voice bubbling up unbidden from men low in the bureaucratic hierarchy, who must be chastised and silenced. Thus a failed Shuntianfu *shengyuan*, awarded a robe and headband, presented a memorial heaping praise on several high officials, military men, and eunuchs, and blame on a few others. Who put him up to this? Anonymous opinion from the streets was all right, but this was clearly illegal.[70] A Confucian school instructor from the provinces, arguing that Jiajing's mother and father needed even more lavish honors, was obviously angling to win favor and promotion.[71] A lowly retired functionary of the Daoist Registry asked Jiajing to preface a compendium of his poorly written poems praising every aspect of current government, surely another grasp for fame and advancement.[72] The same motive animated a lowly county student who submitted an immense revised history of China, for which he claimed a firmer ethical and judgmental foundation than anything ever written before. Jiajing agreed with Xia that the work must be destroyed and the author severely punished.[73] Memorials from a county student and two Embroidered-Uniform Guardsmen, asking Jiajing to disinter his father's corpse and rebury it in the necropolis near Beijing, were likewise opportunistic, and surely some higher-ups put them up to it.[74] And while newly minted *jinshi* must not be silenced altogether, they must route any memorials through their official superiors for vetting and not present them directly to the throne, else we encourage a climate of mindless and troublesome go-getting.[75]

* * *

What kind of stamina and determination did it take to advance in the bureaucratic hierarchy and at the same time deflect the attacks of colleagues at almost every step of the way? There was no escaping the heated interpersonal rivalries and subterranean factionalism of bureaucratic life in mid-Ming China. Many contenders played for the high stakes of influence in the present and fame in future time. For all his scholarly and administrative talent, Xia Yan always had to play this game and engage in the infighting. He was not reluctant to do so.

In September 1529, Xia replied at length to an impeachment sent up by a certain Yue Lun, a vice director of the Messenger Office, which mentioned Xia in passing as an ardent partisan of Zhang Fujing and Gui E, grand secretaries and architects of the Great Rites dispute, "plotting day and night with them, going in and out of their gates." This was a dangerous moment. Reacting to Yue's fierce denunciation of Zhang and Gui as corrupt factionalists—"their power overwhelming, their adherents everywhere, hated by a realm that has been terrorized into silence, and who, as incorrigibly evil men, must be removed to save the state from future disaster"—Jiajing removed both Zhang and Gui on September 15.[76]

From Xia Yan's perspective, how to extricate himself? By giving a detailed account of his career thus far, showing that his return to office in 1528 was not facilitated by Zhang and Gui, that his contacts with either were very few, and that Xue Lun's charges were out-and-out falsehoods. He also said the *kedao* had forced Jiajing into dismissing Zhang and Gui, that Xia himself deserved death for "naively hiding my loyalty and will, shrinking from [defending them] out of fear." That was an astute reply. Xue's attack on him was inspired by angry victims of Xia's anticorruption efforts of 1521–1524, he insisted. Jiajing sent his statement to the Ministry of Personnel for comment.[77]

While Xue Lun's charges were still awaiting Jiajing's decision, censors impeached Xia for "catering to the powerful, overturning the national right." Xia had to make inquiries to find out what they were referring to. It turned out they were referring to his assignments of merit and blame in the Blue Sheep Mountain affair, concluded six months earlier. Xia's response was long, forthright, detailed, and persuasive. The impeachment was, he insisted, prompted by "one or two" men who hated him. The censors who signed on didn't know what they were agreeing to. Public opinion (*gonglun*) was never consulted. Jiajing sent this reply to the ministry. Nothing came of it.[78]

Xia and Wang Hong, censor in chief of the right, were both targets of "surreptitious dissent" voiced by certain unnamed officials who opposed their conduct of Jiajing's ritual reform program. On April 30, 1530, Jiajing sent Xia and Wang an encouraging letter. They were called to the Zuoshun Gate to receive it. "We kowtowed and read it with tears of gratitude," replied Xia two days later. He blamed himself for not having clarified adequately the ruler's intent. Jiajing approved his reply.[79]

On June 12, Xia felt he had to provide a detailed answer to unfair charges against him that Jiajing had already waved off. Censor Xiong Jue had accused Xia of slyly currying favor with the ruler through his work on ritual reform, among other things. Xia was clearly upset. Resentful and jealous enemies were aiming at ruining him, he alleged. Jiajing reassured him.[80]

On August 11, 1533, acting in his capacity as chief supervising secretary of the Office of Scrutiny for Personnel, Xia initiated an impeachment of his own—against Chief Grand Secretary Zhang Fujing and Minister of Personnel Fang Xianfu, no less. He accused them of arbitrarily awarding positions to some half dozen undeserving friends and co-locals. He said Zhang Fujing was dictatorial. He went much harder on Fang Xianfu—an "unintelligent small talent, a drinker who has managed to ingratiate himself, who disrespects the great laws of the court, indulges friends, betrays the ruler's favor, does everything to please [Zhang Fujing], cares little for the post the dynasty has given him, places his co-locals in positions in the two capitals, opens wide the gate of favoritism, and is willing to display traces of bribery."

Jiajing agreed to his plea to scold Zhang and Fang and remind them that "public opinion" must be followed in making appointments. [81]

Zhang and Fang disputed Xia's charges and made countercharges, so Xia submitted a long and impassioned rejoinder. Zhang accused him of relying on Grand Secretary Li Shi to secure a plum promotion, and of leaning on Yan Song, at the time vice minister of rites, to "escape the supervising secretary position." [82] Xia penned an intimate picture of his state of mind and his reactions:

> I heard [these allegations] and at once sent up a vehement protest, but because of a recurrence of a chronic illness, for two days I couldn't attend court. Then on the 24th [*sic*: August 16] I rushed off to the southern suburb, and there I was able to talk to Li Shi, and he said, "When did you ever say that?" Censor in Chief Wang Hong, Vice Minister [of works] Jiang Yao, plus eunuchs and military officers were all there at the time and heard that. So Wang Hong urged me [to protest], and you saw that the allegations were unfounded and said I needn't detail the matter further. During the night, I thought and thought about all this, and I think that the great rite of sacrifice to Heaven is not yet done. My responsibility for it is heavy. I feared that controversy over it was never going to stop, that it was unseemly and harmful, yet I needed to put up with it and bear the slander, which would eventually dissolve by itself. But just now Fang Xianfu has cited what the speaking officials said and joined in with what the [chief] grand secretary said, and the two of them attacked me. They spared no effort. They didn't just scowl. You checked into their allegations and saw they were groundless. What more can I say?

Much more. Xia went on to deny that he ever angled for the plum promotion as alleged. All he did was impeach Huo Tao, who held that position. After some further explanations, Xia proceeded to expatiate on the task speaking officials (*yan'guan*) were expected to do. (Here I paraphrase): Fang Xianfu shows his ignorance of procedure when he says I shouldn't use accusatory expressions. He's wrong to think such expressions can only be used by the legal authorities. And why do Fang and Zhang's charges against me appear to come out of the same mouth? To this, Jiajing replied that he did not want to be bothered by this business any further, that Xia should stay on the job and continue his hard work. [83]

As related in the previous chapter, Xia came out the clear winner in a byzantine plot to destroy his reputation. Jiajing sent Zhang Fujing into temporary exile.

But Xia Yan came under fire six years later, in 1536. He was elevated to minister of rites in 1531 and was extremely busy, designing and building temples for Jiajing's rites reforms. But in doing this, he stirred up a backlog of jealousy and hatred. He found himself the target of another byzantine intrigue.

It happened that one Liu Shuxiang, prefect of Shuntian, the administrative district that included the city of Beijing, plus five subprefectures and twenty-two counties, was in prison. His housemen and in-laws had allegedly been receiving bribes from wealthy households. One of the rich households was that of a certain Fei Wan, an in-law of Xia Yan's. While under arrest, Liu charged that Xia had been personally involved in the bribery.

Xia was stunned to learn this. In a memorial of August 1536, he speculated to Jiajing as to why Liu would make such an accusation. He said there was some bad blood between him and Liu. Xia had scolded Liu for failing to provide enough servants for the ruler's recent trip west to visit the Ming tombs. Liu suspected that Xia had blocked his advice to Jiajing about siting the tombs according to the principles of feng shui. Xia had openly expressed his shock at Liu's hosting a drinking party and an outing at the very time Jiajing was making that solemn visit. That behavior bordered on "disrespect for the throne" (*da bujing*), one of the Ming Code's "Ten Abominations."[84] According to Xia, Liu was put into a state of fear and suspicion when he heard that remark. And that wasn't all. Three years earlier, Xia had secured Jiajing's authorization to exempt certain altar-watching households from regular service obligations. But Liu refused, and continued to refuse, to exempt them. So now he's under arrest, and he uses me, said Xia, as a bridge to others who hate me and might help him. Jiajing agreed with Xia and ordered that Liu be interrogated.[85]

About ten days later, Liu's friends joined the fray and sent up "shameless and shocking" memorials against Xia, who was saddened, he said, to see how low the bureaucratic ethos had fallen, imperiling the *guoti* (the dynastic order). He felt he could no longer stand in court. Chronic illness, nervous exhaustion, and the advice of doctors suggested he take an extended sick leave. Jiajing ordered him to stay on the job and not to memorialize on this matter any further.[86]

But he did. Clearly he felt his reputation in peril, his career on the line, and so was compelled to make yet another statement in self-defense. On September 16, 1536, he responded to new charges lodged from prison by Liu Shuxiang. Liu now alleged that Xia had taken big bribes from Ming princes seeking approval of marriage arrangements and successions. Xia offered a meticulously detailed refutation of all these charges and laid the counter-charge that Liu's friends had bribed the princes into making false statements. Liu also alleged that Xia had taken bribes from a group of four hundred student exam takers who were having their papers graded. Again, Xia refuted the charge, saying the original accusation was a lie made up by a disgruntled Bureau of Ceremonies scribe whom he had dismissed for cause and who was living surreptitiously in Beijing as a hanger-on of the hot-blooded Huo Tao (vice minister of personnel, an original member of Zhang Fujing's Great Rites clique, transferred a few months earlier to Nanjing as minister of rites there). It will be recalled that Huo Tao and Xia were enemies of long standing and that Huo had opposed Xia on the question whether to divide the rites to Heaven and Earth and on the silk rites as well, and Jiajing had backed Xia. So Xia believed Huo Tao's hand was behind this charge of taking bribes from examinees, and Huo believed Xia Yan's in-law, Fei Wan, had engineered his transfer to Nanjing.

Liu Shuxiang made another charge, this one concerning Xia's personal housing arrangements. Xia explained that ever since he achieved his *jinshi* degree (in 1517), he'd moved six or seven times to different houses in Beijing. "Last year," he said, "the place I was living in was cramped and mean, there was no place to draft memorials, so I had a broker look for something else, and he found an empty house belonging to the eunuch Liu Jing, who was willing to rent it. So I placed five hundred taels silver with Yang Hui, a retired usher, and the civilian honoree Ye Guan, and the deal was made. Neighbors in the same alley and official colleagues all know about this. It is now commonplace for officials to rent housing from eunuchs, the military nobility, and imperial in-laws. No one minds it. But now Liu [Shuxiang] alleges that the eunuch Liu Jing bribed me with the house so as to get a post as armory inspector, but that post was abolished long ago! How could that take place now?"

Apparently the strategy of Huo Tao and Liu Shuxiang was to multiply the charges against Xia in the hope that some of them might stick. Jiajing, however, refused to go along with any of them.[87]

Huo Tao wasn't done. He was not going to give up just yet. From Nanjing, he sent up a denunciation of his own, this time accusing Xia of violating the inherited ritual norms by awarding an inappropriate posthumous name to Fei Hong, the recently deceased chief grand secretary. The crime called for decapitation! Xia was ready for this one. He called Huo "a frivolous small man, a contemptible and vindictive no-account." He went on to accuse him of total ignorance of both ritual and law. He patiently explained to Jiajing the procedure for awarding posthumous names. Jiajing accepted Xia's explanation.[88]

In the end, Liu confessed under torture to having taken directions from Huo Tao. He was then released from prison and reduced to the rank of commoner. Huo Tao's salary was reduced; that was all.[89]

* * *

No wonder Xia should have suffered nervous exhaustion and gotten sick during the years he spent as minister of rites. Under bombardment by angry and envious colleagues, managing the ritual rebuilding program, monitoring foreign relations, handling the princedoms, and managing the bureaucratic recruitment system, all with his gimlet-eyed attention to detail, would deplete anyone's reservoirs of energies. And there is another area of responsibility yet to add to his dossier: his involvement in imperial family matters.

There was Jiajing's long failure to produce children. Jiajing and Zhang Fujing discussed this matter at great length. Finally, on September 7, 1533, Beautiful Concubine Yan gave birth to a baby boy, the ruler's first. But he didn't live long. In the early hours of October 28, palace eunuch Zhang Qin notified the Ministry of Rites that the baby had died of illness. The birth had been publicly announced, but the baby had never been formally named heir apparent. Nonetheless, elaborate funeral rites were in order, based in Ming precedent. Jiajing approved the elaborate eighteen-point program Xia prepared.[90]

On January 21, 1534, Jiajing informed the Rites Ministry that his mother had chosen Virtuous Concubine Fang as his next empress, and that he was also promoting Playful Concubine Shen to imperial consort, and Beautiful Concubine Yan to beautiful consort. Xia Yan dutifully prepared a long, eleven-section program for announcing these promotions to the Taimiao and Shimiao, shrines to the Ming emperors and Jiajing's father.[91]

These promotions opened up vacancies for new girls to fill. So an Embroidered-Uniform Guards officer asked Jiajing to order the Rites Ministry to notify the fathers of all good and upright families in Beijing and beyond who had virtuous and mild-tempered daughters with pleasant accents, impressive figures, and beautiful faces that they should bring these girls to the princely hostel for selection. A pool of a hundred was to be gathered, of which the hostel should select ten. The ten selectees should then be taken to one of the gates of the Forbidden City, where Jiajing's mother would make the final selection of three. Jiajing asked Xia Yan to respond to this request.

Xia Yan's reply affords a good look at the inner workings of this process. His advice was first to send out two upright palace eunuchs to each local official office in Beijing, Nanjing, Fengyang, Huai'an, and Xuzhou, plus Henan and Shandong Provinces, to deliver preliminary imperial orders; then send two civil officials to these same places with placards of announcement. Then the local officials should politely have the fathers personally escort their daughters to the local officials' yamens, or to the princely hostel in the case of Beijing residents. However, Jiajing didn't like the proposal to send eunuchs; he thought four-man teams of officials should deliver the placards and that the officials should be warned not to harass or disturb the common people when they did this.

Later, the vice minister of rites of the left, Yan Song (later chief grand secretary; see the following chapter), reported that a motley group of 1,258 girls had arrived in Beijing and that they, or some of them, should be directed to the princely hostel, where palace eunuchs, not civil officials, and Jiajing's own senior palace matrons should do the selecting. Jiajing's reply to that was, yes, send all these girls to the hostel, where the matrons will examine them and send their top choices to Jiajing's mother.

Xia Yan responded to that order. He thought one hundred girls, as originally proposed, too small a pool. He wanted more Beijing girls brought in. He thought three Rites Ministry officials should join the capital censors and police, as well as the civil administrators of the city, in putting out placards and carefully selecting girls from good and well-ordered commoner families. The girls should be fourteen to seventeen *sui* (thirteen to sixteen years old), with fair faces and elegant posture, and be mild and respectful in speech and manner. As many as possible should be assembled in the princely hostel, where the palace matrons would pick the best ten for Jiajing's mother, who would make the final selections. [92]

On August 31, 1536, the ruler's first daughter was born. Xia was asked to work up a program for announcing the joyous event to the ancestors and the realm. On September 18, Jiajing directed Xia to prepare a program for the promotion of six palace ladies to higher honors, and four recently selected virgins to concubine rank. Of course, Xia complied. [93]

On October 20, the ruler's second son was born. Xia prepared a nine-step program for making the public announcements. But there were some recent adverse omens, and Jiajing demanded a brief postponement. Three months later, Xia Yan forwarded to Jiajing a request from the Bureau of Ceremonies that, in light of the baby's survival thus far, ancient ritual be followed and a formal first haircut be administered and a personal name conferred. (Three palace ladies, a "teacher," a "caregiver," and a "protector," would do the haircut rite in the ancestral temple, preserving the shorn hair there.) But Jiajing decided to postpone that, too. He ignored a request to install the baby as heir apparent when he turned six months of age. A bit later, Jiajing asked Xia Yan to gather high-level officials and discuss the detailed procedures for installing the baby as heir apparent. Xia did so, but Jiajing failed to act on it. And he ignored a follow-up prompting from Xia, sometime during the year 1538.[94] It is not clear why Jiajing declined to satisfy what Xia Yan said were the fond hopes of the realm.

It was also among Xia Yan's obligations to take part in Jiajing's excursions out to the Ming tombs, some thirty miles northwest of Beijing. The ruler's frequent processions to the new altars in Beijing's suburbs were elaborate and demanding, as described in the previous chapter. The trips to the tombs were even more so. These trips began in 1536. Xia was closely involved in all the preliminary arrangements, and he accompanied the tour itself.

The ruler called Xia personally to the Wenhua Palace and told him that he intended to visit the necropolis, that he had already sent functionaries to the seven imperial tombs out there to inform the dead of his imminent arrival, and that he was especially concerned to confirm his line of descent at the burial site of the Xuande emperor, his great-great-grandfather. He also told Xia he was bringing his mother, as well as his empress and his palace consorts. They would leave Beijing six days hence, on April 11. They would rest a day near the tombs, do rites on April 14 and 15, pay respects at Xuande's tomb on April 16, and then return to Beijing. Officials were to be sent to Nanjing and Anlu to announce the trip to the spirits of Ming Taizu and his own father. Xia drew up a long program. It was approved.[95]

When the trip was over, Jiajing ordered Xia to assist with the issuing of rewards, the repair of dilapidated tombs, the addition of new facilities, and the siting and construction of a future tomb for Jiajing.[96]

* * *

On January 23, 1536, Xia Yan was at last made a grand secretary. It may have been something of a respite from his work as rites minister. His voluminous file of memorials comes to an end. Save for poems and thank-you notes, nothing like Zhang Fujing's confidential correspondence with the emperor survives. Xia was awarded a seal for such messages in 1534, but what he may have written under that seal is not known. Xia had hoped to save such correspondence as heirlooms, but 405 letters plus the seal were confiscated by Jiajing in 1539, though later returned. They may have been confiscated again when Xia was executed in 1548.[97] On the trip to the Ming tombs, he thanked Jiajing for gifts: four bolts of embroidered silk, a decorated belt, and other rich objects on April 9; fifty taels silver and four gifts of hemp and plain silk, delivered together with an oral message by way of a eunuch while viewing the Nine Dragons Pool on April 10; forty taels silver, two gifts of hemp and plain silk, and a thousand *guan* paper cash on April 17. More gifts followed right after the return to Beijing.[98] But none of these notes and poems would appear to have been secret. So the evidentiary basis for Xia's career in the Grand Secretariat may be missing a good deal of material. We'll have to make do with what we have.

What was Xia Yan like at this juncture? Descriptions of him are few. The *Ming shi* notes that he was intelligent and an excellent writer, given to candor and outspokenness; in appearance open faced, with a fine beard, clear voiced, with no trace of a Jiangxi accent, so Jiajing always paid close heed whenever he lectured at the Confucian seminars.[99]

He entered a depleted Grand Secretariat. Zhang Fujing was dismissed for the last time in 1535. (He was the last of Jiajing's allies in the Great Rites affair of 1524.) Fei Hong died later the same year. That left the low-key Li Shi as the sole remaining grand secretary. When Xia Yan came aboard, Li became chief grand secretary.

Xia Yan's career in the Grand Secretariat cannot be judged a success. It divides, however, into four phases, punctuated by his dismissals. The first phase took up the years 1537 to 1539. Much happened in that short stretch of time.

There was the showdown on the Annam frontier. A large army was slowly assembled, in the face of strong objections, because the northern frontier was being heavily raided at the same time. Xia Yan was hawkish on the issue. His co-provincial and resentful protégé Yan Song, who succeeded Xia as minister of rites, 1537–1542, championed a softer line, and the matter lay unresolved until 1539, when Xia's hard line won out. The Ming army was poised for invasion. Xia drafted the ultimatum. On March 4, news of Mac Dang-dung's capitulation reached Beijing.[100] (There is more to the Annam story; see the next chapter.)

Jiajing made five more excursions out to the Ming tombs. On one of them, while the party was camped at Shahe, fire from Xia's kitchen spread to the tents of Marquis Guo Xun and Chief Grand Secretary Li Shi, burning them down and destroying six memorials from court officials waiting to be read and acted upon. Xia, Guo, and Li, in a joint statement, blamed themselves for the fire. Jiajing was displeased that Xia, as the main culprit, didn't submit a separate statement. Xia begged for mercy. Jiajing forgave him.[101] But this was one more irritant in an accumulating record of them that would bode ill for Xia in the future.

The longest excursion Jiajing ever took as emperor was his 1539 journey back to his childhood home in Anlu, since renamed Chengtianfu. Xia Yan went along as chief grand secretary, Li Shi having died a few months previously. The details of this trip are best left to the following chapter on Yan Song, who as minister of rites was closely involved in its planning and also accompanied it. Suffice it here to say that the three high paladins, Xia, Yan Song, and Duke Guo Xun, all recent recipients of the highest favors, jostled irritably among themselves, envious and spiteful, and eager for even more favor, with Xia and Yan at odds over small details of decorum and ritual procedure. Recently awarded the unprecedented honor of being named a "Supreme Pillar of State," a designation never before given to a Ming civil official, Xia reportedly got a bit arrogant and inattentive to Jiajing's wants, often being away partying with friends rather than on call. In his absence, the ruler would summon Guo Xun, who would use the opportunity to bad-mouth Xia.[102] Nonetheless, while Xia dutifully contributed commemorative poems in response to Jiajing's invitation, his meticulous listing of thank-you notes for every gift Jiajing ever gave him shows a conspicuous gap for the whole year 1539. Reportedly Duke Guo Xun outdid him in receiving gifts from Jiajing.[103]

The imperial party returned to Beijing on May 2. On May 14, Jiajing decreed another trip out to the Ming tombs. Reportedly, Guo Xun and Yan Song's complaints about Xia were deepening the ruler's suspicions about him. Yan Song, two years older than Xia, resented being treated as a protégé (*menke*) of his. At all events, while out at the necropolis, the Grand Secretariat failed to draft rescripts for the memorials sent up by officials back in

Beijing. Jiajing exploded in rage. Xia apologized, but to no avail. Jiajing blistered his ears:

> Xia Yan was just a low-ranking official when I ordered Zhang Fujing to gather opinions about the suburban rituals, [in connection with which] Xia was rapidly promoted in position. He was totally dependent on the throne's favor and should have spared no effort in loyal service to his ruler. But he's been repeatedly dilatory and disrespectful. Just now, most of his recommendations for officials to attend upon the heir apparent have turned out to be men unqualified. He doesn't follow regulations in his secret communications. He just uses a paper seal to suit his own convenience. He doesn't use the [silver] seal with the inscription that I gave him. He needs to hand back to me all the messages I've written him through the years. We know how many there are, so he can't criminally hide them. He needs to introspect and change his ways before he can serve [further]. [104]

Xia wrote an immediate apology. He said he'd been sick during the trip to Chengtian. He admitted fault for the delay in submitting draft rescripts and for not using the silver seal. He wept in gratitude at the chance the ruler was giving him to retrospect and reform. But did he have to surrender the seal and all the emperor's handwritten messages? He'd gathered all those messages into a special file that he wanted to leave to his posterity back home. Perhaps the ruler could come up with a different punishment? [105]

Jiajing would have none of it. "He's been ordered to surrender them," said the ruler. "If in a few days he doesn't hand them over, it means he's ruined or lost them. The Ministry of Rites will collect and hand them in. In light of the fact that I remember his contributions to the suburban rites discussion, I [merely] rescind his honorific titles and order him to retire as a minister and academician." [106] So Xia gathered up the silver seal and some four hundred messages dating from 1530 to 1539 into twelve containers and surrendered them, as ordered, on May 22. He also handed back all the poems and songs written by Jiajing, plus those written by high officials in response, together with their prefaces and annotations. [107]

This turned out to be a very short-lived dismissal. On May 27, Jiajing restored him to his post as chief grand secretary. He'd changed his mind! Maybe his intent all along was just to send Xia a warning. "Grand Secretary Xia Yan was originally my choice for assisting with the suburban rites, and his knowledge being true and correct, his contribution was huge," explained Jiajing to the Ministry of Personnel. "Zhang Fujing laid out the correct ideas that put right the statuses of my father and myself, while Xia Yan bravely aided my restoration of the original Ming rituals." He went on to say that his recent faults did not outweigh this record, and that his assistance was still needed. So he brought him back.

Xia had given his farewell and was about to return home to Jiangxi Province when a eunuch delivered the ruler's recall notice to him. Xia's written reply of thanks—which said he'd been a tall-standing target of hatreds (probably referring to Guo Xun), and which was also blemished by a number of erasures and emendations—annoyed Jiajing, but he let him return anyway. The letters and seal he'd surrendered were given back to him on July 13, 1540. [108]

* * *

Xia Yan's second stint as chief grand secretary lasted two years, from May 27, 1539, to September 16, 1541. These years were fairly quiet, so the ongoing rivalry at the top level of Ming government took up much of Xia's time and attention. Despite the scolding Jiajing had given him, he gave every indication that life as chief grand secretary bored him. He continued to apologize when the ruler mentioned his intermittent derelictions. He fended off the hostile maneuvers of his bête noire, Duke Guo Xun. Perhaps his thickest tie to Jiajing was his ability to write pleasing poems and Daoist prayers, all in response to Jiajing's prompts. These productions seem now like mindless effusions; perhaps they seemed so to Xia Yan as well. [109]

But Xia provides an interesting comment on one such offering. During the night of July 27, 1539, a request came from Jiajing to Xia to write five sacrificial prayers for eunuchs to recite to the soul of Shao Yuanjie, the ruler's house chaplain of Daoism, who had died a few months earlier. Xia was staying in his private quarters in the Forbidden City. It was time for one of the seasonal sacrifices to start, so Xia got into the proper robe and carried the required ancestral tablets out to the Taimiao. The time was four drums (around 1–3 a.m.). When he arrived at the door to the Taimiao, no one else was there, so he sat on the doorstep and composed the five pieces under a lantern. That took less than three *ke* of the water clock (maybe forty-two minutes). These he rushed to West Park, where Jiajing was, just as the sun was coming up. Two Secretariat drafters delivered them to the Wuyi Dian office. Jiajing had been in the Renshou Palace, up all night, asking about Xia's five pieces. Usually it took Xia two or three hours to finish such an assignment. Never before had he done it so fast! This he wanted his descendants to know.[110]

So Xia wasn't always dilatory. He could work at prodigious speed, and here he congratulated himself for his prowess. He sounded like a tired man with a burst or two of energy still left. His dismissal in September 1541 was brought on by a fit of boredom and a sense of uselessness; his plea to resign because of Guo Xun's increasing hostility was denied, but later his written reply to Jiajing's query about what robe the heir apparent should wear for the funeral of the Dowager Empress Zhang was riddled with miswritten characters. Such disrespect! So an angry Jiajing ordered him to step down.[111]

Jiajing was shifting gears. Toward the end of 1539 he moved his main office from the Wenhua Palace in the Forbidden City out to the Wuyi Dian in West Park. An inner circle of close advisors had their offices there as well, on call at any time day or night. They were Duke Guo Xun, Duke Zhu Xizhong, Marquis Cui Yuan, Commandant-Escort Wu Jinghe, Grand Secretaries Xia Yan and Chai Luan, and Minister of Rites Yan Song.[112] That was a combustible mix at the highest level. Jiajing professed an inability to understand why Guo Xun and Xia Yan hated each other so. Right after Xia Yan's dismissal, censors sensed the ruler's preference for Xia and impeached Guo for power seeking and gross corruption. A torrent of accusations against the duke soon followed. Cui Yuan denounced him. An angry Jiajing ordered Guo's arrest and placement in the Decree Prison for interrogation (but recalling Guo's help in the Great Rites battle, he said not to use torture on him). Guo lingered in prison and died there not long after. Xia Yan was called back as chief grand secretary on November 2, 1541.[113]

This time Xia was on the job but half a year. On August 11, 1542, following a bad omen (a solar eclipse), Xia's plea to resign was accepted. The ruler suspected Xia of orchestrating the censorial attacks on Guo Xun. Worse, he was no longer coming to his Grand Secretariat office in the Forbidden City but was doing even his important work at his private home, and he was failing to take the ruler's demands seriously. Jiajing called Xia into West Park. Eight days later, he granted Xia's piteous request to resign.[114]

Xia was gone for about three years. Jiajing ordered him to come back on October 22, 1545, and on January 21, 1546, his arrival in Beijing was announced. Deaths and dismissals had left Yan Song the sole remaining grand secretary. Jiajing thought an effective counterweight to him was needed, and Xia had reminded Jiajing of his existence by sending him annual birthday congratulations. Xia was good at eliciting pity and also at writing those infamous Daoist prayers of which Jiajing was in constant need. So for those and other reasons, Jiajing wanted him back. He was made chief grand secretary again, with Yan Song his unwilling subordinate. Xia did not take Yan into his confidence or consult him. So things seethed until the fateful year 1548.

What brought Xia to ruin was the intensification of Lu raiding led by Altan Khan and others along Ming China's northern frontier. Altan's repeated requests for trading opportunities were denied, leading him, or rather forcing him, to raid and so keep his people, Chinese defectors and refugees among them, fed. The question before Jiajing and his government was how best to respond to this. It was not just a technical question. It involved dirty political infighting at the highest levels. And in that affray, Xia lost his life. He was publicly executed on Jiajing's orders on October 31, 1548. Here I should like to focus on the awful politics that led to this tragedy.

We can begin with the geographical centerpiece of the story, the Ordos region, or Hetao (Yellow River Sleeve), inside and around the great loop the Yellow River makes around Shaanxi Province, dipping due south and then east to the Yellow Sea. The territory is about half the size of modern Spain. It was being used by Altan Khan and other leaders as a base for their raids on China. A Ming capture, or rather recapture, of the region would surely solve the raiding problem. That was the opinion of one Zeng Xian (1499–1548).

Zeng and Xia Yan shared some things in common. Both were civil degree winners from families registered as military. More important, both showed by their career records that they believed bureaucratic activism, getting things done, developing and fulfilling plans, and achieving goals was the right way to advance China's well-being. Both adopted the slogan *zhongxing* (midcourse revival) that had been Yang Tinghe's, but to which the young Jiajing had given only lukewarm endorsement. Xia's deep commitment to Jiajing's ritual-rebuilding program was his way of fulfilling the meaning of that slogan in a very visible way. Before that, he had spent ten years, 1520–1530, in the Office of Scrutiny for War, so military issues were very familiar to him. Zeng focused his energies on China's military inadequacies; as Xia had done, he helped handle a major mutiny (in Liaodong, in 1535) and in 1542 built a massive defense work around the strategic Grand Canal town of Linqing. Then, transferred to Shanxi, by early 1546 he rose in rank to vice minister of war and Shanxi supreme commander, and in that capacity he developed an elaborate plan for the reconquest and occupation by Ming

China of the whole Ordos region. This plan he submitted to the court in January 1548.[115]

By 1548, Jiajing's ritual rebuilding program was drawing to a successful conclusion, with all the temples, altars, and shrines built as he wanted, and all the ritual programs retooled and revised in the light of ancient precedent. So why not continue China's revival in other dimensions? Zeng explicitly linked the recovery of the Ordos to the "midcourse revival." He argued that the Ordos had once been China's, until the Yongle emperor's general pullback of forward defense positions left the Ordos vacant, and so it remained, left to grassland and forest, teeming with wildlife, until 1499, when the Lu, having crossed the Yellow River on rafts and finding it undefended, began nomadizing there and using the region as a staging area for their endless raids on China. Recovering the Ordos would be a huge achievement in the revival program overall. Zeng's argument was compelling, and Jiajing was open minded about it at first.

Zeng's proposal exists now in a book-length portfolio containing, in chronological order, documents about the whole history of the planning: debates among the officials, interim proposals, Ministry of War reactions, and Jiajing's directives. Zeng buttressed his own argument with fascinating and detailed data. Almost every exigency was covered, from the size, recruitment, outfitting, and supply of the main forces to the study of the terrain they would encounter, the likely resistance they would meet, and how to arrange for the postwar occupation.

The argument is persuasive, seductive even. The detail is astounding, as are the many numerical calculations. For instance, just to take the question of firearms, one of the discussants Zeng cites said (and here I paraphrase) that China's gunpowder weapons were one of her advantages, but if they're poorly made, or if powder and ammunition are short, then it's no different from not having such weapons at all. In the recent past, the Shaanxi defenders have had *folangji* ("Frankish guns," i.e., culverins, Portuguese breech-loading cannon), but only forty or fifty of them per camp, not well made, and the gunners were untrained, so only one or two guns were functional. And the supply of powder and lead ammunition was low, so in battle the guns were loud, but not one raider ever got killed by them. After three shots, the guns overheat, and so the defenders have had to use bow and arrow instead. But now we have on hand one hundred thousand well-made guns, and in the early spring (of 1546) we entered the Ordos and shot countless Lu, who panicked and fled. That's how China's advantage should be used. (And the discussant went on to enumerate and quantify how many guns of each type were required, and how much lead, saltpeter, and sulfur had to be collected, and from what sources.) All this Jiajing agreed to, for the time being.[116]

But just as ritual renewal had excited violent internal debate, so too did the plan to invade the Ordos. Was this a case of containment versus rollback, as in the US strategic debates of the early Cold War era? Partly it was. There was a difference of opinion along these lines, but it never developed into a full-blown partisan struggle, because Jiajing single-handedly preempted the debate, wrong-footing both his grand secretaries and radiating fear and trembling through the ranks of all the top Beijing bureaucrats. Ming China was, after all, not a democracy. It was an autocracy, ruled by an emperor who was, by now, at age forty, determined to exercise his legitimate and final decision-making authority.

It's very hard to judge at this distance in time and place whether Zeng Xian's optimistic and energetic plan was truly workable, or whether it was an Operation Barbarossa in embryo, well beyond China's resources and capabilities, despite all the compelling and attractive detail in it.

Xia Yan loved the plan. And given his wide experience and his position as China's top bureaucrat, he was confident that Jiajing trusted him enough to accept his endorsement of it. Word spread among the officials that Jiajing was indeed in favor of it. Officials generally were not prepared to do anything but fall in line with what they at first understood to be Jiajing's preference. However, the emperor, never a committed war hawk, harbored some doubts, never mind his preliminary approvals. Still, he granted two hundred thousand taels silver to Zeng so he could begin rebuilding the badly dilapidated Great Wall as it stretched for some five hundred miles along the Ordos frontier of Shaanxi.[117] He liked a set of maps and illustrations Zeng sent him.[118] He circulated early versions of Zeng's plan among all the top officials for their comments and suggestions. In the late spring of 1547, he rewarded Zeng along with generals Li Zhen and Han Qin for their counter-raid on a Lu encampment in the Ordos.[119] Chief Grand Secretary Xia Yan, his career all along centered on activism, was an enthusiast for Zeng's plan, and he probably drafted Jiajing's interim rescripts relating to it.

There were only a few voices out in the field and in Beijing that opposed Xia Yan and his plan. Qiu Luan's was one. A scion of a distinguished military family, he grew up in Beijing in a modest home on Suzhou *hutong* (alley), northeast of the Chongwen Gate, in the southeast corner of the Imperial City.[120] In 1522 he inherited the title Marquis of Xianning. He was educated. Minister of War Peng Ze gave him the polite name Boxiang and the nameplate Zhizhai for his studio, and so young Qiu got along smoothly in high civil official circles. In 1524, he sided with Marquis Guo Xun in the Great Rites demonstration and crackdown. Though he soon became something of a contrarian, Jiajing was aware of him. In 1539, he was a top commander in the security detail protecting Jiajing on his trip to Anlu; and in 1540–1541, he was part of the war mobilization against Annam. In 1544, he was posted to Gansu as regional commander, and there he soon got into a major run-in with Zeng Xian.[121]

Qiu and a colleague argued that their troops were too few to join one of Zeng's planned raids into the Ordos. Zeng impeached him for insubordination, and on July 7, 1547, Jiajing fined him six months' salary. That didn't satisfy Zeng. He impeached him again. On January 24, 1548, Jiajing ordered Qiu Luan's arrest and imprisonment in Beijing for cruelty and greed, as well as insubordination.[122] So as late as that date, Jiajing was still tilting toward Zeng Xian and his invasion plan.

Another dissenting voice from the field was that of Weng Wanda (1498–1552), supreme commander at Xuan-Da, the frontier bases adjoining Zeng Xian's on the east (in the early months of 1547, Jiajing sent Weng six hundred thousand taels for building some three hundred miles of walls in the Xuan-Da section of the frontier). Weng was a strong advocate of granting tributary status and trading privileges to Altan Khan as the best way to stop his raiding. Realistic opinion in China had it that raiding was a default Mongol policy. Among other things, Altan wanted access to China's farming tools so he could create agricultural settlements. Weng also offered a devastating critique of Zeng's plan. He found fatal flaws in it: China's ignorance of the microgeography, the exhaustion of horses after three days of campaigning, too heavy reliance on untrustworthy guides, and insurmountable supply problems. We're good at defense, said Weng; they're good at attack. Our firearms are for defense, not for field operations. We can raid their nests, but then we haven't the ability to stay and hold the territory. And so on. But Jiajing was still backing Zeng and he did not trust the Lu, so he issued a firm negative to Weng's plea to negotiate tributary relations. He ignored Weng's critique of Zeng's plan.[123]

* * *

Then came the bolt from the blue. Everyone was caught off guard. Barely a month after imprisoning Qiu Luan at Zeng Xian's behest, Jiajing canceled the great Ordos campaign, ordered Zeng Xian's arrest, and for the fourth and last time forced Xia Yan to resign. What on earth happened?

What happened was that Jiajing cast the final and deciding vote on China's national security. A statement sent up from prison by Qiu Luan played a big part in Jiajing's decision. Qiu painted a sad and dark picture of the situation on the northwest frontier. He claimed Zeng Xian hid the facts about a devastating Lu raid that penetrated a hundred miles south into Shaanxi as far as Qingyang, leaving thousands of corpses scattered everywhere. He said this took place in July and August 1546. Zeng Xian extorted 150 taels silver from every military officer, one tael from a thousand different squad leaders, a half tael from each corporal, and a tenth tael from each common soldier. This came to several tens of thousands of taels, which he entrusted to his son, the Imperial University student Zeng Chun, to carry to Beijing and there deliver it to his in-law Su Gang to parcel out as hush money so that no officials would be sent out to investigate the facts of the Lu incursion. On his own authority, Zeng conducted counterraids into the Ordos. One such, in February and March 1547, ended in an utter rout, with the Lu killing three thousand Ming troops and carrying off an equal number of Ming horses. This too had to be covered up, Qiu alleged, and so another silver assessment was laid, and Zeng's son made another payoff trip to Beijing. It was about this time that Zeng impeached Qiu Luan for refusing to take part in any more of his ill-designed counterraids. Zeng cruelly suppressed troop protests. To ensure that the impeachment of Qiu succeeded, Zeng sent one or more of his housemen with ten horses and one thousand taels silver to Su Gang. Qiu said recovery of the Ordos was a good idea, if well prepared. But Zeng's resources are too thin, and his entourage is untalented; his plans leak, his troops are disaffected, and the people of Shaanxi and Shanxi are suffering grievously from his ever-rising demands on them. If this goes on, Qiu concluded, there will be a mass flight from all of China's western regions.[124]

Jiajing was shocked. This was not at all the picture Zeng Xian and Xia Yan had been giving him. Immediately he ordered investigators to go out and check the accuracy of Qiu's statement. Arrest orders went out for Zeng Chun and Su Gang.

Zeng Chun was not in Beijing. The police found and arrested Su Gang and five housemen and servants. Embroidered-Uniform Guards commander Lu Bing sent up a report of their statements, which were probably made under duress. From June 15 to October 27, 1547, Zeng Chun allegedly stayed with three different families outside the Zhengyang Gate (just south of the Imperial City). On the latter date, Zeng Chun and three servants pawned their four riding horses with one of those families for thirty-four taels silver. Then they left two boxes (containing the silver?) with another family for safekeeping. Meanwhile Zeng Chun and a schoolmate were often to be found staying over and drinking at the home of "Bracelet" Li (Li Chuan'er), a female musician connected to the Music Office. Zeng bought her a sable coat and eight gold rings, cost not stated. Tracing interpersonal connections led the police to one Su Deng, a houseman of Su Gang's. Su Deng stated that Zeng Xian twice ordered his son, Zeng Chun, and a houseman to deliver gifts of silver on his behalf to Su Gang. Su Deng didn't know how much silver was involved. Zeng Chun's schoolmate stated that Zeng Chun left Beijing for Shaanxi on January 31, 1548.[125]

Police were sent out to arrest and fetch Zeng Chun. Meanwhile, Qi Yu, chief supervising secretary of the Office of Scrutiny for War, submitted a fierce indictment of Zeng Xian, now also under arrest, in an atmosphere he described as one of general rejoicing that the Ordos campaign was canceled. Jiajing was not pleased that Qi Yu had failed to impeach Zeng Xian earlier on. He demoted him two ranks and listed him for transfer to some post far away from Beijing.[126]

The Ministry of War chimed in. Following court discussions with a wide group of officials, it labeled Zeng Chun "an ignorant small man who defies the law when he brings silver to Beijing and distributes bribes on his father's behalf." Su Gang was a "dangerous villain who defies the law when he dares use his in-law relationship to gain power, makes connections to high frontier officials, and helps advance the plan to recover the Ordos by trafficking bribes to opportunistic officials." And on and on. For the first time, Xia Yan's name came up. The ministry accused him of treason: it said he took some of Zeng Xian's silver as payment for hiding Zeng's failures and backing his plan. And Su Gang? He was none other than Xia Yan's father-in-law!

Jiajing's reaction was to order that Su Gang be forced to repay all the silver, followed by banishment to perpetual military exile in a malarial area. Xia Yan, on the way home after his dismissal, he ordered to be arrested immediately and brought back to Beijing for interrogation.[127]

What had happened here? Originally Xia Yan, with enthusiasm, and Jiajing, tentatively, had favored Zeng Xian and encouraged his ongoing plans to recover the Ordos. On January 10, 1548, Jiajing had the Directorate of Ceremonial print up a hundred form sheets for the Ministry of War to distribute to all the top officials for their reactions to his edict, in which the emperor confessed ignorance of the facts on the ground, feared a possible bloodbath, and, in effect, asked for reassurance. The collective reply was slow in coming, but when it did, it was cautiously positive, in tune with the prevailing winds from on high.[128] Then came Qiu Luan's prison statement and the emperor's abrupt policy shift. However, Qiu's original indictment of Zeng Xian, sent from Gansu on January 30, predated Jiajing's edict of February 9, yet, as Xia Yan pointed out, it incorporated some of the very same language later used in the edict and in a separate memorial of Yan Song's.[129] It appeared Qiu Luan was not acting on his own here but was in fact taking someone's directions.

Angry that he'd been kept in the dark about the situation in Shaanxi, Jiajing thought he'd been lied to, that he'd been a victim of a strategy of "pressuring the ruler to intimidate the crowd" (*qiangjun xiezhong*), so he demanded that Zeng Xian be put to death. A reluctant Ministry of Justice said that it could not find an applicable statute in the Ming Code under which Zeng might legitimately be put to death for his recovery plans. Jiajing demanded that they try harder. Bribing a grand secretary would clinch the matter. And so on that charge, Zeng Xian was publicly executed on April 25, 1548. Alleged were two deliveries from Zeng Xian in Shaanxi to Beijing: first ten thousand taels handed through various intermediaries to Su Gang, who kept eight thousand and handed two thousand to Xia; then later five thousand taels reached Su Gang, who handed one thousand to Xia. On May 5, Qiu Luan was cleared and released from prison.[130]

Xia Yan, reduced to commoner status, departed Beijing for his home in Jiangxi on March 4, 1548. He got as far as Tianjin, when on March 13 the police caught up with him and escorted him in shackles back to Beijing, where on May 9 he was placed in the infamous Decree Prison.[131] His arrest hit Xia in the pit of his stomach. He fell out of the cart he was riding in. "White willow, white willow," someone reported he wailed to a roadside tree. "You know I'll never come this way again." His arrest meant almost certain death.

In prison, or perhaps during the days prior to his arrival, Xia wrote up two very long, detailed, and plaintive cries for the emperor's understanding, pity, and forgiveness. He admitted he was wrong in favoring Zeng Xian's plan, but he favored it out of a belief in it, not because he was bribed. His father-in-law Su Gang was, he said, a "small man of the mountains and wilds, who is ignorant of worldly affairs; when Yan Song earlier on was minister of rites, he befriended Su Gang, called him in day and night to drink and talk, and had him act as a spy and participate in bribe trafficking. I despised Su Gang for his lack of character and refused even to look at him."[132] Xia doubted the possibility that there could have been a ten-thousand-tael silver shipment from Shaanxi to Beijing. One horse, he said, can carry only five hundred or six hundred taels, so the required caravan plus an armed escort of a hundred or more horsemen would have had to pass through some thirty or forty post stations; and such a caravan, if it ever existed, would have been seen by thousands of people. But was it? And where would all this silver have come from? If it originated with an issue authorized by Jiajing, then it ended up in local government treasuries. Zeng Xian would not have had direct access to it, and how, if his troops needed it, could he devise an invasion plan and at the same time impoverish and starve the very troops who were supposed to carry it out? Plus the alleged distribution of the silver bribe, twenty thousand taels to me only, makes no sense. Surely, he said, my in-laws, and other officials down to the lowliest clerks, must have been paid off as well.

Indeed, Xia went on to describe at great length, naming names, places, and dates, an elaborate network of corruption and a tissue of lies developed by Grand Secretary Yan Song and his scoundrel son Yan Shifan for the explicit purpose of destroying him, Xia Yan, and removing him forever as rival for Jiajing's favor.[133]

The legal authorities tried to persuade Jiajing that because of Xia Yan's former eminence as chief grand secretary, the Ming Code should be followed, which stipulated lighter penalties, short of death, for meritorious persons of status who had done wrong.[134]

Jiajing was immune to that plea. "You all are using my powers to offer protection [to Xia Yan] for partisan reasons," he thundered.

> I hired the traitor Xia Yan to be a close advisor. But what did he regard me as? When Zeng first sent up his plan, he pressured me behind the scenes. I never issued any [final] edict about it, yet he dared say that a secret edict favored it. This was something that would set in motion a disaster for the common people. But when I asked him about it, he failed to admit guilt. So I just made him retire. But then he spoke resentful language, saying he was dismissed because he wouldn't wear the scented sash [of Daoist ritual], and because he violated the rules by riding a sedan in West Park. No, he was rejected because for his own benefit he made bad plans on the court's behalf. Is this how a minister

shows decorum? His alibi [about bribery] is that for two months he was on duty in West Park and so could not have seen Su Gang.

Arguments between Jiajing and the legal authorities went back and forth until the ruler's imposition of fines and punishments on the dissenters worked its magic and public execution at the autumn assizes was agreed to. On November 1, 1548, Xia was put to death. [135]

* * *

Xia's eleven years of service, on and off, in the Grand Secretariat were not successful. He did his best work during the twenty years before. He was, in the context of his time, a technocrat. He lacked the psychological awareness and the social skills that would have allowed him to thrive as a politician. As a technocrat, however, his achievements were substantial, perhaps even phenomenal, and they ranged over many different and demanding spheres of Ming governance. He helped greatly in abolishing the excrescences of the Zhengde years—the privileged estates and the bloated military and other rosters. He sorted out and put to rights a messy situation in Blue Sheep Mountain. He handled adeptly the highly complex machinery of the official recruitment system. He understood well Ming China's place in the world as the great power of its time and effectively oversaw its relations with almost every country with which China had contact. He is best known for his well-argued scholarly contributions and on-site architectural planning for Jiajing's revival of ancient ritual—icing on the cake, as it were, for a nationwide preoccupation with reforming and rectifying China's ritual heritage across the board. [136] He was an excellent manager.

But the Grand Secretariat was not a good place for a pure technocrat-manager. It called for political skills. The chief grand secretary needed to be able to mollify on a personal level a highly intelligent but volatile power figure of an emperor. Zhang Fujing had done that well while Jiajing was very young. At the same time, a chief grand secretary needed to develop working relationships with the bureaucratic mandarins in charge of the top ministries and agencies of the outer court. Zhang Fujing did so, until arguments soured and attrition eroded his ties with them, and he had to step down. Xia Yan was not a factionalist. He won enough respect as a technocrat not to be obliged to cultivate an avid following among the bureaucrats in order to get where he wanted to go. And while his know-how and hard work impressed Jiajing, he was fortunate to survive as long as he did in the Grand Secretariat. He survived partly because of his aptitude for writing the Daoist prayers and impromptu poems the emperor constantly demanded from the officials who were in his close entourage. (It was probably his way of monitoring them for loyalty.) Those demands were mind numbing and boring to fulfill, and Xia Yan clearly hated them. And he displeased Jiajing in other ways—by his inattentiveness and a submerged personal dislike and contempt for the ruler that Jiajing surely sensed.

It was Jiajing, acting on his own, who demanded the executions of Zeng Xian and Xia Yan. His reputation suffered for it, in his own time and later. Many people thought the executions wholly unjust. Not long after Jiajing died in 1567, both Zeng and Xia were fully rehabilitated, their offices and good names posthumously restored to them.

And how was Xia Yan, in his role as grand secretary, regarded by later Ming commentators? Zhi Dalun (*jinshi* 1574) regretted the failure of Xia and Zeng to recover the Ordos, deplored their lack of political preparation, questioned their overreliance on Jiajing's favor, and concluded that the whole fiasco inflicted heavy long-term damage on China's military morale.

He Qiaoyuan (1558–1632) noted that Xia early on made himself known for his talent, and at the same time refused to truckle to the high and mighty. He and Yan Song, who was imposing and cultured, were certainly both gentlemen, yet they both came to ruin in the end. This all stemmed from their making a private possession of the ruler's favor. Xia's arrogance evolved into heedlessness. Yan's humility led in the end to disloyalty. These attitudes provoked the ruler's anger.

Wang Shizhen (1526–1590), at the end of his long biography of Xia, said only that the realm regretted his execution because he was the last obstacle to the rise to predominance of the corrupt Yan Song.

Tan Qian (1594–1658) remarked, judiciously, that Xia's talent alone accounts for his eminence. It was his intolerance and pride that handicapped him. He yearned for some world-transforming merit; his resolve was clear in all the dust and fog. Had Zeng Xian's expedition actually taken place and led to his defeat, would Xia have been able to save himself? It wasn't a military defeat that killed Xia; it was slander. It was Yan Song, not a failed campaign, that administered the lethal poison. The evil of penal excess ensnared the topmost official of all. This was a national misfortune, but it did allow Xia to escape blame for a military fiasco. Never before in history was an official of prime ministerial rank ever executed publicly. It was like fulfilling the omen of an exploding star. [137]

The Ming Veritable Records (*Ming shilu*) of the Jiajing reign, published in 1577, put it well. They say that Xia Yan was fearless, highly talented, opinionated, and argumentative. Jiajing got to know him when he was a supervising secretary. He especially won favor in connection with the suburban rites. The emperor was intelligent and probing and didn't like officials who simply chimed in. Xia Yan understood that. Xia was one of the few who dared defy Zhang Fujing. So Jiajing thought him a nonpartisan, treated him well, and appointed him to the highest post. But while Xia's talent was great, his wisdom was not. He used the ruler's favor to act as he liked and paid no attention to Jiajing's subtle objections, or even to his scolding. While the realm held Yan Song culpable for Xia's wrongful execution, it also thought Xia's own defects—his failure to study and his ignorance of the Way—were what got him killed. [138]

NOTES

1. Xia Yan, *Guizhou xiansheng zouyi* (Siku quanshu cunmu congshu, 2nd ser.), 60.549; L. C. Goodrich and Chaoying Fang, eds., *Dictionary of Ming Biography* (New York: Columbia University Press, 1976), 2.1367–1368 (biography of Wang Ch'iung) (hereafter cited as *DMB*; *MS* (any edition), ch. 199 (biography of Wang Xian); Xia Yan, *Guizhou wenji* (Siku quanshu cunmu congshu, 4th ser.), 74.575–577. Xia Yan later forgot all about his earlier indictment of Wang Xian; cf. *zouyi*, 60.554–555.

2. Xia Yan, *wenji*, 74.171–172, 586–592; also *zouyi*, 60.386–390.

3. Xia Yan, *zouyi*, 60.390–393.

4. Ibid., 60.393–397.

5. Ibid., 60.397–398.

6. Ibid., 60.398–400; also Xia Yan, *wenji*, 74.560–562.

7. Ibid., 60.400–401.

8. Xia Yan, *wenji*, 74.592–599.

9. Ibid.

10. Xia Yan, *zouyi*, 60.408–412.

11. Ibid., 60.412–413.

12. Ibid., 60.413–414.

13. Xia Yan, *wenji*, 74.172. Xia was also inspired by a dream in which he rode a horse through the sky to a triumphal entry into the capital city.

14. *MSL*, 75.2172.

15. Xia Yan, *zouyi*, 60.441–468. A later but undated memorial restated at great length Xia's criticisms of the behavior of Shanxi assistant surveillance commissioner Chen Dagang as a commander in this affair. See 60.582–585.

16. Ibid., 60.430–431.

17. Ibid., 60–431–434; Xia Yan, *wenji*, 74.602–605.

18. Xia Yan, *wenji*, 74.602–605.

19. Xia Yan, *zouyi*, 60.441.

20. Ibid., 60.469–470.

21. Xia Yan, *wenji*, 74.605–610.

22. Ibid., 74.610–616; Xia Yan, *zouyi*, 60.437–441.

23. Xia Yan, *wenji*, 74.616–620; *zouyi*, 60.434–437. Some further statements of his while he was supervising secretary in the Office of Scrutiny for War are these: *wenji*, 74.623–625, on horses; 74.620–623, on the Wokou sea raiders; *zouyi*, 60.550–551, impeaching a grand coordinator; 60.549–550, defending a prefect; 60.401–402, a case of undeserved military merit.

24. Xia Yan, *zouyi*, 60.551–552.

25. *Minguo Pingshun xianzhi*, in *Zhongguo difangzhi jicheng: Shanxi fuxian zhiji*, 42.48–49, 108–109.

26. Xia Yan, *wenji*, 74.174–175.

27. Ibid., 74.492–494.

28. *Nangong zougao* (Siku quanshu zhenben, 5th ser., 1973), vol. 109.

29. Xia Yan, *zouyi*, 60.552–554.

30. Xia Yan, *wenji*, 74.553–554. This memorial dates to sometime during 1521–1524, when Li Duo, mentioned in the memorial, was grand coordinator at Xuanfu.

31. Ibid., 74.627–629.

32. Ibid., 74.564–565.

33. Wang Yi-t'ung, *Official Relations between China and Japan, 1368–1549* (Cambridge, MA: Harvard University Press, 1953), 76–77.

34. Xia Yan, *zouyi*, 60.562–564.

35. *Nangong zougao*, 4.7b–9b.

36. Ibid., 4.24b–28a; Xia Yan, *zouyi*, 60.566–567; *wenji*, 74.568–571.

37. *Nangong zougao*, 4.28a–30b.

38. Ibid., 4.30b–36b.

39. Xia Yan, *zouyi*, 60.574–575; *DMB*, 2.1037–1038 (biography of Mansur).

40. Xia Yan, *zouyi*, 60.572–573.

41. Ibid., 60.573. No date for this is given.

42. *Nangong zougao*, 4.1a–7a. See on this John E. Herman, *Amid the Clouds and Mist: China's Colonization of Guizhou, 1200–1700* (Cambridge, MA: Harvard University Asia Center, 2007), 129–131.

43. Xia Yan, *zouyi*, 60.565–566; *Nangong zougao*, 4.20b–24b.

44. Xia Yan, *zouyi*, 60.573–574.

45. Xia Yan, *wenji*, 74.632–633. See also Richard Pearson, *Ancient Ryukyu: An Archeological Study of Island Communities* (Honolulu: University of Hawaii Press, 2013), ch. 9 and appendix 2.

46. Xia Yan, *wenji*, 74.633–634.

47. *Nangong zougao*, 5.35b–40b.

48. Ibid., 5.40b–43b; the *wenji* version is shorter (74.571).

49. Xia Yan, *zouyi*, 60.356–360.

50. Xia Yan, *wenji*, 74.625–627; a shorter version is in *zouyi*, 60.575–576.

51. The Ming and Qing examination systems have been well researched. See Ho Ping-ti, *The Ladder of Success in Imperial China: Aspects of Social Mobility, 1368–1911* (New York: Wiley, 1964); Miyazaki Ichisada, *China's Examination Hell*, trans. Conrad Schirokauer (New Haven, CT: Yale University Press, 1981); and Benjamin A. Elman, *A Cultural History of Civil Examinations in Late Imperial China* (Berkeley: University of California Press, 2000).

52. Du Lianzhe, *Mingchao guanxuan lu*, 36–37.

53. Xia Yan, *zouyi*, 60.424–425.

54. *Nangong zougao*, 1.16a–20b; Xia Yan, *zouyi*, 60.369–371.

55. *Nangong zougao*, 5.1a–2b; Xia Yan, *zouyi*, 60.374.

56. Ibid., 1.8b–13b; 60.367–369.

57. Xia Yan, *zouyi*, 60.362; *wenji*, 74.551.

58. *Nangong zougao*, 1.1a–3a, 3a–4b; Xia Yan, *zouyi*, 60.362, 362–363.

59. Xia Yan forbears to mention the massive *shengyuan* purges ordered by Jiajing's uncle, the Hongzhi emperor, in 1494 and 1504. See John W. Dardess, *A Ming Society: T'ai-ho County, Kiangsi, in the Fourteenth to Seventeenth Centuries* (Berkeley: University of California Press, 1996), 152.

60. *Nangong zougao*, 1.13b–16a; Xia Yan, *zouyi*, 60.369.

61. *Nangong zougao*, 1.20b–22a; Xia Yan, *zouyi*, 60.373; *wenji*, 74.563–564.

62. Nangong zougao, 1.22a–28a.

63. Ibid., 1.4b–8a.

64. Ibid., 1.28a–29a. The date of the memorial was February 23, 1533.

65. Xia Yan, *zouyi*, 60.375–377; *wenji*, 74.573–575.

66. Xia Yan, *zouyi*, 60.377–378.

67. Ibid., 60.378–379.

68. Ibid., 60.379–381.

69. Thus a thorny succession issue in the Shen princedom (Xia Yan, *zouyi*, 60.302–307); the Dai princedom (*Nangong zougao*, 1.39b–43a, 5.7a–9a); princely imprisonment (5.11b–14a); a misdemeanor (5.14a–16a); the Jin princedom (1.44b–49a); the Min princedom (4.56b–60a); the Qinghuai princedom (1.43a–44b); and the Qingcheng princedom (1.49a–50b). Some think "princedoms" are better called "kingdoms." See Craig Clunas, *Screen of Kings: Royal Art and Power in Ming China* (Honolulu: University of Hawaii Press, 2013).

70. Xia Yan, *zouyi*, 60.334–335.

71. Ibid., 60.335–336.

72. Ibid., 60.382–383; *Nangong zougao*, 4.53b–56a.

73. Xia Yan, *wenji*, 74.579–580.

74. Xia Yan, *zouyi*, 60.337–338.

75. Ibid., 60.338–3339.

76. Xia Xie, 4.2041–2042.

77. Xia Yan, *zouyi*, 60.577–578.

78. Ibid., 60.578–580.

79. Xia Yan, *wenji*, 74.639.

80. Xia Yan, *zouyi*, 60.580–581.

81. Ibid., 60.557–558.

82. The supposed promotion was to the position of supervisor of the Household of the Heir Apparent (Zhanshi).

83. Xia Yan, *zouyi*, 60.581–582. The editor's date for this memorial is August 14. Xia must have the right date.

84. Jiang Yonglin, trans., *The Great Ming Code: Da Ming Lü* (Seattle: University of Washington Press, 2005), xvi, 18.

85. Xia Yan, *zouyi*, 60.585.

86. Ibid., 60.585–586.

87. Ibid., 60.586–588; *MS*, ch. 196 (biography of Huo Tao).

88. Ibid., 60.588–589. Fei Hong was chief grand secretary from 1525 to 1527. He followed Yang Tinghe.

89. Xia Xie, 4.2129–2130.

90. *Nangong zougao*, 5.3a–7a, 9ab; Xia Yan, *zouyi*, 60.542–543. The announcement was also elaborately programmed; see 60.352–353.

91. Ibid., 5.22a–29a; 60.348–350.

92. Xia Yan, *zouyi*, 60.351–352. Jiajing's reply, if any, is not given.

93. Ibid., 60.354–355.

94. Ibid., 60.353–354, 360–361. The baby's mother was Luminous Concubine Wang.

95. Ibid., 60.522–525. (One item doesn't belong; p. 524, 16.10a–11b, is part of a response to a different matter altogether.)

96. Ibid., 60.522, 525–528; Xia Yan, *wenji*, 74.524–526, 578–579. On the way to the tombs, the ruler passed through Changping County, remitted two-thirds (or one-third) of its tax load, and gave cloth and grain to the elders there. He noted that Shahe County was very thinly populated and directed that its defenses be improved so as to add to Beijing's security. See Xia Xie, 4.2123–2124; *GQ*, 4.3526.

97. *GQ*, 4.3577.

98. Xia Yan, *zouyi*, 60.474ff. A total of sixty-eight thank-you notes for gifts and other tokens of esteem from the ruler, just for the fifteenth year of Jiajing (1536).

99. *MS*, ch. 196 (biography). Wang Shizhen's biography says much the same; in *GCXZL*, 1.560–568.

100. *DMB*, 2.1029–1035 (biography of Mac Dang-dung); Xia Yan, *wenji*, 74.457–458.

101. See Wang Shizhen's biography (in endnote 99).

102. Ibid.

103. The thank-you notes are in Xia Yan, *zouyi*, 60.474–519.

104. *MSL*, 81.4645. According to *MSL*, 81.4641ff., thirty-seven men were recommended, and most were rejected.

105. Ibid., 81.4645–4646.

106. Ibid., 81.4646.

107. Ibid., 81.4659.

108. Ibid., 81.4669–4670; Xia Xie, 4.2159–2160; *GQ*, 4.3593.

109. Many of these may be found in Xia's *wenji*.

110. Xia Yan, *wenji*, 74.114; *DMB*, 2.1169–1170 (biography of Shao Yuan-chieh).

111. Xia Xie, 4.2182.

112. *GQ*, 4.3587.

113. Xia Xie, 4.2182–2183.

114. Ibid., 4.2190–2191.

115. *DMB*, 2.1303–1305 (biography of Tseng Hsien). Both Xia and Zeng had been honored with living shrines (*shengci*); Xia for his work at Blue Sheep Mountain, and Zeng for handling the mutiny in Liaodong.

116. Zeng Xian, *Futao yi* (Siku quanshu cunmu congshu, 2nd ser.), 60.592–666.

117. Xia Xie, 4.2230–2231; *MSL*, 84.5924–5928.

118. Ibid., 4.2242.

119. Ibid., 4.2237.

120. Hou Renzhi, *Beijing lishi ditu ji* (Beijing, 1985), map on p. 31. *GCXZL*, 1.361, has Zhao Shichun's scathing description of Qiu Luan. Zhao knew Qiu quite well, but his coverage of Qiu's role in the Ordos controversy is minimal. Peng Ze was minister of war from 1521 to 1523, when he died.

121. *DMB*, 1.252–255 (biography of Ch'iu Luan).

122. Xia Xie, 4.2234–2235, 2237. Other opinion had it that if China's capital were in Chang'an, as it was in the Tang, then the recovery of the Ordos made some sense. Others pointed out that a permanent recovery of the Ordos would require a massive emigration of

millions of Chinese people to create the necessary farms, villages, counties, and prefectures. See *GQ*, 4.3711–3712.

123. Ibid., 4.2238–2243. There were other regional officials who opposed Zeng; see Xia Xie, 4.2231.

124. *Bingbu wen Ningxia an* (Xuanlantang congshu, reprint Taipei, 1981), 43–50.

125. Ibid., 50–53.

126. Ibid., 53–61.

127. Ibid., 61–68.

128. Ibid., 1ff.

129. Xia Yan, *wenji*, 74.645–651.

130. Xia Xie, 4.2246; *MSL*, 84.6122–6124; *Bingbu*, 83.

131. *GQ*, 4.3716, says he got as far as Danyang on the Grand Canal east of Nanjing; Xia Xie, 4.2246, says he got as far as Tongzhou. The reason for these conflicting reports isn't clear. I follow what Xia Yan himself says.

132. Xia Yan's second wife, nee Su, was said to have been a onetime courtesan and concubine of talent, allure, and formidable character. See Shen Defu, *Wanli yehuo bian*, new ed. (Beijing: Zhonghua shuju, 1980), 1.140–141.

133. Xia Yan, *wenji*, 74.645–651.

134. See Jiang Yonglin, trans., *The Great Ming Code*, 19ff.

135. *Bingbu*, 97–100.

136. See especially the contributions by David Faure and Joseph P. McDermott in Joseph P. McDermott, ed., *State and Court Ritual in China* (Cambridge: Cambridge University Press, 1999).

137. *GQ*, 4.3724; Wang Shizhen's remark in *GCXZL*, 1.568.

138. *MSL*, 85.6201–6202.

Chapter Four

Autumn

Grand Secretary Yan Song

Xia Yan had many years' grounding in a demanding variety of posts before he became a grand secretary. Yan Song's experience was narrower. He achieved his *jinshi* degree in 1505, twelve years before Xia Yan did, but then he spent eight years on home leave due to some sort of illness.[1]

As an official, nothing Yan Song did was ever ground level or hands on. What he did have, and Xia Yan lacked, was a facade of geniality and a good measure of political adroitness. Tall and slim, with a voice loud and clear, he cut an impressive figure. His ability to turn on charm and his narcissism can be seen in the oversized collection of personal endorsements, many more than was usual, attached to his collected literary works, the *Qianshan tang ji*. Ten prefaces, dating from 1515 to 1551, praise his poems and nonofficial prose items as these accumulated over the years. Twenty-three appreciations, attached to five portraits done at various stages of his career, attest to Yan Song's zestful appetite for flattery. Among his admirers were serious Confucian philosophers (Zhan Ruoshui, Lü Nan, and Ouyang De), and among the officials, Xu Jie, later a grand secretary who helped arrange his ouster. The sincerity of their flattery is open to some doubt.

Yan Song spent nearly all of his early career in rites: vice minister of rites in Beijing from 1529 to 1531, then minister of rites in Nanjing from 1532 to 1536, then the same in Beijing from 1536 to 1542, when he was appointed to the Grand Secretariat, where he remained until dismissed under a cloud in 1562. But rites, civic ritual in the narrow sense, which had so consumed the energies of Zhang Fujing, Xia Yan, and Jiajing himself, were a matter of lesser concern for Yan Song. Other things got his attention, and in what follows, my aim is to figure out what kind of person Yan Song was and to describe and assess his participatory impact, such as it may have been, during a long stretch of the Jiajing era. This is not easy to do, given the hatred he came to provoke and the posthumous condemnation (for "villainy," *jian*) that was imposed upon him. He was a complex character, corrupt certainly, but not ineffective.

Yan himself provides almost all of what little is known of his family and his youth. His story is quite peculiar in some ways. The family home was in Fenyi County in northwestern Jiangxi Province. It was not a commercial hub. The family was registered under the artisan category, but it isn't clear how that mattered, if it did (Zhang Fujing's family were registered as salt workers, Xia Yan's as military).

The Yan social status was modest at best. No forebear was an official. The family cemetery held no ancestor more remote than a great-great-grandfather. Yan Song's father, Yan Huai (1453–1495), seems to have been mainly a professional tutor to young children. At some point he organized a boarding school for them, which some locals ridiculed and others sought to break up. Why? Yan Song, typically for him, never ventured to explain why. Yan Huai married a girl from a well-off family in nearby Xinyu County. She was willing to endure penury and was supportive of her younger husband. She was born in 1447 and died in 1509. For two years she lived with her son in Beijing. Yan Song had by then won his *jinshi* degree, but he said he was too poor to give her a decent burial until many years later. [2]

Yan Song himself, born March 3, 1480, was sickly as a child. His parents took special care of him, fearing he might die. [3] His father saw that he had exceptional literary talent and did all he could to tutor him. Yan Huai died just at a time when Yan Song, age fifteen, was about to get the education intendant's certification to proceed to the provincial capital for the *juren* exams, but now mourning requirements meant he had to wait three years for the next round. The official record shows he passed his *juren* in 1498, sixteenth on the list, good but not spectacular. In 1505, he passed his metro exam as number thirty-eight, but on the final palace exam he came out number five. He'd hoped to be chosen one of the top three and was bitterly disappointed that he failed to make it. [4] Yan's classic of choice was the *Book of Odes*, which surely reflected his preference for poetry over history, rites, or philosophy.

A story, not from a friendly source, has it that the young Yan Song was miserly, shrewd in a small-minded way, and not well regarded by others. Biographer Wang Shizhen (whose father's execution in 1559 Yan Song had declined to impede) also states that at the postexam banquet for the provincial graduates in 1498, an emaciated and badly dressed Yan Song made such a poor impression that his examiner turned his face away. Years later, Yan met the examiner again, as an equal this time, but was again rebuffed. The next day, bearing gifts, Yan crawled to his door and begged to become his disciple. "I've never dared slight you," Yan supposedly said, "but you've long despised me, and I fear you'll reject me forever." "This," wrote Wang, "was how limp, narrow-minded, and excited over petty grievances he was." Fitting, perhaps, that Wang should judge his writing, prose as well as poetry, as "clear, elegant, and dignified, but also soft and devoid of depth and strength."[5]

Yan married a girl surnamed Ouyang and had a daughter by her in 1499. In 1505, Yan was made an elite trainee, a Hanlin bachelor (*shujishi*). Then around 1508 he went home to Fenyi for what turned out to be eight years of sick leave. His one son, the infamous Yan Shifan, was born in 1513. At home, Yan studied and wrote poems, mainly describing scenery, but what else he may have done while sick is not known.[6]

Then one fine day in April 1516, he declared himself cured. His ailment, whatever it was, he later said had left him weak and emaciated for years, until around age thirty, when he recovered and was hardly ever sick again. On April 26, he set forth on a thousand-mile roundabout journey from Fenyi, mostly by boat, that finally ended with his entry into Beijing on August 11. He wrote a daily travelogue of the trip. In it he paid almost exclusive attention to weather, stream levels, distances, and times of departure from one place and arrival at the next. And he carefully collected the calling cards of all the many local and regional officials that he met and ate and drank with. But it seems indicative of the kind of person he was that he showed no further interest in any of them—not their looks, nor their personalities, nor their views, nor anything that they said. He simply gathered them up like so many knickknacks in a collection. In this procedure, there probably lies a key to his successful approach to building a political machine later on in his career: Yan Song would avoid faction and factional fighting; he would take no strong stance on any issue of controversy, any matter of principle. But he was socially outgoing. He would accept gifts and bribes, and in return he would extend preferment and protection, no questions asked.[7]

The stepping-stone to the Grand Secretariat shifted early in the Jiajing era from the Hanlin Academy to the Ministry of Rites. Ambitious men had somehow to get appointed to an office in that ministry. Yan Song managed that, but how? He was not a scholar, or an ideologue, or a specialist in rites. It's not entirely clear how he managed it.

When Yan Song reentered public life in 1516, the ruler was Jiajing's cousin, the unruly young Zhengde emperor. Yan was appointed a Hanlin junior compiler. He steered clear of any involvement in the bureaucratic upheavals of the time: the protests against the ruler's frequent travels to Xuanfu on the northern frontier in 1517–1519, or the cruelly suppressed official demonstration of 1519 against Zhengde's plan to travel south to campaign against the rebel Prince of Ning.[8]

Yan self-reported on several duties he performed during Zhengde's last years. On December 4, 1517, he was called in to serve as a tutor to young palace eunuchs.[9] Early in 1518, he wrote in absorbing detail about a horrendous stampede outside the Meridian Gate, with some men trampled to death, as officials from all over the realm convened for performance evaluations. Later in the year, Zhengde made two short trips to Nanhai, south of Beijing, to watch the hunting; then he went off to Xuanfu.[10] That same year, Yan served as an associate examiner for the *jinshi* candidates, after which he wrote up a precise and detailed account, apparently for his own amusement.[11] In 1518, he was second in command of a delegation sent off in a terrific downpour to Guangxi Province to install a Ming prince there, and of this he wrote a travelogue much like the one he wrote of his trip north in 1516: where he stopped, whom he met, and so on.[12] On return, he stopped at a sacred mountain and conducted a prayer for Zhengde's safety.[13] He was, no doubt about it, a talented if unreflective writer of descriptive prose and verse.

The next years, for all the upheaval associated with Jiajing's controversial enthronement in 1521, the cleanup of corruption, the Great Rites repressions of 1524 and 1527, and so on, are something of a blank as far as Yan Song is concerned. It appears as though he kept a low profile, avoiding any partisan commitments or associations. At some point he was sent down to the Hanlin Academy in Nanjing. Then he came back to Beijing as chancellor of the Imperial University, and in that capacity, he was so impressed by a student named Zhao Wenhua that he adopted him as a son (Zhao later achieved his *jinshi* degree and became an important operative in Yan's machine).[14]

In 1528, he managed somehow to set foot on the ladder of success by an appointment as vice minister of rites. That same year, he undertook a mission south to Anlu, the site of Jiajing's father's tomb, and this time he composed a poetical log of the trip, with topographical annotations. There was an elaborate send-off in Beijing, with Jiajing himself coming to the Fengtian Gate, and a mass of court officials escorting Yan as far as the Chengtian Gate, the southern entry to the Imperial City. The purpose of the trip was to inform the shade of Jiajing's father that his posthumous name had been changed to Ruizong, in effect inserting him into the Ming imperial line.[15] Yan must certainly have been in Jiajing's favor at this time.

From 1531 to 1536, he was sent down to Nanjing as full minister of rites. It's difficult to say whether this was in effect an exile or a step in an upward trajectory.

It may have been partly an exile. In October 1531, at age twenty-four, a still vigorous Jiajing, like a grand marshal, came out of the Forbidden City riding a white horse to the Zhonghua Palace, a large structure in the southeast corner of the Imperial City. He there joined a handful of officials in extended discussions of what the best sites were for building all the new altars and temples. There were several such meetings over the next several weeks. Jiajing would appear sometimes riding a sedan chair, sometimes inside a yellow tent, and sometimes in a heated apartment in the Zhonghua Palace. Discussions also turned to the rehearsing of ritual programs and the need to make immediate appointments to high-level vacancies in the ministries. Both Xia Yan (at the time a chief supervising secretary) and Yan Song (vice minister of rites) were among the attendees. Xia Yan spoke up often, Yan Song not once.[16] That difference, as shown here, was in a way consistent with Xia Yan's aggressiveness and Yan Song's more subdued approach to things. Soon after this, Yan was sent away to Nanjing.

In any event, in 1536 Yan came up to Beijing to deliver a paean to Jiajing on his birthday, and so he happened to be on the spot to be named minister of rites in Beijing. One odd thing about this is that the reason for giving him this high post was in order to put him in charge of a very limited project—to revise the Song dynastic history, which was just one part of a major revision and reprinting of all the basic texts exam candidates were asked to study.[17] Another odd thing is that there already was a minister of rites: Xia Yan. But Xia Yan, though younger than Yan Song, was acting as Yan's sponsor. Their home counties, Guiqi and Fenyi, lay 150 miles apart in northern Jiangxi Province. About this time, Yan Song wrote a fulsome testimonial to Xia's brilliant talent and outstanding achievements in support of Jiajing's ritual reforms.[18] This friendly collusion was not destined to last, however.

On January 23, 1537, Xia Yan vacated his ministry position and became a grand secretary. From that point, Yan Song had sole charge as minister of rites. In 1542, Yan himself became a grand secretary, with concurrent charge of the ministry until May 9, 1543. For those five years, there survives a thick file of memorials Yan wrote as minister, which parallel in coverage, if not in tone or substance, the file compiled by his immediate predecessor, Xia Yan.

* * *

Perhaps at the outset, a few words might be in order describing Yan Song's increasingly comfortable living arrangements. In early 1536, while down in Nanjing, he set up a household ancestral shrine, modestly restricting the occupants to four generations only, following the prescriptions of the Cheng-Zhu orthodoxy, and as befitted someone of high official rank.[19] This seems to have been a step up, because earlier, in Beijing in 1524, Yan wrote about being in great distress. He had brought in a nephew of his wife's, a youth named Ouyang Ru, to serve as his household manager, but an epidemic that raged through Beijing carried him away, together with Yan's own younger brother and a daughter, leaving him without any household management. He had a servant rent a boat to transport the three corpses back to Fenyi for burial.[20] Then, from 1537 to 1539, he lived somewhere in the west part of Beijing, a mile or so away from the Forbidden City, which was too far, because Jiajing was in the habit of calling together the grand secretaries and rites officials two or three times a day to discuss ongoing ritual reforms, and sometimes it was midnight before the talks were adjourned. Messengers might show up at any time day or night with an urgent summons, forcing Yan to ride horseback alone in the dark, as a sedan chair was too slow. So he decided he had to move. He rented a place on Chang'an Boulevard, which lay just south of the Imperial City. He had carpenters, upholsterers, and other workers come in to refurbish the place. When he had to leave Beijing to accompany Jiajing's trip to Anlu, he left his son Yan Shifan, by now twenty-six years of age, in charge of completing the redecoration. Shifan reported a rare and lucky omen—a flock of cranes, circling about, alit for a few moments atop the house. On August 8, 1539, after a half year's work, the job was done.[21]

In later years, after Yan became a grand secretary and moved to live inside West Park, his private home, presided over by Yan Shifan, became a beehive of constant activity as party headquarters, so to speak, for Yan's great bureaucratic machine.

In 1540, flush with money he said he received over the years as gifts from Jiajing, Yan Song decided to build a new home, or estate really, for himself back in Jiangxi. His old home in Fenyi was too flood prone, he said, so he created a new one from scratch at the west wall of Yuanzhou, the prefectural capital, about twenty-five miles east. There lay a large vacant plot, which Yan extended by filling in an adjacent pond and buying out several commoners, who were, he said, very glad to sell him their homes. His son, Yan Shifan, put in charge of the construction, was under strict orders not to impose private labor service on commoners or ask local government for its help. An avenue led in to the estate. In it were living quarters, an ancestral hall, and a library with a separate alcove to shelve all the poems, edicts, and messages he'd received from Jiajing's hand. At Yan's request, the main buildings were given names by Jiajing himself. There was a pleasure garden, with rocks, trees, and another hall, this one for Yan to retire to in his old age.[22] (That he was never able to do; and not long after his death in disgrace, the whole estate was confiscated and fell to ruin.)

* * *

As minister of rites, Yan Song's work on rites specifically was heavy during the years 1538 and 1539. The main contributor to the rites was, of course, Xia Yan, now a grand secretary. Still, there was much for Yan Song to do.

For rites, 1538 was a crowded year. Let it be said that Yan Song performed dutifully. Unlike Zhang Fujing or Xia Yan, he had no plans of his own to offer. Early on, he thought the ruler's father should not be moved from his separate shrine and put in the ancestral temple along with the emperors and made an accessory recipient of the offerings to Shangdi, or have his posthumous name enhanced to Ruizong, in effect making him a ruler posthumously. Jiajing wrote and distributed a tract making the opposite case. Yan caved in immediately.[23] The Yongle emperor's posthumous name, at Jiajing's direction, was at the same time changed from Taizong to Chengzu, on the argument that he and his father, Taizu, were in fact cofounders of the Ming dynasty. (This was a way to pardon Yongle for the crime of usurpation.) Yan Song was put to work writing detailed programs for the carrying out of these ritual changes. The ruler issued a general edict announcing these changes, and Yan Song dutifully saw to the organization of missions to convey copies of the edict to the provinces, princedoms, and Ryukyu, Japan, Korea, and, it was hoped, Annam (Vietnam).[24]

Yan Song deserves some credit for urging Jiajing to make his oldest son heir apparent. The ruler, always striving for ways to ensure progeny, was never in a hurry to make the decision. Did it remind him of his own mortality? Would the elevation make the child a target of unseen evil forces? Or a gathering point for dissent? On February 28, 1537, Yan politely suggested that after sixteen years of rule, and so many accomplishments in ritual reform, it was time for the realm to be assured of a successor. Jiajing's reply was mild but noncommittal. Yan reminded him again on October 29, and he temporized again. But on November 3, in response to an apparently coordinated submission of pleas from the civil and military officials, and especially his own mother, he agreed to do it.[25] And he did it, two years later.

Yan was also involved in elaborate preparations to work up programs for birthday and seasonal celebrations for young Zhu Zairui (1536–1548), in developing procedures for training him for his future role as emperor by having him read incoming memorials, and in editing an appropriate text for his education. The latter endeavor led to trouble.

Two of Ming China's top minds were engaged in the textbook project. In the late summer of 1539, Yan responded to Jiajing's request that he carefully review the text, because it seemed to contain cryptic allusions and slanderous dissent. Yan Song read it and agreed that it did; that the authors, Huo Tao and Zou Shouyi, were eccentrics, given to lofty discourses, but error prone; and that it was entirely up to the ruler to decide what to do about it. Jiajing rejected the text, but on the presumption that the authors meant well, he didn't punish them.[26]

In January 1540, three other intellectuals got into worse trouble for urging that Jiajing include the heir apparent in a congratulatory ceremony at the Wenhua Palace for all of next year's newly minted *jinshi*. This request looked suspicious to Jiajing; were the three—Luo Hongxian, Tang Shunzhi, and Zhao Shichun—perhaps trying to create a dissenting clique, with little Zhu Zairui as their symbolic leader? Yan Song thought they were perverse, impetuous, and lacking in decorum. Jiajing imposed what he called a light penalty: removal from civil service and reduction to commoner status.[27]

Zhu Zairui underwent the elaborate coming-of-age capping ceremony on April 12, 1549.[28] By this time, Yan Song was a grand secretary, joining future grand secretary, now Minister of Rites Xu Jie, and Marquis Cui Yuan as senior officiants in attendance. Except that Jiajing wasn't feeling well and excused himself, the rite was performed as prescribed. On April 13, a mass gathering of civil and military officials did five bows and three kowtows in honor of the heir apparent at the Fengtian Gate inside the Forbidden City. Then on April 14, the boy died. He woke up suddenly ill, and physicians were called for, but to no avail. His last words were "I'm leaving," and he died sitting up. Jiajing had been fond of the boy, and he took his death hard. He never named another heir apparent.

Something of Jiajing's state of mind comes through in the only reply he made to the many memorials of condolence that came in, that from his Daoist guru, Tao Zhongwen. It deserves translation:

> What can I say to your memorial of condolence? I've long followed your promptings, and yet this has happened. We just didn't recognize how special a person the heir apparent was. I was slandered personally for delaying his education, for being flattered by the grand secretaries, for not holding morning court. I have Heaven's clear mandate and ride the cycle of the Great Way, yet small men vilify me. So, I thought, the heir apparent was fourteen *sui* [thirteen years old], and it was time to gradually carry out the installation program, so I had the authorities first conduct the capping ceremony. Who could have foreseen his death? He was not given to common pleasures; he moved about like a sylph, yet this is how he ended up. Some say I should have let him be like a normal child. I would note that I've been vilified, charged with having kept him confined in the Forbidden City, that I should have followed the founders; that if I'd been more compassionate, I'd not have lost him. Yes, he's gone, and no empty talk on paper will bring him back. His death wasn't in defiance of me. He knew I could do nothing about it. My own mother loved him dearly, but she died not long after [he was born]. It's all due to my filial impiety.[29]

Somehow Jiajing never got over this son's death. His next oldest surviving son, Zhu Zaihou, he always shunned and never named heir apparent. He succeeded Jiajing anyway, as the Longqing emperor, in 1567. Perhaps Jiajing thought distancing and disgracing him might in some perverse way be a recipe for keeping him alive.

* * *

Jiajing's mother died shortly after midnight on December 24, 1538. Responsibility for managing her funeral and burial fell heavily on the shoulders of Yan Song. It appears he performed well. Before sunrise, a eunuch told the minister of rites of the empress's death and told him to join the Hanlin officials in preparing the required program. Yan complied. The elaborate funeral observances concluded on January 4, 1539. Jiajing told Yan that he'd been sick off and on throughout that time with fever and cold and an inflamed right eye.

Jiajing earlier ordered that his father's remains be transported north and reburied alongside the other Ming emperors at the Ming tombs west of Beijing, and that when she died, his mother should be interred alongside him there. He made a special trip to inspect the prospective site. Meanwhile, Regional Inspector Chen Rang submitted a memorial arguing on the basis of ancient precedent that Jiajing's father should be left undisturbed, that a cap and robe of his be put in his wife's tomb, and that a cap and skirt of hers be buried in Anlu (Chengtian) alongside her husband's corpse. It was a good idea and cost saving. But Jiajing thought it disruptive of fixed plans and removed the unfortunate Chen Rang from the civil service.[30] Officials were wise never rashly to inject themselves into matters involving imperial family ritual.

After the ruler returned from inspecting the site, Jiajing told the grand secretaries that he'd thought about the matter and changed his mind: his father had lain peacefully in Anlu for twenty years, and his remains really shouldn't be disturbed; and his mother's corpse should be taken to Anlu and there buried alongside him. That arrangement best met the demands of ritual and sentiment. He asked Yan Song and the other rites officials what they thought. Their reply was to recommend staying with the original plan that they had just programmed, as there was no big difference between disturbing his father's remains or his mother's.[31]

Jiajing's change of mind of course won the day, and an edict composed by Grand Secretary Xia Yan informed the realm that the ruler's mother would be buried in Anlu (since renamed Chengtian). Jiajing told Yan Song that it was perfectly all right to bury both of them there and not near Beijing, given that Taizu's resting place lay far off in Nanjing, and Yongle's in the north near Beijing, and no trouble had ever come about because of that.[32] Yan Song was still not so sure. Jiajing answered him on January 21, 1539, with a tirade about "stupid and petty men who fill the world, and though they may study books, they regrettably think ritual is something empty and they criticize me for not stopping it." He informed Yan Song that he was soon going to undertake a journey of his own down to Chengtian to visit his father's tomb and see to its repair and preparation, and he ordered the Ministry of Rites to get busy preparing for that. Several dissenters he ordered imprisoned and interrogated. Yan Song got to work.[33]

On February 14, 1539, Jiajing informed Yan Song that he was going to leave Beijing at the *zi* hour, 11 p.m.–1 a.m., on March 5, and that five days before that, he would personally inform Heaven, Taizu, and his father Ruizong at their respective altars and shrines, and officials would substitute for him at all the other sacred sites.

The logistics and other arrangements for the emperor's trip rivaled those required for a major military expedition. How business was to be conducted in Beijing in Jiajing's absence had to be carefully thought out as well. Programming involved directing a cast of thousands. Though Yan Song had never been taxed with any job like this before, he seems to have risen to the occasion. Last-minute changes could be expected: Jiajing reset the departure time to the *yin* hour, 3–5 a.m., on March 6.[34]

On February 19, the emperor summoned a small group to the Wenhua Palace. He ordered them to gather the next day and agree on a plan to secure Beijing while the emperor was out of town. Involved in the talks were Marquises Guo Xun and Zhu Xizhong, Grand Secretaries Xia Yan and Gu Dingchen, and Yan Song. They met, and Yan wrote up the results of their deliberations; on the 23rd Jiajing gave his approval.

The plan appointed the newly installed heir apparent, Zhu Zairui, not yet three years old, as regent and Jiajing's stand-in, assisted by a grand secretary. They would sign off on routine business and forward all important items down to Jiajing. Security needed to be enhanced at the nine gates of outer Beijing and the four gates of the Imperial City. Detailed instructions were spelled out for handling sacrifices, presentations, requests from the princedoms, issues involving the military and the tribal entities of the southwest, impeachments sent up by the grand coordinators and regional inspectors in the provinces, winter clothing distributions for the army, criminal cases, and various other incoming memorials. The emperor cautioned that Beijing needed to get his approval for the conduct of any important rituals.[35]

Further details were approved on February 25. Informing all the gods and imperial ancestors of the forthcoming journey was a gigantic production, scheduled to begin on March 1 at the *chen* hour (7–9 a.m.). Embroidered-Uniform Guards had to be sent out to clear the roads; then the emperor, empress, and imperial consorts, in sedan chairs, would exit the Zhengyang Gate at the south edge of the Imperial City, leading out to the Altar to Heaven. Six thousand specially trained soldiers, commanded by 120 officers, would escort the imperial cortege, and two thousand others would ensure proper parade order, lining the route, conveying messages, and such like. Three thousand horses were to be made available to be ridden in rotation so as not to tire them out. When the trip itself got under way on March 6, all the officials who were staying behind in Beijing were instructed to wear their festive robes and, ahead of the departure time, assemble in rank order outside the Xuanwu Gate on the southwest edge of the Imperial City.

In Jiajing's own terse log of the journey, he noted that twenty-one separate pleas for protection were directed on March 1 to the gods and ancestors, four of them by Jiajing himself, the rest by designated high officials.[36]

Accompanying the trip down to Chengtian, plans called for a mobile central government of 191 senior officials, 518 lower functionaries, 127 clerks, 8 dancers, and 200 musicians. All were to ride mules or take carts. An escort army of six thousand men would provide protection—two thousand men each at the front and rear, five hundred on either flank to transmit messages, and a thousand others to manage the horses. The Ministry of War would have charge of all this.

Minister of War Zhang Zan got Jiajing to agree to the following: 120 Embroidered-Uniform Guards officers and 8,000 banner bearers were to follow alongside, with 3,000 horses, the army itself to provide the fodder and incentive pay; wherever the emperor stopped for the night, the regional military officials were to provide for his security (which is why, when Jiajing's traveling palace burned down, the regional *fu'an* [grand coordinator and provincial inspector] were held accountable); all obstructions were to be cleared from the road, and all narrow archways torn down; alongside the traveling palace, ten or so smaller portable structures were to be set up to house the ruler's close guards; two officials from the Court of the Imperial Stud were to procure six thousand horses at each of several stages of the journey and extend the use of the Henan horses if none were locally available; horses exhausted by the long journey were to be compensated for by the same court; every prefecture, subprefecture, and county the procession passed through was to be allotted silver enough to hire up to ten thousand locals as servants; these places were also to be paid government silver for the rent of some four hundred carts; anyone in the procession was to be punished for extorting more food than their per diem allotment allowed; from Beijing down to Zhuozhou (about thirty miles south), the ministry was to hire servants and carts from its own funds and borrow 4,500 trained cavalry horses from the Training Divisions; and finally, the ministry was to appoint ahead of time in each province one official to manage labor, a second to manage carts and horses, and a third to manage food supplies, the *kedao* (supervising secretaries and censors) to impeach any who might be guilty of dereliction.[37]

The *fu'an* through whose jurisdictions the imperial entourage passed were to provide stations as well as military horses for the emperor's own use.

The Ministry of Revenue had advised that North Zhili, Henan, and Huguang Provinces were short of resources due to recent natural disasters, so Jiajing ordered officials to be sent to the Taicang treasury to fetch two hundred thousand taels silver—thirty thousand for North Zhili, seventy thousand for Henan, and one hundred thousand for Huguang. That was to pay the *fu'an* for laying up fodder and grain supplies. The musicians and dancers were to be paid Taicang silver as well—four taels per dancer, three for each musician, and five for their conductors.[38]

The Ministry of Works was, in conjunction with the Directorate of Palace Eunuchs, to make sure the roads and bridges were passable and take care of the traveling palace and other temporary offices constructed of mats.[39]

* * *

On schedule, this huge procession departed Beijing. Provincial officials posted notices along the road ahead of time warning locals against price gouging, and those on the march against extortion. As the procession came within ten miles of each county, military garrison town, subprefecture, or prefecture, the inhabitants were assembled to wait at the roadside, ready to kneel and kowtow when the ruler arrived. Then all the local officials, clerks, students, and elders, wearing festive robes, were ushered into the traveling palace to do their five bows and three kowtows. Imperial princes of the first rank received a banquet as part of an elaborate protocol designed just for them. Jiajing noted in his log his reception for each such prince.

On March 28, advance groups of the cortege finally arrived in Chengtian, the trip having taken twenty-two days, at an impressively fast pace of thirty miles per day. Jiajing himself arrived on March 30. Lu Shen's diary shows that they all traveled in rain or shine, and at night too, especially when the moon was out.

The only big trouble occurred at Weihui, about forty miles southeast of Kaifeng. At three drums (11 p.m.–1 a.m.) or four drums (1–3 a.m.), during the night of March 18–19, a fire of unknown origin burned down Jiajing's traveling palace. Lu Shen could see the blaze in the night sky. Some eunuchs and, it seems, palace ladies were burned to death. Some special traveling equipment was lost as well. Where was Jiajing? His bodyguards didn't know. Somehow Lu Bing, commandant of the Embroidered-Uniform Guard, found him unscathed and hustled him into a cart. The next day, the Henan grand coordinator and provincial inspector were impeached, arrested, shackled, put on display, and then imprisoned. Zhang Yunqing, vice minister of war, who was responsible for the emperor's personal security, was arrested and removed from civil service. Jiajing sent a message back to Beijing to tell everyone he was well and stanch any wild rumors people there may have heard about the fire.[40]

The emperor seems to have enjoyed revisiting his old home. He spent much of his time holding court, conducting sacrifices, visiting his father's tomb, and issuing instructions for its repair and enlargement so as to accommodate his mother's remains.

Diarist Lu Shen, supervisor of the Household of the Heir Apparent and concurrent Hanlin academician, had failed to show up for escort service when the Prince of Tang came to pay his respects on March 26 at Xinye, just north of the border of Huguang Province. A mix-up in the program was apparently the cause. Jiajing issued a scolding, punishment pending. In Chengtian on March 31, Jiajing held court. Lu expected to hear what his punishment was. But the ruler discussed timber for tomb construction with Pan Jian, vice minister of works, and that was the only item on the agenda that day. At court on April 1, at the *ji* hour, 9–11 a.m., he heard the verdict— a salary reduction of two grades. "I was overjoyed and fearful at the same time," he wrote. "I announced my name and rendered my thanks. By nature I'm a bit diffident; it's hard for me to thrust myself forward, and it's likely I disappointed the ruler. When I heard the verdict, I saw there was deep affection behind it. Still, the pain of my shame was worse than if I'd been ordered to be flogged or executed. It's hard for me to deal [psychologically] with disfavor. Other accompanying officials will know what I mean."[41] Indeed, during the trip, Jiajing punished many officials in varying degrees for a range of failures and derelictions, not just those committed at Weihui.

On April 11, Jiajing left Chengtian to return to Beijing. He accomplished his main purpose, which was to prepare and enlarge his father's tomb so his mother could also be buried there. The mausoleum, recently restored, sits today in what is now Zhongxiang County, Hubei Province. The building is sited at the foot of a small forested hill, majestic yet delightfully understated in the impression it makes.[42] How much of the artistry is attributable to

Jiajing personally, given his intense interest in architecture, is open to speculation.

The return journey required that everything done on the way down be done again on the way back: offerings at each sacred site, receptions for each prince, and such like. On May 2, at sunrise, the emperor entered the same Xuanwu Gate through which he had departed. Lu Shen calculated that the whole trip took sixty days and covered 5,400 *li* (about 1,800 miles). Immediately, Jiajing and a squadron of officials fanned out to give thanks at the same altars and shrines where blessings had been asked for earlier on. (Yan Song's assignment was to inform the spirits of the Chenghua emperor and his consort, whom he'd also visited on departure.)

Was this journey, for all the enormous effort and expense invested in it, a wanton exercise in profligacy, or were larger purposes somehow served?

For the masses of officials and people of Ming China, it would appear that the main purpose, self-evident and in no need of any extensive propaganda, was to express and reinforce society's central ethical norm—*xiao*, or filial piety. Everyone could relate to it. And the ruler tried to ensure that the trip was paid for and did not inflict unwelcome economic burdens upon anyone. Indeed, local people may well have profited from imperial payments for food, lodging, and other services.

Upon his departure from Chengtian, the ruler offered some words for the local people. "I've heard filial piety is the sages' main consideration in ruling the realm, and it is a model for the common people," he told them. He also told them that he had come to look after his parents' tomb in person and that he had been greeted by the officials and the princes, but he was mindful of the people's hardships, so starting the next year he was ordering a reduction of two-fifths of the field tax they were presently paying and a reduction of one-third for the people of Henan and North Zhili. In another statement, this one in colloquial language, he addressed a gathering of locals:

> I talk to you old local neighbors. In emperor Xiaozong's time, my parents were enfeoffed here, and they did many virtuous things, and they produced me, who's become emperor, so today for my parents' sake I've returned here. Today I see you all, elders and those born after me too, and my two parents have gone to Heaven, and I lack all virtue. Do you see my bitter situation? My business here is done, and I'm returning to Beijing, so I say these few words to you. All you who are sons must exhaust filial piety. Fathers must teach their sons and grandsons. Seniors must care for juniors, and juniors must respect their seniors. Work at your livelihoods; be good people, and heed what I say. I

can't be literary here, so I speak aloud to you, for the sake of those of you who
can't read and write, so you can reflect on what I say, and bear it in mind. [43]

The expedition also created opportunities to reinforce ties binding the
princedoms to the imperial center. Princes who made every effort to show
courtesy and respect to the ruler as he came within reach of their estates got
generously rewarded with boosts of three hundred to five hundred *shi* in their
annual grain stipends. One prince failed to appear and was punished by
having his management team put under interrogation.

The formidable organizing capacities of the Ming state were put on national display for two months, but contemporary propaganda made no mention of this fact. Were foreigners watching? How many Chinese, beyond
those in the direct path of the excursion, knew about it? Many probably did,
because Jiajing's speech to the common people in Chengtian was, at Yan
Song's insistence, printed up for nationwide distribution. [44] If they knew
about it, what lessons might they have drawn from it? These questions elicit
no clear answers. However, it might be conjectured that Jiajing's energetic
and sustained commitment to resuscitating ancient ritual and centering it in
its familial dimension restated and refocused a national sense of identity.
Devotion to that ritual defined what it meant to be a Ming Chinese, and the
supreme shaper of that definition was no less a figure than the emperor
himself. All his grand secretaries assured him that he possessed the necessary
authority to make all final decisions on ritual (and everything else). In a more
modern setting, all this could serve as ingredients for the concoction of a very
powerful nationalist-chauvinist dictatorship.

* * *

Yan Song accompanied the Chengtian excursion. Its needs kept him busy. So
did Jiajing's demands for commemorative and banquet poems. Jiajing's
poems, edicts, and sacrificial prayers were, at Yan Song's urging, printed up
for general circulation.

The next extravaganza involving rites, programmed and directed by Yan
Song, was the shipment of Jiajing's mother's remains from Beijing to their
final resting place in Chengtian. This was another big exercise in filial piety
and another big logistical challenge. Moving an empress's coffin was no
simple affair.

At first, it was proposed to move her coffin overland; then it was decided to use an all-water route. To move the coffin from the Forbidden City to the Grand Canal at Tongzhou, the Ministry of Works and the Directorate of Palace Eunuchs put up temporary palaces ahead of time at the docks at both Tongzhou and Zhangjiawan, and shelters at each location along the twenty-mile route from the Zhaoyang Gate east to Tongzhou, where offerings were to be made. The Works Ministry was directed to inform the local authorities everywhere along the all-water route to Chengtian that they were to erect temporary facilities for sacrifices at each docking place so that offerings might be made to the local gods of mountains, rivers, and streams, thus ensuring a safe trip.

Two days before the coffin left the Imperial City, all the high civil and military officials were to join the palace in wearing mourning robes and conducting the rites of grieving. An elaborate program of last rites was worked out for the emperor and empress themselves to follow, as well as all the other palace women. A further list of detailed instructions for everyone from Jiajing on down to observe while the imperial mother's coffin was being carried from the Forbidden City out to the Grand Canal will not be detailed here (to the relief of the reader, no doubt; nor will the rest of the observances be listed, involving a cast of thousands, singers and all, placing Ming filial piety on spectacular display).[45]

June 3, 1539, was chosen as the lucky day of departure. The empress's coffin was loaded into a "dragon boat" at Zhangjiawan, and at midnight it headed down the Grand Canal. The Court of Imperial Sacrifices laid on incense, candles, and other goods needed in rituals. The Hanlin academicians prepared texts for use in prayers and announcements to the gods and ancestors. A high military noble was put in charge of the escort guards, and also to serve as grand master of ceremonies alongside a high official from the Ministry of Rites. Eunuchs were to go, too. A vice minister of the Court of Imperial Sacrifices led a delegation of eighteen functionaries, as did a vice minister of the Court of State Ceremonial. A vice minister of the Court of Imperial Entertainments would lead four subordinates. There would be one commander and four subordinate officers of the Embroidered-Uniform Guard; there would be *kedao*, two supervising secretaries and two censors, as well as an official and two subordinates from the Directorate of Astronomy. A delegation of high officials would participate in the send-off at Zhangjiawan, then return to Beijing. All this, just to move a coffin.

Down in Chengtian, the enhanced importance and increase in traffic connected to the construction going on at the Xianling, Jiajing's parents' tomb, required the raising of the city's status from subprefecture to a full prefecture and the posting there of a eunuch grand commandant and a special circuit censor. After a long and in places difficult journey, the imperial mother's coffin arrived at the Chengtian water station on August 19.[46]

The movement of the funeral boat was closely monitored and reported upon every step of the way, such that, after the trip was over, on October 15, Jiajing was able to respond to a long, consolidated accounting sent up by Yan Song. Merits were assessed and graded; among others, five officials were rewarded for guiding the boat through the locks and across the Huai River. Thirteen men earned merit for getting the boat across the Yellow River.

Many officials deserved censure. Impeachments lodged against six men, for dereliction or imposing extortionate taxes, needed to be double-checked. Two deserved dismissal for failure to provide deckhands. Three mismanaged and needed to be arrested and interrogated. Thirteen officials failed to provide food. Eight were negligent in directing sacrifices. Six failed to police the misbehavior of their subordinates. All, Jiajing agreed, should be arrested and interrogated.

There were two mixed cases. The Shandong provincial administration commissioner, though recently retired, was still on hand and should have come forth to greet and send off the coffin, but he didn't. For that, his retirement should be changed from voluntary to forced. And then at Nanjing, Grand Coordinator Ouyang Duo did very well in handling a difficult job, except that he didn't go after the boatmen who deserted. Jiajing fined him a month's salary.

There was a follow-up. Ouyang Duo memorialized detailing further meritorious cases of officials posted along the Yangzi. The dragon boat had to hug the Yangzi shoreline, and there were trouble spots in several places: rocks and dangerous eddies on one side and a swift head current on the other, and places too narrow for oars, where the rocks had to be broken up and the boat hauled by ropes. Jiajing sent the memorial down to Yan Song for his reaction. Yan agreed that three more officials deserved rewards for that. Jiajing agreed too, on January 7, 1540.[47]

Thus, for being the topmost official in charge of arranging and managing two extremely involved and difficult logistical operations, both in the service of ritual and doing the job successfully, a good deal of credit must be tallied up in Yan Song's favor. These successes surely helped make him a credible candidate for eventual appointment to the Grand Secretariat.

* * *

Xia Yan was minister of rites from 1531 to 1536, and Yan Song directly followed him in that post, from 1536 to 1543. It would make sense to take up the same issues affecting the ministry in the same order: foreign relations, schools and exams, then princedoms and the rest. The purpose of this is to compare the two men's performance in two successive but different periods of time.

Yan Song presided at a time when formal relations between China and Japan were deteriorating, as Japan edged ever closer to anarchy (relations would end altogether in 1549, when Yan was chief grand secretary).

In late May and early June 1539, Zhejiang provincial inspector Fu Feng-xiang and the eunuch grand defender Liu Fu informed Beijing that three Japanese boats appeared on the coast, flying flags bearing the words "Bring-ing tribute from the *guo* [state] of Japan." Ming naval officers and interpret-ers came aboard and contacted the head of the mission, a Buddhist monk named Koshin Sekitei, whose letter apologized for the violence that occurred in 1523, forcing Beijing to break relations. (Xia Yan, at that time a supervis-ing secretary in the Office of Scrutiny for War, unleashed an unsparing blast at China's weak defenses, as was noted in the previous chapter.) Sekitei pleaded that the main culprits responsible for the earlier violence were dead, and he humbly beseeched the court to reestablish the status quo ante. The provincial authorities didn't think it appropriate to summarily refuse him, and they asked the emperor to consider the plea and make a ruling.

Jiajing sent this memorial to the Ministry of Rites for comment. Yan Song thought the visitors might be lying about the fate of the earlier rioters. He recommended that the coastal authorities reinterrogate them and let them proceed to Beijing if their statements panned out. On August 20, Jiajing agreed and permitted fifty Japanese to come present tribute, threatening can-cellation and worse if the envoys turned violent again.

That was the last mission, as things turned out. When the issue came up again, in 1540, Ding Zhan, chief supervising secretary of the Office of Scru-tiny for Rites, concluded after a long review that the Japanese lacked deco-rum and righteousness, and the celestial court should never deal with such *guo*. Jiajing agreed and sent his statement to the Ministry of Rites, ordering a general court discussion of the question. Yan Song reported the consensus conclusions. They were three. First, the conferees urged reinstituting an older rule: one mission every ten years, no more than a hundred envoys, three ships, no weapons, and if they misbehave, stop the mission. It would be a bad idea to stop them if they're sincere. Second, they urged a retrial of the suspects still in custody; and third, they urged serious and far-reaching improvements in Ming China's coastal defenses: recruit fighters, prepare weapons and war boats, put up signal towers, monitor the weather, prosecute bad officials, forbid all contact between the envoys and the local people, and send troops to throw a cordon around the envoys there now. On July 11, 1540, Jiajing stated his full agreement with this reply.[48]

Given Xia Yan's passionate outburst of 1523 about the shame of China's flimsy coastal defense, it is remarkable that, nearly two decades later, little or nothing had been done about it. The lethargy was amazing. The great bureaucratic machinery obviously needed a jolt of electricity to get it moving. But even now, little was done. Jiajing was focused on ritual issues and wasn't forced to give his full attention to coastal military defense until the Wokou violence blazed forth in the 1550s.

Central Asia was quieter, although it was still sending bloated embassies representing "kings" of dubious authenticity. It's hard to see any improvement in the situation. Yan Song could only reiterate the need to enforce existing regulations. There was one new wrinkle. A Tianfang envoy by the name of Shaikh Shams ad-Din asked permission to go sightseeing. He wanted to see the coast before he went home. Yan Song urged Jiajing to forbid this. The man was a probable spy. No such permission was ever granted by the Ming. Denying his request will teach him that the court's predominance cannot be challenged, and all the outside Yi (foreigners) will respect China's paramountcy as well. On February 14, 1538, Jiajing agreed.[49]

In 1539, Zhao Zai, grand coordinator in Gansu, sent up a twelve-point proposal based, he said, on his eleven years' experience on the frontiers. He said Gansu was like a wedge, with Tatar raiders to the north, Hui Yi (Muslims) to the west, Qiang to the south, and Fan (non-Chinese) living inside. There were no civil prefectures or counties, only military settlements (*weisuo*). He hoped the ruler would authorize court discussions of all the issues he raised. Jiajing complied. Two of the issues came under the purview of the Ministry of Rites. One was a need for full and clear regulations for handling the Yi to the west, and the other was the need to improve the corps of interpreters necessary for dealing with those Yi. So Yan Song of course had the ministry discuss those two issues, and then he reported the results in detail to Jiajing.

On the first question, Yan explained that the western Yi were too disorganized and unruly to be fit into the same set of rules that applied to Japan, or the Uriyangkhad, say. We must above all make sure that China's dignity is preserved. The Ming will provide carts and servants for their delegations. It will forbid any private trade as they proceed to Beijing, and all local officials and other personnel who demand bribes or share information with them must be punished.

On the second point, Yan used his talent for description to go into a long and interesting rumination on the comparative anthropology of Chinese as opposed to foreigners. The focus was the corps of a hundred or so ushers (*xuban*) attached to the Court of State Ceremonial, whose job was to herd the foreign envoys through the rituals and other rules that governed caravans and envoys' sojourns in Beijing. At present, he said, the ushers consist of *semuren* (West Asian residents of China) who are of Yi origin. Would it be possible to replace them with Chinese-speaking Muslims (Han Hui), of which there are many in China? They categorize themselves socially as elites, peasants, artisans, and merchants, as do all Chinese. But in their funerals, they follow Yi rituals. They refuse to eat pork, so they stand apart. When we try to get them to change, they gather in crowds and protest. Even their wives and children persist in this separatist perversity. They all cleave together like close kin. They consider the *semu* who serve as ushers as close kin too. They look on us as strangers. They even go so far as to incite the envoys into doing wrong, advising them while they're in Beijing to raise their demands, and while on the road, to deal illegally in tea and contraband goods. As a result, the Yi envoys "look lightly on [ethnic] Chinese, as though we didn't exist, and think only their co-ethnics can translate their language." So the obvious policy change to make was to have only ethnic Chinese in the Translators Institute (the Siyi Guan, attached to the Court of Imperial Sacrifices) and have them study foreign languages, because "they won't leak China's affairs, and they'll be proof that the people of China can do anything. This is one way to defend ourselves against the outside Yi." On February 10, 1534, Jiajing approved Yan's recommendation.[50]

On August 9, 1540, Jiajing agreed with Yan Song and the Gansu and Shaanxi officials that a large Central Asian delegation that showed up a year too early, and had ignored their assigned schedule in the past, should be kept blocked outside China. And so the Central Asian situation simmered on low heat, well below crisis proportions.

Xihai, Tibet, and Kaili, which made it to Xia Yan's desk earlier, made no noise during Yan Song's tenure. The Uriyangkhad did, squeezed as they were between the broad expanses of Mongolia and Manchuria. They were a key component of Ming China's northern defense. On May 16, 1541, Jiajing agreed to this piece of business: Gelantai, an Uriyangkhad chief bearing the Chinese title *dudu* (commissioner in chief), accompanied by a hundred of his tribesmen, came down to the frontier pass at Jizhou. There he requested that in light of his having captured "Tatar bandits," he be allowed to expand his twice-yearly tribute missions to six hundred men. The "bandits" were apparently the same ones mentioned in the case Xia Yan handled in 1533. Yan Song argued effectively that Gelantai's claim to have captured bandits might be false, that his request should be denied, and that China's border defenses should be put on the alert. [51]

Gelantai made no threats when he got Beijing's disappointing response. Instead he kowtowed, acknowledged his guilt, and apologized. So the frontier officials allowed him and a party of three hundred to proceed. All of them were given salt, rice, cloth, wine, and meat. Gelantai said his job was much more demanding than it had been and asked for aid for the "Tatar bandits," who lacked for food and clothing. Ming border officials said a resumption of raiding would be calamitous and recommended a policy of generosity. Jiajing asked the Ministry of Rites for an opinion. Yan Song replied that while Gelantai and his party behaved submissively when they arrived at their quarters in Beijing and made no further demands, they didn't show up at the scheduled time. Gelantai said they'd been delayed by rain and by a raid from the "yellow-haired Tatars" (whoever they were; Cossacks, perhaps?). Yan was inclined to believe this excuse but thought they should be warned not to delay again. On September 24, Jiajing agreed to that, plus a onetime enhancement of their subvention. [52]

The Jurchen made no waves, and Korea was quiet as well. The Ryukyu Islands, however, turned troublesome. No longer radiating a bright beacon of civilized virtue, as they had in 1535, the islands and their king, Sho Sei, had by 1542 befouled themselves in a complex morass of illegal trade. Yan Song sent up a long memorial about that problem, urging a tightening of controls, a range of punishments, and a threat to cut all ties if the problem continued. On June 1, Jiajing agreed. [53]

* * *

Without question, the biggest foreign relations headache for Yan Song as minister of rites was Annam. When Xia Yan left the Ministry of Rites and entered the Grand Secretariat, Beijing was still uncertain about how to continue relations with a recognized state (*guo*) in such a dismal state of civil strife and systemic breakdown. A Ming military intervention was readied and could not be ruled out. Yan Song must be credited with helping to obtain a peaceful solution to the problem over the years 1537–1541.

It was nearly impossible to get accurate information about what was going on in Annam. There were various claimants to the throne, all fighting each other: the Tran, the Trinh, the Le, and the wily Mac Dang-dung—a fighter, politician, and Confucian-style state builder, whose power and legitimacy as Annam's would-be ruler were fiercely contested by his rivals. Roads were blocked. Violence and destruction everywhere discouraged Ming attempts to go in and gather facts.

Opinion in Beijing varied widely over what, if anything, should be done about it. However, the issue never rose to the level of partisan ferocity that disputes over the Great Rites had kindled, even though Annam impinged on Ming China's rites-related system of international order. Annam lay very far away, 1,200 miles south, and Jiajing had to remind the officials not to look on it as unimportant as, over and over again, he directed the court to meet and discuss and come up with some consensus about how to handle it. The urge to intervene militarily, as the Yongle emperor had done in similar circumstances in 1406, was blunted by the general realization that China's security was much less threatened here than it was on the northern frontiers or on the east coast. Thus the degree of disagreement between the aggressive Xia Yan and the peace-seeking Yan Song was fuzzed, not sharp.

Much ink was expended on long memorials agonizing over the issue. As early as 1522, Xia Yan himself, as part of a delegation sent to deliver an imperial announcement to the Annam king, found the roads impassable and entry into the country impossible. Since then, various combatants in the civil wars had signaled a desire for Ming recognition, but the authenticity of their claims could not be verified, and the true facts on the ground were too dim to discern.[54] On November 1, 1536, Jiajing responded to a detailed memorial from Xia Yan, just as he was about to leave the Rites Ministry and enter the Grand Secretariat. He explained how spillover from the Annam civil wars was creating violence inside the Ming frontier, and he thought it time for all the relevant officials in Beijing and on the frontier to gather and plan a major military buildup. Jiajing agreed. Annam's misbehavior and its cessation of tribute embassies were equivalent to a rebellion against China, and it was time for the Ministry of War to plan a punitive invasion.[55]

Then in 1537, Beijing received a long account from Le Ninh, the former king of Annam, who was trying to restore his shattered dynasty. The onetime king rehearsed the whole recent history of the troubles, how his family's supporters had tried to contact the Ming court and restore tribute relations but found all roads blocked, and so now he had commissioned a party of ten headed by a "chief" (*toumu*) by the name of Trinh Duy-lieu to board a merchant ship from Guangdong that happened along and try to reach Beijing by sea route.

Jiajing read the account. It raised his suspicions. It didn't read like anything a foreigner might write. The envoys, who had reached Beijing, must be queried about it through interpreters.

Yan Song reported the results of the interrogation. The envoys said that the date of Le Ninh's account was May 29, 1534, and that the party of ten had divided into two groups, each taking a boat separately and secretly. Trinh and his party of six sailed south to Champa. There they lingered until 1537, when at last they were able to get a boat to take them to a post station on the coast of Guangdong. From there, they took another merchant boat to Gaoyou on the Grand Canal, and then they continued by land to Beijing. One of their number, an interpreter, died of illness along the way. Trinh said he didn't know the fate of the other party.

Yan Song had doubts about this statement. Annam had not sent tribute for twenty years. So why now, suddenly, when the Ming was commencing army mobilization, do they ask to restore relations? Why, when Trinh and his party reached Guangdong, didn't they just get passports from the officials there and come by official route to Beijing? Agents need to be sent into Annam to check into the facts behind all this. Meanwhile, given that war continues in Annam, the roads are still blocked, and Le Ninh hides somewhere in the grass and dirt, while Mac Dang-dung occupies the national capital. Trinh might be housed here for a bit, then sent to wait on the Guangxi frontier.

To all this, Jiajing assented, except that he ordered the Embroidered-Uniform Guard to keep Trinh in Beijing under sequestration, with no contact with outsiders allowed; the Court of Imperial Entertainments was instructed to give him the same food that it gave to Korean envoys.

A few months later, a plea filed by Trinh reached Jiajing. The prisoner said he didn't understand why he was being detained, that he didn't know what was happening back in Annam since he'd been absent so long, and that he was a useless drain on Ming resources. Jiajing asked the Ministries of Rites and War to confer about this. Yan Song replied that things now seemed a bit clearer; Le Ninh is the legitimate ruler, while Mac Dang-dung is a usurper. A military intervention must be carefully planned, and Trinh should be sent down to Guangxi to await developments. Jiajing complained that this response was not satisfactory, and he ordered further discussion.

The war and rites officials did as their ruler demanded. Yan Song replied by reciting for the ruler's edification a potted history of China-Annam relations since Han times down to the present, and by giving a roundup of the latest facts emerging from that sorely distressed country, plus a review of the turmoil as it had leached into China's border province of Yunnan. The ministries urged more fact gathering and a large-scale war mobilization. Jiajing concurred.[56]

By all the signs, a Ming invasion was imminent. Yan Song reported the results of another general court discussion. The decades-long rupture in Annam's tribute missions was now understood to have been caused by Mac Dang-dung and not the deposed and beleaguered Le Ninh. A list of ten crimes charged against Mac was gotten up as clear justification for a Ming intervention. Assassinations, murders, massacres, shutting down all connections to China, and, curiously, setting up a bureaucracy modeled on China's were among the main criminal acts charged against him. The pitiful pleas of Le Ninh and his envoy Trinh Duy-lieu were cited in support. The need for an invasion was now as clear as daylight. It looked like war was on. On April 17, 1537, Jiajing agreed.[57]

A few months later, however, the scenario changed. A lengthy report from Yan Song asserted some new facts. Le Ninh controlled only 10 to 20 percent of Annam. Mac Dang-dung held 70 to 80 percent of it. The defeat of the Tran forces reduced the contending parties from three to just these two. Both Le and Mac had signaled a desire to restore tribute relations. Both admired Jiajing's virtue and feared Ming power. So the recommendation now was essentially to wait and let the Annamese sort things out. To that, Jiajing, no war hawk, agreed on April 3, 1538.[58]

Half a year after that, a large Mac delegation came to the Yunnan frontier, acknowledged guilt, and argued that Le Ninh was in fact an impostor and that the Mac enjoyed wide support from the people of Annam, so the Mac now asked for Beijing's recognition and petitioned to be allowed to resume the tribute relationship. Ming officials on the spot were willing to listen to all this but were wary. The Ministries of Rites and War discussed the matter at length. Yan Song's memorial duly noted the Mac argument but maintained that Beijing should ascertain whether or not the Mac claim to have popular support was true. On April 3, 1538, Jiajing agreed.[59]

The Mac kept up the pressure, this time at the Guangxi frontier. The Ming officials there agreed that Le Ninh's claims to legitimacy were very weak, and the Le hopes for a restoration were unrealistic. At the same time, however, the Mac were usurpers, no doubt about that. Both the Mac and the Le were using Ming-issued seals, but one of them must be a forgery. Which one? They asked for Beijing's direction as how best to proceed now that the Mac had submitted maps and a census, and expressed terror and sincerity. Yan Song was accompanying Jiajing's trip to Chengtian at the time, but he endorsed Beijing's suggestion to send another mission down there to ascertain the facts. That was on July 13, 1539.[60]

Then the frontier officials reported sickness and several deaths among the Mac envoys being detained at Zhennan on the Guangxi-Annam border. They wanted to send them all home, as it was no use having them die there. Yan Song agreed. Jiajing did not. The emperor was still waiting for clear results from their interrogation. How could they be sent back? He ordered a rethink. That was on August 18. In October, Beijing was still contemplating the likelihood of war.[61]

Yan Song has no further statements about Annam on record. The whole issue was successfully resolved in the theatrics Mac Dang-dung displayed on November 30, 1540, in obedience to Ming demands and in the face of a massive Ming war mobilization. Personally he led a delegation of forty-eight men to the Guangxi border at Zhennan, each man fettered by the neck, barefoot, and inching forward on his knees, where they surrendered copies of maps, official and military rosters, and a long written promise to accept humiliating terms if the Ming court allowed the Mac to resume tribute relations.

Jiajing put the whole problem to bed with his long edict of April 28, 1541. He forgave Mac Dang-dung all his sins and crimes and permitted the resumption of tribute relations. The Le royal line was declared to be extinct. Annam was demoted from the dignity of *guo* status to that of a hereditary pacification office, along the lines of the *tusi* (native administration) system imposed on the tribes of China's southwest. The Mac rulers were not to be recognized as "kings" but as pacification commissioners only. For special praise in settling the Annam troubles, Jiajing singled out Chief Grand Secretary Xia Yan for planning mobilization but refraining from invading, Grand Secretary Chai Luan for aiding Xia in that, and Marquis Guo Xun and Minister of Rites Yan Song for their constructive contributions. All were rewarded with gifts of silver and cloth. Further rewards and promotions went to the key officials on the China-Annam border. [62]

Contemporary opinion was, on balance, favorable to this outcome. Relations were restored, and war was avoided. Everyone seemed to understand that, as far as Annam was concerned, the ethical and ritual foundations of Ming foreign policy (that in return for their submission, China would protect legitimate rulers against usurpers and rebels) had to be compromised. Everyone knew that the Xuande emperor, after withdrawing the Ming occupation forces from Annam in 1427, had set the precedent when he recognized the Le outlaws and usurpers as legitimate tributaries and as kings of a *guo*. Jiajing outdid him by refusing to go quite that far. No one in Beijing was willing to risk all by denouncing the settlement as an evil violation of a basic moral principle, in the style, say, of the Great Rites controversy. Yan Song was very comfortable in the stance he took. Standing fearless and tall for moral principle was never a weapon in his political arsenal. Compromise was always the ace in his deck of cards.

* * *

The Ministry of Rites had a big part to play in managing Ming China's systems of education and bureaucratic recruitment, as was made clear in the previous chapter, featuring Xia Yan as minister of rites. How did Yan Song handle the responsibilities? Some of the problems that landed on his desk were different from those Xia Yan had dealt with.

Yan Song took a rather harder line than Xia Yan with regard to the quality of the written answers to civil service exam questions. Yan seems to have been reacting to problems rather than initiating change on his own. But he made a strong statement, in which Jiajing concurred on February 26, 1538, that the candidates' writing was intimately tied to their moral makeup and their later behavior in office. He said that until the Zhengde era, test questions were centered squarely on the classics and on orthodox Neo-Confucian commentary, but during that time, the candidates' answers began showing signs of a heightened competitiveness, in particular a penchant for striking, clever, and unorthodox expressions. Xia Yan had addressed this issue in 1532, he said, but the abuse had since gotten worse. Winning answers just now submitted in the provincial exams were full of these perversions, especially in Guangdong Province. The examiners had been held to account and punished. Jiajing agreed to issue a general proclamation about the matter.

The 1531 Guangdong exam at issue here was viewed in Beijing as a scandal of disturbing proportions. Singled out for excoriation as bad models for the examinees were two figures: Lun Wenxu (1467–1513) and Chen Xianzhang (1428–1500). Lun Wenxu was a literary, behavioral, and examination superstar, the number-one *jinshi* of 1498, who died prematurely. Why he was targeted isn't clear. The other was famous nationally for pioneering a dissenting form of Neo-Confucianism, tainted with what many took to be Buddhist ideas. So targeting Chen was understandable. In any event, Yan Song urged a harsh crackdown. He listed by name two examiners and six assistant examiners for arrest and asked that the teachers in all the local state-run Confucian schools be disciplined. On December 9, 1537, Jiajing ordered arrests and interrogations of all the violators. [63]

One of the new features of the Jiajing era was the rise of Guangdong Province from its obscurity and remoteness from Beijing into something of a hotbed for new developments in Confucian thought and a nursery for a new cohort of top-level officials as well. The Cantonese luminaries included Huo Tao and Fang Xianfu, important backers of Jiajing in the Great Rites controversy. Chen Xianzhang was the philosophical superstar. In his wake came his fervent disciple, Zhan Ruoshui (1466–1560), also a Cantonese. Zhan was rich and gregarious, and a major founder of private academies, as many as thirty-six of them, well funded, all of them honoring the name and legacy of Chen Xianzhang. Zhan rose to high office in Beijing and Nanjing, but he was a bit unsure and inept as a player in the high-stakes game of politics. He and his friendly rival, Wang Yangming, who died in 1529, were the two leading lights spearheading the important reconfiguration of Neo-Confucianism that dominated the intellectual scene in China in the middle and late sixteenth century. [64]

Violators were to be found elsewhere than in Guangdong. Nan Zhili, Huguang, Jiangxi, and Henan Provinces were also called on the carpet. In response to Yan's detailed report and recommendations for indictments, dated October 27, Jiajing noted not only the failure of all the examiners in Nanjing to list their own names on the official report; he also saw that many of the students' answers to questions on ritual and military matters were mocking and hypercritical. He agreed to the arrest and interrogation of all the examiners, two of them to be fetched to Beijing by the Embroidered-Uniform Guard, the rest to be prosecuted by the provincial authorities.[65]

What to do about Zhan Ruoshui and his academies came up for discussion and decision in 1537. Nan Zhili regional inspector You Jujing (a descendant of a high disciple of the Cheng brothers, thus with both state orthodoxy and personal legacy at stake) pointed up the menace in these new departures. He sent up a memorial to the throne:

> In recent years, dissident intellectuals have promoted novel ideas and set up tight gatherings (*menhu*) to delude younger students, many of whom are tired of normality and seek novelty, and so become disciples of those who pursue the offbeat in their quest for fame. Many fine *shi* get led astray by the extreme ideas of the many misguided followers [of those dissidents]. The result is that exam candidates reecho this and thereby pass, and that then becomes the prevailing current. . . . One of the promoters of this is Nanjing minister of personnel Zhan Ruoshui. His teaching competes with that of the world-famous minister Wang Shouren [Wang Yangming], now deceased. Wang's precept of *liangzhi* [the "good conscience"] derives from the *zun dexing* ["honor the virtuous nature"] of the Song Confucian Lu Jiuyuan [Lu Xiangshan]. All you need is that "good conscience," and there is no further need to consider good behavior. That this is an extreme view is obvious. As for Zhan's teaching, *tiren tianli* ["embody heavenly principle"]—that surreptitiously coincides with Wang's precept, just changing the words so as to attract fame seekers who adopt it for selfish reasons. Wang, because of his forceful help in suppressing the rebellion of Zhu Chenhao [Prince of Ning], had pro-regime loyalty and effective talent that criticism cannot erase. Zhan, however, is just a dissident academic intellectual without talent or learning. Whatever his ideas, his behavior fails to match.

You Jujing went on to ask Jiajing to dismiss Zhan, ban the writings of both him and Wang Yangming, destroy or turn to other uses all the academies built by their followers, and warn all students to stay away from them. Jiajing directed the Ministries of Personnel and Rites to respond.

Personnel said Zhan was a sincere proponent of ancient classical authority and that not everything he advocated was wrong; he has some peculiar views, but on the classics he is illuminating. His disciples are on the increase, however, and many of them are villainous, which is what prompted You Jujing to speak out. The academies appear to be unauthorized and should be torn down or repurposed.

Yan Song echoed this opinion. He went on to urge education intendants everywhere to investigate the academies, in cities as well as in rural places, and turn them all into "community schools" (*shexue*), with all students warned not to stray from the orthodox curriculum. Jiajing agreed and warned that any further builders of private academies would be prosecuted. [66]

We see here the fine hand of Jiajing's governance technique in action. Rather than repressing deviant thought by mass arrests, incarceration, forced recantations, or executions, as Ming founder Taizu might have done, Jiajing took an institutional approach, kicking away the underpinnings—banning the texts and closing down the schools before they swamped the realm with who knows what results. Issue warnings, punish the leaders, and let everyone else go, just as he had earlier directed in the suppression of the Blue Sheep Mountain bandits. Yan Song, no zealot, was glad to go along with him.

The same approach held for the Buddhist church, which Jiajing personally found abhorrent, as we've seen in the case of his mother's devotion to it. In the same year the academies were ordered to be suppressed, 1537, Li Qin, a supervising secretary in the Office of Scrutiny for Justice, asked Jiajing to conduct a harsh crackdown on the church. Send all builders of monastic centers into military exile on the frontiers. Reduce all illegally ordained monks to commoner (*min*) status. Confiscate the idols and tear down the shrines. These things had been ordered earlier, he said, but the local officials ignore or circumvent the edicts. Exempt from exile all who volunteer to return to lay life.

Yan Song's response to this counseled moderation. He advised Jiajing not to overdo it. Buddhism was a foreign faith, and it was harmful because in its modern form it wandered far from what it was originally. The church provides food and clothing to poor peasants who work the fields attached to the monasteries, thus relieving them of their responsibility to pay taxes and render services to the state. But should this abomination be abruptly ended? No. A mass laicization in a time of natural disaster, floods and the like, would cause social upheaval. Defrocked monks would become desperate refugees. Local officials would steal from the confiscated properties. It would be best just to encourage voluntary laicization, forbid repairs to moldering temples, forbid *min* children from taking tonsure and becoming monks, and prosecute their parents and neighbors if they do. Set the church on a path of gradual decline. Blanket the realm with warning placards. To this, Jiajing agreed. [67]

* * *

As minister of rites, one of Xia Yan's concerns had been to alleviate the difficulties faced by students who lived on the frontiers and in other remote places. Yan Song continued this concern. The problem persisted because China's population was growing, and once-unpopulated places were filling with settlers. Jiajing authorized new schools and enlarged degree quotas as soon as Yan brought these matters to his attention.

The Jinshan military settlement, located in Songjiang Prefecture in the richest part of China, had a Confucian school, and, like a regular county, it was allowed to send up one tribute student to one of the imperial universities every two years. Never did it have a granary or stipends on offer, however. Jiajing agreed to follow the precedent of what was done for the Pinghai military settlement in Fujian: set up a locally funded granary and issue monthly stipends of one *shi* to their twenty top students.

Along a major Yunnan highway, sixty miles northeast of Kunming, lay Malong Subprefecture, on what was then considered a remote frontier. No school existed there. Students had to travel two hundred *li* to attend the school at Xundian, about twenty-five straight-line miles to the west. Yunnan was acculturating to Ming norms, and local people were willing to pay to build a school. Likewise Lufang County, forty miles west of Kunming, whose students had to travel a like distance southeast to the school in Anning Subprefecture. So Jiajing authorized new schools and agreed to appoint instructors and granary attendants.

In Guizhou, there were but ten locales with schools, granaries, and stipends in the whole province. There were thirteen military communities with schools, but no stipends. These were poor places, but the numbers of talented students were on the rise. Each of those schools was allowed to appoint twenty stipend students. Detailed instructions were issued to them about how and where to obtain the stipend grain.

Wuchuan County, isolated in northern Guizhou, got its plea for a school and a government-appointed teacher approved, as talents were increasing there. Longan County in Guangxi, newly created, needed a school, teachers, stipends, and various attendants, and received all of them.

In Yun County in Huguang, a region opened to pioneer settlement only sixty years earlier, a rise in the population of young local talents prompted the need for a school there. Yan Song reported that there were 170 students in the now-crowded Yunyang prefectural school, so the county's request for a school, teachers, granary for stipends, and all the rest won Jiajing's approval.[68]

Population pressure made itself felt in demands to expand the civil service examination degree quotas, most of which Yan Song noted and Jiajing agreed to. Huguang Province was allowed to raise its quota from eighty-five to ninety. Not the Beijing (Shuntian Prefecture) quota, however. The prefecture hosted the North Zhili provincial exam, and a quota of 130 every three years was in effect. The capital was swarming with some five thousand students of the Imperial University, almost all of them eligible takers of the exams, but the fear was that raising the quota would attract "expelled *shengyuan* [local students] from all over the realm, who would change their names, falsify their registry, or hire substitute exam takers" and throw the whole system into an uproar. It was agreed only to verify identities and not expand the quota.[69]

The metropolitan exam quota for 1538 was 320. The examiners, however, reported a total of 548 passing exams. Yan Song said that Ming China had many more talents than it ever had before. There were requests from the provinces to appoint more *jinshi* degree winners as subprefectural and county magistrates in order to upgrade administrative quality. At present, only 10 to 20 percent of such magistrates held the metropolitan degree. Jiajing, for whatever reason, kept the quota as it was.[70]

* * *

Yan Song's duties as minister of rites also obliged him on occasion to descend into the lowest levels of Beijing's governing apparatus and deal with its denizens.

Imperial message bearing was one of the most sought after of all the low-level functions. It was supposed to be the exclusive job of the Messenger Office, staffed by newly minted *jinshi* who had finished low on the ranked list. But messenger duty was a chance to stay away for as long as a year to sightsee, make home visits, and tend to private matters. The Court of Imperial Entertainments was strictly a food service. The Court of State Ceremonial provided ushers for embassies. The Secretariat drafters were palace copyists. The Court of Judicial Review studied legal appeals. The managers of these organs must not let their subordinates go off as messengers, and the whole messenger service needed to be tightened up. So Yan Song stated on August 21, 1538. Jiajing agreed.[71]

The Imperial Academy of Medicine had its share of scandal and unde-sired growth in numbers of untrained but practicing physicians. Yan called Jiajing's attention to Beijing's being a magnet for discharged clerks and expelled students from the provinces; here they live illegally, under false registry, hoping to land government jobs. Some are the younger brothers, nephews, sons, and grandsons of legitimate physicians, who though ignorant and untrained themselves get jobs nonetheless. Jiajing agreed that this had to be forbidden and controls tightened.[72] Then there were shortfalls and fraud in drug quotas and delivery requirements imposed on the provinces. Although Jiajing was himself a consumer of drugs, he agreed just to remind the region-al inspectors to exercise diligence. He declined to prosecute.[73] Whether Jia-jing was in a forgiving mood or ready to fly off the handle was not easy to predict.

The labor demands of Jiajing's revised imperial ritual were quite heavy, as can be seen in the required number of cooks of sacrificial meals. The Court of Imperial Entertainments had charge. On hand in 1537 were some four thousand cooks, of whom many were incompetent menials who con-sumed as salary an enormous quantity of government grain. The court wanted to add 150 more, at a salary of one *shi* per month. These men needed to be given a test to ensure they really knew how to cook. A complaint filed by a supervising secretary of the Office of Scrutiny for Revenue stated that this was too many cooks; numbers needed to be cut to save expenses. The court replied that the original quota for cooks was 6,884. But only 4,093 were presently on duty. Dead or absconded cooks came to 2,791. And now the demand for cooks has risen because of the four suburban rites, ancestral temple rites, and the imperial visits to the Ming tombs. Yan Song proposed adding seventy or eighty as a compromise. Jiajing endorsed that.[74]

Evidently cooks were scarce. Absconded cooks were a problem. Cook recruitment was abusive. It had become routine to arrest runaway cooks, like Wang Qin and nee Pan, a married woman, both of them from Shaanxi, and have someone from a rich household send them back to Beijing. Costs for food and travel were laid on the local taxpayers and service providers (*lijia*). Just now the commoners were suffering poverty, and this imposition is caus-ing an uproar among them. This procedure must stop, Yan argued. The emperor agreed.[75]

Finally, there were the ushers, interpreters, and translators essential to receiving foreign embassies. In an undated memorial, Yan endorsed the statement of Wei Jing, chief minister of the Court of State Ceremonial, that they were short some ten interpreters and had none at all for some languages. Jiajing approved Yan's solution, which was to have all the regional inspectors on the frontiers recruit upright and properly registered local youths, age nineteen or younger, either living there or in Beijing, whose families were law abiding. The court would screen them and forward them to the ministry. Also, police from the Beijing Warden's Office were directed to scout the neighborhoods for presentable candidates and forward them to the ministry for testing on their pronunciation, basic literacy, and handwriting. Those chosen would apprentice under a senior interpreter of the particular language, or anyone competent in the language; then they would be sent to the relevant frontier for a year, then return for a test, and those who showed proficiency would be allowed to wear a plain headband as a mark of status. After three years, they'd be given salaries in grain, and after six, a cap and belt as well. Those who failed the tests were to be sent home and forbidden to linger on in Beijing. Yan went on to explain that the job of interpreter was to accompany foreign missions. Interpreters had to be dressed well and speak well. But too many candidates were being sent in. The system was growing lax and abusive. The regulations presently on the books needed to be reemphasized. [76]

Impeachments for corruption hounded Yan Song year after year; the earliest serious one came up again and again, and it had to do with the recruitment of translators, no less. He was accused of taking bribes from candidates for positions as apprentice translators in the Translators Institute. Yan's discussion of the issue, the question of his guilt or innocence notwithstanding, affords another close look into a submerged but important sphere of Ming governance.

When Yan first became minister in 1537, he sent students to the Translators Institute, at which point the speaking officials impeached him for taking bribes, because many of those students were the sons and younger brothers of rich Beijing merchants. At the same time, Yan said, he was being deluged by the calling cards of high officials from the ministries and Censorate who were scrambling to get their own juniors accepted as apprentices. But he was new on the job and ignorant of how things were run, so he just picked young boys who looked promising and sent them to the institute to study, with the idea of making final choices after the three years were up. "I was too hasty," he said, "and didn't check carefully into their backgrounds." Only after the impeachment did he learn that two brothers, or cousins, from the same rich Beijing family of merchants had gotten certification from two different offices, which fooled Yan, and he'd been tainted by this mistake ever since, which the speaking officials must know, but they just want to use that as a pretext to attack him. So now, three years later, those same students have passed the test, so Yan felt he need not respond to the accusations, as it would look as though he had indeed been paid to protect them. But now the charge has been raised again, which is why he must bother Jiajing over the matter. He has since discovered that twenty-three of those successful examinees (he lists each by name) are in fact all members of big rich Beijing merchant families with huge fortunes that everyone knows about. Yan said he never knew any of them personally. They solicited endorsements from the local authorities. The documentary evidence for that is available. "This is a blot on the national dignity [*guoti*]," he asserted. "I can take the dirt, but those street-smart and corrupt types, who've wormed their way in by bribes, fouling the official hierarchy, makes us all indignant. National law cannot tolerate it." He asked Jiajing to reduce them all to commoner status. Others, most of whom come from official families, should be expelled too, for fear of the future harm they may cause. That would leave ten translators available for hiring.

Jiajing refused to go that far; he agreed to expel those of merchant background only. Again, the ruler was loath to conduct deep purges or witch hunts against corruption, dissent, or any other offense.[77]

* * *

As with the review of Xia Yan's work in the Rites Ministry, space constraints discourage anything more than a brief review of other matters that piled on Yan Song's desk. Handling some twenty complicated disputes and pleas generated by the princedoms demanded in each case careful adjudication and resolution.[78]

All omens had to be interpreted. Good omens, like multiheaded wheat stalks, the appearance of the so-called sweet dew, or a predicted solar eclipse that didn't happen, required the ministry's response.[79] Bad omens brought Yan's facility for description into play. The whole body of government— emperor, palace, and bureaucracy—had to come to a stop while everyone did penance, conducted elaborate rites, and reflected on what lapses might have triggered Heaven's anger. Thus it was when a lightning strike in the early evening of April 30, 1541, burned down an imperial ancestral temple.[80] Earlier, before dawn on June 28, 1537, lightning hit the Jinshan Palace, one of the big halls in the Forbidden City, and set it on fire. Three days of penance and introspection were mandated. Did injustices in the legal system cause this? Or corruption? Or tax inequities? Military abuses?[81] Small portents of evil omen reported from the provinces were from time to time consolidated by the ministry into long lists and brought to Jiajing's notice.[82]

Comets, like the one reported on May 10, 1539, stirred unease too. As did frightening or worrisome weather phenomena. The spring of 1540 brought ten days of skies dark with dust. In the late afternoon of April 19, a major dust storm billowed up, the northwest wind kicking up a smothering blast of yellow and red air, blowing away the arches marking streets and wards, flagstaffs, roofing tiles, gates, and metal fixtures along Chang'an Boulevard. The storm eased as night came on. Everyone panicked and took cover, then went out to view the wreckage. Once-sturdy structures lay strewn about like so much rotten wood. Jiajing agreed that this was a major omen, calling for special vigilance on the northwest frontier.[83] Droughts, too, caused anxiety. Yan Song reported on May 15, 1538, a persistent drought, a little occasional drizzle only, dust storms, and dry soil. Animals were suffering, spring planting was delayed, and there was outright starvation east of Beijing, with corpses everywhere along the roads. Refugees sprawled about at the Chongwen Gate (along the southeast side of the Imperial City), wallowing in hunger, disease, and death. Jiajing endorsed Yan's plea for prayers and famine relief.[84] Omens accompanied an alarming epidemic in the capital in 1542. Again there was drought. Yan had his people print up copies of a pharmacopoeia for physicians to consult. He sent a copy to Jiajing.[85]

The Ministry of Rites had a hand in so many sectors of Ming governance that the name "Rites" hardly conveys any idea of the broad range of its responsibilities: foreign relations, cooks, translators, interpreters, physicians, schools, examinations, recruitment, and princely disputes, not to speak of a ministerial hand on the erratic pulse of nature's cosmic and climatological forces. Service in the Rites Ministry was good preparation for anyone stepping up from it into the Grand Secretariat.

* * *

In his official capacity as minister of rites for six years, Yan Song comes across as bland, competent, diligent, and ingratiating, and not much more than that. He was no ideologue, no contrarian, and no firebrand. There was another side to Yan Song, however, and his fellow bureaucrats were very much aware of it. He wanted to exercise dominance. Yan seems to have hidden this urge even from himself. His copious writings never allude to his aims, his hopes, his plans, or his dreams. He fed his ambition surreptitiously, through bribery under the table, an activity he more and more farmed out to his sole son, Yan Shifan, to keep his own hands clean. He needed above all to keep pleasing Jiajing, and he was a master of that.

Jiajing appointed Yan a grand secretary on September 24, 1542. Yan was sixty-two. His son was twenty-nine. Jiajing was thirty-five.

Jiajing was changing. Twenty intense and demanding years of ruling China, not only reconstructing its rites but participating in so many of them personally, on top of all the other obligations he tried earnestly to fulfill, were wearing him out. The battles over the Great Rites, the fight to build separate altars to Heaven and Earth and remove the idols from all the Confucian temples nationwide; the struggle to redesign and rebuild the ancestral temples, the trips to the Ming tombs, the trip to Chengtian, his conduct of all the public rites—huge, spectacular productions, daylong processions, thousands of singers, dancers, cooks, and police; meeting the court every day at dawn—all this was getting to be too much. Jiajing was coming close to mental exhaustion and physical collapse.

In 1536, he attended his last Classics Mat tutorial.[86] On September 10, 1540, he called a special meeting in the Wenhua Palace of the grand secretaries and Minister of Rites Yan Song. He had a personal confession to make to them. He said that since 1534 he'd stopped holding dawn court and that he now had to send substitutes to conduct the various sacrifices. "I'm just like a corpse in office," he said. "Recently my vitality (*xueqi*) has diminished, my hair and beard have half fallen out, my energy has declined, and I wasn't like that before." He said the realm, meanwhile, needed attention: governance was getting disordered, omens were becoming more frequent, finances were depleted, and the common people were not secure in their daily lives. These problems disturbed him even in his sleep, he said. In his mind, he felt as though he were teetering at the edge of an abyss. He said he'd like to take a year or two off to recuperate and get his health back. Perhaps his four-year-old heir apparent could act as regent during that time, as he'd done when Jiajing took his trip to Chengtian the year before.

The emperor wanted a general court discussion of the matter and a reply within three days. He may have been fishing for a vote of confidence in this, expecting the officials to protest his stepping down. Apparently they did just that. Yan Song won great favor by arguing that the ruler was concerned for the realm, he was mentally alert, and he should just delegate his ritual duties and continue to issue decisions and decrees from his palace quarters. (A Palace Guard vice commander ventured to disagree and was sent to prison for interrogation under torture for his temerity.) In an aside, Yan Song said that none of the documents about this matter were ever released and made public. [87]

Although Jiajing no longer took part in the grand state sacrifices, he remained serious about otherworldly things. His religion never focused inwardly upon the soul. It was always cosmic and outwardly directed. From early on, one can discern his deep feel for the unseen forces: Heaven, ancestors, the gods, signs and omens, the power of weather.

Fortunately for him, these forces were reachable through easier and more immediate channels than the great state rituals. Daoism showed the way. Daoism was a system of worship that was widely observed in the many princely houses scattered through central and north China. [88] Although it isn't known for sure, it might have been practiced in the Xing princedom that was Jiajing's childhood home. Or, more likely, it was palace eunuchs who first introduced him to *zhaizhao*, small, nondenominational altars that could be placed in any convenient palace room, where they could be used on any occasion for any length of time. Chief Grand Secretary Yang Tinghe had once joined the other high officials in demanding their removal. On May 19, 1523, the boy ruler caved in, resentfully. [89]

In 1524, Jiajing was introduced to a learned Daoist adept by the name of Shao Yuanjie, whom he made, in effect, a palace chaplain in 1526, a personal channel of access to the forces beyond. (Circumstantial evidence strongly suggests that Xia Yan was the key intermediary; Shao was living in a Daoist temple in Guiqi County in Jiangxi when Xia returned there in 1524 on mourning leave, and it was Xia who later composed Shao's epitaph, on Jiajing's orders.) Shao also became head of the Daoist church nationwide, with an office headquarters of his own in the Xianling Temple just west of the Imperial City, an annual salary of one hundred *shi*, forty Embroidered-Uniform Guardsmen, thirty *qing* (about fifty acres) of tax-free farmland, plus much else. The initial interview between Shao and the young emperor went very well, and Shao's prayers seemed to elicit immediate responses from the weather gods. Wisely and circumspectly, Shao deflected Jiajing's words of praise and attributed the gods' responses to the ruler's own "refinement and sincerity." But Jiajing still thought Shao's prayer sessions responsible for finally bringing on the birth of his first son in 1529 (and he was not faulted for the baby's death two months later). Tall and impressive looking, Shao "carried himself like a god, knew the classical literature from his youth, and later on absorbed the mysteries of Daoism; he could truly grasp the creative forces, control their workings, and direct wind and thunder with the greatest of ease." So Xia Yan wrote in Shao's epitaph.[90]

Jiajing's Daoist devotions would intensify as the years wore on. Grasping at his main chance, Yan Song would act as an eager and faithful supporter of and participant in Jiajing's personal religion. That was one big reason for his rise to the Grand Secretariat and his ability to stay there so long.

* * *

The year 1542 saw heightened Lu raids along the northern frontiers. Ming defenses weren't holding the line very well. Jiajing took advantage of a momentary lull to express his unease with the situation. After Xia Yan's dismissal on September 10, only one grand secretary, Chai Luan, was left. He was not a commanding figure, and Jiajing tended to sidestep him. On September 10, the emperor called in the ministers of revenue and war plus Yan Song, still minister of rites, and demanded their considered written opinions about how best to remedy China's border security lapses.[91]

National defense was untried waters for Yan Song; asking him to plan strategy was perhaps a qualifying examination for promotion to the Grand Secretariat. If it was, Yan passed it. He replied the next day. He noted the tendency of the Ming defense establishment to seesaw from panic to complacency and back to panic again. Ming defenses were riddled with weaknesses that Lu spies discover and the raiders exploit. Border-dwelling Chinese troops should replace the unmotivated provincial outsiders, who are there now, and are thin and weak due to supply failures. The border-dwelling Chinese are every bit as good fighters as the Lu and have the incentive of defending their own homes and families, but they must be well fed and well armed. As things stand, frontier service is such a hardship that our troops defect to the enemy because life as a raider is so much easier. Yan's remedies were obvious: find better leaders and tighten all the disciplinary bolts. Indeed, he ended by saying there was nothing out of the ordinary in his statement. Jiajing liked it.[92] Yan was formally made a grand secretary two weeks later, on September 24.

Ming commentators and historians hostile to Yan Song link his promotion not to his calm response to Jiajing's asking for his opinion on defense strategy, nor his hard work as rites minister, but to his fawning subservience to the emperor. There is some truth in that.

No sooner did Yan become a grand secretary but an impeachment of September 26 targeted him. Shen Liangcai, chief supervising secretary of the Office of Scrutiny for Personnel, charged him with greed, corruption, and self-seeking flattery. His promotion has dismayed the whole realm. Yan offered to resign. Jiajing ordered him to stay on.[93]

Another impeachment came in on October 21. Tong Hanchen, regional inspector of Shanxi, indicted Minister of Personnel Xu Zan for gross negligence, Minister of War Zhang Zan for corruption, and Yan Song for avarice, excess, and cunning evil. He said it was courting disaster to entrust such a man as Yan Song with government duties. Jiajing didn't buy that and absolved them all.[94]

Still another impeachment of Yan came in on November 10. Supervising Secretary Wang Ye, of the Nanjing Office of Scrutiny for Personnel, joined Censor Chen Shao and charged Yan with corruption and sly cunning, and for allowing his "despicable and evil son" Yan Shifan to traffic in bribes, encouraging official wrongdoing and inviting disaster for the Ming state. Jiajing sent this one out to court for discussion. Yan Song begged to resign. Whatever the result of the discussion, his resignation was not allowed.[95]

Impeachments sent up by speaking officials were seldom backed by evidence, and they weren't here either. They were allegations only. The emperor alone could authorize arrests, investigations, interrogations, and prosecutions.

Soon after, Sichuan regional inspector Xie Yu impeached a group of high officials, including Yan, as the "four evil ones," whose extermination would be an act of justice that would benefit the whole realm. To this, Yan replied with a statement laced with self-pity. The world knows of this impeachment, he said, thanks to the *Dibao* (*Capital Gazette*) and its circulation to officials everywhere; everyone is being led to believe an evil clique of villains is in power. Jiajing rejected the impeachment with anger and sarcasm and threatened retaliation against anyone who in the future might make more such allegations.[96]

Yan spent no small fraction of his time in the Grand Secretariat fending off impeachments. As time wore on, these impeachments became more specific in their allegations of wrongdoing. In tandem with that development, Jiajing's punishments for speaking out grew ever more severe.

On July 30, 1543, Yan answered a damning accusation endorsed by Minister of Personnel Xu Zan, but not initiated by him, relating to a certain Qian Kejiao, an Imperial University student he'd known since 1505 when he was a Hanlin junior compiler. The charge was serious. It appeared to catch Yan in flagrante delicto, as it were. The *Ming shilu* puts it this way:

> Grand Secretary Chai Luan sought on behalf of Zhang Weiyi, bureau secretary in the Ministry of Rites, a shift of position to the Ministry of Personnel, while Grand Secretary Yan Song sought the position of magistrate in Dongyang County for Imperial University student Qian Kejiao. [Xu Zan's] memorial impeached them. Also he sent up under seal letters sent by [Chai and Yan] to Wang Yuling, director of the Bureau of Appointments, ordering him [to make those appointments]. [Xu Zan] said this was just two instances [of corruption]; there must be much more. We protest these mountainous crimes, and you, the ruler, must agree with us; otherwise two powerful villains preside on the inside, while a pack of their eagle-dog adherents cooperate on the outside. . . .
> We hope you'll forgive us for doing our duty and send Zhang Weiyi and Qian Kejiao to the legal authorities for prosecution. That will send a warning to all unprincipled go-getters.

Jiajing sent this bombshell to the grand secretaries for their reply. Chief Grand Secretary Chai Luan said he'd been Zhang Weiyi's examiner on the Shuntian exams, that he was first on the metro exam and fourth on the final palace exam. "He did so well, and he was straight in character, so when a vacancy came up in personnel, I recommended him for his learning and behavior, and I so stated to Wang Yuling. I daresay this impugns my service to the ruler, and it all took place some years ago."[97]

Yan replied in shock and amazement. He said he had to explain this one in detail. The student's father, Qian Yu, from Zhejiang, was a skilled physician, and Yan was very ill back in those days, and he used to go to Qian Yu for medicine. Last winter, Qian Kejiao came to Beijing to see me, said Yan. He asked me for a note authorizing him to go see Xu Zan. I asked him for what purpose. He replied that his older brother Qian Rucheng was a good physician, and when Xu Zan held office in Zhejiang, he was impressed with his skills and kept up contact with him. Qian Rucheng sent me a letter asking for a note so he could come see me. Qian Kejiao wanted my help in getting him a position. "I refused," said Yan. "I don't dare interfere in Ministry of Personnel affairs, and so your elder brother should arrange to seek that for himself." Yan ordered a servant to escort Qian Kejiao out the door. That was the last he saw of him, he said. So it needs to be investigated how this note got falsely attributed to me. Yan said he and Xu Zan were on respectful terms, but perhaps he resents me. He urged Jiajing to order the Embroidered-Uniform Guard to arrest and interrogate Qian Kejiao and find out who forged the note and sent it to Xu Zan.

The interrogation was carried out. It turned up the information that a cabal had been formed; that Wang Yuling, director of the ministry's Bureau of Appointments, had somehow urged or forced Xu Zan to endorse the accusation; and that several others of Yan Song's detractors were involved. Jiajing defended Yan. He let Xu Zan stay. On Wang Yuling he was lenient, merely sending him home reduced to commoner status. The others he sent to posts in the provinces. He ordered Qian Kejiao to be imprisoned and interrogated further.[98]

Jiajing personally wrote the response to Xu Zan's charges. "I've read your memorial," the *Ming shilu* records him as saying. "Your intent is certainly to be supportive, but you all base this on one single directive, one single note, and without these you have no case. And Xu Zan didn't initiate this. He bent to pressure from Wang Yuling and those in his clique who backed him up. Chai Luan wrote his note long ago. Yan's note was forged. There is no big fact-based case of bribery here.[99]

Wang Yuling went home, with his reputation for honesty and integrity not only undamaged but enhanced. He hated corruption. Reportedly, morale in the Ministry of Personnel collapsed when he was removed. It is said that the Embroidered-Uniform Guard, on inspecting his baggage as he left Beijing, found nothing in the way of ill-gotten gains at all.[100] Another confrontation of righteousness versus power seemed to be building up. How far would it go?

Quite far. No sooner did Jiajing settle the Xu Zan/Wang Yuling issue, but an attention-grabbing dissent was sent in by Zhou Yi (1506–1566), a supervising secretary of the Office of Scrutiny for Personnel, and a much younger man than Xu or Wang, fired up since his student days by an ideal of fearlessness—"Don't avoid the cauldron; don't forget the ditch." This was, to be sure, not Yan Song's recipe for a life in politics. Zhou Yi exercised the powers of his position to the maximum, sending one official after another into dismissal. He decided to destroy Yan Song, and indeed he braved the seething cauldron when he did so.

He wrote two attacks on Yan Song. The first seems to be a draft that was not actually sent in. Even so, it deserves translation, because it shows another side of Yan Song and affords a window into what many bureaucrats in

Beijing were probably thinking but were too cowed to articulate. (Zhou sounds a bit like Cicero fulminating against Catiline.)

A fervent plea that the emperor will terminate a bad situation early on and sternly put an end to villainous and sycophantic grand secretaries, who lie and act dictatorially:

I learned on September 23, 1542, that you made Minister of Rites Yan Song a grand secretary. We [speaking officials] said at that time that a bad man shouldn't have such a high position, but you rejected all the protests and defended Yan all the more firmly. Is Yan so worthy that you should back him so completely? Or is it that you think we're all wrong?

Yan Song has been busy at your side for years now, so his corrupt mindset, his vile behavior, and the shallow crudity of his opinions have become fully evident. Right now you've let him have his way, and when he displeases you, you let him admit his shortcomings, and you test him, so that he'll be grateful to you and give good service. So Yan Song knows shame and works hard to reform and renovate himself. He doesn't necessarily lack a conscience. He replied to one impeachment that it was like falling into a bitter sea. He also said the impeacher was raising matters from long ago. Yan Song would do well to reflect that you were especially kind to choose him at a time when everyone was angry and suspicious of him. He should also feel shame that he has such an evil reputation among those below him. He should introspect, vow to turn over a new leaf, to fulfill at least a little your expectations for him, and quiet some of the adverse things others say about him. He must stop his lying and his meanness, and not keep on betraying the dynasty's favor and hating what's impartial and right. . . .

During March–April 1543, you gave him a silver seal bearing the words: "loyalty, diligence, acuity, thoroughness." . . . When you chose those four words, didn't you expect him to live up to them? Did you think that the monetary value of it would embarrass him, so that he'd perform loyally, diligently, discerningly, and thoroughly? Maybe your aim was to have him reflect inward, rise early and retire late, to fulfill those words and enhance your brilliance as a judge of men, and be the help to you that his position demands.

While Chief Grand Secretary Chai Luan was on sick leave, Yan Song was able to seize and monopolize power, yet during that time, everyone could see your brilliance and hear your thunder. Everyone at court was prodded into self-correction, and everyone, inside and out, was spurred into creating good policy. The job of the grand secretaries is simply to be your aides and draft replies to memorials. It's the throne that decides whether to agree or not. Who dares seize that prerogative? . . . Yan Song gladly seizes it. His private gate fills with the carts and horses of men in trouble or seeking favors. Any who displease him are gotten rid of. Thus recently the case of Wang Yaofeng—despised by everyone everywhere, as everyone except Yan Song seems to realize. For some unknown reason, Yan protected him on the pretext that you favored him. He arranged for Minister of Personnel Xu Zan to come to the Dongge [in the Forbidden City] to receive your directive, that since the ministry hadn't gotten the facts and hadn't recommended him, when they get this directive, they must send up the names of two men [including Wang]. So then they recommended Wang Yaofeng, who got the appointment. That shocked everyone. But no one protested, as they all thought this was your firm intention, so they just let it pass, and if Wang did well, that would end the matter, and if he didn't, it wouldn't be too late to impeach him.

Now the Nanjing *kedao*, Zhang Rudeng and others, sent up impeachments. In response your directive clearly said, "As the previous directive said, it's forbidden to recommend Wang Yaofeng. Recommend two other men for the vacancy." This rescript, in your own hand and in your own voice, cheered everyone with its clarity and decisiveness. . . . Who would think that Yan Song would dare, in such an enlightened age, to be so dishonest? Even if you intended to appoint Wang Yaofeng, he should have firmly dissuaded you, declined to accept such an edict, and refused to be a sycophant until you changed your mind. If that was not your intention, then the penal code's stipulation on fraud clearly applies.

Yan Song also told people that Chai Luan was out due to chronic illness and that he told you it would be hard for him to assume the whole load, but that you told him the Duke of Zhou [in China's Golden Age] did it. Whether that's true or not, I don't know. If you did say that, then he should be sweating and trembling in fear that he can't fulfill such a charge and constantly try to comply. Should he happily brag of it to others in order to inflate himself?

A grand secretary's main duty is to advance worthy men and block the unworthy, to encourage the good and condemn the evil, to enhance the ruler's virtue, and to leave behind a model legacy. Right now things are busy. We have a critical need for worthy talents. The realm has no shortage of valiant men. Surely some are available to fill vacancies. Can Yan Song claim he doesn't know of them? If he knows of them, then he should tell you and recommend their immediate appointment so as to fix problems. But we've heard nothing of that. So is he blocking worthies? If he doesn't know of them, he should be exerting every effort to find them. He shouldn't be complacently blathering away over fine food and mouthing off to the court inside and on the streets outside.

Fan Jizu ingratiates himself with the powerful; like a housefly or a dog, he leaves foul traces that are too many to recount. So I'll just cite two instances. He and the former Military Defense Circuit vice commissioner at Bazhou, Wang Fengling, colluded in brick manufacture for frontier wall building, from which they skimmed such a huge amount of silver that a few months later no silver was left. They profited from depleting and weakening the army. They were larcenous officials who deserve death. I regret [Fan's survival]. But Yan

Song protected him, and he was never prosecuted. He would have been fortunate just to enjoy old age and die at home. But now he's been recalled as minister of works and censor in chief to collect big timber in Huguang. This is an urgent task, but many men at court in Beijing and outside could handle it, so why pick the criminal Fan Jizu? Yan Song must explain that to you, but he hasn't said a word. [101]

Zhou Yi's draft impeachment, torn off at the end, goes on to make a few more allegations. It looks as though there was hard evidence for some of it, especially the case involving Wang Yaofeng. Yan Song was conducting his own appointments business, keeping Jiajing in the dark about it. On the other side of the coin, no surviving biographical sources about Fan Jizu, so damningly portrayed here by Zhou Yi, hint at any corruption. Fan comes across as highly literate and as wise and effective in every post he ever occupied. [102] Which is the true story? Typically in the case of emotionally charged politics, it's very hard to say.

Zhou Yi wrote another impeachment targeting Yan Song (and others). This one he did submit, and it provoked a response from Jiajing. The focus of it was different. It sidestepped fraud and corruption and instead targeted disharmony. Again I translate, to bring to light currents of a mounting bureaucratic opposition to the ruler and his grand secretaries:

> Any who serve the ruler, high or low in rank, inside or outside, are loyal if they exert all efforts to identify themselves with the state (*ti guo*), and harmonious if they all cooperate to achieve things. They're disinterested when they put others before themselves, impartial when they forget enmity and join worthies. Never has it been possible to achieve order otherwise. And certainly not when grand secretaries compete at court, and top defense officials compete on the frontiers. Yet now Grand Secretaries Chai Luan and Yan Song and Minister of Personnel Xu Zan accuse each other of villainy, while on the frontiers [four officials all have conflicting views]. This is ominous, and disaster looms for the state. . . .
>
> The grand secretaries stand atop the court, looked up to by the whole realm, taken as exemplars by the bureaucracy. They are observed and closely imitated. So when there's a crack of disagreement, crevices of flattery and praise open up outside. And when the highest officials vie heatedly, then a disastrous situation of combat breaks out below. This has always been the case.
>
> You've been ruling now for twenty-two years. Early on, you eagerly sought good order, and now your concern is to assuage the common people. That's wholly to the good. We live in an age of great peace, and foreigners

everywhere come and submit. Recently, however, you've turned to [Daoist] prayers and sacrifices, yet everywhere floods and droughts persist. You've instituted silver collection, yet the treasuries haven't filled. You've issued tax remissions, yet the common people still suffer. You've issued orders to select commanders and train troops, yet there is no quiet on the frontiers. Why is this? Why, despite your worries and anxieties, is no one willing to obey your commands? What times are these, when inside, finances are exhausted and demands of all sorts rise? When outside, our enemies flourish while our frontier defenses lie depleted? . . .

[The grand secretaries should be remedying this], but Chai Luan and Yan Song rely on your favor and act selfishly. They bless and threaten, sell protection and wreak vengeance.

I've heard that they approach you separately with their disagreements and mutual denunciations. They're not harmonious. How can we make them get along? The grand secretaries, the Nine Ministers, and all the other officials are ranked high and low, but they all form one body of eyes, ears, hands, and feet of willing obedience. They need to cooperate, not fight. They need to tell the Ministry of Personnel of all the good and bad candidates they know of so the ministry can make recommendations. Then everyone is convinced [that the procedure is fair]. They shouldn't use their powers selfishly and impose unsuitable choices. The ministry must show integrity, as heroes and heroines do, so they earn respect and so that powerful men can't wrongfully interfere. The ministry shouldn't just cave in and develop a compliant habit to the point where it can no longer protest.

Right now, Yan Song dominates all, and he overpowers the bureaucracy. He's assumed such command that any who want to memorialize their doubts and fears must first dance attendance at his gate and get his approval before they dare send their statements up to you, the emperor. So officials everywhere have no fear of you. They just fear Yan Song. Chai Luan just cringes and can't make his own case. Weak as he is, he can't get men to side with him, yet his position is high enough that he constitutes a hindrance to Yan Song. Minister Xu Zan is one of three in two generations of his family who have served in the Ministry of Personnel. He can be taken to be a hereditary official. He's cautious and respectful, but his sense of what's right is too weak to withstand the demands of the powerful. You as ruler know this perfectly well, so you know I'm not lying to you. . . .

High officials secretly squeeze and openly press, accusing each other of villainy. What sort of ruler do they think you are? What kinds of minds have they, that they don't foster healthy spirits, protect talents, and plan together to resist humiliations, but just vent their personal resentments?

Earlier, Censors Xie Yu and Tong Hanchen impeached the grand secretaries, but they were blamed and removed. . . . I'm afraid there will be no one to speak up. . . . And this is ominous and frightening. [103]

This attack Yan Song had to reply to (and here I provide a close paraphrase). He said that when he came on board, it was already an established routine that officials could confer with grand secretaries whenever they wished. I've not followed that, and Xu Zan and others can be asked to confirm it. As to the other officials, I seldom meet them when I'm on duty, and this the people of the capital know full well. So what Zhou Yi says I do, and how I actually behave, are at complete odds. I and Chai Luan are yearmates, and we have no rift, though we have differences of opinion. We just want to get things right. . . . We have harmony despite our disagreements, and we serve the ruler. We don't denounce others before you, so you know perfectly well his allegations are false.

Jiajing replied on July 30, giving Yan his full support. Types like Zhou Yi, he said, are out to win at all costs and will stop at nothing. Some of Zhou's barbs were even aimed at himself. [104]

So which side is to be believed here? Some bureaucrats in a self-righteous, angry state of mind, or the topmost guardians of the Ming realm? Or neither? [105]

In the late afternoon of July 30, Zhou Yi said he received the following personal message from Jiajing himself:

> Zhou Yi says when officials don't get along, they betray the ruler and invite disaster. That's right. But his real mind is on slander. He says I do daily prayers and sacrifices when it would be better to get harmony and virtue into the minds of the top men than to get the gods to listen through clouds of incense. But I serve Heaven, and the gods all provide protection. In a realm as big as ours, of course there will be flood or drought somewhere. As to good order under Heaven, that will be the case when all you officials act loyally and impartially, harmoniously and sincerely, joining minds to help the ruler. What horror can't be remedied then? If officials inside and outside aren't harmonious, and you know who they are, then why haven't you named them in impeachments? Reply with the full case.

Zhou Yi replied, "in fear and trepidation," grateful that the emperor didn't condemn him to death. He apologized for his "ignorance and shallowness" and promised a full statement.

He may not have had time to compose it. Jiajing replied with a crushing rescript. "This memorial's undertone slanders the ruler and blames the Ministry of Personnel. . . . It pretends to be an impeachment, but actually it's [a ploy] to gather a clique and harm the good. . . . Hatred for the grand secretaries is his idea of [preaching] the Great Way for assisting in rule. . . . It's perverse and has nothing to do with the Way. I order the Embroidered-Uniform Guard to bring him up to the front of the Meridian Gate and there flog him forty times with the big stick, as was done with Yang Jue. Then put him in prison in fetters for an undetermined period."[106]

* * *

Back in 1524, Jiajing's insistence on his own version of the Great Rites had cost seventeen men their lives. Now it appeared as though in 1542–1543 another wave of official dissent was heading toward a crest, this one targeting Jiajing personally, plus his grand secretaries, plus Duke Guo Xun, in the atmosphere created by the ruler's detachment from his earlier orthodox commitments to an intensified preoccupation with religious Daoism. Another civic pantheon of martyrs in the cause of righteousness appeared to be in the process of formation. And Yang Jue's prison writings certainly helped such a process along. Yang was horribly abused in prison and denied food, and he noted that upon his arrival, Zhou Yi was also being starved. Both prisoners relied on inmate Liu Kui to share his rations with them, and so they managed to survive.[107]

Yang Jue (1493–1549) hadn't targeted Yan Song. He tangled head-on with Jiajing himself. A censor, he fired some heavy ordnance. An early shot reveals vividly the dissenting frame of mind. Returning north from a mission to Huguang in 1529, Yang reported a terrible famine in the countryside, indeed nearly a catastrophe. People have to eat before they can be taught, he said. And only after being taught can rites and music be performed. "But now in the afflicted areas, 60 to 70 percent of the people have died. The survivors turn to banditry. Even families with some food supplies can't protect them. The situation is growing out of control. But the court ignores it. It argues about whether to separate [the sacrifices to Heaven and Earth]! . . . Today is not time to revive rites and music. We must instead rescue the common people from death. Always it's been the case that the Mandate of Heaven disappears and dynasties collapse when the people become poor and turn to outlawry and the rulers don't care to take notice."[108]

Jiajing ignored Yang's sarcastic stabs at his program of ritual reconstruction; he simply sent the statement down to the Ministry of Revenue and ordered the officials there to provide relief.

It was Yang's long and scathing critique, sent up on March 1, 1541, that prompted Jiajing's angry and cruel retaliation. Yang found China to be in sorry condition under Jiajing's misguided sway. He now raged at weak frontier and coastal defenses, rampant corruption, sycophancy, and ominous portents. Yang denounced Chief Grand Secretary Xia Yan for his obsequious complacency and Duke Guo Xun for his wormlike rottenness. Yang saw with his own eyes eighty corpses in the southern suburbs of Beijing, and who knows how many more there must be elsewhere? Where are the funds for relief? Construction has been going on now for ten years, the Ministry of Works has added dozens of officials, and thunder altars are being built far and near at the behest of the Daoist [Tao Zhongwen]. And the ruler has given up the classics tutorials, no longer meets court, and no one ever sees or hears him. All the highest officials are sycophants; extraordinary honors and rewards go to Daoists. How much worse can things get? How much greater a laughingstock can the ruler become? His recent intolerance of criticism has cost excellent men like Luo Hongxian their careers. Nothing short of a complete end to all this will do. [109]

Jiajing read this unwelcome screed, and instead of sending it down for general discussion, replied directly to it by having the Embroidered-Uniform Guard arrest and interrogate its author. Apparently he wanted Yang to confess guilt and express remorse. Flayed and fettered, Yang refused to give in. His prison statement to Jiajing bristled with classical, historical, and earlier Ming instances of how rulers should and should not respond to loyal dissent. He repeated his earlier complaints of military and financial misrule and why and how these outrages must end. He noted how the emperor had sent spies from the Eastern Depot to ferret out his true intentions. "When first imprisoned," he wrote,

> The prison guards Ni Min and Sun Gang, owing to your fierce anger and my deep guilt, stopped my food and drink. They allotted me daily government rice, which made me sick, and I nearly died. Then Tao et al. let my houseman provide gruel and wheat soup twice daily, and so it's been for some forty-five days. That's allowed me to live. That's thanks to your virtue and grace. You don't want me to die and thereby give your government a reputation for killing dissenters who might not be disloyal to you. Now, however, the three or four men from the Eastern Depot and the Embroidered-Uniform Guard prison officials and guards are nervously on edge day and night, starving me as though they want to kill me. I don't mind dying, but killing me by starving me is not something a sagely mind should entertain. I'm afraid liars and deceivers have spread rumors that have gained traction with the crowd, and so things have come to this. If you judge me guilty, you must publicly execute me as a warning to the disloyal. Or exile me to a frontier garrison. Or send me home.

That's a sagely gesture of forgiveness. If I were truly guilty, I couldn't hope for that.[110]

The prison asked that Yang's case be tried at court by the legal authorities. Jiajing refused. Apparently, the off-and-on starvation regimen imposed on Yang was the ruler's own idea.[111] A few men were brave enough to protest the unjust abuse heaped on Yang. On or about May 23, a bureau secretary in the Ministry of Revenue, Zhou Tianzuo, pleaded with the throne for Yang's release. Jiajing ordered him flogged sixty times and imprisoned alongside Yang. Heavily wounded, he died three days later, at the age of thirty. Yang wrote his obituary. On or about November 3, Pu Hong, the regional inspector of Yang's home province, Shaanxi, begged again for Yang's release. Jiajing ordered mounted police to go out to Shaanxi and arrest Pu. They brought him to Beijing and the Decree Prison on December 30, 1541. He was taken out and flogged a hundred times on January 15, 1542, and placed in shackles. He died on January 21. Yang vividly described the awfulness of it all in his obituary.[112]

Zhou Yi and Yang were joined on October 24, 1542, by another learned cell-mate, and as avid a Confucian as they. Liu Kui, vice director of the Bureau of Forestry and Crafts (a Ministry of Works subsidiary) was alarmed at the cost of all the new Daoist construction going on in West Park. Several new halls were still being built, and on top of that, the erection of a "Thunder Altar for the Protection of the Dynasty and the Well-Being of the People" was about to begin. Liu advised Jiajing that the project should be postponed for a lack of funding for it. Jiajing thought this simply an anti-Daoist ploy, and so he ordered Liu to be flogged and sent to the Decree Prison.[113]

The cruel and unjust punishments Jiajing personally imposed on Zhou, Yang, Liu, and several others, described in gruesome detail by Yang, underscored the bad odor that would forever cling to Jiajing's long rule. This repression echoed on a smaller scale the Great Rites crackdown of 1524. It was a bad stain on the Ming escutcheon, with the Decree Prison a sort of Guantanamo of law-defying injustice and long-term physical abuse. If, as is likely, its purpose was to frighten the rest of Ming officialdom and discourage any thought of another mass protest and demonstration, it worked.

* * *

And Jiajing's Daoism intensified. The ruler's attraction to religious Daoism seems deeply felt and genuine. It was consistent with his lifelong embrace of natural processes and supernatural essences generally. He was coming to the belief that adepts could by esoteric means make influential contact with the terrestrial, atmospheric, and spiritual realms. He took real pleasure in good portents and took warning from bad ones, beseeching the thunder god for rain, or snow, or good harvests, or protection from frontier raids. It was also possible to converse with the spirit world by way of the planchette and get yes-or-no answers to judicial or other queries that way. Elixirs and alchemy rounded out the menu.

West Park was a big preserve inside the walls of the Imperial City, on the west side of the separately walled and smaller Forbidden City. By degrees, Jiajing built it into a holy city, a sort of Daoist Vatican, presided over by Shao Yuanjie, then by his protégé Tao Zhongwen, who were the ruler's personal chaplains as well as heads of the Daoist church nationwide. (Tao accompanied the ruler on his trip to Chengtian in 1539 and, they say, predicted the fire that would destroy the traveling palace; thus forewarned, the ruler survived it.)

But Jiajing's turn to Daoism was not at all an escape from his decision-making obligations as ruler. West Park gradually replaced the Forbidden City as the center of Ming government.[114] The death of Jiajing's mother freed him of any further obligation to spend time in the Forbidden City, and he spent more and more of it in West Park. But what drove him to live in West Park permanently, never, until he died, to return to the main palace, was an event the emperor himself described as something unprecedented in all of recorded history. It was indeed horrifying.

As nearly as can be ascertained, sometime during a night in November 1542, a gang of nine palace girls, all listed by name, entered the apartment of the attractive Upright Consort, currently in high favor, where Jiajing lay fast asleep, and tried to kill him by strangling him with a cord. They stuffed cloth in his mouth so he couldn't yell. But they didn't tie the knot correctly, or else couldn't pull it tight enough. Jiajing gurgled and thrashed about. Four or five other girls, part of the gang, never had a chance to get into the action. Apparently the girls were acting under the direction of a certain Restful Concubine nee Wang. (One can also imagine that they all suffered abusive treatment from Jiajing.) Consort Cao, mother of one of the ruler's daughters, had no part in the plot, which was planned over time and would appear to have been prompted by Concubine Wang's jealousy. The girls who hadn't yet taken part, seeing that the assassination attempt was not going well, and surely but vainly hoping to escape blame, ran and told the Empress Fang of what was going on. The empress, with her eunuchs, hurried into the apartment and rescued Jiajing, whose throat was injured so that he couldn't speak. Physicians were called in, and they got the bleeding stopped. Empress Fang had her eunuchs conduct a hasty inquiry. To Jiajing's lifelong regret, Consort Cao was wrongly named as a conspirator and was executed. Empress Fang, it seems, was behind that.

The retribution was swift and terrible. By a directive to the Ministry of Justice, Jiajing ordered the following: "This gang of palace girls, Yang Jinying and the rest, plus nee Wang, plotted to kill me in my bed. Death is too light a penalty for such a heinous crime. You will interrogate and get things clear. Arrest them all, leaders and followers, and put [the guilty] to slow slicing, as the Ming Code stipulates. Confiscate properties. Don't prosecute Ai Furong, as she tried to stop it."

On November 26, 1542, the ministry replied and reported that they went to the Yinghe Gate [unidentified] and received the above directive from eunuch Zhang Zuo of the Directorate of Ceremonial. They also received the cord used, plus the cloth used as a gag. These they put in storage. The Embroidered-Uniform Guard commander Chen Yin handed over sixteen girls, who were taken tied up to a marketplace, where each was put to death by slow slicing. Their corpses were then dismembered and their severed heads put on public display. A list of all the dead girls by name was appended. (There was no mention of Consort Cao or Concubine Wang.)

The medical treatment given Jiajing was conducted by Xu Shen (1478–1543), a well-respected head of the Imperial Academy of Medicine. He vowed to commit suicide if he failed to heal the emperor. A concoction of peach pits, safflower, and rhubarb got the bleeding stopped in the 7–9 a.m. time period. At 1–3 p.m., Jiajing could stand up and make sounds. He coughed up quite a bit of blood. By 3–5 p.m., he could speak again. Further doses of the concoction soon brought him back to normal.[115]

Jiajing left Empress Fang behind and, as noted, moved permanently out of the Forbidden City and took up permanent quarters in West Park. That was on November 28. Yan Song, newly elevated to the Grand Secretariat, advised Jiajing that he should issue an edict and reassure the realm that he was well. The ruler did so on December 8. He gave a brief account of the girls' attempt on his life and said they were led by two "palace ladies" (*yushi*). Jiajing seems at this point to have believed that Consort Cao was a conspirator. He noted the girls' lawful execution by slow slicing and the beheading of all their close relatives. He mentioned sending officials to thank all the gods and ancestors and said the purpose of the edict was to put an end to any rumors and tell everyone in China that he had happily survived.[116]

* * *

Personal attacks and impeachments, well founded or not, trailed Yan Song throughout his career. He always managed to defend himself adroitly before the only judge and jury he had to face—Jiajing. As grand secretary, there wasn't much of importance for him to do, no crisis until 1550. He had ample time to attend to Jiajing's unending demands for written Daoist prayers, maneuver against rivals in the Grand Secretariat, and run his bureaucratic machine—with his son and aide Yan Shifan doing much of the actual work.

The only noticeable difference between Yan Song and Jiajing, and it was a minor one, was the ruler's trust in Daoist elixirs and Yan Song's caution. There may have been an unstated rivalry with the ruler's Daoist guru, Tao Zhongwen, in play here. Xu Shen had healed Jiajing's throat wound with herbal medicine, but Shao Yuanjie, and after him Tao Zhongwen, were purveyors of a different type of medicine, alchemical rather than herbal, and featuring "red lead" (i.e., cinnabar) and "truth-holding cakes," the latter concocted of blood taken from the mouths of newborn babies.[117] Around 1540, as minister of rites, Yan responded to an edict of Jiajing's, to the effect that while Daoist "techniques" were worldly and not Heaven centered, there was something authentic in it, and the ruler wanted benefits from it. Yan replied that the ruler needed to be on guard; if the adepts were simply offering to translate base metals into gold and silver for use as funds to pay construction costs, that was fine, but if they claim longevity effects if ingested, then history shows that this is likely to be charlatanism, as gold and silver may be harmful if eaten.[118] Yan doubted, in a gentle follow-up memorial, whether a certain alchemist, long resident in Beijing, could really make gold and silver. Perhaps he can, but he should be tested. Have loyal and honest eunuchs take copper cash from the imperial treasury and watch and see what the adept can do with it. If construction costs can be eased this way, that's fine. But eating it for the sake of longevity is another matter.[119]

The unnamed alchemist here in fact refers to Duan Chaoyong, a crook and impostor introduced to Jiajing through the good offices of Duke Guo Xun. Duan was arrested and died in prison in 1543.[120]

Then there was Gu Kexue (d. 1560), who caused some trouble for his *jinshi* year-mate, Yan Song. Gu's story has it that after he left, or was ousted from officialdom, he went home and took up alchemy, specializing in the manufacture of "autumn stone," pills made from children's urine, said to prolong one's life when swallowed. Yan Song recommended him to Jiajing. Eager to use Jiajing's quest for drugs as a way to return to official life, he reportedly paid Yan a huge bribe and came to stay in Yan's house in Beijing. Yan had to explain to Jiajing what was going on, because Gu's presence was public knowledge and was causing a stir. Yan admitted that Gu and his many housemen, coming in and out day and night, were a nuisance, but he swore to the sincerity of Gu's hope to help with Jiajing's health needs. [121] Rumors, however, had it that Gu's pills contained unknown and suspicious ingredients. Yan suggested that the Imperial Dispensary and the Imperial Academy of Medicine test them. [122] Then Yan grew uneasy with Gu. Rumors targeting Gu, he said, were really aimed at bringing about Yan's own dismissal. "I'm a grand secretary," Yan explained, "and my house has to be carefully guarded, but [Gu's] kinsmen and servants come in and out noisily, and his friends and relatives come by to visit him, and I can't stop their eavesdropping." Yan suggested it might be best if the emperor ordered Gu to go back home. [123] There was a backup; Yan at the same time supported another ex-official and manufacturer of autumn stones, Sheng Duanming (1470–1550), a more modest, less controversial figure than Gu. [124]

In fact, Yan Song was publicly impeached in 1546 by Censor He Weibo over his sponsorship of the two pill makers. His response is a good example of his political adroitness in action. First, he pointed up errors of fact in the censor's allegations, which both Yan and Jiajing could easily spot, but then he reminded the ruler that no outsider could know what people at the highest level know, and that the censor should be forgiven, because it was, after all, his job to impeach. Jiajing, however, thought He Weibo was a stalking horse for others. He was arrested, imprisoned, flogged, and removed from civil service. By that, Jiajing showed his firm support for Yan Song, and for pill makers everywhere. [125]

* * *

The Grand Secretariat followed their ruler's permanent move to West Park. They lived there, conferred with the emperor on decision making there, dressed up in Daoist costume for rituals there, and were on call day and night to write the special prayers whenever Jiajing was moved to plead to the thunder god or other divine entities. Without a skilled and willing hand to write these boring texts, one was hard put to gain the ruler's favor. Yan Song cheerfully performed this duty until his very last years, when he tired of it.

When Yan was first brought into the Grand Secretariat in 1542, it was shortly after Xia Yan's dismissal, so he became junior to the new chief grand secretary, Chai Luan, in a two-man Secretariat. One thing Yan could not long abide was being some other official's subordinate.

Chai Luan (1477–1546) was a Beijing native and a *jinshi* of 1505. In his career, he showed literary talent; he made his way into Jiajing's notice and favor with his lecturing on the classics, and the ruler liked his modesty, assiduity, fine appearance, and good Beijing accent. From 1527 to 1533, and again in 1540, he served as a lower-ranking grand secretary, drafting re-scripts. Military issues were his specialty. He also wrote nice congratulatory poems on felicitous omens. In 1539, Jiajing sent him on a yearlong tour of the entire northern frontier, a task Chai carried out conscientiously and effec-tively, building defense works, boosting troop morale, issuing rewards, and showing everyone on the frontiers that the ruler cared about them and hadn't forgotten them.

Many believed that Yan Song, from behind the scenes, masterminded Chai Luan's ruin. On September 14, 1544, two supervising secretaries of the Office of Scrutiny for Justice charged seven officials with corruptly facilitat-ing the surprising successes, all at the same time, of Chai's sons plus their tutor and in-law through both the Shuntian and metro exams. What was going on here? Jiajing sent the impeachment down to the Ministry of Person-nel and Censorate for their reactions. Before those organs answered, Chai Luan sent the ruler an explanation and asked that those charged be allowed to retake their exams. That, reportedly, angered the ruler. "Chai Luan is under impeachment," he roared. "I directed a review. He didn't wait for that, but on his own sent up this unhelpful retort. He claims he was on duty in West Park the whole time, sharing the sedan chair with Yan Song, yet he alone gets indicted. His attitude is defiant; he dares lie to me, saying he was busy writing rescripts and taking part in Daoist observances, that he has to be on duty early in the Grand Secretariat, inasmuch as I don't hold dawn court [anymore]. His two sons may have the requisite talent, but how can anyone expect me to accept them simultaneously? That is just too provocative."

He ordered the ministry and Censorate to offer no excuses and propose penalties. On the grounds that this offense clearly befouled the ancestors' recruitment system, Jiajing reduced Chai Luan and all four exam takers to commoner status. All their examiners were overawed by the examinees' connection to Chai Luan, but they took no bribes from him. There were other bribes and irregularities, however, so the emperor ordered three main examiners flogged sixty strokes and removed from civil service, with the others also punished.[126]

So Chai Luan, after many years of good and faithful service to Jiajing and to Ming China, was abruptly and dishonorably discharged, thanks to the bad impression made by his sons and his own indignant reaction. Chai Luan's ouster made Yan Song the chief grand secretary. But did Yan really have a hand in that? He may have spoken to Jiajing off the record. Who knows? Certainly there were suspicions that Yan prompted the supervising secretaries to launch the impeachment.[127] But when Chai died at home in 1546 and his three sons buried him in the family grave site outside the Chongwen Gate (southeast of the Imperial City), who did they ask to write the inscription for the spirit-way stela? Yan Song! His remarks were brief, fulsome, and non-controversial.[128] His hand, if it did facilitate Chai's ouster, was well concealed.

* * *

Yan Song's last rival for Ming China's highest post was Xia Yan. Thinking it not a good idea to have Yan dominate everything, Jiajing recalled Xia for the last time in 1545 to serve as chief once again, with Yan unhappily subordinate to him. The previous chapter detailed how Xia's dismissive attitude toward Jiajing, plus his disastrous support for the failed plan to recapture the Ordos, led to his final removal in 1548. But Xia was not simply dismissed; he was, in an unprecedented and shocking act, publicly executed. The question here is, what role did Yan Song play in that?

The Ordos controversy was a political minefield, full of danger, and Yan's acumen was seriously challenged to deal with it safely. The key was to read correctly the ruler's state of mind, which was positive at first, but then turned doubtful on the realization that the Ming lacked the resources necessary to allow such a campaign to succeed. The ruler was beginning to think those favoring the plan were frivolous and light-minded and pointing the dynasty toward the verge of an abyss. Xia Yan enthusiastically backed the plan. Jiajing solicited Yan Song's opinion.

Yan's reply was deft. Why, he asked rhetorically, had the recovery of the Ordos never been advanced as a plan before this? Our armies are weaker now than ever before. Our finances are in even worse shape. The main planner, Zeng Xian, thinks five million or more taels silver will be needed to support 120,000 troops over three years of combat. This we cannot do. The harm to the civilian population will be incalculable. Beijing officials all know full well that the plan is impossible, but they're too afraid to say so. "As for Xia Yan," he concluded, "he and I are colleagues, and he has done well in every other respect. I, on the other hand, have been useless, and I ask you to dismiss me."

Jiajing replied to this on February 13, 1548. He said he had never been taken in by Xia Yan's enthusiasm for the plan but had just quietly played along with him, and everyone misread that as an approval. He denied Yan's request to resign.[129]

That caught the outer court by complete surprise. In fear, the opinion of the officials swung suddenly and completely away from their earlier support of the plan. On February 15, Jiajing ordered Xia's dismissal, and the Embroidered-Uniform Guard was sent out to Shaanxi to arrest Zeng Xian.

Yan Song, meanwhile, successfully slithered away from the circle of blame. He admitted he was on duty the whole time, but Xia Yan had cut him totally out of the loop, so he was never told anything about the Ordos plan. He fully endorsed the criminal charges of bribery the judicial organs had laid against Zeng and Xia. Documents proved the case. But he advised Jiajing to preserve the *guoti* and not impose too harsh a penalty on Xia Yan.[130] So he saw to it that all blame for harsh cruelty would fall on Jiajing solely and personally. Yan Song would avoid it. He could in all conscience say he urged leniency.

Zeng Xian was publicly executed on April 25, 1548. Xia Yan's moment came on November 1 of the same year. These "killings," as posterity labeled them, were Jiajing's unassisted handiwork. They certainly added to his growing reputation for cruelty and injustice.

* * *

After Xia Yan's execution, the supreme governing organs of mid-Ming China, the emperor together with his grand secretaries, entered a long period of unusual stability. Jiajing lived and did as he liked as a devotee of religious Daoism, yet he never relaxed his grip on power. The bureaucracy lived in fear of his often venomous rescripts and edicts. The Grand Secretariat evolved into a troika, with Yan Song in control and two younger subordinates, Xu Jie and Li Ben, under his thumb and offering no overt challenge to him. This arrangement lasted fourteen years, from 1548 until 1562, when Xu Jie at last engineered the octogenarian Yan's ouster. The troika steered the realm through the crisis years of 1550–1559, when Lu raids on the north and Wokou raids along the coast imposed a severe strain on Ming China's resources and coherence as a system. The question here is, how did Ming China cope with this decade-long crisis, and what was Yan Song's role in it? Did he help or hinder a national survival strategy?

Just two years after the debacle of the aggressive Ordos recovery plan, which had the aim of ending Lu raiding altogether, the Lu, under the guidance of Altan Khan, made their deepest raid ever, coming within sight of the walls of Beijing itself with a demand that China open tribute and trade relations.

Jiajing was no war hawk, but he was irascible and impatient to see positive results from his officials. We know Yan Song had never been a military administrator and lacked a head for grand strategy, as he openly admitted on several occasions. We know him to prefer compromise solutions to any difficult problem. He was no radical or diehard. Xu Jie did have military connections, was forceful by nature, and as a rule pressed for clear-cut victories rather than compromises with enemies. There lay a potential explosion between him and Yan Song, but both men seemed tacitly to understand that such a rift could rip China apart, and so they found ways to sidestep an all-out confrontation. The third member of the troika, Li Ben (1504–1587), kept a low profile, avoided controversy, deferred to Yan and Xu, and involved himself mainly in routine work. Like Xu Jie and Chai Luan, he'd come to Jiajing's favorable attention by way of the Classics Mat tutorials, in which he participated in 1537. Unlike any of the others, he'd never served in the Ministry of Rites.[131]

This was the makeup of a very stable top layer of the Ming system, and Yan Song surely helped make it so. His personnel machine, liberally oiled by corruption, caused widespread abhorrence and a drumbeat of impeachments, but Jiajing's fearsome lash kept the detractors at bay and the machine running. Yan Song spent nearly all his time inside West Park, so he had to leave the daily management of his machine to his son, Yan Shifan, known politely as Donglou (East House), at the Yan home somewhere on Chang'an Boulevard, immediately south of the Imperial City. A few effusive and elliptical letters survive, written by officials to Yan Shifan, because he was the main conduit to his father and thus favor and appointive office. [132] (Yan Shifan was intensely hated, and in 1565, that would cost him his life.)

The combination of a complacent Yan Song at the top of the Grand Secretariat and an extremely energetic Xu Jie as the number two man was a tactic of Jiajing's deliberate invention. Fond as he was of Yan Song personally, he never wanted him in total control. He'd tried to use Xia Yan as a counterweight to him earlier. In Xu Jie, he found a much more politically skilled and creative source of the desired tension.

At the time of Altan Khan's raid, Xu Jie was still minister of rites, but he lived in West Park as a kind of candidate member of the Grand Secretariat, and he would soon use the raid as a springboard to full membership.

In the autumn of 1550, Altan Khan's Lu forces penetrated the thin defenses directly north of Beijing and in a spectacularly brutal display of slaughter, arson, and plunder reached the outer walls of the Ming capital itself. He sent a captured eunuch with a letter for the Ming court. Yan Song received it and shared it with Jiajing, Grand Secretary Li Ben, and Rites Minister Xu Jie in an emergency meeting in West Park to decide how to respond to it. The letter, written in Chinese, was a demand to extend recognition to Altan Khan as a tributary and open frontier markets to the Lu. Although Altan Khan had no intention to conquer any part of Ming China, the crisis was serious. Crisis management was not one of Yan Song's skills. At first, he declined to recognize it as a crisis. It was just starving bandits on a rampage. No full-scale army mobilization was necessary. Insofar as the matter involved foreign relations, he thought the Ministry of Rites should handle it. Xu Jie was eager to do just that, and more.

Xu's plan, which worked, was to doubt the authenticity of a Lu message written in Chinese and buy time to organize defenses by informing Altan Khan that he must return to the steppes and present his letter in written Mongolian (Fanwen) at the Xuan-Da frontier. After some twenty days of looting and destruction, Altan Khan led his forces, hauling carts laden with plundered goods, back north to the steppes, sent in a proper request at Xuan-Da, and so unilaterally put an end to the crisis.

Through all of this, Yan Song and his machine did not fare well, but they survived. The leading defender of Ming China at the time of Altan's raid was General Qiu Luan, the very same literate, clever, and ingratiating figure whose testimony had sent Zeng Xian and Xia Yan to their graves in the Ordos fiasco of 1548. He was a political general, not a fighting general.

Jiajing liked him. Reportedly he paid a handsome bribe to Yan Shifan in the summer of 1550 to secure the command of Ming forces at Datong. Reportedly he gave rich gifts to Altan Khan to make him leave Datong alone and attack China somewhere further to the east. He authored a memorial, which Jiajing found plausible, arguing that the Lu fighters were better informed and decidedly superior to those of the Ming, and that it would be best not to engage them in battle but to meet their demands by opening frontier markets and placing those markets under tight central control. Qiu was Yan Song's man, and Yan saw to his extraordinary designation as supreme commander over the whole anti-Lu resistance. Jiajing gave him a special seal, allowing him to bypass the bureaucracy and communicate with him secretly and directly.[133]

Judging from the action on the ground, it appears that Yan Song and Qiu Luan's tacit strategy was to avoid at all costs fighting the Lu head on, for fear of being punished for suffering certain defeat. Instead, they preferred to put their ill-fed and ill-trained troops inside walled cities, in the hope, often realized, that the Lu would prefer looting the undefended countryside to assaulting the walls. The problem was that Jiajing was temperamental and easily angered by poor performance, with the result that commanders cautioned by Yan Song to avoid battle found themselves under impeachment for exactly that. That's how the unfortunate Minister of War Ding Rukui ended up publicly beheaded on October 6 when Yan chose not to try to shield him from Jiajing's wrath.

The "crisis of 1550" (*gengxu zhi bian*) left behind a thick residue of suspicion and recrimination. Why were China's defenses so weak and its commanders so inept? Yan Song was the obvious man to blame. Attacking him directly was very dangerous, but several heroes took up the challenge.

On November 29, 1550, Xu Xueshi, a young bureau director in the Ministry of Justice, submitted a scorcher. Yan Song, he charged, was wholly and personally responsible for the debacle just ended. Why? (And here I paraphrase.) Because of his extraordinary corruption. Everywhere, the grand coordinators and regional commanders gouge the troops and civilians for silver and valuables to fill Yan Song's sacks. This is what fomented the Lu disaster. You, the ruler, never punished him. Yan argued the strange notion that militarization was not a good plan. He let his son Yan Shifan take two thousand taels silver from the failed Li Fengming and got him appointed regional commander at Jizhou. And he took three thousand taels from the long-dismissed regional commander Guo Zong and got him appointed to the Grand

Canal administration. The entire bureaucracy is indignant, but no one dares say anything. This has long been the situation. Shifan has intruded upon his father's status, such that all memorials of any significance must get his approval before they can be submitted to the ruler. Yan Song's powers are absolutely overwhelming. While he can't openly punish dissenters, he secretly gets others to denounce them at evaluation time. I can't list all such cases, but the former supervising secretaries Wang Ye and Chen Kai, and the Censors Xie Yu and Tong Hanchen, may have been forgiven, but where are they now? So the whole realm thinks Yan Song and his son to be vermin. Why would they rather be angry but dare not speak out, as though they had some awful disease? Because they fear these sly denunciations. The ruler must get rid of Yan Song and his son, regain control at the top, and let the six ministries do their jobs.[134]

Yan Song offered his own and his son's resignations. He admitted that his wife, son, and grandchildren all lived in Beijing. He denied taking any bribe from Li Fengming. That was an emergency appointment to a desolate place wrecked by the Lu; why would he pay two thousand for a hardship post like that? Xu Xueshi was just recycling rumors. Yan said he himself was old and not so alert anymore and should be allowed to retire.

Jiajing told Yan that Xu Xueshi was a scoundrel disloyally hoping to provoke the ruler's anger, but he, the ruler, refused to take the bait. He disallowed Yan's request to retire. He ordered Xu Xueshi to be imprisoned and interrogated under torture. He was then removed from civil service. Reportedly, Jiajing was actually persuaded by Xu's charges until his Daoist chaplain, Tao Zhongwen, advised him that Yan was friendless and totally loyal, while Xu was just a vengeance seeker.[135] So Yan Song's weak rebuttal won the day, and Xu Xueshi added his name to a growing honor roll of victims and martyrs who dared speak truth to power.

Unfortunately for the accusers, all the indictments of Yan Song and his son tended to be tactically inept, mixing unfounded and dubious charges in with everything else. Unlike a modern reporter or lawyer, the speaking officials lacked the time, resources, and investigative powers to make a careful case. Offense was hamstrung; defense was easy. All Yan Song needed to do was explode one or two allegations, and as long as Jiajing's support lasted, the rest of the indictment would collapse like a house of cards in a windstorm. This is evident in the most damning impeachment Yan Song ever got, that sent up on January 31, 1553, by Yan Jisheng, a newly assigned director of the Bureau of Military Appointments in the Ministry of War.

Meanwhile, some major changes had taken place since Altan Khan's raid of 1550. Of them, the biggest was the alleged treason and posthumous dismemberment of the corpse of Yan Song's protégé Qiu Luan. Next came the ineffectiveness and subsequent closure of the frontier horse markets and the collapse of Yan's policy of appeasing the Lu. In the wake of these reversals, Yan tacitly conceded frontier policy to Xu Jie. He also reached out to promote Yang Jisheng, earlier brutally tortured in the Decree Prison for his opposition to opening the horse markets in the first place. This was a clever personnel ploy, but it exploded in Yan's face. Yang Jisheng was no machine cog. He'd long groomed himself to be a hero.

Yang's very long bill of indictment repeated many of the charges made by earlier attackers, and it reads less like a judicial brief than a political broadside; but as such it provides a full look at the nature and workings of a private empire of corruption so pervasive, so beyond Jiajing's control, so impervious to nationwide discontent, and so effective in blanketing the realm in fear that the very future not only of the Ming but of China's very civilization was being eroded to a point of no return.

This was sensational. But Yang made two big mistakes. One was calling as witnesses Jiajing's two surviving young sons, who (he guessed) might corroborate his portrait of the Yan Song regime. That provoked Jiajing's immediate suspicion and anger. The other was his failure to produce hard, incontrovertible evidence against Yan.

Jiajing's response was swift. He absolved Yan Song of all charges. He sent Yang Jisheng to the Decree Prison again and ordered him flogged a hundred times and interrogated under torture. Yang's searing autobiography and prison notes rank alongside those Yang Jue wrote earlier. While he lost his case, and after a horrible prison experience was publicly beheaded in 1555, he prevailed in the long run, as posthumously he helped to destroy Yan Song, making him a hated national villain and himself a brave and shining hero.[136]

Yan sent Jiajing a short thank-you note. The ruler had said Yang's motive was simply personal revenge and his statement nothing but a collection of unfounded rumors, and why did he drag in the two princes?[137] Yan offered his pro forma resignation, but he echoed Jiajing (here I paraphrase his remarks). Yang thought an excess of personal venom would be enough to unseat me, but it wasn't. Then he befouled your own father-son relationship with the princes. Then he said my monopolizing power subverts the ancestral system, but you, Jiajing, are my witness here, and you know perfectly well that's nonsense. All we grand secretaries do is draft rescripts and send up requests. You, the ruler, make all the decisions. But I've been in office too long and I've grown too old (age seventy-three at this juncture), and I hope you'll dismiss me. [138]

Jiajing kept him on board for another nine years.

* * *

Yan Song's deficiencies as a strategist and policy maker came clear in the wake of Altan Khan's raid of 1550. He was probably too old to change his ways, and he was not moved even to try to reinvent himself. Thus when he turned his attention to handling the crisis along the coast in the 1550s, occasioned by an upsurge in the intensity of raiding, he dealt with it in much the same way, patronizing a corrupt general commander (Hu Zongxian in this case) and looking for compromise solutions to the raiding problem short of all-out war. But unlike Qiu Luan, Hu Zongxian was an able man, and he had some success.

The northern frontier troubles and those far away on the seacoast were surprisingly alike in some ways. Neither was state sponsored. Both the Lu and the Wokou were multiethnic, with many participants being impoverished young local Chinese. Both sets of raiders specialized in arson, massacre, and especially looting. Neither aimed at permanent conquest. The open steppes of Mongolia were the Lu safe haven; the sea, offshore islands, and Japan were bases of operations for the Wokou. The ultimate cause of all the raiding was Jiajing's stubborn and unrealistic refusal to allow anything like open private commerce with the outside world and his determination to keep foreign relations of any kind under narrowly limited and tight central control. But population growth and a rising world circulation of silver were bursting the seams of the Ming straitjacket.

The sea raiders' counterpart to Altan Khan, which is to say a leader with some degree of control over the whole, was no foreigner, nor even a Japanese, but a Chinese merchant and entrepreneur by the name of Wang Zhi, who sported informally the title "king" at his base of operations off Kyushu, across the sea some six hundred miles from the China coast.

The situation was, briefly, as follows. By the mid-sixteenth century there had developed along the China coast, mainly from the Yangzi Delta on south, a growing socioeconomic quicksand of a smuggling trade with the outside world. In it were big illegal profits for China's coastal elites, who provoked violence by refusing to pay their debts to the smugglers, a mixed lot of Japanese, Southeast Asians, Portuguese, and especially Chinese adventurers. Many of the leading Chinese merchant-entrepreneurs were not coastal dwellers but natives of the inland prefecture of Huizhou, in present-day Anhui Province. That was the home of Wang Zhi, as well as his nemesis, Hu Zongxian.

At the top level, the conduct of the war against the Wokou was, by 1555, divided, as Yan Song and Xu Jie tried to stay out of each other's way. From Beijing, Xu Jie oversaw a northern sector of the coast, with field headquarters in Nanjing, while Yan supervised a southern and more important sector, with Hu Zongxian his main man in Hangzhou. Xu and Song had different management styles, with Xu's much more hands-on and personally involved. Yan instituted his accustomed corruption-tinged machine approach. Here we focus on Yan. Xu Jie is featured in the following chapter.

After a number of civilian field commanders were tried, found wanting, and removed, the highly talented Hu Zongxian (1511–1565) was made supreme commander of three coastal provinces in April 1556, with his headquarters at Hangzhou. A civil official (*jinshi* 1538), he scored some outstanding successes against the Wokou and managed to last an extraordinary six years in the post. He gathered an entourage of civil and military talents, advisors such as Tang Shunzhi, Mao Kun, and Xu Wei, and fighters such as Yu Dayou and Qi Jiguang. He sponsored a peaceful invasion of Huizhou merchants into Hangzhou and other coastal cities, and he also sponsored the printing of popular literary works, gazetteers, and other writings. Wine, women, and song and banqueting embellished life in his Hangzhou headquarters. Hu's skills were best seen less in combat operations than in diplomacy, cajolery, and guile, tools through which he lured first the ex-monk and Wokou leader Xu Hai, then the grand old man himself, Wang Zhi, into negotiations and then into captivity. This was in 1556 and 1557.[139]

In order to have any success, Hu Zongxian needed someone in Beijing supporting him. It seems he could have found a powerful backer in Xu Jie, but he made the deliberate choice to link up with Yan Song instead. In the medium term, that was probably the better option, as at the time Yan Song was a more powerful figure than Xu Jie, and friendlier to bon vivants.

Xu Jie's mode of operation was to blizzard operatives out in the field with thoughtful personal letters of suggestion and advice. Yan Song's preferred way of doing things was to forge a close tie with one top man. On the northern frontier, Qiu Luan was that man, but after his demise, Xu Jie maneuvered to ensure that there was no true replacement for him, and so Yan's communications with Jiajing about problems on the northern frontier turned dithering in tone, deploring this and worrying about that, with no firm plan in mind. As raiding heated up along the coast, however, Yan Song did rather better. He got Jiajing to send his adopted son and close follower Zhao Wen-hua—who had developed plans for handling the Wokou and was at the time a vice minister of works—down to the coast to sacrifice to the sea god and, more important, scout out and report on just what the situation was.

The date of Zhao's appointment was March 14, 1555. Zhao conducted the sacrifice to the sea god at Songjiang on April 27. Then he spent the next several months on the scene, during which time he leveraged the removal and arrest of several key officials, among them Supreme Commander Zhang Jing and Assistant Regional Commander Tang Kekuan. Xu Jie had counseled both men and had tried to save them, but could not (Zhang Jing and several others were put to death in Beijing on November 12, 1555). Zhao also made contact with Hu Zongxian, who'd already been on the job for a year as Zhejiang regional inspector. It was through Zhao's good offices that Hu was leapfrogged upward to the post of supreme commander in April 1556.

Zhao Wenhua made victims of many high regional officials. He was deeply hated for this in his own time, and posterity later assigned him a slot in the Ming dynastic history as an "evil minister" alongside Yan Song. His corruption, large and blatant, was probably real, even though it was based on allegations and never fully documented. The same goes for Hu Zongxian, whose documented bribery, if such it can be called, was capped by his twice forwarding to Beijing white deer captured on Chusan Island. Jiajing received these felicitous animals with great pleasure and fanfare. The white deer are said to have turned away the ruler's anger at Hu for suffering some military reverses. So corruption tied Hu to Zhao to Yan Song, and Hu directly to Jiajing, after Zhao's own demise in September 1557.

But the point to be made here is that corruption and effective official performance were not necessarily antithetical. Zhao Wenhua's letters to Yan Song and Xu Jie show that he was no ignoramus, but knowledgeable and astute about how to handle the Wokou. He was also a talent spotter. And Yan Song played his part too, assuring Jiajing of Zhao's competence and the accuracy of his reports from the coast. (And then, just as he had done with Qiu Luan earlier, Yan Song completely washed his hands of Zhao Wenhua when Zhao's corruption and misbehavior overwhelmed his competence.) But it was the efforts of all four—Jiajing, Yan Song, Zhao Wenhua, and Hu Zongxian, that by 1559 turned the tide against the coastal raiders. [140]

* * *

Yan Song spent his last years as chief grand secretary on a downward slide, as old age more and more diminished his customary alertness and energy. His eightieth birthday was celebrated to wide acclaim, as was that of his wife, nee Ouyang, a year later. When his wife died, Yan received special permission to let a grandson escort her coffin back to Jiangxi, on the grounds that he depended on his son to manage his household and assist him in handling official business. But as a son in mourning, Shifan was barred entry into West Park, which was bad for Yan Song.

Yan's attention had begun to waver and lose focus, such that Shifan had to step in and write his rescripts for him. Shifan's street smarts came into effective use in this respect, as he paid eunuchs tips to get their reports on Jiajing's state of mind. Personnel decisions Yan Song used to make himself he turned over to Shifan to make.

In 1561, Yan Song fumblingly misread Jiajing's mind and angered him by saying that rebuilding the burned-down Wanshou Palace was too costly. These were not good signs. Jiajing's urgent palace messages, scribbled and often hard to read, but usually deciphered by Yan father and son in discussions, now suffered from breakdowns in communication between the home-bound Shifan and his father in West Park. Jiajing began leaving Yan Song out of the loop, relying for advice and assistance on Xu Jie instead. Even Yan Song's Daoist prayers, which he now got others to write for him, were no longer up to standard, and that displeased the ruler. And word reached Jiajing that Shifan, who should have been immersed in deep sorrow and ethical reflection during the mourning period for his mother, was instead indulging in wild partying and lascivious behavior. It was not good that someone as devoted to filial piety as Jiajing should hear such things. The gods, too, were restive. Through a planchette, they replied to a query of Jiajing's that Yan Song and his son were bad for Ming China.

Was now the time to fire off an impeachment of Yan Song? Zou Ying-long was a newly minted *jinshi* and censor. One day he ducked into the house of a palace eunuch to escape a summer rainstorm. While he was waiting it out, the eunuch leaked to him details of the situation inside West Park. On that information, Zou decided the time might be right to impeach Yan

Song—not directly, but by way of a denunciation of his son, at the time vice minister of the Ministry of Works. Still, this was risky. Zou was well aware of the roster of horrible experiences suffered by protesters earlier on. His statement bears translation:

Yan Shifan uses his father's eminence to satisfy his insatiable obsession with advantage. He privately dishes out honors and rewards and takes in bribes from everywhere. He charges new appointees on a sliding scale according to the rank of the position in question. For promotions, he charges according to the desirability of the new post. This has wrecked the selection system by commercializing it. The more competitive the buyers, the higher the price he demands. Thus Bureau Secretary Xiang Zhiyuan of the Ministry of Justice paid twelve thousand silver through houseman Yan Nian to get transferred to the Ministry of Personnel as a secretary in the Bureau of Records. The provincial degree holder (*juren*) Pan Hongye paid 1,200 [or 2,200] for a subprefectural magistracy at Linqing. Yan Hong brokered that. There are more than a hundred men who broker such transactions. Tops among them are [Shifan's] sons Yan Hao, of the Embroidered-Uniform Guard, and Yan Hong, a Secretariat drafter. Also his family slave Yan Nian and the Secretariat drafter Luo Longwen. Yan Nian is the worst of these. Yan Shifan treats him like a close intimate. From everyone who comes to Shifan's place, he takes a tenth of the sales price. Villainous place seekers fawn on him and call him "Master Haoshan," not daring to use his given name. Every year he sends Yan Song ten thousand taels as a birthday present.

Yan Song and his son have their registry in Yuanzhou Prefecture, Jiangxi, but they also have a dozen or more large estates in Nanjing and Yangzhou and other places. These are managed by their evil servant, Yan Dong. He's oppressive, and everywhere the common people hate him.

It's remarkable that when Shifan's mother died, you let him stay to look after his father and directed his son Yan Hao to escort the coffin home. Though in mourning, Shifan entertained guests, consorted with women, and danced and sang all day and night. Yan Hao is a stupid rodent, a lover of lucre, who used the funeral trip as a chance to extort. His demands caused trouble everywhere. All along his trip to Jiangxi and back, local officials catered to him, exhausting all their resources.

Now in the realm we have had repeated floods and droughts, and crises north and south; the common people are being fleeced to destitution, all due to the limitless greed of Yan Shifan and his father. Their rapacity grows, governance is conducted through bribery, and positions are for sale. Everywhere the lowest functionaries gouge the people to recoup what they paid to get their posts. This impoverishes the people and depletes the public treasury, so of course natural and human disasters recur.

I would ask that you behead Yan Shifan, to show everyone what happens
to a disloyal and unfilial figure. His father Yan Song has not repaid the generous favor he's been given. He mindlessly loves his son and uses his power to
enrich himself, and he should be dismissed forthwith to cleanse government. If
I speak falsely, I ask to be decapitated as an apology to Yan Song and Yan
Shifan. [141]

Zou's charges, quite specific about the inner workings of the Yan machine, were sent up on June 20, 1562. Having taken this step, Zou waited,
petrified by fear, anticipating the imprisonment, torture, and death that might
well follow the firing of this incendiary missile. How would Jiajing respond?

Jiajing's response was politically apt. He was fond of Yan Song and
disgusted with Yan Shifan, but unwilling at this moment to set in motion a
general clean-out of Yan partisans. He is recorded as saying that Yan Song
was painstaking and loyal, cautiously respectful of ongoing conditions, and
of great help in Daoism, for the sake of my longevity and his love of the
dynasty. Yet for many years he's been hated. He has unstintingly indulged
his villainous son, whose advice he listens to and acts on. He doesn't give
any thought to the favor I've given him. I hereby dismiss him. He can go
home using the postal system. The local officials will issue him one hundred
shi rice annually. The Embroidered-Uniform Guard will arrest and send all
the others named in [Zou's] memorial in shackles to the Decree Prison for
interrogation. Zou will be rewarded for his loyalty; the Ministries of Personnel and Rites will suggest a post to which he might be promoted. [142]

So Zou was saved. The middling post of assistant commissioner of the
right in the Office of Transmission was his reward. Yan Shifan was exiled to
a military garrison in a malarial area. Yan Hao, Yan Hong, and Luo Longwen
were made soldiers in far-off frontier garrisons. Yan Nian was to be kept in
prison until Shifan's ill-gotten gains were recouped. Yan Hong was allowed
to escort his grandfather home and serve as his aide. The place seeker Xiang
Zhiyuan was arrested and later died of abuse in prison. Place seeker Pan
Hongye and estate manager Yan Dong were sent to garrisons. [143] Yan Shifan's frantic attempts to bribe his way out of trouble were unavailing.

It was with profound sadness, not anger, that Jiajing dismissed Yan Song,
who for twenty years had been his closest supporter. He rewarded Zou Ying-
long, but he threatened to punish anyone else who memorialized further
about all this for any reason. Censor Zhang Jia didn't listen; he asked Jiajing
to rehabilitate everyone punished earlier for impeaching Yan Song. That
angered Jiajing. He ordered Zhang to be shackled, imprisoned, and interro-

gated. [144] Despondent, the ruler confessed to Xu Jie, now chief grand secretary, a wish to abdicate and devote all his time to his religious devotions. Xu talked him out of it.

* * *

The Yan Song saga wasn't quite over yet. There was a very unpleasant ending to it.

Yan Shifan slipped his guards on his way to exile and returned home to Yuanzhou. So did Luo Longwen. Luo's home was in Huizhou Prefecture, which was also the home of both sea raider Wang Zhi, now dead, as well as his captor, Hu Zongxian. Yan Shifan had wealth, and Luo Longwen had contacts in the bandit and raider underworld. Allegedly, they then began concocting a rebellion.

This allegation was lodged in an impeachment written up and submitted by one Lin Run, a Nanjing-based censor and an aggressive dynamo. [145] He got young Li Qi (1531–1578), prefectural judge at Huizhou, to spy out what Luo and Yan were up to. On the basis of what Li and others dug up, Lin submitted a memorial, which was received in Beijing on December 5, 1564. Lin informed Beijing that his reconnaissance had turned up information that the escapees Yan Shifan and Luo Longwen had assembled many raiders; that Luo had built a mountain base, outfitted himself like a lord, and behaved like a rebel; that he and Yan had been overheard denouncing the government; and that one or both of them had gathered some four thousand men to build a residential compound. The roads were full of talk of an impending uprising. He urged the two men's immediate arrest. Jiajing so ordered. [146] Shifan's son Yan Shaoting, on duty in Beijing as an Embroidered-Uniform Guardsman, tried to warn both his father and Luo, but he couldn't reach them soon enough. [147]

Arrested without much difficulty, the two suspects were brought to the Decree Prison in Beijing. On April 24, 1565, Nanjing minister of justice Huang Guangsheng consolidated Lin Run's and other reports and submitted the formal case against them.

It was shocking. How much of it was based on solid evidence is open to question. In any event, the charges mushroomed. Now it was alleged that the conspirators were planning to ally with the raiders in both Mongolia and Japan with the aim of overthrowing the Ming dynasty altogether.

I paraphrase Huang's bill of indictment. Let us not forget, Huang wrote, the colossal sums Yan Shifan collected while he was still in office in Beijing, which have still not been repaid. Beyond that lies this: the Wokou leader Wang Zhi had marriage relations with his Huizhou compatriot Luo Longwen, and through him conveyed one hundred thousand taels to Yan Shifan to buy himself a post, a deal that nearly worked, save for Jiajing's vigilance.

Then there is the site of the Jiangxi provincial treasury in Nanchang. A medical official by the name of Peng Kong claimed the site had a "royal aura," and so the storehouses were torn down [by Shifan] and a residence was built there on a royal scale with double walls and nine sections.

Then, continued Huang, there's Yangzhou, located at a choke point for northbound tax shipments; there [Shifan] built an estate, under the management of the household slave Yan Dong, who seized people's properties and netted commercial profits, and committed evils beyond all reckoning.

You, the ruler, sentenced [Yan Shifan] to military exile in Leizhou and remitted the death penalty. Instead of showing gratitude for that, Yan was resentful and was openly determined to live in [his home county] of Fenyi instead. And Luo Longwen escaped from the garrison at Xunzhou [in Guangxi Province] and returned home to plot with Yan. They gathered outlaws and bandits from everywhere, plus a number of false prophets and soothsayers, some four thousand men in all, supposedly to build the residence [at Nanchang]. They secretly recruited military trainers. They hired ten or more assassins to kill enemies and silence dissent. They trained a hundred or more spies who formed a constant stream going to Beijing and back.

Luo Longwen gathered in five hundred former Wokou of Wang Zhi's, and he and Yan planned to send them to Japan and contact others still there. And Niu Xin, one of Yan's foremen (*bantou*), escaped from the garrison at Shanhai[guan] and ran to the Lu in order to get them to coordinate in an assault. Shifan's son Yan Zhaoting, undercover in Beijing as an Embroidered-Uniform Guardsman, lay low with the aforementioned assassins and spies and waited.

Yan Song blindly loves his son, and, ignoring the law, lets him stay in Fenyi, while he tried to petition the court for his release. This is the acme of deceit and disloyalty. Shifan was under more than one indictment entailing the death penalty, and he and Luo should be beheaded. Shifan should have two million taels confiscated, and Luo two hundred thousand. The properties at Nanchang and Yangzhou should be sold off by local officials there, with the proceeds sent to the ministry. The original owners of the seized fields should get them back. All his villainous sons and nephews who have official registry should have it removed. The Jiangxi regional inspector should prosecute Peng Kong, all plotters and outlaws, the powerful slave Yan Zhen, and all those who protected outlaws and seizers of wives, daughters, and fields.[148]

Jiajing's response to Huang's memorial was to ask whether such an extraordinary indictment was truly credible. Lin Run was the sole source for it. Would it convince the realm? He ordered the Beijing Censorate, Court of Judicial Review, and Embroidered-Uniform Guard to double-check. Huang Guangsheng asserted that the charge that the Wokou and Lu had been contacted in the cause of rebellion was true and well founded, that not all the prisoners' crimes had been mentioned, and that their execution should be carried out forthwith.

Jiajing agreed to their execution. Further, he ordered the regional inspectors to conduct a thorough confiscation of their properties. Yan Song, he said, was afraid of his son and betrayed his ruler, and so he and his grandsons who held offices of any sort were ordered to be reduced to commoner status. All other adherents were ordered to be removed from office. Jiajing said he would ignore the failure of the indictment to state what legal stipulation applied to the case. All the ill-gotten gains of the Yan and their crowd were to be confiscated. Peng Kong and five others were given death sentences. Twenty-seven family slaves were given a variety of punishments.[149]

Yet the case nearly collapsed! Chief Grand Secretary Xu Jie saw that the original indictment mentioned Yang Jisheng, the great Yan Song detractor executed nine years earlier at Jiajing's personal direction. Mentioning him would incite the ruler's anger and force him to reject the entire indictment. Xu was able to remove Yang Jisheng's name before Jiajing saw it, and so he saved the day.[150]

* * *

A chance survival of the original inventory of the Yan estate, sent up by Huang Guangsheng and Lin Run, makes for an astoundingly detailed picture of a private empire, probably Ming China's largest private fortune. Rather than being exaggerated, as some have claimed, it might if anything be understated, given the tendency for accountants to pilfer. But it certainly looks complete.

Start with gold. The accountants found 13,171.65 taels in ingot, strip, cake, leaf, granular, and shard form. There were 3,185 gold dishes, cups, and plates, weighing 11,033.31 taels. Dishes and other items featuring gold inlay: 253 such, weighing 403.92 taels. Gold jewelry and other adornments: 1,803 such, 2,792.26 taels; 21 gold combs, 99.63 taels; 267 pairs gold earrings, 149.83 taels; 62 gold necklaces, 179.26 taels; 309 gold hairpins, 92.54 taels; 105 gold bracelets, 421.1 taels; miscellaneous gold jewelry, 776 items, 997.03 taels; 35 gold hat tops, 77.17 taels; 208 gold neckpieces, 1,113.09 taels; and 68 gold buckles, 235.75 taels. The checkers totaled all the gold objects at 3,938, weighing 6,558.2 taels—a fortune in gold right there. (Each item is carefully described: thus "four gold butterfly-loving-flowers hairpins, 3.5 taels," and on and on.)

Then silver: 2,013,478.9 taels in bulk; 1,649 silver dishes and the like, weighing 13,357.35 taels; and jewelry, 628 items, 253.85 taels. A total of 2,277 items, 13,610.2 taels, and together with the bulk silver, 2,027,090.1 taels.

Proceeding to a miscellany of jade and other items of every description, the checkers found 857 items weighing 3,529.5 taels. Included were 202 jade belts, 124 belts inlaid with horn, amber, and other materials; 563 objects featuring both gold and silver, 1.331.7 taels; 2,682 gold, silver, and ivory chopsticks; 5 "dragon egg" pots; 63 pearl crowns, 306.3 taels; 260.5 taels worth of amber objects; 69 objects of coral, rhino horn, and ivory; miscellaneous vessels and objects of crystal, glass, ivory, tortoiseshell, etc., single or in pairs; 13 jars and boxes of perfume, bear gall, etc.; 3 containers of raw cinnabar, 385 taels; regular cinnabar, 250 catties, 6 taels; 291 sticks of various fragrances, 5.058 catties, 10 taels.

Bolts of silk of various kinds, plus 57 bolts of kudzu cloth, plus more of ramie, came to 14,331 altogether. In view of the importance of Chinese silk in world trade, research into the exact nature of all these meticulously described bolts, which I will not attempt here, might yield interesting results. All this silk would appear to be enough to clothe a large number of upper-class people. Then there was a large stock of ready-to-wear clothing. Without going into details, there was a total of 1,304 garments of every sort and description.

The checkers moved on. There were 27,308 fans, 54 musical instruments, and 16 ink slabs, plus countless stationery items and knickknacks of all sorts; 108 screens; and 1,127 ancient bronze vessels together with pewter vessels, altogether weighing 6,994 catties, 2 taels. The checkers also found 9,475 copper coins and two packages of paper cash. And there were eighty-eight titles of books in 2,613 volumes. Rubbings of calligraphy came to 358 scrolls. Most outstanding was the Yan art collection—3,201 scrolls and albums, not further described.

Then the checkers calculated sales prices for various categories of goods. So 27,288 bolts of cloth came to 15,047.6 taels silver. Men's and women's ready-to-wear clothing came to 17,043 garments, fetching 6,205.7 taels. The 3,506 bronze vessels totaling 19,689.6 catties sold for .076 per catty (a catty consisted of 16 *liang*, or ounces, so the implied total would be 1,496.4 taels silver). The 4,791 pewter vessels, 6,954.1 catties, were valued at .06 taels silver per catty. Together these came to 1,928.083 taels silver, according to the checkers.

There were 5,852 sets of basic classics, histories, and Confucianist texts; these were to be distributed to the local Confucian schools. Buddhist and Daoist temples were to receive the 914 sutras and Daoist texts. The 6,688 stationery items fetched 250.25 taels silver. The blank paper was worth 29.3 taels.

As to furniture, 640 fancy couches and beds came to 2,127.85 taels. Bedding, blankets, and the like came to 22,427 items, valued at 2,248.6 taels. Thirty-five sedan chairs totaled 70 taels silver. Tables, chairs, and cabinets and such were 7,444 in number, valued at 1,415.56 taels. Containers and plates of bamboo, wood, and porcelain were counted up: these totaled 94,926 items, which together with a few other items were worth 1,235.95 taels. Parts for musical instruments, drums, and lamps came to 46.74 taels. Niches for religious items numbered 41 in all and, at .1 tael each, were worth 4.1 taels altogether.

There were 341 weapons and armor, including 4 iron helmets, 4 pieces of iron body armor, 4 iron axes, 15 bows and crossbows, 2 Japanese swords, 53 single and double-edged iron swords, 21 iron spikes, 6 bronze and iron clubs, 34 iron cannon, 20 fowling pieces, 82 long and short spears, 16 insignia, 23 flags, 5 quivers, and 50 religious musical instruments and leather bags. These totaled 341 items, which would be distributed to soldiers for training purposes. This is an interesting collection of weaponry, but it seems far from enough to equip a rebel army.

So much for movable items. The inventory goes on to detail the Yan holdings in Jiangxi residential real estate. In Nanchang city, capital of the province, a large complex of various buildings, vegetable plots, and empty lots, carefully described, was assessed at 7,850 taels total. In Nanchang

County, properties and houses totaled 31,498 taels. Xinjian County properties came to 6,783 taels. The total for the Nanchang-area houses, shops, and
so forth came to 1,680 rooms valued at 47,496 taels.

In Yan Song's home prefecture, Yuanzhou (Yichun County), the accountants found 19 residences, houses, shops, and so forth, containing 3,343
rooms, with a value of 20,163.2 taels. Yan Song's original county of residence, Fenyi, contained twenty places, with 1,624 rooms, valued at 18,647.6
taels. Some of these are ascribed to Yan housemen (*jiaren*), for example, 42
big houses with 887 rooms in them in Yichun, worth 3,574.2 taels. In Fenyi,
Yang Song's grandson Yan Hong's residence had 67 rooms, valued at 900
taels. In Pingxiang County, six farmhouses fetched 46 taels. The checkers
totaled all this real estate as worth 86,350.8 taels.

Farmland and bamboo forest were confiscated too; some of it was held in
pawn. The Yan holdings were spotted about in several northern Jiangxi
counties: Nanchang, Xinjian, Yichun, Fenyi, Pingxiang, Xinyu, Qingjiang,
and Xinchang. I omit the details. The total value was 44,493.4672 taels.
There was much livestock: water buffalo, yellow cows, horses, and mules
totaling 856 head, plus cranes, deer, pigs, sheep, ducks, geese, chickens, and
dogs. Their total value came to 2,022.017 taels.

The total of everything, according to the checkers, was 2,342,731.7772
taels. There were late additions to all the above categories of confiscations,
which amounted in value to 16,516.002 taels. So the grand total was
2,359,247.7792 taels silver.[151] A gigantic fortune, indeed. And not included
in this reckoning were the properties at Yangzhou, or Yan Shifan's Beijing
mansion and estate, said to have spread over four wards and to have included
a large pond plus rare animals and plantings.[152]

This extraordinary document opens a window on what may well have
been the largest private estate in Jiajing's China. This information deserves
an econometric analysis, but this isn't the place for it. There are, nonetheless,
two crude points than can be made. One is that the confiscation, directed by
Lin Run, appears extremely thorough. The report that Yan Song, his beloved
son beheaded, his status reduced to commoner, died alone at age eighty-five
in a hut by his parents' tomb in 1565 is probably correct. He had no more
house or home, and nothing in the list of confiscated properties refers to tomb
sites, so he was probably allowed to live there in penury. The other conclusion is that none of these data would appear to show that Yan Shifan was in
any way ready to organize a rebellion or military coup, at least not one with a
Jiangxi base. That he and his ally Luo Longwen were arrested so easily

suggests that such an uprising, if contemplated, must have been in a very preliminary stage of development. In addition, the charge of allying with Japan and Mongolia eerily reminds one of the same sensational charge, probably also groundless, lodged against the doomed Prime Minister Hu Wei-yong in 1380, and against Qiu Luan in 1552.

* * *

Thirty-three years in office, twenty as a grand secretary, thirteen as chief grand secretary, and for Yan Song, it all ended in ignominy and utter ruin. But while he was in office, did he bring nothing to the table, at least to preserve the Ming, if not to reform or improve it? His talents were limited, but several of them were important in a conservative cause. He was effective in coordinating large nonmilitary operations, such as Jiajing's visit to Anlu (Chengtian) in 1539 and the shipment of his mother's remains there later the same year. And while it's hard to gauge these things, it does seem that Yan Song had an unexpressed but outsized ambition to dominate others. Emotionally aloof, no one's close friend, and occasionally ruthless, it also seems he radiated a certain charm. Men sensed he was upward bound, going places, and thus a good horse to ride.

It's also hard to assess all the charges of corruption that hounded him throughout his career. How many of these allegations were true? If they were true at least in part, what did they mean for Yan Song personally and for Ming governance overall? More than one source attests to Yan's home in Beijing being a gathering spot for ambitious place seekers. Given that, it is likely they paid bribes or offered gifts to have their pleas heard. As minister of rites, Yan could have collected large sums from princes wanting their claims heard, from *tusi* (native administrators) on the southwestern frontier wanting their legitimacy validated, from officials seeking honors for their parents, or from descendants seeking the same for meritorious ancestors. The imagination takes over when the hard evidence runs out. Yet it is hard to believe a private estate worth over two million taels silver could ever have been created by honest methods in just a few decades.

Corruption fed faction, Yan and his son took bribes, and in return they dispensed favors. Many officials had little tolerance for this sort of thing, and a few brave souls risked health and life when they voiced their objections. There is a case to be made, however, that a regime that tolerates corruption and suppresses dissent creates stability, not over the long term, but over the medium term. (One thinks of the Soviet Union under Brezhnev, or indeed Russia under Putin.)

In Jiajing's China of the sixteenth century, the key to so many years of stable governance was the personal connection between the emperor and his chief grand secretaries. Xia Yan never developed a good working arrangement or meeting of the minds with Jiajing, but Yan Song did. How he did it is in some ways a puzzle, as neither man discussed it in so many words. Yan Song's willing and dedicated involvement as a participant in Jiajing's Daoism was emphasized often to the exclusion of all else by Ming commentators. Surely that was important, but there was more. Gu Yingtai noted Yan's ability to read the emperor's moods and manipulate his easily aroused anger, making impeachments of himself look like covert attacks on the ruler.[153] Yan must also have been a model physically for Jiajing. Here was a man twenty-seven years older than he, a father figure surely—tall, vigorous, and a model of health and longevity for a ruler susceptible to hypochondria. And as Jiajing downshifted from the demanding regimen he followed in his early years to the slower pace of his life in West Park, Yan Song's conservative and unambitious agenda for governing China proved to complement the ruler's diminished energies very smoothly.

Then why did Yan Song's career end in such calamity? Jiajing was sad to see him go but felt he had no choice. Yan left with full honors. Soon Jiajing had to take those away too. The old man died alone, impoverished and unmourned.

Self-doubt accompanied Jiajing's sadness and depression. Maybe he was a poor judge of the characters of men. How could he have been so misled by Yan Song? The new chief grand secretary, Xu Jie, reassured him. Yan Song, he said, had talent and was a good choice early on. It was his son's aggressive corruption that laid him low. Had the speaking officials been given free rein to speak out, he advised, things might never have come to such a pass.[154]

In fact, however, Yan Shifan's corruption had been brought to Jiajing's attention many times, and the impeachers suffered heavily for it. Jiajing adamantly refused to rehabilitate any of them, despite pleas that he do so.[155] As the *Ming shi* has it, "Shizong [Jiajing] was not a feebleminded ruler. Yan Song was twenty years a grand secretary, and his greed was boundless. Men bravely impeached him for this, only to be dismissed or killed, and they were never able to make the emperor wake up to it."[156] The *Ming shilu* has this editorial comment: "Yan Shifan was an evil presence. He was able to corrupt court government because his father Yan Song had long been in office, while the ruler isolated himself in West Park, devoted to Daoism, and having no further direct contact with the officials outside. That's how the ruler was kept in the dark, and why [Shifan] was able to wield such power."[157] It was also a case of Jiajing's blind affection for Yan Song and Yan's blind affection for his son, and no affection at all between Jiajing and Yan Shifan, that in the end brought about the collapse of the whole machine.

NOTES

1. Yan Song, *Liguan biaozou* (1912 printed ed.), 11.9a–10 (hereafter cited as *LGBZ*). There exist two detailed modern biographies of Yan Song. One is Zhang Xianqing, *Yan Song zhuan* (Hefei: Huangshan shushe, 1992). The other is Cao Guoqing, *Yan Song nianpu* (Beijing: Zhongguo renshi chubanshe, 1995).

2. Yan Song, *Qianshan tang ji* (Siku quanshu cunmu congshu, 4th ser.), 56.280–283 (hereafter cited as *Qianshan*). Her surname is also spelled "Yan" but is written with a different character and is pronounced with a different speech tone.

3. So he said in a poem; *Qianshan*, 56.65.

4. *Mingdai dengkelu huibian* (reprint Taipei, 1969), 5.2424; *Qianshan*, 56.64.

5. *GCXZL*, 1.570.

6. Du Lianzhe, *Mingchao guanxuan lu*, 53; *Qianshan*, 56.225, 345–346; *LGBZ*, 11.9a–10a.

7. *Qianshan*, 56.229–233.

8. John Dardess, "Protesting to the Death: The *fuque* in Ming Political History," *Ming Studies*, no. 47 (Spring 2003): 99–109.

9. *Qianshan*, 56.238.

10. Ibid., 56.236–237.

11. Ibid., 56.237–238.

12. Ibid., 56.233–236.

13. Ibid., 56.222–223.

14. *MS*, ch. 308 (biography of Zhao Wenhua).

15. *Qianshan*, 54.21–24, 222.

16. Li Shi, *Nancheng zoudui* (Siku quanshu cunmu congshu, 2nd ser.), 46.601–606.

17. *GQ*, 4.3528.

18. *Qianshan*, 56.170.

19. Ibid., 56.229.

20. Ibid., 56.226–227. In 1518, Yan explained in reply to an impeachment that one Yan Yin, a Jiangxi provincial government clerk and a relative of his mother's, lived with him and took punishment for a late submission of military registers on Yan Song's behalf to the Censorate. See *LGBZ*, 9.1a–3a.

21. *Qianshan*, 56.196–197.

22. Ibid., 56.191–192.

23. *MS*, ch. 308 (biography of Yan Song); Xia Xie, 4.2147–2148. Jiajing's tract, called the *Mingtang huowen*, can be found in Siku quanshu cunmu congshu, 2nd ser., 268.769–772.

24. Yan Song, *Nangong zouyi* (Xuxiu siku quanshu) (Shanghai: Guji chubanshe, 2002), 476.263–283, 284–293 (hereafter cited as *NGZY*).

25. *NGZY*, 476.295–298.

26. Ibid., 476.302–303.

27. Ibid., 476.303.

28. *MSL*, 85.6254–6266.

29. *MSL*, 85.6268–6269.

30. Xia Xie, 4.2152–2153.

31. Xia Xie, 4.2153; *NGZY*, 476.309–314.

32. *NGZY*, 476.317–319.

33. Ibid., 476.320; Xia Xie, 4.3155.

34. *NGZY*, 476.335.

35. Ibid., 476.338–340.

36. Zhu Houcong (i.e., Jiajing), *Yuzhu dashou longfei lu* (Siku quanshu cunmu congshu, 2nd ser.), 45.180–216.

37. *MSL*, 81.4552–4553.

38. Ibid., 81.4551–4552.

39. *NGZY*, 476.335–338.

40. *MSL*, 81.4603, 4605; Lu Shen, *Shengjia nanxun rilu* (Siku quanshu cunmu congshu, 2nd ser.), 46.607–618; Zhu Houcong, *Yuzhu dashou longfei lu*, in ibid., 45.204; Tu Shan, *Ming zheng tongzong* (reprint Taipei, 1969), 6.2299. Lu Shen says Zhang Yunqing was only fined six months' salary; perhaps Jiajing relented. Exactly who rescued Jiajing is not entirely clear; see Shen Defu, *Wanli yehuo bian*, 1.142–143. Carney Fisher's article on Jiajing's trip is well worth reading; see his "Center and Periphery: Shih-tsung's Southern Journey, 1539," *Ming Studies*, no. 18 (1984): 15–34.

41. Lu Shen, *Shengjia nanxun rilu*, 46.612–614.

42. See the color photo of it in Craig Clunas, *Screen of Kings: Royal Art and Power in Ming China* (Honolulu: University of Hawaii Press, 2013), 59.

43. Zhu Houcong, *Yuzhu dashou longfei lu*, 45.206–207.

44. *NGZY*, 476.348–349.

45. *MSL*, 81.4650–4665; *NGZY*, 476.321–325.

46. See *[Wanli] Chengtian fuzhi*, 24–66. The construction costs were huge—some 998,900 taels silver from 1539 down to the end of Jiajing's reign.

47. *NGZY*, 476.330–333.

48. *NGZY*, 476.499–502; Wang Yi-t'ung, *Official Relations between China and Japan, 1368–1549* (Cambridge, MA: Harvard University Press, 1953), 78–81.

49. *NGZY*, 476.496–497.

50. Ibid., 476.493–496; also Chen Zilong, ed., *Huang Ming jingshi wenbian*, 14.461–472. This vast work reproduces very little of Yan's vast output, save for his memorials on foreign relations. The rest of this memorial of Yan's is a tirade against Muslim Yi as the worst among the aliens China has to deal with, and the Chinese Muslims as not quite so bad. He followed with practical suggestions about testing, appointing, and monitoring the interpreters and translators.

51. Ibid., 476.502–503.

52. Ibid., 476.503–504. In the *Huang Ming jingshi wenbian* copy of this memorial, an interlinear note takes Yan Song to task for thinking that chiding the foreigners for delay was a good control technique; see 14.481. In a subsequent memorial, Yan said it was a bad idea to excite their cupidity by being too openhanded with them; a onetime gift of cloth should be enough. Jiajing agreed on October 14. *NGZY*, 476.504.

53. Ibid., 476.504–506.

54. Xia Yan, *Guizhou xiansheng zouyi* (Siku quanshu cunmu congshu, 2nd ser.), 60.356–360.

55. Ibid., 60.575–576; a longer version is in his *Guizhou wenji* (Siku quanshu cunmu congshu, 4th ser.), 74.625–627.

56. *NGZY*, 476.473–474, 477–480.

57. Ibid., 476.480–481.

58. Ibid., 476.482–484.

59. Ibid., 476.485–488.

60. Ibid., 476.488–491.

61. Ibid., 476.491–492.

62. *MSL*, 82.4966–4973; *GQ*, 4.3601–3603; see also Jung-pang Lo, "Policy Formulation and Decision-Making on Issues Respecting Peace and War," in *Chinese Government in Ming Times: Seven Studies*, ed. Charles O. Hucker, 63–66 (New York: Columbia University Press, 1969); *DMB*, 2.1029–1035 (biography of Mac Dang-dung).

63. *NGZY*, 476.429–430, 433–434; *GCXZL*, 2.771–772 (biography of Lun Wenxu).

64. *DMB*, 1.36–42 (biography of Chan Jo-shui); John Meskill, "Academies and Politics in the Ming Dynasty," in Hucker, *Chinese Government in Ming Times*, 152–156; Meskill, *Academies in Ming China: A Historical Essay* (Tucson: University of Arizona Press, 1982); David Faure, "The Emperor in the Village: Representing the State in South China," in *State and Court Ritual in China*, ed. Joseph P. McDermott, 282–297 (Cambridge: Cambridge University Press, 1999).

65. *NGZY*, 476.434–435.

66. *MSL*, 80.4191; *NGZY*, 476.422–424; Meskill, *Academies*, 95. See also Sarah Schneewind, *Community Schools and the State in Ming China* (Stanford, CA: Stanford University Press, 2006), esp. 160–161.

67. *NGZY*, 476.450–452. *MSL*, 80.4292, is much briefer.

68. *NGZY*, 476.418–421. A military community in Liuliang, Yunnan, was for some reason allowed a school, but no stipends.

69. *NGZY*, 476.430–431.

70. Ibid., 476.432; *MSL*, 80.4333.

71. *NGZY*, 476.443–444.

72. Ibid., 476.446–447.

73. Ibid., 476.447–448.

74. Ibid., 476.448–449.

75. Ibid., 476.449–450. The Court of Imperial Sacrifices also needed cooks. It isn't clear whether there was a common pool of cooks, or whether each court had its own.

76. Ibid., 476.445–446.

77. Ibid., 476.444–445; also in *LGBZ*, 2.12b–14b.

78. *NGZY*, 476.397–415.

79. Ibid., 476.384–386.

80. Ibid., 476.389–391.

81. Ibid., 476.391–392.

82. Ibid., 476.392–394.

83. Ibid., 476.394–396.

84. Ibid., 476.396.

85. Ibid.

86. Hung-lam Chu, "The Jiajing Emperor's Interaction with His Lecturers," in *Culture, Courtiers, and Competition: The Ming Court (1368–1644)*, ed. David M. Robinson (Cambridge, MA: Harvard University Asia Center, 2008), 197.

87. *LGBZ*, 1.5b–8a; *MSL*, 81.4868. The Veritable Records indeed mention only the dissenter.

88. See Richard G. Wang, *The Ming Prince and Daoism: Institutional Patronage of an Elite* (Oxford: Oxford University Press, 2012).

89. *GQ*, 4.3279; *MSJSBM*, ch. 52 (Jiajing's devotion to Daoism).

90. The epitaph is in *GCXZL*, 8.5285–5260; also *MS*, ch. 307, and *DMB*, 2.1169–1170 (biography of Shao Yuan-chieh).

91. *MSL*, 82.5247–5252.

92. *LGBZ*, 1.8a–12a.

93. *MSL*, 82.5259–5260; *LGBZ*, 10.5a–6a.

94. *MSL*, 82.5269.

95. *MSL*, 82.5282; *LGBZ*, 10.6b–7a.

96. *LGBZ*, 10.7a–11b.

97. *MSL*, 83.5396–5397.

98. *LGBZ*, 10.12b–14a. Yan later wrote the inscription for a spirit-way stela for Xu Zan. It does not mention this incident at all.

99. *MSL*, 83.5397–5398.

100. *GCXZL*, 2.1121–1122 (account of conduct of Wang Yuling by Zhan Shichun); *MS*, ch. 207 (biography of Wang Yuling).

101. Zhou Yi, *Naqi zoushu* (Siku quanshu zhenben, 9th ser., 1979), 17a–22a.

102. For example, Guo Tingxun, ed., *Mingdai fensheng renwu kao*, in *Mingdai zhuanji congkan* (Taipei: Mingwen shuju, 1991), 138.563–564; Tang Bin, ed., *Qian-an xiansheng Mingshi gao*, in *Mingdai zhuanji congkan* (Taipei: Mingwen shuju, 1991), 159.766–776. Another long memorial by Zhou Yi, dated June 8, 1543, details five crimes against Fan Jizu, but leaves Yan Song out of the picture (22a–27b).

103. Zhou Yi, *Naqi zoushu*, 36b–43a.

104. *LGBZ*, 10.14a–15b.

105. See, generally, Zhang Xiangming, "A Preliminary Study of the Punishment of Political Speech in the Ming Period," *Ming Studies*, no. 62 (2010): 56–91.

106. Zhou Yi, *Naqi zoushu*, 43b–44b.

107. Yang Jue, *Yang Zhongjie ji* (Siku quanshu zhenben, 5th ser., 1974, vol. 356), 2.11a.

108. Ibid., 1.1a–4a.

109. Yang Jue, *Yang Zhongjie ji*, 1.1a–4a, 4a–11b. See also *GCXZL*, 5.2882 (biography of Yang Jue).

110. Ibid., 1.11b–18b.

111. Xia Xie, 4.2175.

112. Ibid., 4.2177–2178; *GQ*, 4.3611, 3619; Yang Jue, *Yang Zhongjie ji*, 3.7a–12a.

113. *MSL*, 82.5269–5270; *DMB*, 2.1506–1508 (biography of Yang Chueh).

114. Jiajing's predecessor, the Zhengde emperor, also hated the Forbidden City, and so he moved his base of operations to the Leopard Quarter, also in West Park. See James Geiss, "The Leopard Quarter during the Cheng-te Reign," *Ming Studies*, no. 24 (1987): 1–38.

115. Shen Defu, *Wanli yehuo bian*, 1.65, 2.469–471; *MS*, ch. 114 (biography of Empress Fang).

116. *GQ*, 4.2634; Fu Fengxiang, ed., *Huang Ming zhaoling* (1548; reprint Taipei, 1967), 4.1964–1967. See, generally, Bao Hua Hsieh, "From Charwoman to Empress Dowager: Serving Women in the Ming Palace," *Ming Studies*, no. 42 (1999): 26–80.

117. Shen Defu, *Wanli yehuo bian*, 2.471.

118. *LGBZ*, 6.1ab.

119. Ibid., 6.1b–2a.

120. *DMB*, 2.1266 (biography of T'ao Chung-wen); *MS*, ch. 307 (biography of Duan Chao-yong).

121. *LGBZ*, 11.2a.

122. Ibid., 11.2a–3a.

123. *GCXZL*, 2.1393 (biography of Gu Kexue); *MS*, ch. 307 (biographies); *LGBZ*, 11.3ab.

124. Yan explained that the recipe for autumn stones was classical and not esoteric at all. Sheng was respected by such Confucian stalwarts as Zhan Ruoshui and Ouyang De.

125. *LGBZ*, 10.15b–17a; *MS*, ch. 210 (biography of He Weibo).

126. *MSL*, 83.5567–5569.

127. *GQ*, 4.3660 (quoting Xu Xuemo); *MS*, ch. 193 (biography of Chai Luan).

128. See *Qianshan*, ch. 34. Xia Xie (4.2211) thinks that Chai bribed his way back into the Grand Secretariat after his tour of the frontier, and so his reputation was already diminished before the exam scandal broke.

129. *LGBZ*, 13.6a–8a.

130. Ibid., 6.6b–7b.

131. *GCXZL*, 1.587–591 (biography of Li Ben by Wang Daokun). After leaving office in 1561, he changed his name to Lü Ben.

132. For example, Wang Weizhen, *Wangshi cunsi gao* (Siku quanshu cunmu congshu, 4th ser.), 103.176, letter to Yan Donglou.

133. For the events of September–October 1550, see *MSL*, 85.6482–6512ff.; Gao Dai, *Hongyou lu* (1557; reprint Taipei, 1977), 1422–1442; *MSJSBM*, ch. 59 (the crisis of 1550); *DMB*, 1.252–255 (biography of Ch'iu Luan).

134. *MSL*, 85.6547–6549. Gu Yingtai adds the further detail of Yan Song's "private adherents" returning from the south accompanying tens of baggage wagons, forty carts of other kinds, and ten or more tower boats, storing their contents under official seal. See *MSJSBM*, ch. 54 (Yan Song in power).

135. *MSL*, 85.6549; *LGBZ*, 14.7a–8b; Xia Xie, 4.2275.

136. Yang's story has been vividly recounted in Kenneth J. Hammond, *Pepper Mountain: The Life, Death, and Posthumous Career of Yang Jisheng* (London and New York: Routledge, 2007).

137. *MSL*, 86.6912; Xia Xie, 4.2306–2307.

138. *LGBZ*, 15.4b–6a.

139. *DMB*, 1.631–638 (biography of Hu Tsung-hsien); Charles O. Hucker, "Hu Tsung-hsien's Campaign against Hsu Hai, 1556," in *Chinese Ways in Warfare*, ed. Frank A. Kierman Jr. and John K. Fairbank, 273–307 (Cambridge, MA: Harvard University Press, 1977); John E. Wills Jr., "Maritime China from Wang Chih to Shih Lang: Themes in Peripheral History," in *From Ming to Ch'ing: Conquest, Region, and Continuity in Seventeenth-Century China*, ed. Jonathan D. Spence and John E. Wills, 201–238 (New Haven, CT, and London: Yale University Press, 1979).

140. There are *DMB* biographies of many of the principals cited here—Zhao Wenhua and Hu Zongxian among them. Also, *LGBZ*, 12.1a–12a; Zhao Wenhua, *Zhaoshi jiacang ji* (Siku weishou shu jikan, ser. 5), 19.229–239 (letters and orders).

141. Zou's statement differs slightly in the various sources. See *MSL*, 90.8386–8388; *GQ*, 4.3977; Xia Xie, 4.2429–2430; and *MS*, ch. 210 (biography of Zou Yinglong).

142. *MSL*, 90.8388–8389.

143. Ibid., 90.8389–8390; Xia Xie, 4.2430.

144. *MSL*, 90.8890–8891.

145. *DMB*, 1.924–926 (biography of Lin Jun). Luo Longwen was reportedly the son of a merchant, and a skilled navigator, whom Hu Zongxian had sail to Japan to bribe Wang Zhi into surrender. See *GCXZL*, 4.2676 (biography of Lin Run). It was through Hu's good offices that Luo entered Yan Shifan's circle and became a Secretariat drafter.

146. *MSL*, 91.8737.

147. *MS*, ch. 210 (biography of Lin Run).

148. *MSL*, 91.8789–8791.

149. *MSL*, 91.8792.

150. See John W. Dardess, *A Political Life in Ming China: A Grand Secretary and His Times* (Lanham, MD: Rowman & Littlefield, 2013), 142–143.

151. These data, later given the title *Tianshui bingshan lu* (alluding to the susceptibility of great wealth to erosion) can be found in *Zhibuzu zhai congshu* (reprint Taipei, 1964), 6.3705–3840. There is a listing of the Yan holdings of art and calligraphy in Zhang Xianqing, *Yan Song zhuan*, 375–391.

152. *MS*, ch. 308 (biography of Yan Shifan).

153. *MSJSBM*, ch. 54 (Yan Song in power).

154. Dardess, *A Political Life*, 147.

155. *MSL*, 90.8391; Xia Xie, 4.2453.

156. *MS*, ch. 210, at the end.

157. *MSL*, 91.8792–8793.

Chapter Five

Winter

Grand Secretary Xu Jie

Would the long-hoped-for end of Yan Song and his machine also be a har-binger of the demise of the Ming itself? Would things from here go from bad to worse? How could a regime survive with its autocratic head self-secluded in a sacred park and his top advisory board forced to live in that holy precinct alongside him, and thus no longer in direct touch with the regular agencies of government? The office of chief grand secretary was also a magnet for all the resentment, dissent, and outrage that might be boiling up in the bureaucratic ranks at any given time. To the present-day observer, it looks for all the world like a crazily built structure that is ready to collapse at the slightest touch.

But it held. The "winter" of the long Jiajing reign, 1562–1567, constituted an upward turn out of a dangerous downward trajectory, and a rejuvenation, a reenergizing of the system, a refocusing on getting things right again in China. The main author of this turnabout was a chief grand secretary who differed from his predecessors. Xu Jie (1505–1583) brought to the office a new way of thinking and innovative practical approaches to the problem of how one can possibly govern as huge and complex a realm as Ming China. Xu Jie showed that in an autocracy, a single powerful personality, other than that of the autocrat, can have a major impact on the whole apparatus.

Xu Jie was a man of a new generation. He was four years older than the emperor he served, but twenty-three years younger than Yan Song, twenty-one years younger than Xia Yan, and twenty-eight years younger than Zhang

Fujing. He knew them all. Zhang Fujing interviewed him in 1523, right after he'd finished third in the *jinshi* competition that year. By pure chance, his father's death in 1524 took him out of the deadly Great Rites protest of that year. Like Yan Song, home on sick leave, and Xia Yan, in mourning for his mother, Xu Jie escaped the likely career-damaging effects of being on hand for that awful confrontation. Xu was a Hanlin junior compiler, and had he been in Beijing, he would almost certainly have joined his Hanlin colleagues in their support for Yang Tinghe and their failed career-ending demonstration against Jiajing's Great Rites.

Xu came to Jiajing's notice later in the 1520s, when he served as an occasional lecturer in the ruler's Classics Mat tutorials. (That was how, before the sessions ended in 1536, Jiajing got some idea of who the up-and-coming stars of his administration might be.) Xu's contacts with Xia Yan were not very friendly. Yan Song he came to know very well, because he served under him for ten years in the Grand Secretariat.

But let us not jump ahead of the story. I propose to do with Xu Jie as I did with Zhang, Xia, and Yan and address first the question of what skills and experiences each brought to the job of chief grand secretary, and second, how Xu's personality and operating style compare to those of his predecessors, and how the sort of man he was shaped his relationship to Jiajing and his interactions with the bureaucracy in Beijing and beyond. How was he ever able to steer the Ming in a better direction?[1]

* * *

One vital character trait Xu shared with Zhang, Xia, and Yan was a seldom-expressed but powerful drive either to excel or dominate by any and all available means. Where ambition of this sort comes from is a mystery, but lavish attention from parents, fathers especially, was an element in the early lives of Xia Yan and Yan Song (and indeed Jiajing as well), which undoubtedly enhanced their confidence and self-esteem. Zhang, Xia, and Yan had middling success at the examinations; Xu far outshone them. None of them came from wealthy or privileged family backgrounds.

Because Xu Jie belonged to a later generation than they, he was attracted at a young age, when he was a student in the county school in Huating (in Songjiang Prefecture, Nan Zhili, present Jiangsu Province), to the new form of the standard Neo-Confucianism that was held in suspicion in Beijing but elsewhere was on the upsurge, sweeping the country, inviting students, officials, and even commoners into its warm embrace. Wang Yangming was the leading exponent, teacher, and practitioner, but there were others, Xu's county magistrate and instructor Nie Bao among them. Xu Jie never met Wang Yangming, and Nie Bao declared himself Wang's disciple only later, but no matter; Xu was close friends with Ouyang De and others, who were direct Wang Yangming disciples. Discussing, interpreting, and internalizing the main precepts of this inward search for ethical certitude became a life-long preoccupation for Xu. He rose to become an important sponsor of the special study gatherings (*jiangxue*) in which these precepts were shared and discussed, in Beijing and all over the realm. This was something new. "Extending the good conscience" (*zhi liangzhi*) was the Wang school's central slogan. It meant radiating one's rediscovered ethical identity, polished by discussion and inward reflection to a high gloss, until it shone like a light, affecting and attracting others.

What Xu Jie did was to introduce this mode of personal conduct into the world of high-level politics, and this made him a very different kind of grand secretary—unlike Zhang, a hard-edged ideological warrior; or Xia, a brilliant technocrat; or Yan Song, a corruption-based machine politician.

It took some years for Xu to develop this technique. A first step was his felt need to establish his bona fides with his contemporaries in officialdom. His absence from Beijing at the time of the 1528 crackdown put his loyalties in doubt. When he returned from mourning leave, he evidently thought he needed to undergo the same risk to life and career that many of his friends in the defeated and silenced underground had undergone. He needed to confront power. Engaging in the politics of protest was not at all in the new philosophical style. Xu had never done this before, and he never did it again.

The controversy in question had nothing to do with the Great Rites. It was, however, an important element in Jiajing's continuing program for China's ritual reconstruction. Jiajing was determined to force a complete overhaul of the existing cult of Confucius. That entailed, among other things, the erasure of the title "king" from the sage's posthumous honors and the removal of all the statues of Confucius that stood in his shrines nationwide. This was a respectful iconoclasm of purification, not a downgrading. Jiajing and Zhang Fujing wrote up the rationale for making these changes, and they sent out their statement for the Hanlin academicians and Rites Ministry officials to comment upon.

Of course they expected everyone to approve, or at least not object. Everyone did as expected, with the sole exception of Xu Jie. Mourning period over, he was back in office as a Hanlin junior compiler. He said he was at work in the History Office on November 17, 1530, when Minister of Rites Li Shi handed him a copy of the statement. He read it over several times. He appreciated the ruler's not acting as a lone decider (*duduan*) and being willing to ask for reactions, so he felt he had to share his doubts and voice his objections to making any changes in the existing cult. One objection he raised was the fact that both the Ming founder Taizu and Yongle had sanctioned the title and the statuary. What of that? He asked that his objections be sent out for discussion. On November 20, Jiajing did so. [2]

Xu probably understood that his objections stood no chance of acceptance. The *kedao* (supervising secretaries and censors) did rally to his support, led by Censor Li Guan and Supervising Secretary Wang Rumei. They elaborated on Xu's argument. Jiajing thought Li had the hidden aim of attacking the Great Rites settlement. He was arrested, interrogated, and removed from civil service. He went easier on Wang. [3]

Xu Jie himself was called to the carpet in the Grand Secretariat. Zhang Fujing wanted some answers. Why these objections to a plan to simplify the cult? Xu ventured to explain. Taizu, he said, had removed the titles from all the mountain and river gods, but he let Confucius's title stand. Zhang said Taizu was young then, and we can't use that as a precedent. Xu replied, "How can you say young? Taizu founded the dynasty first; then he turned to discussing the rites. Anyway age doesn't matter. When you redid the suburban rites, why did you cite Taizu's earliest directive?" Score one for Xu Jie. Zhang's cheeks reddened. Then he asked Xu whether the statues of Confucius were of ancient origin. "They aren't," answered Xu, "but they've been there a long time, and how can you bear to destroy them?" It was Zhang's turn to score a point. "The Cheng brothers said, if one hair is not that of my father, how can you call it parental?" Xu's retort to that was a bit shaky. "If the hair looks like my father's, how can you destroy it? Plus how do you know whether any portrait of a sage or emperor is exact in every respect? You don't." Zhang felt he'd been outfoxed. "You're rebelling against me," he asserted in anger. Xu's reply to that was death defying. "To rebel means I must have once been an adherent of yours, but I've never been that, so how can you say I'm rebelling?" The two other grand secretaries, Gui E and Chai Luan, who'd sat silent through all this, urged Xu to apologize. Xu made no apology. He bowed and left.

Jiajing, told of this, demanded Xu's retraction and apology. Xu agreed to accuse himself of ineptitude only. He would not recant. He asked to be dismissed. Jiajing apparently developed a liking for Xu, based on his Classics Mat lectures and other brief encounters. So he imposed a light penalty, sending him to a low post away from Beijing.

But when Censor in Chief Wang Hong, a pro–Great Rites loyalist, saw that directive, he protested it. Demotion and transfer weren't harsh enough. Xu's statement was perverse, an affront to the "national dignity" (*guoti*), and he needs to be heavily punished as an example to others.[4] That terrified Xu, less for himself than for the welfare of his terminally ill wife and new baby son.

Thus, representatives of the Hanlin, the Censorate, and the supervising secretaries, the same bloc that had manned the front lines demonstrating against Jiajing in 1524, ventured another assault here in 1530, this time over a different issue involving ritual, and this time Xu Jie was not to be left out. He led. He stood up and stood out. Clearly he was no palace sycophant but a member and indeed a leader in the moral underground, wounded but still alive.

Xu feared he might face death in prison after prolonged abuse there. That was the fate suffered by many a dissenter. Fortunately for him, Jiajing was not just then of a mind to crack down that hard, and he ordered Xu demoted to the post of prefectural judge in war-damaged Yanping Prefecture in far-away Fujian Province. Xu was much relieved.

* * *

Xu Jie spent the next nine years, 1530–1539, out in the provinces, gaining experiences of a kind his predecessors as grand secretaries never had. (Xia Yan's work at Blue Sheep Mountain was on a much higher bureaucratic level.) He made good use of his time. As prefectural judge, he adjudicated cases for three years. He also helped formulate strategy to eradicate a gang of bandits. He cracked down on corruption in the local silver mines. And, attracted as he was to the new Confucianism, he copied his mentor Nie Bao (and indirectly Wang Yangming) by voluntarily adding to his assigned functions that of teaching the local youth. Again, this expanded significantly his portfolio of experience and made him in due course a grand secretary of a very different stripe.

From prefectural judge in Fujian, Xu's philosophical interests and teaching prowess won him promotion to the position of education intendant, first for Zhejiang Province, then Jiangxi. He was on track to achieve some sort of outstanding success, but in what field? What did he want to do with his life? He thought about, but firmly rejected, the opportunity to become a full-time Confucian teacher-evangelist. He toyed with the related idea of becoming a thinker with a published body of texts to his credit. As things worked out, he would retain strong interests both in teaching and in developing and expanding Confucian doctrine, but he decided that his career should involve administration above all else and that it should entail activating the "good conscience" of the Wang Yangming school and radiating the polished sense of a moral self into the dangerous and shark-infested waters of Jiajing's bureaucracy, so as to make China a better place in which to live. That was to put revisionist ethical doctrine to its intended practical use.

Xu Jie also brought to the table a liking for the military, for soldiers and military affairs. He did not shy away from the occasional need for lethal violence in human affairs. Nor, indeed, did the great ethicist, Wang Yangming.[5] He had friends and in-laws who were hereditary military people. (A younger son of his later married a daughter of Lu Bing, of hereditary military descent; and when Lu was made head of the Embroidered-Uniform Guard, he became China's top policeman.) Xu's social ease with rough men and their bloody trade, as well as his long intellectual interest in security and defense, proved essential to his effectiveness as a grand secretary.

Besides that, Xu also developed skills as an overseer and manager. While he always professed an inability to understand correctly the full import of the precept "extend the good conscience," despite all his devotion to "discussion and study" (*jiangxue*), Xu acted as though he did get it. Why would he be so diffident about this?

Had he claimed to grasp the precept fully, he would have been compelled to become a full-time evangelist for it, and that he did not want to do. Without claiming he understood what the "good conscience" was, he simply went ahead and "extended" it, whatever it was. This stance, as it turned out, produced positive results in bureaucratic life. As education intendant, he made himself a good dean: he demanded discipline, but without provoking discontent, resentment, or wrath among the students. Just the opposite, he won respect.

The next few years had their ups and downs, but from 1539 Xu had several opportunities, which he eagerly seized, to expand his portfolio of challenges successfully met. In 1539, he was called back to the Hanlin Academy, apparently because tutors were needed for the young heir apparent, and Jiajing, as the years went by and his rancor over the Great Rites opposition eased, recalled Xu Jie fondly as a good man for the job. As little Zhu Zairui was all of three years old, duty was light, and Xu had ample free time in which to gather a *jiangxue* circle with several of Ming China's current intellectual lights—Luo Hongxian, Zou Shouyi, Tang Shunzhi, and Zhao Shichun among them. Xu Jie was the kingpin, as only he was equally at ease with inward self-realignment and an outward urge for real-world knowledge and action. All these men were soon sent away or were removed for composing a text for the child containing passages deemed critical of the ruler (that was Zou), or for proposing that the tot be a New Year's Day stand-in for his sick father (Luo, Tang, and Zhao). Where was Xu? At home, in mourning for his mother, and thus out of danger. Once more, Lady Luck had him under her wing.

When he returned, he was appointed chancellor of the Imperial University. The demands of that post were mainly supervisory and administrative, not far different from those of a provincial education intendant. Again, Xu imposed discipline without stirring up resentment. Students who'd finished their course of studies and held traineeships were forbidden to ask or bribe higher officials to help them land regular posts; they were to go strictly by seniority and wait in line. Archivists were directed to keep account books for all payments for food and the like. Xu promised he'd handle any complaints personally. He instituted monthly logs to record the behavior of each student. He'd wear a celebratory robe when reading aloud the log for good behavior on the first of each month, and a mourning robe when reading out the log for misbehavior. "You'll be on this list if you don't respect your teachers and seniors," he would warn. The students reportedly took note.[6]

Xu was made a vice minister of rites on November 23, 1544. Rites was a stepping-stone to the Grand Secretariat in Jiajing's time, but Ming bureaucracy was always in a bit of a churn, and Xu hardly had time to do anything in rites, because on February 23, 1545, he was shifted to the post of vice minister of personnel. This was a new and different challenge. He met it eagerly and aggressively.

One habit of his was to hang a poster on the wall of his office, reminding both himself and his visitors of his commitments and priorities. So after thinking about it, he hung this reminder: "If I don't show total loyalty, if I plant a faction, if I chase bribes, if I turn against the public interest for the sake of salary, may the gods destroy me! I must strive to befriend guests, consult widely about governance, and discover any hidden ills the common people may be suffering."[7] Apparently he hung another poster (or the same one was remembered differently). This one said, "You won your *jinshi* degree at twenty-one *sui*, and at forty-three you're vice minister of personnel. The dynasty has treated you well. How can you not exhaust loyalty and exert every ounce of effort? Will you plant faction and reject worthy men? Chase bribes and sell decisions? Forget impartiality and fawn on superiors? Take salary just to feather your own nest? May the gods destroy you and your progeny if you do!"[8]

As a voluntary code of conduct, openly announced and seriously meant as a guide to the actions he promised to undertake, Xu's admonitions to himself seemed to fly in the face of the high-level status quo. What was going on here?

There were some major turnovers in the Grand Secretariat. Xia Yan was temporarily ousted in 1542. That made Chai Luan chief grand secretary from 1542 to 1544, with Yan Song serving under him. On September 14, 1544, Chai was ousted and reduced to commoner status due to a big examination scandal involving his sons. That brought Yan Song temporarily to the top as chief. Jiajing admitted two new men to the Grand Secretariat: Xu Zan and Zhang Bi, both on September 27.

Xu Zan (1473–1548), minister of personnel from 1536, was a major sponsor of Xu Jie's (they were unrelated; their surnames are written with different characters and are pronounced with different speech tones). It was Xu Zan who in 1539 recommended appointing Xu Jie and several other intellectual stars to positions in Beijing. And here the story gets a bit convoluted. Xu Zan had joined in an impeachment of Yan Song in 1543 and was temporarily forced out of office when Jiajing rejected it. Yan Song did not object to Xu Zan's entry into the Grand Secretariat in 1544 because Xu Zan had been chastened and would not dare challenge Yan Song again. Plus he was thought to be corrupt as well as soft and controllable. Yan Song cut both him and Zhang Bi out of the loop, giving them no role in drafting rescripts (imperial replies, usually decisions, to incoming official memorials). Xu Zan complained of being taken out of a substantive post as minister of personnel and relegated to being a mere bystander in the Grand Secretariat. He wanted out. Jiajing removed him in December 1545.[9]

Xu Zan's replacement as minister of personnel was Xiong Jie (1478–1554), one of the small cohort of officials who twenty years earlier had joined Jiajing's side in the Great Rites dispute. Nonetheless, Jiajing removed him on the same day he removed Xu Zan because he had protested Jiajing's building a special facility, a Jixiantai, or "Terrace for Consulting the

Immortals," which the ruler intended to visit whenever he wanted to contact the Daoist gods. Xiong was escorted home in shackles. [10]

Xiong's replacements as ministers of personnel were two old men, first Tang Long (1477–1546) and then Zhou Yong (1476–1547). They were in poor health and low on energy. Both were glad to let Xu Jie step forward and act on their behalf. Spotting the opportunity, Xu Jie was glad to oblige. Jiajing was aware of the arrangement and was happy to let it be.

That, in brief, was the state of play in which Xu Jie found himself at an important stage in his career. He was de facto minister of personnel. This is when he hung the placard or placards on the wall. In addition, he is described by his admirer, Wang Shizhen, as actually setting a new standard of conduct when he refused to act as his ministry predecessors had done, treating lower-ranking officials with icy hauteur and never allowing them a chance to talk at length. No, Xu Jie treated them with deferential respect, sat down with them, and questioned them tirelessly and at great length about frontier affairs and local problems. By doing that, Xu got a picture of how things were in Ming China and the kinds of men he was dealing with. When he liked them, he helped them. That won him acclaim across the board. Xiong, Zhou, and Tang all valued him, as did all those whose reports he listened to and whose careers he advanced. Xu refused to play a quiet, low-key role. He helped good men whose honesty and diffidence had so far hindered their careers. He blocked the career paths of obnoxious go-getters. [11]

How does this behavior, if it is accurately recounted, square with his professed principles? The sticking point is that Xu did not admit even to himself his own powerful ambition for the highest of offices, yet he always kept alert for the next opportunity. When he spoke of "exhausting loyalty," this works well as cover language. The higher one rises, the greater the loyalty he can exhaust. When he promised never to "reject worthy men" or "plant faction," this did not mean that he had no interest in cultivating a bureaucratic following. Could such a following, though, be considered a faction (*dang*)? In the 1620s, this question was argued heatedly and philosophically. In the 1540s, it wasn't.

The word *dang* can mean a party, clique, faction, or indeed a gang, as in a bandit gang. But it's slippery. Belonging to an "evil faction" carried the death penalty, and the Ming Code defined it so loosely that Jiajing (or the Daoist gods he consulted) could stretch it as he liked and impose it at will. "If officials at the court form cliques to disorder the government of the court," reads the code, "they shall all be punished by decapitation. Their wives and

children shall be enslaved, and their property confiscated by the government."[12] So Xu Jie had to step gingerly here, and he did. His moves were
politically brilliant. He avoided the corruption route taken by Yan Song. He
avoided sounding off in a provocative way, which would "disorder government" and invite the ruin of himself and his admirers. He never challenged
Jiajing's Daoist procedures, seeing what happened to Xiong Jie. He never
attacked that grand marshal of machine politics, Yan Song, seeing what
happened to everyone courageous enough to try it. And he avoided being
pressed into factionalism; his persistent but brilliant refusal to understand the
term "good conscience" shows this, because if he had claimed to know what
it was, he would have helped to create a shibboleth, a factional identifier,
rewarding all who subscribed to it, rejecting all who did not, and surely
triggering the code's "disruptive" clause. As it was, he could embrace as
followers and supporters a wide range of talented men, some of them Wang-
school adherents, but many of them not. In fact, he championed no school at
all, or even any circumscribed cause, such as rites.

But Xu Jie had his eye on the main chance, and he saw early on, as did
Xia Yan, that to get ahead in Jiajing's world, a demonstrated interest in and
facility with rites was going to be essential. Despite his vow not to, he did
indeed "fawn on superiors." One simply cannot thrive in hierarchy if one has
never attracted the notice, goodwill, and favor of superiors. Lacking any
special appreciation of rites for their own sake, he made himself knowledgeable about them, beginning with assisting in their editing in the late 1520s.
And he didn't stop there.

* * *

Then Xu's stint as virtual minister of personnel came to an end. On February
17, 1547, Wen Yuan (1480–1563) was appointed minister, but unlike his
predecessors, he insisted on taking sole charge of things. Unhappy about
such a restraint on his freedom of action, Xu sought and got a concurrent
appointment as a Hanlin academician, with a new responsibility for instruct-
ing the latest crop of bachelors, top winners of the *jinshi* degree. Reportedly,
he had by this time already won renown as a man to be respected and
reckoned with, yet he bent conscientiously to his new duties, reviewing all
the trainees' writings and chiding them for using the elegant antithetical style
in their essays, urging them instead to express directly what they really
meant. If this wasn't exactly the "good conscience" in action, it certainly

came close. The bachelors accepted his criticisms, as well as his advice to study government, and later on some of them credited him with aiding their success.

One of those bachelors was none other than Zhang Juzheng, who became chief grand secretary and virtual dictator of China early in the reign of Jiajing's grandson, the Wanli emperor. He and Xu remained close.

* * *

On March 13, 1549, Xu Jie was appointed minister of rites, a sure preliminary to eventual elevation to the Grand Secretariat. Xu would hold that position until 1552. In July 1549, Jiajing invited him to live inside West Park as minister of rites. How did he perform?

As to rites in the restricted sense, business was heavy and Xu did his duty, but he lacked Xia Yan's zest for the job. Before Xia Yan became a grand secretary, he had been a technocrat. Every official paper Xia wrote over the years carried a passionate sense of urgency, almost as though the fate of civilization itself hung on his handling every matter correctly and expertly and expressing it forcefully. Xu Jie cared greatly about China's military security and about fine-tuning his political and bureaucratic relationships, but his technical papers are flat, as though the issues bored him, and so his heart wasn't really in it. Just the opposite of Xia Yan.

What rites-related issues came up? Xu tried annually for six years running to persuade Jiajing to formally install as heir apparent his oldest surviving son, the future Longqing emperor. The ruler pigeonholed the first two requests, "noted" the third, denied the next two, and on the sixth try told Xu to stop. So Xu Jie, reluctant to be too confrontational, backed off. (As noted earlier, Longqing was never made heir apparent, but he assumed the throne anyway.)

There were occasions when Xu showed as much in the way of planning and organizing skills as any of his predecessors had shown. He worked out the elaborate program for the funeral observances for the heir apparent Zhu Zairui in 1549.[13] He successfully pressed Jiajing for his approval, a year late, of capping and marriage ceremonies and educational arrangements for the two surviving princes in 1552.[14] And Xu would successfully arrange the huge funeral for Jiajing himself in 1567.

A knotty problem came up in 1547 with regard to installing Empress Fang's tablet in the imperial ancestral temple. The temple had just been reconfigured to conform to the ancient rules, which severely limited the space available for new admissions. A general discussion by various high officials suggested removing the Hongxi emperor's tablet to make room for hers. Xu Jie and a colleague disagreed with that but said nothing at the meeting. Instead, Xu sent Jiajing his dissenting opinion by way of a secret memorial. Jiajing was unreceptive. He wondered why Xu didn't speak out at the meeting. This looked like dishonesty. Xu backed down, trembling, he said, with fear. [15] This was a serious misstep, but nothing came of it.

In March 1550, north China was in the grip of a serious drought. No snow had fallen over the winter, and there had been no precipitation at all for 150 days. There were bad dust storms. There was an earthquake in Liaodong. Epidemic disease. Frontier raids. The cause? Government malfunction, corruption, and judicial cruelty. Xu Jie urged Jiajing to authorize a full-scale appeal to all the gods and a pause for ethical reflection and introspection by all the officials. Jiajing agreed and conducted a rain prayer of his own in West Park. Officials offered sacrifices at six different altars, and all offices, including the Hanlin Academy (for prayer texts) and the Directorate of Astronomy, were mobilized for a full-court press. [16] It was a major undertaking, and it fell to the Ministry of Rites to arrange and direct it.

* * *

Xu Jie was knowledgeable about rites, and he showed he could organize large public events. But what really seized Jiajing's favorable attention was Xu's ability and willingness to write Daoist prayers (*qingci*) and his fawning composition of paeans and celebratory poems in honor of signs of celestial favor. Since taking residence in West Park, Jiajing had become obsessed with this sort of thing, and an ambitious man like Xu knew how to take advantage of it. Much of this was, to be sure, required routine, and some of it was ghostwritten for him by others. Jiajing demanded congratulatory statements on, for instance, his birthday, on the winter solstice and New Year's Day, on the completion of major construction projects, on the capture of rebels, on installing the heir apparent, on retitling the empresses, on drought-breaking snow and rain, and on the presentation of yellow and white rabbits. [17] It was a joyous sign when "sweet dew" fell on the Xianling, Jiajing's father's tomb, and celebratory lyrics were demanded. Ming princes were occasional recipients of lucky omens as well, such as in 1552 when a hunter presented the Prince of Yiyang with a white macaw, a bird normally black, and a talking bird as well. Xie Jie checked the omen literature, but he found nothing about white macaws, so he ventured to associate it with Jiajing's benevolent care for high culture and with good results in the recent provincial exams. Multiheaded grain stalks presented to Jiajing by the Prince of Lujiang were a sign of harmony and unity in the realm.[18] Poem after poem of Xu's joined those of Yan Song in celebrating banquets and boat rides and other such occasions with Jiajing. We will spare the reader. Jiajing demanded this sort of literary trivia from his top officials; it was a kind of test of their commitment to him.

* * *

On a more serious level, Xu as rites minister conducted a thorough review and reform of testing procedures in the Imperial Academy of Medicine, adjusted management rules for the four thousand cooks attached to the Court of Imperial Entertainments, and set up recruitment procedures to restock a sadly depleted corps of translators attached to the Court of State Ceremonial. Personnel rosters also had to be ironed out for all the cooks, musicians, and dancers attached to the Court of Imperial Sacrifices.[19] All in a day's work for the minister of rites.

The question of Xu Jie's personal relationship to the emperor, whether it was tentative or solidly enough founded to withstand the occasional rift, came into view several times while Xu was minister. One such occasion was over the placement of Empress Fang's tablet, as noted above. Another involved the rank order of the tablets honoring Jiajing's two dead empresses. Jiajing wanted the tablet of the Empress Fang (d. 1547) to precede that of the disliked Empress Chen (d. 1528). Xu Jie argued the opposite. Jiajing's own reaction was firm but subtle. A chief supervising secretary for rites, Yang Sizhong, submitted a strong memorial backing Xu Jie's. So, early in 1553, the emperor had Yang publicly flogged a hundred times over a different matter and removed him from civil service. Xu Jie he let alone. And Xu Jie got the message. Confrontation was not his style.[20]

In 1549, Jiajing invited Xu to come into West Park and live there permanently, alongside the grand secretaries and a handful of other favorites.

Not long after, the whole arrangement threatened to unravel. Xu Jie's son Xu Fan (a rival to Yan Song's son Yan Shifan in his corrupt opportunism) was caught cheating on the provincial exams held in Nanjing. An official who was a philosophical friend of Xu's hurried a messenger to Beijing with the bad news before a censorial impeachment made the whole scandal public. (A similar scandal had led to Grand Secretary Chai Luan's ouster in 1544, as we saw.) Was this the end for Xu Jie? It was, if the emperor were waiting for a good excuse to dump him. The impeachment apparently reached Beijing on September 5, 1549. Xu sent the emperor a secret apology. Jiajing simply ignored the matter. Neither Xu nor his villainous son was ever punished.[21] If proof were needed, this affair shows Jiajing's strong liking for Xu Jie. It also showed Xu Jie how heavy a debt he owed Jiajing. Such were the power games played in the holy Daoist precincts of West Park.

* * *

Foreign relations came under the purview of the Ministry of Rites, as we have seen. During Xu Jie's tenure there, quiet reigned among most of China's tributaries. One exception was Japan. Xu Jie submitted a long and detailed discussion of China-Japan tribute relations on July 9, 1548.

Little did Xu guess that he was dealing with the last official contact between the two countries until the late nineteenth century, 250 years in the future. The end of the relationship was partly due to Japan's descent into civil war (as with Annam, not long before), and partly to China's failure to understand the explosive growth of the world silver economy and the impossibility of sustaining the politically mandated chokehold on foreign trade under such conditions. To continue to limit Japan's access to the China markets to three ships at ten-year intervals, to dock at the one port of Ningbo only, from which an official delegation to Beijing was limited to fifty men, defied all reason. Xu Jie's many talents and virtues did not include a gift for grand strategy. The one high official who might have boasted such a gift was Xia Yan, but he was in deep trouble and was soon to be decapitated in the wake of the failed plan to recover the Ordos. So Xu Jie's careful review, which won Jiajing's endorsement, simply recommended some minor adjustments in order to palliate complaints from the Japanese side. Xu had a good tactical, local-level understanding of maritime smuggling and the violence it occasioned, but he did not paint this into a larger strategic picture. He saw no fault, no causative role from China's side for the coastal raiding. He noted that Japan's "king," Shogun Yoshiharu, wanted to be allowed to provide his fleet with armed escorts because of the rising menace of seaborne banditry. He noted, too, how Zhu Wan (1494–1550), only just appointed to a very powerful position created just for him on the Zhejiang-Fujian coast, was ruthlessly destroying the smuggling trade, raiding illegal offshore trading ports, and prosecuting the onshore "nest lords," Fujian elites whose chronic nonpayment of debts to the multinational smugglers was fomenting their retaliatory raids. He noted also that Chinese merchants and adventurers were making illegal trade-related visits to Japan. But all he could think of was to make minor adjustments to the trade ban.[22]

* * *

The biggest foreign relations problem was not Japan but Altan Khan and his raiders (Lu). Altan's often-repeated demand was that China should afford him trading opportunities. Jiajing kept refusing to deal with him. Altan then turned to raiding China's frontier.

Insofar as this was a foreign relations question, Xu Jie was on Jiajing's side. Just as he sought no basic rethinking of Ming relations with Japan, he had no new approach with respect to Altan and his people. But in 1550, Altan's shocking raid, deep into China, right to the walls of Beijing itself, turned a question of foreign relations into something else—what Xu argued was a major security crisis. Security was not a file in the Rites Ministry portfolio. That belonged to the military. But there was Xu Jie, at the emperor's beck and call, sitting right inside West Park. Security was an issue he was beside himself with eagerness to plunge into, and he wasted no time putting himself in the virtual driver's seat of an existential effort to save China—not by rethinking its grand strategy or redesigning its institutional order, but by a hands-on, inspirational relationship with its key civil and military personnel. That was a context in which "extending the good conscience" could show itself to good effect. That, together with subtle intrigue against men he didn't like, was Xu Jie's way.

The year 1550 was a bad one for China's security generally. Intrigue and lobbying by coastal elites, their fortunes imperiled by Zhu Wan's war on smuggling, managed to bring about his dismissal. An arrest warrant pending, Zhu Wan committed suicide. A blanket of fear among officials deterred for a while any further discussion of how to reestablish maritime security.[23]

Then early in the fall of 1550 came Altan Khan's spectacular raid on Beijing. It was a disaster for China, exposing huge holes in its defenses, but it opened up a big opportunity for Xu Jie to step forth and put his interpersonal skills, and his so far untested leadership potential, on public display.

There was the hastily called meeting on October 1, of Jiajing, Grand Secretaries Yan Song and Li Ben, and Xu as minister of rites, to decide what to do about a letter from Altan Khan written in Chinese demanding that he be given tributary status and trading privileges. This was a question of foreign relations. Yan Song was happy to pass the letter along to Xu Jie. Yan Song thought the raiders a bunch of starving bandits. Jiajing toyed with the idea that they might be bought off. Xu Jie disagreed with both, and his argument won the day. These weren't simple bandits, he exclaimed. They are right outside our gates, wreaking terrible havoc! And paying them off was a terrible idea. No, the thing to do was to doubt the authenticity of the letter written in Chinese: who really wrote that? We need to stall for time until we can get our defense in better shape. So we'll tell Altan Khan that he has to go back home to the steppes and submit his demands in his own language (Fanwen, "foreign writing") to China's frontier authorities for further transmission to Beijing. Jiajing demanded a general court discussion of Xu's proposal. But the ploy worked. Altan's raiders, sated with loot, were itching to go back home with it.

Back up a bit. For some days before this, reports had been coming into Beijing about Altan's advance. Something had to be done in a hurry to protect the Imperial City. This was an emergency. It had nothing to do with rites. Nonetheless, Xu Jie was eager to have a hand in it.

Altan Khan was making short work of the Ming defenses. Beijing and the whole surrounding region were thrown into an indescribable state of confusion. Out on the frontier at Xuan-Da, Qiu Luan, earlier a key witness against Zeng Xian and his plan, reportedly bribed Yan Shifan and through his good offices was appointed regional commander there at some point in 1550. When he arrived, Altan was busy attacking the frontier. On August 20, Qiu sent Jiajing a report stating that his men were not in fighting trim, and his strongpoints were too widely spaced to keep the Lu at bay. So he proposed consolidating the strongpoints, putting the best troops there, and reserving the weak ones for patrol duty. He also said that something needed to be done to deny the Lu access to certain hilltops, from which they could see what was going on inside Chinese territory. Jiajing liked this and sent it down to the Ministry of War, where Minister Ding Rukui gave it a generally positive critique.[24]

On August 23, Jiajing ordered Yang Shouqian, grand coordinator at Baoding, 150 miles southwest, to move two contingents, one Chinese and the other Tatar, to Tongzhou (twenty miles east of Beijing) and Yizhou (sixty miles southeast) for training. Six regional commanders were ordered to take contingents to each of the main frontier passes directly north of Beijing. Jiajing ordered the Ministry of Revenue to distribute silver from the Taicang treasury—3.5 taels to each officer as bonus money, plus .5 tael for cloth, and for each soldier 1.5 and .5 taels. Yang Shouqian's Chinese and Tatar officers were each to get 2 taels, and each soldier 1 tael. Censors Wang Yu and Zhao Shen recommended a major reorganization of the command structure of all forces around Beijing, and Jiajing approved on September 1.[25] Defenses looked to be getting ready, but were they?

On September 4, a spy's report came in from Datong stating that the Lu cavalry had been near the frontier and were headed east. Jiajing ordered three detachments to head them off. From Xuanfu came a spy's report on September 8 that the Lu had moved camp and were now at a place called Guchengchuan, only twenty *li* (six miles or so) from the frontier. Jiajing ordered the mobilization of three more detachments. The emperor also issued one hundred thousand taels silver to Datong for the next year, plus thirty-five thousand to Miyun and thirty-five thousand to Changping to pay for rations for newly arrived troops. These and earlier allotments were all diminished by widespread pilferage, however.

The crisis grew. On September 11 came word that the Lu chief Altan had gathered together the Ordos tribesmen for a big campaign; he had gotten as far as Dushikou, a frontier choke point some one hundred miles northwest of Beijing, and was camped at Jinzihe, just outside China's territory.

On September 13 came news that the Lu (not Altan's men, apparently) had been successfully beaten back at Xuanfu. The next day, Jiajing ordered troop detachments to proceed to Miyun and Huailai counties as backups for Xuanfu and Jizhou. On the 14th, the Ministry of War stated that the Lu, frustrated at Xuanfu, would likely move east to assault Ji-Liao, so the garrisons there needed to be put on alert. Also, Dushikou was the gateway to the Ming tombs and Beijing, so on the ministry's recommendation, Jiajing ordered a detachment of Liaodong troops to White Horse Pass (some 125 miles southwest of Beijing), and another consisting of Han and Tatar troops to Gubeikou, about fifty miles northeast.

Earlier, on September 8, Jiajing ordered Qiu Luan to deploy all outside troops and join Zhao Guozhong, regional commander at Xuanfu, in an anti-Lu defense. When the Lu attacked Xuanfu earlier, Qiu moved his forces to Huailai, and Zhao his to Longmen and Chicheng (generally, north and east of Xuanfu), at which time Jiajing put Qiu in charge of outside forces and ordered Zhao to back him up with his regulars. On the 12th, reports said the Lu, unable to break through at Xuanfu, had moved east to Daxingzhou, some 170 *li* (about 60 miles) north of Gubeikou. Qiu accordingly moved his forces to Juyongguan (not far northwest of Beijing) and sent an urgent message that the Lu cavalry were moving ever further eastward, threatening Jizhen (fifty miles east of Beijing), and he asked for orders as to what he should do: harass the Lu from the rear, or come directly to Tongzhou to defend Beijing?

Meanwhile, Grand Coordinator Wang Ruxiao, posted at Jizhen, misled by a false report that the Lu were headed northwest, begged the ruler to stop Qiu Luan from coming east and send him back to Datong. So Jiajing ordered Qiu to stay at Juyongguan until backup reached Jizhen, then go back to Datong.

But on September 14, the Lu attacked at Gubeikou, fifty miles northeast. The defenders there failed to stop them. On the 16th, the Lu used a feint that fooled Wang Ruxiao's defenders and broke through the Great Wall in several places. Wang's army disintegrated. That opened the way to the interior. The Lu ravaged the counties of Miyun and Huairou, thirty odd miles northeast of Beijing. But when they learned that Baoding defenders were inside Shunyi County, about twenty miles northeast, they bypassed it and headed directly toward Beijing.[26]

It was at about this time that Qiu Luan sent up a thoughtful if controversial analysis of China's whole defense strategy. It certainly challenged anything Xu Jie had in mind. Qiu said that Xuan-Da could not be defended. The Lu encampments were inside the frontier, so our night watchmen and soldiers from the forts regularly visit them in order to trade, and they've forged mutual ties. The Lu have taken over some of our forts, they pasture their horses in our territory, and they know everything about us. Earlier the regional commander Zhou Shangwen surreptitiously let his men trade with the Lu, and a civilian escapee named Shen Jirong and a defecting commander named Wang Chen became spies for the Lu. This made the frontier ungovernable. Qiu said the Lu population was large and dependent on China for sustenance, and when their demands for it aren't met, they turn to raiding. They double their strength by grouping together, while our men are few and scattered. They know all our movements, while we're ignorant of theirs. That's why their yearly raids succeed and we can't stop them. When earlier the court refused the Lu request to establish tribute relations, Zhou Shangwen feared they'd retaliate, and so, while a decision on their demands was pending, he traded with and bribed them, which brought some peace to the frontier. He had no other choice. Rather than let our frontier commanders break the ban and trade illegally, pocketing the profits themselves, Qiu advised, why not have the emperor open the trade? There now are markets at Liaodong, Gansu, Jizhou, and Xifengkou. If the ruler sent messengers with proclamations to [Xuan-Da], opening strictly regulated horse markets there, then the Lu will be grateful. It will be much better than the present smuggling.

Jiajing was impressed with Qiu's argument and sent it down to the War Ministry for their reactions.[27]

Meanwhile, reports were coming in from all over, among them an alarm that the Lu had placed spies inside Beijing and were going to destroy Ming horses and fodder stores. Plans were approved to move horses inside walled cities. Students who had come to Beijing to take their military exams were asked to volunteer for day and night patrols. All Hanlin and *kedao* who had plans to offer were urged to offer them.

On September 17, the Lu, having made a wide swing around Tongzhou, were for the moment stopped at the river there and couldn't attack Tongzhou itself. So they made camp on the east bank and plundered four counties north and west of Beijing. The capital was put on alert. Qiu Luan was ordered to come down from Juyongguan to help defend the city. Calls went out for troops to come in from Jizhen, Henan, and Shandong to assist.[28]

Would the Lu breach the walls of Beijing? The Forbidden City was inside the Imperial City. Both were walled, and both lay inside the walls of greater Beijing, with its Nine Gates. A military noble together with a civilian official were put in charge of each of the Nine Gates. Guards were placed at each of the widely spaced four gates of the Imperial City as well.

Minister of War Ding Rukui's proposals won Jiajing's quick acceptance. He asked for five hundred troops at each of the thirteen gates. He wanted four camps, with ten thousand infantry and cavalry each, placed on four outskirts of Beijing. To protect the dense population in the wards, he asked that the residents build barriers, dig ditches, and post sharpshooters; residents of unwalled villages in the surrounding counties were to scorch the earth and flee to Shuntian Prefecture in and around Beijing; more defenders were needed at Tongzhou. There were more details. Yan Song also had a few suggestions.[29]

But Xu Jie had little use for Ding Rukui's proposals, and he let Jiajing know about that in a long memorial. He excused himself for exceeding his authority as rites minister, but, he said, the crisis situation forced him to speak out. The Ministry of War was merely planning by the book, either in ignorance or out of fear. The truth was, our troops lack training, and our military nobles have no fighting experience, so what use are they? Xu listed by name eight experienced commanders presently languishing in prison because of some infraction or other, who should be released at once and put in command. Further, we must anticipate that several hundred thousand refugees from the wards may come inside the walls, so we need to have food and accommodations ready so they won't all fight and kill each other. Ding's proposal for four outside camps to protect the wards is bound to fail, because untrained troops will flee and cause yet more panic. Qiu Luan's forces need to do this job, but they will be exhausted from their long march from Datong and will need to be issued double amounts of cloth and grain. The War Ministry, he said, apparently hasn't thought of any of this. Jiajing heartily endorsed Xu's corrections. [30]

Meanwhile, the Baoding forces led by Yang Shouqian arrived and were positioned outside the Chongwen Gate. Other newly arrived forces were told to make camp outside the Zhangyi Gate. These moves reportedly eased for the moment the fears of people inside Beijing.

On September 27, Xu used his privilege of secret correspondence with the emperor to tell him that he'd heard that among the Lu were many Chinese defectors. They'd changed into Chinese clothes at the frontier and had come here as spies, claiming to be our men. This has happened in the past, and we need to watch out for this now. He urged Jiajing to return temporarily from West Park to the Forbidden City for safety's sake. Also, he said, it was risky to discuss security measures by open memorial; secret messages were essential. Furthermore, all high officials should be told to discuss their strategic plans with Jiajing face to face so as to prevent leaks. Jiajing replied that he preferred secret messages to face-to-face meetings.

On the same day, Xu used the same secret channel to advise Jiajing not to shut the Nine Gates of the outer city too fast. Next morning, let me tell all the officials on the watch to scout first for the presence of raiders before they shut them. Also, Yang Shouqian's forces have been posted, but Qiu Luan's Xuan-Da troops are still straggling in, and Qiu should be posted outside as well, not brought inside. Also, many officials inside and outside aren't obeying your orders; you must tell the Ministry of War to get your permission to do major things, but let them do the small things and take emergency measures and report these things afterward. [31]

The Lu were on the move, meanwhile. On September 28, they were raiding villages barely six or seven miles away. Troops were sent to patrol Chang'an Boulevard, just south of the Imperial City. Yang Shouqian moved his camp to the east side of Beijing. A moat was ordered to be dug around the entire outer wall of Beijing, altogether about twenty miles in length. In response to Jiajing's earlier call, a blizzard of helpful suggestions for Beijing's defense threatened to overwhelm the Grand Secretariat's handling capacity. Troops at Miyun were issued fifty thousand taels silver, those at Changping twenty thousand. That was to pay for food.

On the 29th of September, the Lu conducted massacres, burned down stables for horses, and captured eunuch Yang Zeng, whom they would very soon use as a bearer of a message to Jiajing.

It seems never to have been a part of Lu strategy to seize any of China's walled cities. They much preferred plundering the undefended countryside. So they declined to assault Tongzhou, the walled city at the terminus of the Grand Canal, even though they were camped very nearby to the east. The Embroidered-Uniform Guard commander Lu Bing said Qiu Luan's troops were the reason Tongzhou still held out, but they were undermanned (only 1,700 defenders) and starving. They needed reinforcements and food immediately. Jiajing flew into a fit of anger over this lapse and endorsed Lu Bing's urgent request.

Zhang Binghu, chief supervising secretary of the Office of Scrutiny for Personnel, pleaded with the emperor to return to the Forbidden City. The West Park walls were thin, he said, and shouts and screams from outside could easily be heard there, surely disturbing the ruler. Besides, the people's morale would improve. Jiajing replied in a friendly way, but he refused to move.

Refugees from the wards were pressing into the city, and the price of rice was rising ominously. Jiajing ordered the government to sell fifty thousand *shi* at half a tael per *shi*. That was too high. The ruler agreed to reduce the price to .35 taels.

Rewards of money and promotions were put on offer for enemy heads, proof of bravery, and extra efforts by the troops.

On September 30, the Lu crossed the river east of Tongzhou, and in the late afternoon a vanguard of seven hundred horsemen reached the training field outside the Anding Gate, on the north edge of Beijing's outer perimeter wall. They were joined the next day, October 1, by many more. They made no move to storm Beijing but went about looting villages and setting fires. Eunuch Yang Zeng brought Altan Khan's message to West Park, and there Jiajing, Yan Song, Li Ben, and Xu Jie discussed how to respond to it. As already noted, Xu's argument to reject it won out.[32]

On September 30, Xu Jie sent an urgent message to Jiajing about Beijing's thin city defenses. He said the guards so far posted at the Nine Gates lacked armor and weapons and were wholly undisciplined. The officials in charge were doing nothing about this. The realm was now in such peril that he felt compelled to step out of line and ask to be permitted to join Lu Bing and officials from the Revenue, War, and Works Ministries to tour the gates and determine just what needed to be done to fix this.[33]

* * *

It might be noted here that the Ming sources are a near blank about what these Lu were really like.[34] Altan Khan is barely a name, with no personality attached. The so-called Lu are ethnically indeterminate and faceless as well. Many were horsemen, and many were not Mongols but Chinese renegades. Some of their advisors were Chinese. Beyond that, the Ming sources and officials showed no interest at all in their enemies. Why did they never build Altan up into a ravening beast, an icon of evil? Evidently they saw no need to. Their intense focus of interest was always directed to their internal responses to the Lu, never to the Lu themselves. It's obvious from the behavior of the Lu overall that they had no intention of occupying China, no plan to create a new Mongol Empire. They wanted to be accepted as a Ming tributary with frontier trading privileges. They had a large and needy population to care for. Yan Song's characterization of them as "starving bandits" wasn't so far off the mark.

The discussion in West Park continued. The question turned to whether Jiajing should respond to the pleas made earlier by various officials, and now raised again by the grand secretaries, that he needed to come out of West Park, show himself publicly, and deliver an edict that would alleviate everyone's anxieties. Reluctantly, Jiajing gave in.

Right after this meeting, Xu Jie left West Park and conducted a general meeting of officials, probably at the Meridian Gate, entryway to the Forbidden City. Under discussion was how to meet the Lu threat. Opinions were voiced. A low-ranking official, Zhao Zhenji, director of studies in the Imperial University, dared yell out that if Shen Shu were released from prison and Zhou Shangwen given posthumous honors, it would showcase both merit and outspokenness, raise everyone's morale, and compel the Lu to withdraw.

That shout stunned the crowd. Mentioning these two names opened a running sore. It was a partisan wedge issue, which might raise the morale of some but alienate others, and so put a unified Ming response to the Lu at serious risk. Zhou Shangwen (1475–1549) was regional commander at Datong, a gruff and controversial figure and an effective fighter, especially against Altan Khan. In life he was well rewarded, but after he died of natural causes, posthumous honors were denied him. Why? Because he had unfortunately run afoul of Yan Song and his son Yan Shifan. He'd denounced Shifan, who at the time held a low post in the military bureaucracy, to his face. Yan Song had to apologize for his son and move him to a different position.[35]

Shen Shu (1514–1581), a supervising secretary in the Office of Scrutiny for Rites, made a fervent protest in Zhou's behalf on June 5, 1549. He put the blame for this mindless travesty on the disloyalty and caprice of "officials in charge," that is, Yan Song. This enraged Jiajing. He reminded Shen that the dead general was a self-promoter, full of hatreds, who didn't respond well to leniency. Shen should have impeached him. Why does he champion him? Because he's deceitful, grabs for power, and sells favor. Jiajing sent the case to the Ministry of Personnel and the Censorate for their judgment, which was that Shen was simply naive. Jiajing exploded again. "To organize a faction and deceive the ruler is no small matter," he thundered. He docked the minister (Wen Yuan) and the censor in chief (Tu Qiao) three months' salary. Poor Shen Shu was arrested, publicly flogged, and jailed for an indeterminate length of time in the Decree Prison. (There he joined the likes of Yang Jue, Zhou Yi, Yang Jisheng, and other suffering victims and martyrs; fourteen years later, after Yan Song's demise, he was released.)

No wonder Zhao Zhenji's loud voice stirred the crowd. A eunuch sent to eavesdrop on this assembly was evidently an enemy of Yan Song's. Zhao's words inspired the unnamed eunuch to invite Zhao to enter the Forbidden City and write up a proposal. This Zhao did. He proposed having trusted officials visit each camp and distribute rewards and encourage the troops. Wisely, he said nothing of Zhou Shangwen or Shen Shu. Jiajing was happy to promote him and issue him fifty thousand taels for that very purpose. Zhao received the silver, but he had to go to West Park to get Yan Song to order up an escort and transportation in order to carry out his mission. Yan Song sabotaged him. He declined to issue him the required authorizations. Zhao had to go find his own transportation. He was unable to reach the camps and had to return with his funds unspent. Yan Song charged him with dereliction. By now, Jiajing had learned of his brief for Shen Shu; he ordered him flogged fifty times and sent him away to a low post in the far south.[36] Thus even in the thick of a crisis, partisan politics managed to insert its ugly head, and a model fighting general had to wait until the Longqing era for his posthumous honors.

Meanwhile, Qiu Luan was made a generalissimo—"Great General who Suppresses the Lu"—with the freedom to punish at will all but the highest-ranking officials and commanders. He moved his camp from Tongzhou to the Dongzhi Gate, on the east side of Beijing's outer wall. Yang Shouqian was promoted as well. Neither man went on the offensive.

On October 2, as he had promised the day before, Jiajing left West Park and came to the Fengtian Gate inside the Forbidden City and delivered his speech. The officials all massed and kowtowed outside the Meridian Gate. What their ruler said was relayed to them by functionaries from the Court of State Ceremonial, a body attached to the Ministry of Rites. Jiajing offered no inspiring words of commitment and hope. What he delivered instead was a harsh scolding. According to the Ming Veritable Records (*Ming shilu*), this is what he said:

> While the Lu chief listens to our defectors and enters deeply into our territory, our officials neglect their duty. They say, "The emperor never meets court, so why should we do our jobs?" They say, "The emperor relaxes while we labor." They use the Sage's adages for their own benefit; this is how far their disloyalty has gone. Actually, the ruler worries while the officials belittle him, and that's not how things should be. Even at night I'm on the job, with the grand secretaries assisting me all day and night. Not even for a moment are our minds off the military situation. What good would my holding court do? You creatures who defy Heaven and turn your backs on the ruler have never yet been impeached by the *kedao*. Instead, you've forced me to come to the Forbidden City, and you've filled me with fright. What the *kedao* needs to do is impeach each and every malefactor who sells fine reputations, prettifies cliques, and cheats the ruler because they fear the traitors higher up. Everyone else needs to cooperate on national affairs. Any of you with ideas about how to smash the Lu needs to speak out. Any who just look on as you've been doing will be punished according to military law. [37]

At least the bureaucrats could rest assured that Jiajing was alert and doing his job. The *kedao* got the message and sent up a number of impeachments of nonperforming officials.

On October 3, Xu Jie memorialized the results of the court discussion of October 1. The officials agreed with Xu Jie's plan to demand that Altan return to the steppes and present his plea in written Mongolian (Fanwen) to the frontier commanders, and if he refused to do that, to mobilize for all-out war.[38]

It was over. On October 3, reports came in that the Lu had begun a withdrawal. On October 5, the capital-city alert was lifted. The Lu plundered villages as they left. Prolonged rains created mud, slowing the retreat, and plans were made to take advantage of that and strike at the enemy's loot-laden columns. On October 6, the Lu surprised Qiu Luan by suddenly doubling back on him, killing or disabling a thousand of his men and nearly capturing the generalissimo himself.

Punishments of nonperforming officials proceeded apace, topped by the public executions of Minister of War Ding Rukui and Grand Coordinator Yang Shouqian. Flogging was administered to many others. That was on October 6.

On October 8, reports said that all the Lu had exited China and returned to the steppes. Neither Qiu Luan nor anyone else was in any condition to harass their retreat. And thus ingloriously did the "crisis of 1550" (*gengxu zhi bian*) come to an end.[39]

* * *

China desperately needed better appointees than those who performed so badly during Altan's raid. On October 9, Xu Jie, acting as though he were already a grand secretary, made a strong case. He said that men's talents aren't all the same, and their limitations differ as well. They shouldn't be miscast. Right now we need men of vigor and initiative. But high-level talent evaluators have for too long emphasized "cultivation and caution" (*xiujin*) in candidates for positions. In normal times, that's fine, but such conformity will never do in a crisis. We need to search out and bring back men who've shown their contempt for the usual credentials.

So, in that connection, Xu Jie recommended two men: one was none other than his old mentor and philosophical guide, Nie Bao (1487–1563). Indeed, since his promotion from the Huating magistracy, Nie had built up a dossier of military experience, a bit like his idol Wang Yangming. As prefect of bandit-infested Pingyang in southcentral Shanxi Province, he financed and organized an effective militia. For that, Yan Song and others supported his promotion to vice commissioner in the Shaanxi Military Defense Circuit, only to be arrested, imprisoned, and dismissed by Xia Yan on the basis of rumors that he had profiteered while at Pingyang. Xu said he'd been dumped because he was an inept player of political games. [40]

The other man was He Dong (1490–1573), an energetic official, ousted as grand coordinator at Datong on partisan grounds in 1532. Xu Jie wanted him back. Jiajing at once gave both Nie and He suitable appointments. [41]

Xu addressed several other remedial issues. If it did nothing else, Altan's raid exposed a broad range of deficiencies in China's defense preparedness and gave Xu welcome opportunities to show initiative and convince Jiajing of what needed to be done right away. Beijing became a beehive of postraid military rebuilding and reorganization. Xu's contributions by no means overbore everyone else's, but his descriptions throw shafts of light on a number of problems and show his style of thinking, matters of importance later on.

Thus on October 17, while the emperor and the grand secretaries were engaged in wide-ranging discussions of army reorganization and relief to the war ravaged, Xu Jie weighed in with a secret message. Following up on an idea to plant spies among the Lu, he noted uneasily that Altan's original letter of demand was probably written by a Chinese turncoat soldier, and that Beijing was unprepared for the raid and had no intelligence sources among the Lu, yet he doubted that planting a spy now was advisable. He agreed with Jiajing that the present situation was wholly unlike the disastrous year 1449, when Esen Khan captured the Zhengtong emperor. He added that the winter cold hadn't yet set in, and the Lu might well raid us again, so we must be ready for that. The ruler is right to consider Beijing's defense needs before checking the routes and sending troops to the frontiers. Xu said he was especially worried about another Lu raid because they'd never been beaten in any engagement the first time. The Ministry of War has detained seven frontier contingents, and the rest of them are still here, so if we keep them all here for defense, it will eliminate the need for a return march. Of the frontier troops, the best are those at Yan-Sui, followed by those at Datong. If we increase [defenses at Beijing], only Yan-Sui troops will do. However, frontier troops all have their proper sectors, so if the Lu lay deceptive plans and conduct a diversion, then the frontier troops have to stay there, while those here will surely be unsettled in mind. I think we must deploy frontier troops; still, Beijing's affairs desperately need fixing. Qiu Luan has been put in charge of all the capital-area camps, so he needs to press ahead with that. Wang Bangrui and Jiang Fu were put in charge of the Nine Gates, so they should now take care of the city defenses. We must also at once rebuild all the watchtowers from the suburbs out to Jizhou and the frontier wall, and from the capital out to Gubeikou and Baiyangkou. We've got to get weapons and cash and grain ready. Everywhere, troop recruiters must be sent out, but if the recruiters are bookish civilian officials, probably they'll recruit useless troops. And if one man recruits but someone else commands the recruits later, his heart won't be in it. It would be best to have a team of two or three officers go recruit and then command and train the men they've recruited. Let them control their men and get the full use of them, just as the frontier officers do with the *jiading* (family servants) they've recruited.

Winter will soon be here, and we must work on all this day and night. I hope you will so order all the officials. As for finding out what the Lu are up to, only the night watchmen at Datong can do that, and only the people who flee down from Xuan-Da can discuss it. I ask you to order [the generals] Xu Jue and Zhao Guozhong to send men out from everywhere to scout and report at once what they've learned so we'll be prepared. [42]

Obviously rushed, and based on a rapid recall of topics raised at a meeting, Xu Jie was here wholly involved with immediate defense needs, not in planning grand strategy. But his remarks relating to troop morale were psychologically acute and based in concrete realism.

Sometime in the immediate wake of the raid, Xu Jie submitted on behalf of his old mentor Nie Bao a detailed set of things that needed correction in order to make Beijing safer in the likely event of another Lu raid. Xu Jie had been intensely involved in securing the Nine Gates at the time of the raid itself, so he knew a great deal about the matter. Nie Bao had only just been appointed to a post in the Ministry of War and was not up on the issue, so he was no doubt willing to let Xu write the memorial for him.

Speaking for Nie Bao, Xu recommended that unless the Nine Gates had to be shut in the case of a raid, they should be opened at sunup and shut at sundown; and we need to keep careful watch for spies, forbid begging, and stop the police from extorting money and goods from commoners entering the city. Second, we must prevent the riotous anarchy that broke out when refugees streamed into Beijing during the raid. We should have the city censors put up notices telling all refugees with friends or relatives who live in Beijing to seek shelter with them. All other refugees, if they bring children, are to move in rent free with commoners; if they don't bring children, they're to stay in Buddhist or Daoist temples. Coal, rice, salt, and vegetables must be sold to them at reasonable prices. Starvelings will be fed gruel. The Warden's Office will manage all of this. Third, we can't allow the outbreak of criminal behavior that occurred last time, so the fire patrols must arrest drifters and vagrants, and troops must be ready to be called in to suppress any gang activity. Fourth, while the government can always supply grain, it cannot supply coal if the camel caravans that bring coal in from the mines to the west are blocked, as they were during the raid, when coal was stolen and fought over. The coal route can and must be protected by armed escorts. Fifth, instead of constantly shifting forces from one spot to another, troops must be assigned permanent sectors to defend; otherwise they feel badly led and will not exert themselves, and will even mutiny, as was seen at the time of the raid. Last, too many rules have created bureaucratic mismanagement, such that deserving fighters never got rewarded, and the Ministry of Works hadn't prepared flags, weapons, and gunpowder ahead of time. We have to streamline demand-and-supply procedures. [43]

From all this, we get a good sense of the panicky chaos and the angry frustration Altan Khan's raid created. Next time, Beijing would surely be better prepared.

Xu Jie also sent up on his own an undated riposte to a Ministry of War proposal. In it, he stated that the barbarian (Rong-Lu) nature was controlled by a "shameless love of profit," that "benevolence and righteousness" simply do not register with them, and that they respect us only after we've forcefully defeated them. He further stated that Qiu Luan had not so far adequately trained the troops that had failed so utterly last time. This just invites another Lu raid. But, he noted, there has been taking place a groundswell of military voluntarism. The sons and younger brothers of frontier officials, and Imperial University and county students everywhere, have been readying saddles, horses, weapons, and their housemen (*jiading*) and bringing them to Beijing. They want to fight. They're strong and capable. Officials at the Nine Gates must put them on salary, issue them grain and fodder, organize them into units, and train them. So if another big Lu raid comes, we already have forces outside, and now, unlike last fall, we'll have forces at the walls which will resolutely battle the raiders. When things quiet down, we can issue them rewards and send them all home. [44]

It is interesting to note here that there had welled up, in the wake of the Lu raid, a strong surge of something like patriotism, with a determined and purposeful edge to it. Xu Jie wanted to mobilize this urge and harness it to the task of contributing to the defense of Beijing. One side (Ming China) puts ethical values first and can rally its people on that basis; the other values only profit, and a good punch in the nose will send its people reeling in demoralization.

* * *

On the one hand, the raid of 1550 sparked a surge of patriotism. What else did it do? It triggered a spate of executions ordered by an angry Jiajing for commanders who failed to engage the enemy. And it appears, too, that the Ming regime very much needed a sacrificial scapegoat. A scapegoat would help resolve a deep and lingering sense of public shame and unanswered suspicions over Ming China's abysmally feeble response to Altan's incursion. Could a villain, indeed a traitor, be found who could be plausibly fingered as responsible for it all? It turned out that Qiu Luan was just that man.

Aside from Yan Song, who'd sponsored him, no one stood higher in Jiajing's esteem and affection than Qiu Luan. He was assigned living quarters inside West Park. His title, "Great General Who Pacifies the Lu," gave him complete command of all the Ming forces in the north. He was given a special seal, which allowed him to bypass the Ministry of War and correspond directly with the ruler himself. But he was, to repeat, not a fighting general. His own policy statement, cited earlier, made this clear. Like Yan Song, he was always ready to avoid combat and make deals with the enemy. Somehow he escaped immediate blame for the debacle of 1550, and thanks to his special connections, he exerted great influence over Ming China's defense posture for the next several years. He and Yan Song arranged to open a frontier horse market for Altan Khan, a move that prompted Yang Jisheng's fiery but unavailing dissent, as described in the previous chapter. Other dissenters were badly abused as well.

On June 2, 1551, it was reported that Altan traded 2,700 horses at the market at Datong. When it closed, on June 21, Qiu Luan thought China should offer rewards to the Lu and open another market at Xuanfu. Rumor had it that this was to buy their neutrality, as Qiu Luan was planning an assault on the Uriyangkhad. The Uriyangkhad were a soft target, but he needed the battle credentials. So a market at Xuanfu opened on June 26, and two thousand more horses were traded there. Jiajing agreed that besides silk, which is what the well-off Lu wanted, for which they traded horses, the poorer Lu could trade oxen and sheep for what they wanted, grain. Objections to that idea were overridden and the dissenters punished.

But the problems had become insurmountable. Despite tax increases, revenues were failing to meet defense costs. The poorer Lu had no choice but to begin raiding again when the frontier markets closed on schedule, leaving their food needs unmet. Severe famine hit Xuan-Da itself. Early in 1522, Altan resumed raiding, and not long after that, the frontier market at Xuan-Da closed down for good.

Qiu Luan was ordered to lead forces to Datong on March 30, 1552. And on April 2, Xu Jie was promoted to grand secretary.

By April 26, Qiu had marched some two hundred *li* (seventy miles) into the steppes north of Datong, looking for a Lu encampment to assault, when he was ambushed at a place called Maoerzhuang (cat farm), site of an abandoned fort of the Yongle era (1402–1424). A report said he lost over four hundred men and two hundred horses. But Qiu reported victory: five heads cut off, thirty horses captured. This sounded a bit fishy, and both Jiajing and Yan Song began to have doubts about him. On May 25, Jiajing called him back to the capital, as Altan had allied with the Uriyangkhad, thus increasing his forces, and was knocking holes in the frontier walls, making raid after raid. Qiu wanted to abandon Xuan-Da and pull the Ming army southeast to defensive positions closer to Beijing. His request was denied. Beijing was in a panic, fearing another raid.

Just about this time, the generalissimo fell seriously sick with a cyst on his back, perhaps a symptom of a terminal cancer. Too ill to serve any longer, he was ordered to surrender his seals and sash of authority. He died on August 31, 1552.[45]

At the time he died, Qiu's relationship with Yan Song had deteriorated completely. He and Yan had traded devastating attacks on each other, both men exploiting their secret communications channels to Jiajing. Xu Jie, meanwhile, kept his voice down, but he too turned against Qiu Luan. Xu's brother-in-law, the Embroidered-Uniform Guards commander Lu Bing, once a supporter of Qiu's, also turned against him. Qiu had no more friends in West Park.

Yan Song and Xu Jie were both determined to prove that Qiu Luan was not only corrupt and self-serving, but a traitor who had been plotting with the Lu to join forces and stage a coup d'état. Lu Bing (1510–1560) was their spear-carrier in this. To be sure, Lu Bing had his good side. At the time of the 1550 raid, he had ordered Beijing's gates opened to the huge crowds of refugees massed outside and had arrested the leaders of a city gang who were poised to join the Lu raiders. In the epitaph he wrote for Lu Bing, Xu Jie explained further that "the rebel [Qiu Luan], commander of both frontier and frontier troops, had gathered many daredevils and was plotting an uprising, so Lu Bing asked Jiajing for permission to set up a shooting range so his officers and men could take turns at target practice, this as a subtle way to deter Qiu, who indeed was frightened and decided not to act."[46] Did Qiu gain the impression that his West Park colleagues no longer trusted him?

Xu Jie, meanwhile, took steps to frustrate Qiu. On May 31, 1552, he secretly urged Jiajing to reject Qiu's plan to evacuate Xuan-Da.[47] On August 28, with Qiu on his deathbed, Xu argued—successfully—that no generalissimo should replace him, that frontier and capital commands should henceforth be put in separate hands.[48]

After Qiu died, Lu Bing proceeded full bore with a probe into just what the generalissimo had been up to. Xu Jie in a secret message (not to be found in his collected works) apparently told Jiajing that Qiu had made treasonous contact with the Sino-Japanese coastal raiders.[49] This allegation shocked Jiajing, and he ordered Lu Bing to conduct a secret investigation. Lu Bing had already had spies report on every small villainy Qiu and his entourage were involved in, but on the day before Qiu died, Lu Bing didn't think his evidence was yet good enough, so he secretly sent a man to falsely warn two housemen (*jiading*) of Qiu's, Shi Yi and Hou Rong, that they were in trouble and had best flee to the Lu for protection. Shi and Hou believed the warning and fled, but they were intercepted, arrested, and brought back to Beijing for interrogation under torture.[50] The two captives confessed, or were forced to state, that when he was first posted as commander at Datong in 1550, Qiu had made a private deal with the Lu, offering to exchange silk and other goods with them if they'd give him an arrow and a flag in token of a promise not to attack Datong. Shi Yi and Hou Rong were the contact men in this arrangement. Fearing the exposure of this deal, they'd tried to escape to the Lu, hoping to get them to invade.

In high anger after reading this report, Jiajing ordered Lu Bing to meet with the *san fasi* (the Ministry of Justice, Censorate, and Court of Judicial Review) and formulate the indictment. They met and returned a charge of high treason (*mou fan*), which called for posthumous dismemberment. So the ruler ordered Qiu's coffin to be opened and his head to be cut off and exposed at the Nine Frontier Garrisons; his parents, wife, and children, plus Shi Yi and Hou Rong, to be decapitated; his concubines and granddaughters to be given to meritorious officials as slaves; his properties to be confiscated; and his other dependents and adherents to be exiled.[51]

This butchery looks like a case of overkill. The vengeance shown was attention grabbing. Two detailed accounts by eyewitnesses to some of what happened are evidence of that. One account is by Gao Dai, who happened to be in Beijing because he'd just won his *jinshi* degree. Gao Dai attested to the ferocity of the debate whether or not to grant Altan his demand to open frontier markets. It wasn't just Yang Jisheng. At the frontier, Commander Shi Dao favored trade, but Commander Su You was bent on war. No one knew which one to follow. When the markets did open, the Lu demanded payment for the thin and worn-down horses they offered. The Lu who traded at Datong raided Xuanfu, and those at Xuanfu raided Datong; then they'd all trade peacefully by day and raid by night. The Lu made a ruin of the Datong area, while the Ming defenders cowered inside their walled city. So Beijing closed down the markets and in effect followed Qiu's plan to write off the whole region. Gao Dai went on to describe deep unhappiness with Qiu, but Jiajing's crushing of all dissent left everyone too terrorized to speak out. Qiu meanwhile had gotten up big plans to mobilize the resources of all China and lead some sort of massive attack on the Lu when his cyst erupted and his death followed.

Gao Dai didn't know Xu Jie, but he closely echoed Xu's feelings over the whole matter. "I witnessed the crisis of 1550," Gao wrote. "Everyone had led a life of ease. Officials were tied down by rules and precedents and avoided responsibility. The troops were idle. Elites partied even after the Lu had broken through at Gubeikou." Qiu Luan, he wrote, was a violent man of low quality who enjoyed exceptional favor, who, when facing the enemy, just folded his arms with no plan at all. He was corrupt. The emperor hoped he'd do well and was unaware of his treachery. "Some feared he'd rebel," Gao concluded, "but I said he won't, or if he does, he'll be easily quashed, like an orphan piglet or putrid rat. . . . With all the forces he commanded, he couldn't even stop an isolated Lu army deep in our territory, so for sure he couldn't pull off a rebellion."[52]

The other account is by Zhao Shichun (1504–1562), a brilliant young firebrand and a good friend of Xu Jie's. He writes about his personal experiences as first a bureau secretary in the Ministry of War, who, at the time of the raid, trained militia (he was adept at riding and shooting), then was sent out to Shandong as assistant, then vice provincial surveillance commissioner, his task being to fetch four thousand militia up to Tongzhou, which he did. As bureau secretary, hearing that Qiu Luan favored opening frontier markets, he braved arrest when he replied that this was like Qin Kui's policy of appeasing the Jurchens, which led to the collapse of the Song dynasty. He said Qiu's title was "Generalissimo Who Pacifies the Lu," so why does he think like a merchant? Zhao said he himself was eager to volunteer to march north and battle the Lu. His bravado and combativeness certainly tilt his account against Qiu Luan, portraying him as no more than a corrupt buffoon.[53]

The "crisis of 1550" was an event not soon forgotten. The whole Ming system shivered on the edge of collapse. Its military defenses proved to be porous. The passivity and ineptitude of its leadership were put on view for all to see. The volatile emperor, sequestered in West Park, easily manipulated by his in-house favorites, made decisions that appeared foolish. (Somehow he reminds me of the dysfunctions of that other final source of all legitimate authority, the Continental Congress in the American Revolution.) Yan Song and Qiu Luan aimed to appease and palliate the invader by abandoning the frontier and opening the markets. Qiu Luan, however, did offer several harebrained schemes for a gigantic invasion of the steppes, which Jiajing listened to but in the end disallowed.

But a contrary current abroad in the land, patriotic in tone and coming close to nationalism, demanded a thorough purge of corrupt and inept leaders, the appointment of better men, and a radical revitalization of the dynasty's defense systems. Inside West Park, it was Minister of Rites Xu Jie, soon to be made a grand secretary, who championed this way of thinking. His was a strong hand behind the posthumous condemnation of Qiu Luan for treason. The symbolism of that very public act of decapitation, exhumation, and family slaughter helped show why the Ming armies had performed so wretchedly—they were led by traitors! And the retaliatory violence inflicted on Qiu Luan and his kin robbed Altan Khan of agency; Qiu Luan was made to appear a greater threat to the Ming than Altan Khan and his raiders.

The appeasement line was weakened but not totally discredited because Yan Song remained in Jiajing's good graces for another decade.

* * *

As of 1552, on the eve of his becoming a grand secretary, how does Xu Jie's career dossier look, as compared to those of Zhang Fujing, Xia Yan, and Yan Song at the comparable moment of their careers? It is varied and rich.

Zhang Fujing's moment of entry into the Grand Secretariat came in 1527. Until then, he'd held a middling post in Nanjing, then was head of the Hanlin Academy in Beijing, but his whole career had been focused almost exclusively on the fierce intrabureaucratic struggle over the Great Rites. He was a scholar-ideologue and a partisan fighter and not much else. Xia Yan's moment came in 1537. By that time, he had put together an impressive file of accomplishments as a supervising secretary in the Office of Scrutiny for War and in the Ministry of Rites. His knowledge and ability ran in several different directions, leading me to style him a technocrat, and a good one. Before Yan Song became a grand secretary in 1542, his whole career was spent in the Ministry of Rites, first in Nanjing, then in Beijing. Neither an ideologue nor a technocrat, he was a rather effective organizer, both of large-scale rites-related activities and of his own political machine. Xu Jie's background shows that he was a technocrat, though not as passionate a one as Xia Yan was, but he was more than just that. As a Hanlin junior compiler, he'd led a protest over changing the rites to Confucius. As a prefectural judge in Fujian, he showed himself to be a self-motivated activist. As an education intendant, he'd come to know many young and promising juniors. He also plugged himself into the leading intellectual-philosophical currents of the day, inspired mainly by Wang Yangming's Confucian revisionism. In Beijing, he virtually ran the Ministry of Personnel. Then he became minister of rites and had a leading hand in defending the city in the 1550 crisis, as we've just seen. The shock value of Altan's raid dwarfed anything Zhang, Xia, or Yan had ever faced. Xia Yan was an inept politician. Yan Song, on the other hand, was adroit; but while with one hand he stirred the sweet glue of corruption, with the other he inflicted intimidation and pain on his detractors. Xu Jie outshone them all—in his ability to get nearly as close psychologically to Jiajing as Zhang and Yan had; in both the depth and breadth of his background experience; and in the way in which he dealt politically with the bureaucratic world, using a potent combination of open goodwill and a surgical thrust of the stiletto when the occasion seemed to call for it. He was a partisan, but a subtle one.

* * *

For ten years, the Grand Secretariat was a troika consisting of Yan Song, Xu Jie, and Li Ben. It was, given their differences, a remarkably stable arrangement. In 1561, Li Ben left, and Yuan Wei replaced him. Both Li and Yuan were unobtrusive, and Yan and Xu kept their natural rivalry under wraps. In 1562, upon Yan's dismissal, Xu became chief grand secretary. I should like here to focus on Xu Jie's part in ruling China from 1552 to 1562. He was a major determinant of whether there would be stability or disorder at the very top of the Ming ruling system.

What Yan Song and Xu Jie worked out was something along the lines of a treaty of peaceful coexistence, an icy one to be sure. He deferred to Yan Song's seniority and his bonding with Jiajing. Yan Song was in the habit of issuing orders to whichever officials in the ministries were his men, telling them what to do, what decisions to take. He and his machine inevitably generated unhappiness and occasional denunciatory outbursts. While Jiajing always backed Yan and crushed his critics, he was also glad to have Xu Jie on hand as a counterweight to Yan, and so Yan's power never became too overwhelming.

So Jiajing let Xu Jie cultivate a bureaucratic following of his own. As noted earlier, Xu used the crisis of 1550 to secure the post of minister of war for his old mentor Nie Bao, a post he held from 1553 to 1555, after which Yang Bo, a friend of Xu's and a superb talent, followed him as minister from 1555 to 1566. Also, when Xu entered the Grand Secretariat, he was able to get Jiajing to agree to the appointment of his longtime friend in philosophy, Ouyang De, as his successor as Minister of Rites. Ouyang died unexpectedly of natural causes in 1554, and in the sorrowful epitaph he wrote for him, Xu said he had been hoping and planning that his friend might soon join him as a grand secretary.[54]

Party organization in Ming China was illegal, so machines and followings had to be put together under the radar, so to speak. Bribery was by its nature covert. Xu Jie won over officials one by one by his listening attentively to their views, and even more by sponsoring gatherings, small ones nationwide and large ones in Beijing, all of them devoted to *jiangxue*, where students, examination candidates, and junior officials "discussed studies." *Jiangxue* was not an obvious partisan label. It was neutral and in general use. When Jiajing was a young man attending Confucian tutorials, he was said to be engaged in *jiangxue*. For Xu Jie, it was a bit of a cover term, because what was discussed in the meetings he sponsored was the dissenting Confucianism of mainly Wang Yangming and sometimes Zhan Ruoshui, with an emphasis on the Wang school's slogan: *zhi liangzhi* ("extend the good conscience").

Xu Jie was cautious about not making it look as though he was "planting faction." But there is no doubt whatever that these actions of his were aimed at creating in the Ming bureaucracy a pro-Xu constituency that might effectively counterbalance Yan Song's machine. Jiajing must have known about it too, because the great *jiangxue* meetings of 1553 and 1554 were held in a

Daoist temple, the Lingji gong, located just outside the wall of West Park, and Jiajing's Daoist chaplain, Tao Zhongwen, ran that facility. Both Nie Bao and Ouyang De met, spoke to, and mingled with hundreds of eager attendees over a period of several weeks at those meetings, which were unofficial and thus off the record. It was not corruption but a more spiritual substance that attracted these young men and created an alternative recruitment base for later appointments and official positions. Xu helped to see to it that these two partisan groups, his and Yan's, though potentially implacable enemies, avoided the extreme polarization of the pro– and anti–Great Rites factions of the 1520s. Xu, for example, refrained from trying too hard to rescue Yang Jisheng from his tormentors. And blanketing officialdom with a suffocating, boilerplate ideological orthodoxy was never his purpose. His purpose was to discover by whatever means a corps of honest, talented, vigorous, and innovative men who could help restore China's defensive capabilities and prevent another security collapse like that of 1550.

But as Yan Song and his son knew, capable officials could also be found among those who had expensive tastes and liked high living and had no qualms about extortion, pilfering, and greasing the palms of the higher-ups.

It is said that one day Jiajing, peering out from West Park, where a new pavilion of his own was undergoing a construction delay, noticed the upper story of a large mansion on Chang'an Boulevard. He wondered whose it was. He was told that it belonged to Yan Song's close adjutant Zhao Wenhua and that half the Ministry of Works' store of big timbers had been diverted to build it. That news displeased Jiajing, and it was a factor in Zhao's dismissal in 1557.[55] In 1561, Nanjing censor Lin Run impeached one Yan Mouqing, unrelated to Yan Song, but appointed through his auspices to superintendent of salt distribution, with power over all north China salt, a power never before given to anyone (Yan Song liked to give field operatives total powers, witness Qiu Luan and others). Lin Run charged him with, among other things, gross corruption and a lavish standard of living. On his tours of prefectures and counties, selling government monopoly salt at extortionate prices, Yan would bring along his wife and parade her about in a sedan chair painted in five colors and borne by twelve women, an amazing sight.[56] Yan Shifan's corruption was legendary; his wanton lifestyle in his luxurious Beijing estate featured Bai Qichang, a chief minister of the Court of Imperial Entertainments in Nanjing, who would powder his face and do female impersonations. Prostitutes could be found in his bedrooms, and other visiting officials like Tang Ruji and Wang Cai could be seen sneaking in to see them.[57] Perhaps these remarks can be read as egregious examples of a wider addiction to materialism, hedonism, and high living in Yan Song's political-bureaucratic machine.

In the public record—the Ming Veritable Records (the *Ming shilu*)—Xu Jie's ten years as second-ranking grand secretary are nearly invisible. He very rarely appears in it. His personal collected works, however, are full of off-the-record material, including hundreds of personal letters to officials in the field that show what an active role he played. These letters were invariably addressed to men using their polite, informal names, not their standard legal names. This usage shows that Xu was bypassing the regular bureaucratic communications channels and activating a network of his own. His secret messages to Jiajing never entered the public record either. Secret messages to rulers were nothing new in Ming history. But Xu Jie by all appearances was a pioneer in the use of personal letters of advice to officials beyond Beijing. Neither Zhang Fujing, nor Xia Yan, nor Yan Song ever did this.

As a grand secretary, Xu Jie had no authority to issue orders to anyone. That was the emperor's prerogative. His close proximity to the ruler, however, lent weight to any advice or suggestion that he saw fit to convey to officials in the provinces. There was a seamless congruence of Xu's personality, his philosophy, and his politics in all this. Xu Jie was an activist. He was friendly and outgoing. He was an idealist, though a well-grounded one. While never claiming that he fully understood the precept "extend the good conscience," he enjoyed the friendship of many devotees of the new-wave Confucianism, and he seems to have put the precept into effective daily use as a builder of goodwill. And that was Xu's technique for creating, not a clique, which he professed to abhor, but a wide and deliberately unorganized following throughout the ranks of Ming officialdom.

And it was China's persistent security crises at the Great Wall and along the coast that prompted all these letters of Xu's. As pointed up earlier, Xu Jie's interest in military matters was lifelong. His letters from Beijing to officials he knew in the field began in the 1540s, when he shared his knowledge of the state of play in Beijing politics with Weng Wanda, then supreme commander at Xuan-Da. He shared with Weng his thoughts about how to handle Lu raids and how to react to the negative reactions that Weng's larger strategic plans were receiving at court. Open debate about such issues was a good thing, he counseled. Weng (1498–1550) was an avid participant in *jiangxue* and an advocate of opening frontier markets. And Xu urged Sun Jin, grand coordinator at Xuanfu, to ignore the usual procedures and make every effort to find fighters who could do the job and treat them with dignity and respect. And in a letter to Wang Bangrui (1495–1561), grand coordinator at Ningxia, way out on the west end of Shaanxi Province, he reminded Wang of their recent conversations in which Xu had tried to convince him of the impossibility of Zeng Xian's Ordos recovery plan; Xu chided Wang for forgetting about that and reassured him that Jiajing's cancellation of the plan was a good thing for everyone. [58]

Shortly after the raid of 1550, a grand secretary in all but name, Xu got busy sending detailed suggestions to officials charged with walling Tong-zhou and recruiting more troops in Shandong. Xu's special worry, expressed in his letters, was that with the Lu having returned to the steppes, the pressure was off the officials, leaving them free to resume their former complacent habits. The decision to open markets at Xuan-Da just encouraged this com-placency. As an inhabitant of West Park, Xu had access to all the latest military reports coming in from the field, and he freely shared his inside information with friends and colleagues on the front lines in the north, bring-ing Jiajing's powers to say yes or no into the equation, suggesting what the Lu might be up to, and encouraging vigilant good service because Xu himself could influence the hiring and firing of key personnel. Xu was proud to tell everyone of his success in getting Jiajing to divide Qiu Luan's old unified command into two, with one official in charge in Beijing and the other at Xuan-Da. He had a gentle way of chiding and scolding and urging better performance that well suited a man with influence but no executive authority of his own.

Frontier military personnel management was a particular concern of Xu's: find good commanders, rough and illiterate though they may be, and treat them well. Food supply was vital. And firearms. And the manufacture of war carts. And proper accountancy of receipts and expenditures. And cracking down on the constant pilfering of funds and supplies. If frontier officials feared being too frank in their memorials, they should write Xu confidential-ly and Xu would pass it on. How to assess commanders whose troops de-fected to the Lu? How to soothe inept and sulking players of the political game? All these efforts plus the hostility of people who hated him wore on Xu Jie, and to friends retired from officialdom he several times described the great stress he was under. [59]

In his secret messages to Jiajing, Xu provided the ruler with detailed reports on the situation on the northern frontier, and suggestions about the edicts the ruler should promulgate in order to remedy this or that foul-up.

* * *

As raiding eased a bit along the Great Wall, Ming China's maritime frontier came under a mounting level of violence from the so-called Wokou, Sino-Japanese seaborne bandit gangs, during the years 1552–1559. Xu Jie's home county and prefecture (Huating and Songjiang) lay within range of the Wokou raids, and indeed his involvement in efforts to foil these raids was even more intense than his concern for improving the northern defenses. No wonder he felt himself overstressed.

Ever the activist, Xu Jie's letters to operatives in the field here already began in the 1540s, just as they did in the north, before all the big troubles arose. In the case of the south, Xu mainly focused on the grand coordinator and regional inspector at Nanjing, capital of the Southern Metropolitan Province (Nan Zhili, nowadays Jiangsu). Beijing was suffering fiscal shortfalls, and Suzhou and Songjiang Prefectures were, as Xu would tirelessly point out over the years, China's major producers of tax revenues, but they were suffering from a prolonged drought. Xu's letters bristle with detailed suggestions about tax reform, hydraulic engineering, silk manufacture, corruption control, price-fixing, and such like. He was in favor of commuting taxes-in-kind (rice) to assessments in silver taels, a step toward the later "single-whip" system. The problems were vexing in the extreme: backlogs of unpaid taxes, unfair silver assessments, badly kept tax registers, and peasants without the resources to resume farming. And then the raids began.

There developed a de facto division of responsibilities between Yan Song and Xu over management of the coastal defenses. Following more or less their peaceful coexistence policy, they tended to stay out of each other's orbits. Yan Song's reach extended through his adopted son and close aide Zhao Wenhua down to Hu Zongxian, after 1556 supreme commander of three coastal provinces, with headquarters at Hangzhou. Xu Jie didn't deal with him, as he belonged to the rival bureaucratic network. He dealt with the officials at Nanjing, who were technically under Hu's jurisdiction, but too far away from him geographically (150 straight-line miles), and so free to listen to Xu Jie and act on their own. So while Hu controlled the coast of Zhejiang Province, it was mainly the officials at Nanjing who handled the coast of Nan Zhili.

For a few years, the main problem in this arrangement for Xu Jie was Yan's man on the scene, the capable but notoriously corrupt Zhao Wenhua.

As a special envoy sent down from Beijing, he joined Hu Zongxian in military operations and lodged vehement and damning impeachments of virtually everyone outside the Yan network. Xu Jie anxiously sent letters of advice to officials in danger, warning them of their vulnerabilities in an effort to save their necks, but to no avail. Xu's old mentor Nie Bao was ousted from his post as minister of war in part because he refused to give a blanket endorsement to a proposal of Zhao's. Then Zhao himself was ousted in 1557, when his mendacity angered even Yan Song. Through it all, Hu Zongxian proved effective in suppressing the Wokou in Zhejiang; and Xu Jie, despite all his frustrations, never gave in but persisted in his determination to help shape the restoration of coastal security, with his stream of letters to the top officials in Nanjing, to the occasional literate general, and even down to prefectural and local officials. Ground-level developments were his main concern: local militias versus outside northern troops and non-Chinese fighters from the southwestern frontiers of the realm; defense versus pursuit; logistics; personnel management; weaponry; reconnaissance; espionage; and local social and economic rehabilitation. Nothing exceeded his vision or his competence. He handled, even micromanaged, the very difficult job of clearing his three hundred miles of shoreline of Wokou raiders. He was always aware of the pitfalls of trying to cope with these matters from far away in Beijing; it took several weeks for a courier to take a letter and return with a reply. [60]

* * *

Xu Jie suffered ten difficult years as junior grand secretary under Yan Song. During those years, he was an active force in Ming politics and administration like no predecessor had ever been. It was not easy. He had to please Jiajing. He had to mollify Yan Song and his son Shifan, keeping his deep dislike of both and his hatred of the corruption they sponsored well hidden. He had to encourage *jiangxue*, but not to the extent that it aroused charges of factionalism or the suspicions of Jiajing and others about Confucian revisionism. He had to befriend as many officials as he could, whether or not they were converts to the "good conscience." He might just have sat passively, reading the incoming memorials and drafting Jiajing's rescripts, and let it go at that. But no. He was a man of ambition. He became a one-man tornado of activity. After the crisis of 1550, he devoted himself tirelessly to the task of mending Ming China's tattered northern frontier defenses. Then in the subsequent Wokou crisis, he acted as a sleepless manager of every challenging threat to, and every breakdown in, the coastal defense apparatus. When, after 1559, the raiders evacuated the coasts of Nan Zhili and Zhejiang for riper targets farther south, Xu was no less eager to assist in arranging postwar rehabilitation. By 1562, his official portfolio glowed, his popularity among many officials was unparalleled, and, all important, he stood high in Jiajing's favor, as much for his willingness to write Daoist prayers and participate in the ruler's religious exercises as for his effectiveness as a grand secretary.

Then in 1562 he helped engineer the dismissal of Yan Song and his son, using all the political skill that such an operation demanded. And in 1565 he followed that up with an expertly wielded knife, followed by a machete, which brought about the public execution of Yan Shifan; the imprisonment and death by abuse in prison of none other than the anti-Wokou hero Hu Zongxian; the reduction of the aged Yan Song to commoner status; the confiscation of the enormous riches of the Yan family and their adherents; and the concoction of an allegation, most likely groundless, that Yan Shifan and his friends were about to ally with both the Lu and the Wokou and bring off a coup d'état. The treason charge made possible the purge of several of Yan Song's top supporters. Xu Jie was now able at last to openly vent his long-buried hatred of the Yan family and his disgust with the corruption of their machine, now in a state of total ruin.

Xu Jie held the post of chief grand secretary from 1562 down to Jiajing's death in early 1567. He kept that position under Jiajing's successor, Long-qing, until he was pressured into retirement in 1568.

The years of his tenure as chief grand secretary were, on the whole, less stressful than the ten years he spent under Yan Song. He now had unfettered access to Jiajing. The security crises persisted but were winding down. He remained as engaged as ever through his letter writing to officials in the field. He even went so far as to resume Zhang Fujing's old role as tutor and psychological counselor, this time to a flailing and weeping ruler who was beginning to lose his grip.

Xu Jie openly formulated three rules of procedure, explicit guidelines for how government should and would be conducted in the post–Yan Song era. Note that this was not the supposed despot, Jiajing, giving Xu Jie directions; it was Xu Jie telling Jiajing how things would be done. Could Xu Jie be called a constitutionalist? His first rule was to restore all decision-making power to the emperor. Jiajing puzzled over that; didn't he already have that power? Xu explained that in the lower levels of the bureaucracy, his edicts were routinely ignored. Xu Jie did not go on to explain who was ignoring them and why, but the likelihood is that Yan's political machine had surreptitiously quashed them.

His second rule was to let the Six Ministries manage their affairs without dictation from the Grand Secretariat. This rule negated Yan Song's way of doing things. Xu Jie in other contexts had expressed a distaste for rule by fiat (*duduan*). Yan's domineering over the ministries was a charge often raised in impeachments. And the third rule was to let "public opinion" have once again a leading role in hiring, firing, rewarding, and penalizing. This meant opening the "avenue of speech" (*yanlu*) to the censors and supervising secretaries (the *kedao*, frightened and suppressed for so many years). When Jiajing wondered aloud how he could have gone so wrong in trusting Yan Song, Xu Jie reassured him that Yan Song was talented and a good choice early on, that it was his evil son who caused his downfall, and that if the "avenue of speech" had been open earlier, if it had not been so savagely beaten back, then the impeachment process would have brought about his removal long before his corruption ever reached such an extreme.

Xu also conducted a seminar with Jiajing over the nature and function of the Grand Secretariat. After forty years of rule, why would a fifty-five-year-old Jiajing wish to discuss such a question with Xu Jie? Didn't he know by now? Perhaps influenced by Yan Song, Jiajing said that the chief grand secretary was just like a prime minister, even though he no longer bore that title. Xu Jie disagreed. In a complex exchange of messages, Xu insisted that, in effect, it was the emperor who was prime minister. The grand secretaries and the minister of personnel held positions so vital that they had to be the personal choices of the emperor. They could not be men recommended by the bureaucracy. The minister of personnel had to be someone the grand secretaries could not intimidate. It was fine for the court to send up ranked recommendations of candidates for all other posts, but not those. So when the death of Yuan Wei in 1565 left Xu Jie the only grand secretary, he patiently explained to Jiajing why he could not do the job alone, why at least two more men were needed at once, and why he couldn't recommend anyone for the job. The ruler knew his own top officials, and he must make the choices by himself. That was the ancestral system.

Jiajing more than accommodated Xu Jie. He chose two more southerners, Yan Na and Li Chunfang. Yan Na (no relation to Yan Song) was an honest and hardworking minister of personnel. Li was the son of peasants and minister of rites. All three—Xu, Yan, and Li—were, or had been, devotees of *jiangxue*, followers of the schools of Wang Yangming, Zhan Ruoshui, and others. This was a remarkable team, harmonious in outlook and deferential toward Xu Jie, their chief. But it was short-lived. Yan Na left for health reasons late in 1565. Jiajing wanted to replace him with Dong Fen, another southerner, but Dong was a onetime adherent of Yan Shifan's; and Xu Jie, for all his insistence on the emperor's sole authority, objected violently and got Jiajing to change his mind. Too confident, perhaps, of his fairness and his ability to charm all comers, Xu Jie warmly endorsed the appointments of two northerners to the Grand Secretariat: Guo Pu and Gao Gong. Gao proved to be a major player of the power game, refused to defer to Xu Jie, and in 1568, in the post-Jiajing era, engineered Xu's removal from government. Xu never returned, and he died in 1583.

Jiajing did not take lightly the dismissal and disgrace of Yan Song. For several years, Yan's departure from West Park deeply saddened him. He thought of abdicating—as he had back in 1521, when his mother was being denied due ritual respect on her entry into the Forbidden City. Forty years later, in 1562, he thought of stepping down and devoting the rest of his life to his religion. In 1565, he expressed the same wish. In 1566, distressed by Hai Rui's famous memorial criticizing him personally, Jiajing said he wanted to retire to a palace in Nanjing. Then he said he wanted to revisit his old home in Chengtian and visit his parents' mausoleum there. It was Xu Jie's delicate job, well performed, to dispel Jiajing's repeated bouts of depression and self-doubt and convince him to stay put and on the job.

* * *

For Jiajing the end came around noon on January 23, 1567. His desperate calls for remedies, pills, and elixirs were unavailing. Xu Jie was on the spot, the man of the hour, and his task now was to deliver the ruler's final edict, manage the elaborate funeral and burial rites, and arrange the formal accession, twelve days later, of Jiajing's surviving eldest son, the unloved Zhu Zaihou, known as the Longqing emperor. These duties he carried out to perfection.

The final edict, written as though Jiajing himself had composed it, which he had not, was an expert piece of political craftsmanship, except for one mistake. Xu Jie cut the other grand secretaries, the two northerners and Li Chunfang, out of the loop. Instead of them, he asked a brilliant protégé of his, Hanlin academician Zhang Juzheng (mentioned above, later the last of Ming China's powerful grand secretaries), to help him with it. They worked on it all day and night. The edict was issued on January 24, the day following Jiajing's death. It seemed to answer positively to what the realm had been waiting for, and, with the exception of the two northern grand secretaries, the edict was received with widespread rejoicing. It did two main things. First, Jiajing was made to renounce totally his long devotion to Daoism. Not a single voice was raised in defense of his religion. Immediately the whole complex of altars and shrines Jiajing had built in West Park was torn down and their materials recycled for other construction projects. Only one palace was left standing. Second, everyone who had ever been punished for speaking out, dead or alive, had his honors and status restored. Over two hundred victims of the Great Rites protest of 1524 and the Great Case of 1527, plus all other upstanding targets of Jiajing's wrath, were raised at the stroke of a pen from the garbage pit of ignominy to that special Valhalla reserved for China's moral heroes.[61]

* * *

How were Jiajing and his era remembered? Did the era end in men's minds on this note of relief from grievances of many years' standing? No.

Late Ming commentators judged the era in a surprisingly positive light. The official Veritable Record of the Jiajing reign, the *Shizong shilu*, edited by Zhang Juzheng and others in 1577, downplays the unpleasant aspects and gives the whole reign a ringing endorsement. There were good things accomplished on the watch of this emperor, with his "prominent nose, fine beard, godlike presence, decisiveness, and knowledge of government." There was his repeal of all the evils of the preceding Zhengde reign, giving the realm a new lease on life (actually this was the work of Chief Grand Secretary Yang Tinghe, but no matter). There was his resolutely correct stance on the Great Rites issue. There was his equally resolute follow-up in reforming the rites to Heaven and Earth and all the rest, such that "since the founding of the Ming, this was the unprecedented pinnacle of civil order." He was active and energetic early on, and harsh with his officials, but ever solicitous of the hardships and sufferings of the common people. He walled off the "barbarian miasma" in the north and cured the "maritime disease" to the south. He handled his bureaucrats with apt skill. His filial piety was deep and sincere. The sadness on his face as each year he observed his father's death anniversary caused everyone present to shed tears of sympathy. Even in his late years, when he turned to Daoism, he continued to serve as an active ruler.

"His great enterprise of dynastic revival outshone [the legacies] of his predecessors," and he can truly be called "a godlike sage [of a sort] that rarely appears in the world."[62]

Other Ming appraisals generally echo this positive line.[63] The commentaries of the succeeding Qing, however, weighed in with a different judgment. The Ming dynastic history, *Ming shi*, published in 1736, acknowledged Jiajing's cleanup of the mess left by Zhengde; thought his Great Rites program fairly on target; but wondered whether some of it wasn't excessive, too adversarial, and too vitiated by politics. Worse, while frontier wars and internal banditry raged on, Jiajing turned to Daoism, carried out unorthodox rituals, overindulged in construction projects, and exhausted the treasury, such that China's long-standing peace and prosperity began its decline during his time on the throne. Although he suppressed powerful villains and kept the levers of power in his own hands, he was "a ruler of middling talent."[64]

My own assessment lies somewhere between the positive and the negative. My respect for his assiduity and understanding of power pulls in one direction, but my distaste for his lifestyle and abhorrence of his cruelties pull in the other. I've tried to understand Jiajing, but I must confess I rather dislike him. My aim in this book, however, was not so much to pass judgment on him personally, but rather to explore the lives and experiences of his chief grand secretaries and gain from them a generous store of concrete pictures of the Ming regime in action over a considerable span of its history. I hope I succeeded in doing that.

NOTES

1. For what follows in the next several pages, source citations can be found in my *A Political Life in Ming China: A Grand Secretary and His Times* (Lanham, MD: Rowman & Littlefield, 2013).

2. Xu Jie, *Shijing tang ji* (Siku quanshu cunmu congshu, 4th ser.), 79.476–477 (hereafter cited as *SJTJ*).

3. Xia Xie, 4.2066–2067. Li Guan had an interesting career; see *GCXZL*, 5.2854–2855 (epitaph by Huang Zuo). Wang's argument was strong; see *MS*, ch. 208, for biographies of both him and Li. Also *MSL*, 77.2823–2833. On the Confucian temple issue, see Deborah Sommer, "Destroying Confucius: Iconoclasm in the Confucian Temple," in *On Sacred Grounds: Culture, Society, Politics, and the Formation of the Cult of Confucius*, ed. Thomas A. Wilson, 95–133 (Cambridge, MA: Harvard University Asia Center, 2002). Also see her "Ming Taizu's Legacy as Iconoclast," in *Long Live the Emperor! Uses of the Ming Founder across Six Centuries of East Asian History*, ed. Sarah Schneewind, 73–86 (Minneapolis: Society for Ming Studies, 2008).

4. Wang Shizhen, account of conduct for Xu Jie, in *Yanzhou shanren xugao* (reprint Taipei, 1970), 13.6246–6250.

5. See George L. Israel, *Doing Good and Ridding Evil in Ming China: The Political Career of Wang Yangming* (Leiden: Brill, 2014).

6. Ibid., 13.6254.

7. Shen Shixing, *Sixian tang ji* (Siku quanshu cunmu congshu, 4th ser.), 134.471–477 (epitaph for Xu Jie).

8. Wang Shizhen, *Yanzhou shanren xugao*, 13.6254.

9. Xia Xie, 4.2211; *MS*, ch. 186 (biography); *DMB*, 1.608–609 (biography of Hsu Tsan). Ironically, Yan Song wrote his spirit-way stela epitaph and, no surprise, said nothing beyond bland praise. See *GCXZL*, 1.581–583.

10. *MS*, ch. 197 (biography); *GCXZL*, 2.1033–1034 (epitaph).

11. Wang Shizhen, *Yanzhou shanren xugao*, 13.6255; *MS*, ch. 203 (biography).

12. Jiang Yonglin, trans., *The Great Ming Code: Da Ming Lü* (Seattle: University of Washington Press, 2004), 58.

13. *SJTJ*, 79.461–462.

14. Ibid., 79.459–460.

15. Ibid., 79.463–464.

16. Ibid., 79.486–487.

17. Ibid., 79.501–512.

18. Ibid., 80.146–149.

19. Ibid., 79.483–485, 489–490.

20. Dardess, *A Political Life*, 23.

21. *GQ*, 4.3737. In error, the *Guo que* has another and wrong entry for this (4.3704).

22. *SJTJ*, 79.481–483.

23. *DMB*, 1.373–375 (biography of Chu Wan); Xia Xie, 4.2265.

24. *MSL*, 85.6462–6463.

25. Ibid., 85.6466, 6470.

26. Ibid., 85.8464–6483.

27. Ibid., 85.6483–6484.

28. Ibid., 85.6484–6485.

29. Ibid., 85.6486–6488.

30. *SJTJ*, 79.490–491 (the *MSL* version of this is abridged; 85.6488–6489).

31. *SJTJ*, 79.369.

32. *MSL*, 85.6489–6495.

33. *SJTJ*, 79.369–370.

34. For a closer look at Altan Khan, see Johan Elverskog, *The Jewel Translucent Sutra: Altan Khan and the Mongols in the Sixteenth Century* (Leiden: Brill, 2003). In 1594, Xia Daheng helped fill this gap with his "Customs of the Northern Lu" (*Bei Lu fengsu*). See Henry Serruys's French translation in *Monumenta Serica* 10 (1945): 117–208.

35. *MS*, ch. 211 (biography of Zhou Shangwen).

36. I've amended slightly what I said about this incident in *A Political Life*, 26–27.

37. *MSL*, 85.6497–6498.

38. *SJTJ*, 79.491; *MSL*, 85.6500–6501, is abridged. The *shilu* goes on to editorialize that Jiajing's policy of refusing tribute yet failing to improve China's defenses was disastrous. Corruption and mismanagement might well have led to the Ming collapse but for the residual loyalty the Chinese people had for the Ming imperial house.

39. *MSL*, 85.6501, 6506–6509.

40. *MS*, ch. 202 (biography of Nie Bao).

41. *SJTJ*, 79.491–492; *MSL*, 85.6509–6510; *GCXZL*, 4.2425–2426 (epitaph for He Dong).

42. *SJTJ*, 79.370–371.

43. Ibid., 79.493–495.

44. Ibid., 79.495–496.

45. Xia Xie, 4.2279–2297.

46. *SJTJ*, 79.737.

47. Ibid., 79.371. Apparently Xu talked Jiajing out of backing Qiu's plan to invade the territory of the Uriyangkhad to avenge their having sided with Altan. Xu argued that the loss of the Uriyangkhad security hedge would be to Altan's advantage, because the Ming had no way to occupy that territory permanently. See Wang Shizhen's account of conduct for Xu Jie in *Yanzhou shanren xugao*, 13.6270.

48. *SJTJ*, 79.371.

49. Xia Xie, 4.2297. Xia may be reporting hearsay evidence.

50. Xu Jie's epitaph for his brother-in-law puts all this rather differently. "When Qiu died, his daredevils had long been acting aggressively in the capital, and they feared indictment and so thought of an uprising, but Lu Bing spoke kindly with them and had them sent back to their garrisons, so the capital stayed peaceful. After Qiu's coffin was opened and his severed head sent to the Nine Frontier Garrisons for exhibit, Lu Bing sent officers to nab his clique, including Shi Yi and Hou Rong, and prosecuted them both. Both had been in contact with the Lu. Had it not been for Lu Bing, they would have made good their escape to the Lu" (*SJTJ*, 79.737).

51. *MSL*, 86.6827–6828.

52. Gao Dai, *Hongyou lu* (1557; reprint Taipei, 1977), 1422–1442. Xu Jie also targeted Beijing's high-living lifestyle in a memorial that he prepared at the time he was made a grand secretary, but he did not submit it for some reason, perhaps for fear of offending Yan Song. "In recent years, officials high and low compete in luxury and splendor in their gourmet dinners, their drinking, clothes, homes, sedan chairs, horses, and social visiting. Salaries aren't adequate to pay for all this. Officials make the necessary extra income by selling favors and protection, and by extortion from soldiers and commoners. This of course directly affects China's anti-Lu defense." He urged a police crackdown on makers and merchants of luxury goods (*SJTJ*, 79.497–498).

53. See *GCXZL*, 1.360–363, for the account. Also see *MSJSBM*, ch. 59 ("The Crisis of 1550"); *DMB*, 1.252–255 (biography of Ch'iu Luan); Dardess, *A Political life*, 47ff.

54. *SJTJ*, 80.16–20 (spirit-way stela for Ouyang De).

55. Xia Xie, 4.2366–2368.

56. Ibid., 4.2421. The *MSL* abbreviates this; 90.8267. Jiajing disallowed the impeachment.

57. Ibid., 4.2435–2436.

58. Dardess, *A Political Life*, 43–47.

59. Ibid., 47–65.

60. Ibid., 89–137.

61. For citations to sources for Xu Jie's term as chief grand secretary, cf. Dardess, *A Political Life*, 139–170.

62. *MSL*, 91.9065–9068.

63. *GQ*, 4.4037–4038, lists several. The compiler, Tan Qian (1594–1668), thought Jiajing ranked somewhere in the middle of China's list of long-lived emperors of the past.

64. *MS*, ch. 18.

Cast of Principal Characters

Gui E (d. 1531). From Anren, Jiangxi. One of Jiajing's earliest backers in the Great Rites controversy. He and Zhang Fujing cooperated closely.

Guo Xun (1475–1542). A scion of a distinguished military family, he inherited the title marquis and was later made a duke. A powerful supporter of Jiajing in the Great Rites controversy and later a participant in Jiajing's Daoist observances. He died in prison, under indictment for massive corruption.

Hu Zongxian (1511–1565). From Jiqi, in present-day Anhui Province. A partisan of Yan Song's and a bon vivant, he nonetheless played a major role in the suppression of coastal raiding, 1554–1562. Arrested in connection with the confiscation of Yan Song's estate, he died in prison.

Huo Tao (1487–1540). From Nanhai, Guangdong. A hotheaded controversialist and early on a backer of Jiajing. He and the other Great Rites partisans later parted ways.

Jiang, Dowager Empress (d. 1538). She was Jiajing's birth mother and a strong-willed personality who was close to her son and shared his passion for ritual correctness.

Qiu Luan (1505–1552). From a Ningxia military family, he inherited the title of marquis. A Jiajing backer in the Great Rites dispute, and later in Jiajing's Daoism, Qiu helped to end the plan to recapture the Ordos. Appointed a generalissimo to command Ming China's defenses at the time of Altan Khan's raid of 1550, he performed poorly. Accused of treasonous collusion with the enemy, he was posthumously beheaded, and his immediate family members were executed.

Wang Yangming (1472–1529). From Yuyao, Zhejiang. Probably Ming China's greatest all-round talent. His revisionist ethical teachings made an empire-wide impact and strongly shaped Xu Jie's approach to life and politics.

Xia Yan (1482–1548). From Guiqi, Jiangxi. Energetic and omnicompetent, Xia was a major architect of Jiajing's project to reconstruct the ancient system of public worship. He served as a grand secretary from 1537 to 1548. In 1548, Jiajing had him executed for his role in the Ordos recovery dispute.

Xu Jie (1505–1583). From Huating, in present-day Jiangsu Province. A Confucian ethicist, he cultivated a loose but fervent bureaucratic following that included many converts to Wang Yangming's teachings. He rose to prominence during Altan Khan's 1550 raid on Beijing. He was a grand secretary from 1552 to 1568. He helped engineer Yan Song's downfall and was the main author of Jiajing's final edict, which put an end to the ruler's Daoist establishment and rehabilitated all of his political and judicial victims.

Yan Shifan (1513–1565). Yan Song's only son and manager of his political-bureaucratic machine. Ousted on charges of corruption in 1562, he was executed on charges of treason in 1565.

Yan Song (1480–1565). From Fenyi, Jiangxi. He served as a grand secretary from 1542 to 1562, the longest such tenure in Ming history. A machine politician, his effectiveness was compromised in the end by his colossal corruption. He died in disgrace.

Yang Tinghe (1459–1529). From Xindu, Sichuan. As chief grand secretary, he helped arrange Jiajing's enthronement in 1521. He opposed Jiajing in the Great Rites controversy and retired in 1524. In 1528, Jiajing reduced him to the status of commoner.

Zeng Xian (1499–1548). From Jiangdu, Yangzhou, in present-day Jiangsu Province. His elaborate plan to recapture the Ordos region was, in the end, rejected by Jiajing, who had him executed.

Zhang Cong. In 1531, Jiajing changed his name to Zhang Fujing.

Zhang Fujing (1475–1539). From Yongjia, Zhejiang. A rites scholar, ideologue, bureaucratic fighter, and intimate personal advisor to Jiajing. He was a major player on Jiajing's side during the Great Rites dispute. He served as a grand secretary from 1527 to 1535.

Zhu Houcong (1507–1567). The personal name of the Jiajing emperor.

Zhu Houzhao (1491–1521). The Zhengde emperor, Jiajing's cousin and predecessor. He had no brothers or sons, thus opening the way for Jiajing's accession.

Zhu Youtang (1470–1505). The Hongzhi emperor. He was Zhu Youyuan's half-brother and Jiajing's uncle. Jiajing's refusal to become his son by post-humous adoption prompted the Great Rites controversy and crackdown of 1524.

Zhu Youyuan (1476–1519). Jiajing's father and Prince of Xing. The question of how he should be honored polarized Ming bureaucracy, a standoff won resoundingly by Jiajing in 1524.

Timeline

1507	Zhu Houcong, the future Jiajing emperor, born September 16 in Anlu (nowadays Zhongxiang County, Hubei Province), seat of the Xing princedom.
1519	Jiajing's father, Prince of Xing, dies.
1521	Jiajing arrives in Beijing, as successor to his cousin, the childless Zhengde emperor.
1524	The Great Rites demonstration and crackdown. Also, a serious mutiny breaks out in Datong.
1527	The Great Case crackdown.
1528	The Blue Sheep Mountain bandits are at last suppressed.
1530–1531	The key years for reviving ancient rituals and constructing the required temples.
1533	The second mutiny in Datong.
1535	Chief Grand Secretary Zhang Fujing, a grand secretary since 1527, is dismissed for the last time.
1536	Xia Yan enters the Grand Secretariat.
1539	The Annam invasion is called off, as Mac Dang-dung capitulates. Also, Jiajing visits his boyhood home in Anlu (since renamed Chengtian).

1542	The palace girls' assassination of Jiajing fails. Jiajing vacates the Forbidden City and moves to the Daoist complex he was still in the process of building in West Park.
1548	Jiajing cancels Zeng Xian's plan to recapture the Ordos. Zeng Xian is executed. Xia Yan is executed as well. Yan Song is made chief grand secretary.
1550	Altan Khan's raid on Beijing.
1552	Generalissimo Qiu Luan, accused of treason, is executed. Xu Jie is made a grand secretary.
1555–1559	The climax years of the coastal raiding.
1562	The dismissal of Yan Song. Xu Jie becomes chief grand secretary.
1565	Yan Song's son Yan Shifan is executed. The huge Yan estate is confiscated.
1566	Hai Rui sends up his famous memorial excoriating Jiajing. He is arrested.
1567	Jiajing dies on January 23. His son, Zhu Zaihou, the Longqing emperor, succeeds him.

Bibliography

SOURCES

Bingbu wen Ningxia an. Xuanlantang congshu ed. Reprint, Taipei, 1981.

Chen Zilong, ed. *Huang Ming jingshi wenbian*. 30 vols. Reprint, Taipei, 1964.

Fu Fengxiang, ed. *Huang Ming zhaoling*. 4 vols. Reprint, Taipei, 1967.

Gao Dai. *Hongyou lu*. Reprint, Taipei, 1977.

Gu Yingtai. *Mingshi jishi benmo*. 80 chapters. Any edition.

Gui E. *Wenxiang gong zouyi*. Siku quanshu cunmu congshu, 2nd ser. (1996), vol. 60.

Guo Tingxun, ed. *Mingdai fensheng renwu kao*. In *Mingdai zhuanji congkan* (Taipei: Mingwen shuju, 1991), vol. 138.

Huang Zongzi. *Mingru xue'an*. 62 chapters. Any edition.

Huo Tao. *Weiyai wenji*. Siku quanshu cunmu congshu, 4th ser. (1997), vols. 68–69.

Jiao Hong, ed. *Guochao xianzheng lu*. 8 vols. Reprint, Taipei, 1965.

Li Chunfang. *Li Wending gong Yian tang ji*. Siku quanshu cunmu congshu, 4th ser. (1997), vol. 113.

Li Shi. *Nancheng zoudui*. Siku quanshu cunmu congshu, 2nd ser. (1996), vol. 46.

Lu Shen. *Shengjia nanxun rilu, dajia beihuan lu*. Siku quanshu cunmu congshu, 2nd ser. (1996), vol. 46.

Ming shi. 332 chapters. Any edition.

Ming shilu. 133 vols. Reprint, Taiwan Academia Sinica, 1962.

Ming Shizong (Zhu Houcong). *Huojing huowen*. Siku quanshu cunmu congshu, 2nd ser. (1996), vol. 57.

———. *Yuzhu dashou longfei lu*. Siku quanshu cunmu congshu, 2nd ser. (1996), vol. 45.

Mingdai dengkelu huibian. 22 vols. Reprint, Taipei, 1969.

Minguo Pingshun xianzhi. Zhongguo difangzhi jicheng: Shanxi fuxian zhiji, vol. 42.

Shen Defu. *Wanli yehuo bian*. New ed. 3 vols. Beijing: Zhonghua shuju, 1980.

Shen Shixing. *Sixian tang ji*. Siku quanshu cunmu congshu, 4th ser. (1997), vol. 134.

Tan Qian. *Guo que*. New ed. 6 vols. Beijing: Guji chubanshe, 1958.

Tang Bin, ed. *Qian-an xiansheng Mingshi gao*. In *Mingdai zhuanji congkan* (Taipei: Mingwen shuju, 1991), vol. 159.

Tianshui bingshan lu. Zhibuzu zhai congshu ed. Vol. 6. Reprint, Taipei, 1964.

Tu Shan. *Ming zheng tongzong.* Reprint, Taipei, 1969.

Wang Shizen. *Yanzhou shanren xugao.* 18 vols. Reprint, Taipei, 1970.

Wang Weizhen. *Wangshi cunsi gao.* Siku quanshu cunmu congshu, 4th ser. (1997), vol. 103.

Wanli Chengtian fuzhi. Reprint, Beijing: Shumu wenxian chubanshe, 1990.

Xia Xie, *Xinxiao Ming tongjian.* New ed. 6 vols. Taipei, Shijie shuju, 1962.

Xia Yan. *Guizhou wenji.* Siku quanshu cunmu congshu, 4th ser. (1997), vols. 74–75.

———. *Guizhou xiansheng zouyi.* Siku quanshu cunmu congshu, 2nd ser. (1996), vol. 60.

———. *Nangong zougao.* Siku quanshu zhenben, 4th ser. (1973), vol. 109.

Xu Jie. *Shijing tang ji.* Siku quanshu cunmu congshu, 4th ser. (1997), vols. 79, 80.

Yan Song. *Liguan biaozou.* 1912 printed ed.

———. *Nangong zouyi.* Xuxiu siku quanshu, vol. 476. Reprint, Shanghai, 2002.

———. *Qianshan tang ji.* Siku quanshu cunmu congshu, 4th ser. (1997), vol. 56.

Yang Jue. *Yang Zhongjie ji.* Siku quanshu zhenben, 5th ser. (1974), vol. 356.

Zeng Xian. *Futao yi.* Siku quanshu cunmu congshu, 2nd ser. (1996), vol. 60.

Zhang Fujing. *Taishi Zhang Wenzhong gong wenji.* Siku quanshu cunmu congshu, 4th ser. (1997), vol. 77.

———. *Yudui lu.* Siku quanshu cunmu congshu, 2nd ser. (1996), vol. 57.

Zhao Wenhua. *Zhaoshi jiacang ji.* Siku weishou shu jikan, 5th ser. (1997), vol. 19.

Zhou Yi. *Naqi zoushu.* Siku quanshu zhenben, 9th ser. (1979), vol. 117.

MODERN STUDIES

Cao Guoqing. *Yan Song nianpu.* Beijing: Zhongguo renshi chubanshe, 1995.

Chu Hung-lam. "The Jiajing Emperor's Interaction with His Lecturers." In *Culture, Courtiers, and Competition: The Ming Court (1368–1644),* edited by David M. Robinson, 186–230. Cambridge, MA: Harvard University Asia Center, 2008.

Clunas, Craig. *Screen of Kings: Royal Art and Power in Ming China.* Honolulu: University of Hawaii Press, 2013.

Dardess, John W. *A Ming Society: T'ai-ho County, Kiangsi, in the Fourteenth to Seventeenth Centuries.* Berkeley: University of California Press, 1996.

———. *A Political Life in Ming China: A Grand Secretary and His Times.* Lanham, MD: Rowman & Littlefield, 2013.

———. "Protesting to the Death: The *fuque* in Ming Political History." *Ming Studies,* no. 47 (2003): 86–125.

Ditmanson, Peter. "Imperial History and Broadening Historical Consciousness in Late Ming China." *Ming Studies,* no. 71 (2015): 23–40.

Du Lianzhe, ed. *Mingchao guanxuan lu.* Ming Biographical History Project, Monograph No. 1, 1966.

Elman, Benjamin A. *A Cultural History of Civil Examinations in Late Imperial China.* Berkeley: University of California Press, 2000.

Elverskog, Johan. *The Jewel Translucent Sutra: Altan Khan and the Mongols in the Sixteenth Century.* Leiden: Brill, 2003.

Fisher, Carney T. "Center and Periphery: Shih-tsung's Southern Journey." *Ming Studies,* no. 18 (1984): 15–34.

———. *The Chosen One: Succession and Adoption in the Court of Ming Shizong.* Sydney: Allen & Unwin, 1990.

Geiss, James. "The Significance of the Reign Title Chia-ching." *Ming Studies,* no. 30 (1990): 37–51.

Goodrich, L. Carrington, and Chaoying Fang, eds. *Dictionary of Ming Biography*. 2 vols. New York: Columbia University Press, 1976.

Hammond, Kenneth J. *Pepper Mountain: The Life, Death, and Posthumous Career of Yang Jisheng*. London and New York: Routledge, 2007.

Herman, John E. *Amid the Clouds and Mist: China's Colonization of Guizhou, 1200–1700*. Cambridge, MA: Harvard University Asia Center, 2007.

Ho Ping-ti. *The Ladder of Success in Imperial China, 1368–1911*. New York: Wiley, 1964.

Ho Yun-yi. "Ideological Implications of Major Sacrifices in Early Ming." *Ming Studies*, no. 6 (1978): 55–73.

Hou Renzhi. *Beijing lishi ditu ji*. Beijing: Beijing chubanshe, 1985.

Hsieh Bao Hua. "From Charwoman to Empress Dowager: Serving Women in the Ming Palace." *Ming Studies*, no. 42 (1999): 26–80.

Hucker, Charles O. "Hu Tsung-hsien's Campaign against Hsu Hai, 1556." In *Chinese Ways in Warfare*, edited by Frank A. Kierman and John K. Fairbank, 273–307. Cambridge, MA: Harvard University Press, 1977.

Israel, George L. *Doing Good and Ridding Evil in Ming China: The Political Career of Wang Yangming*. Leiden: Brill, 2014.

Jiang Yonglin, trans. *The Great Ming Code: Da Ming Lü*. Seattle: University of Washington Press, 2005.

Lam, Joseph S. C. *State Sacrifices and Music in Ming China: Orthodoxy, Creativity, and Expressiveness*. Albany: SUNY Press, 1998.

Lo Jung-pang. "Policy Formulation and Decision-Making on Issues Respecting Peace and War." In *Chinese Government in Ming Times: Seven Studies*, edited by Charles O. Hucker, 41–72. New York: Columbia University Press, 1969.

McDermott, Joseph P., ed. *State and Court Ritual in China*. Cambridge: Cambridge University Press, 1999.

Meskill, John. "Academies and Politics in the Ming Dynasty." In *Chinese Government in Ming Times: Seven Studies*, edited by Charles O. Hucker, 149–174. New York: Columbia University Press, 1969.

———. *Academies in Ming China: A Historical Essay*. Tucson: University of Arizona Press, 1982.

Miyazaki Ichisada. *China's Examination Hell*. Translated by Conrad Schirokauer. New Haven, CT: Yale University Press, 1981.

Mote, F. W. *Imperial China, 900–1800*. Cambridge, MA: Harvard University Press, 1999.

Mote, Frederick, and Denis Twitchett, eds. *The Cambridge History of China*. Vol. 7, *The Ming Dynasty, 1368–1644. Part I*. Cambridge: Cambridge University Press, 1988.

Pearson, Richard. *Ancient Ryukyu: An Archeological Study of Island Communities*. Honolulu: University of Hawaii Press, 2013.

Schneewind, Sarah. *Community Schools and the State in Ming China*. Stanford, CA: Stanford University Press, 1999.

———, ed. *Long Live the Emperor! Uses of the Ming Founder across Six Centuries of East Asian History*. Minneapolis: Society for Ming Studies, 2008.

Sommer, Deborah. "Destroying Confucius: Iconoclasm in the Confucian Temple." In *On Sacred Grounds: Culture, Society, Politics, and the Formation of the Cult of Confucius*, edited by Thomas A. Wilson, 95–133. Cambridge, MA: Harvard University Asia Center, 2002.

———. "Ming Taizu's Legacy as Iconoclast." In *Long Live the Emperor! Uses of the Ming Founder across Six Centuries of East Asian History*, edited by Sarah Schneewind, 73–86. Minneapolis: Society for Ming Studies, 2008.

Taylor, Romeyn. "Official Religion in the Ming." In *The Cambridge History of China*, vol. 8, *The Ming Dynasty, 1368–1644. Part 2*, edited by Denis Twitchett and Frederick W. Mote. Cambridge: Cambridge University Press, 1998.

Wang, Richard G. *The Ming Prince and Daoism: Institutional Patronage of an Elite*. Oxford: Oxford University Press, 2012.

Wang Yi-t'ung. *Official Relations between China and Japan, 1368–1549*. Cambridge, MA: Harvard University Press, 1953.

Wills, John E., Jr. "Maritime China from Wang Chih to Shih Lang." In *From Ming to Ch'ing: Conquest, Region, and Continuity in Seventeenth-Century China*, edited by Jonathan D. Spence and John E. Wills Jr., 201–238. New Haven, CT: Yale University Press, 1979.

Zhang Xiangming. "A Preliminary Study of the Punishment of Political Speech in the Ming Period." *Ming Studies*, no. 62 (2010): 56–91.

Zhang Xianqing. *Yan Song zhuan*. Hefei: Huangshan shushe, 1992.

Index

About the Author

John W. Dardess is a professor emeritus of history at the University of Kansas. To date, he has written seven books about China. He enjoys writing, cycling, socializing, and keeping up with the latest from his granddaughters, Lea and Maya.

Lightning Source UK Ltd.
Milton Keynes UK
UKOW01f1043260218

318485UK00001B/302/P